FRANCE 1848–1945
AMBITION & LOVE

FRANCE 1848–1945

AMBITION & LOVE

By

THEODORE ZELDIN

OXFORD   NEW YORK   TORONTO   MELBOURNE
OXFORD UNIVERSITY PRESS
1979

Oxford University Press, Walton Street, Oxford OX2 6DP

OXFORD LONDON GLASGOW NEW YORK TORONTO
MELBOURNE WELLINGTON CAPE TOWN NAIROBI
DAR ES SALAAM KUALA LUMPUR SINGAPORE JAKARTA
HONG KONG TOKYO DELHI BOMBAY CALCUTTA MADRAS
KARACHI

*First published as the first two sections of France 1848–1945 by
The Clarendon Press, 1973. First issued with additional material, as
an Oxford University Press paperback, 1979*

British Library Cataloguing in Publication Data

Zeldin, Theodore
    France, 1845-1945.
    Ambition & love
    1. France-Civilization-1830-1900
    2. France-Civilization-1901-
    I. Title
    944.07   DC33.6   79-40578
    ISBN 0-19-285090-3

*Reproduced, printed and bound in Great Britain by
Cox & Wyman Ltd, Reading*

CONTENTS

LIST OF MAPS

LIST OF FIGURES

PREFACE

FRANCE 1848–1945 may be read in the same way as one would a series of novels, each of which tells the story of a family or a community from a different point of view. Each chapter and each volume may be read independently. Each has its own surprises, for I aim to show that France was not what it seemed to be; each has its own constellation of heroes or anti-heroes, because I do not see France as dominated by one man, one class or one set of principles. Taken as a whole, however, these portrayals of the many faces of the French are designed to make it possible to judge anew, and less partially, the idiosyncracies, the poses and the torments of a nation that has always irritated its neighbours, even when it has won their admiration and sometimes indeed their affection.

The analogy with the novel is more than that, for I have tried to combine the preoccupations of the historian with those of the novelist. Historians have by custom concerned themselves mainly with public lives, with issues and movements. So they have left private lives, the emotions of the individual, to the novelists. Since I believe that behaviour is muddled and obscure, and cannot be presented truthfully as simply a search for some ideal, like glory, justice or liberty, and since I do not presume to be able to prove anything when it comes to discussing human motivation, I have not written a general national narrative, held together by a more or less plausible string of causes. Instead, I have made the individual my starting-point, and have tried to show him beset by a multitude of pressures, internal as well as external. I have grouped his struggles around six passions: ambition, love, anger, pride, taste and anxiety.

This volume deals with the first two. The study of ambition— of hope and envy, of desire and frustration, of self-assertion, greed and imitation—puts class conflict, the bug held responsible for so many of society's ailments, under a microscope. I focus on how people feel about themselves, without taking for granted that their behaviour is determined principally by their economic situation. I investigate the rival attractions of money,

security, fame, power, happiness, amusement, which divide
a country as much as its more obvious structures; I seek to
penetrate the significance of the choices people make about
their careers, about the direction they give to their lives, what
they understand by success and what they do to achieve it. I
try to show how Frenchmen were tortured and inspired by
competitiveness. They made many miscalculations in their
frenzy.

Love was another revolutionary force that needs to be incorporated into investigations of change. History usually takes
the activities of the male adult population as determining the
course of events. The problems which this minority had in
coping with the ambitions of women and children have barely
been chronicled. Men did not altogether dominate society
through the family, for it is a myth that family life was the basic
norm, as I shall show. Women were indeed placed under
severe disadvantages in certain respects, in the world that men
ran, but women also had a world of their own, in which they
had a different kind of power. Children likewise developed
their own forms of resistance both to families and to schools.
To study love is to see how ineffective laws and regulations
were, how rebellion could flourish, even if it had to do it discreetly, and how tension and ambiguity were concealed by the
facade of respectability.

My method is to hold up a multitude of mirrors around the
French, so that they may be seen simultaneously from different
angles: and my other volumes pursue these themes into other
recesses of their personalities. To adapt to the kaleidoscopic
vision I offer, the reader must, of course, be willing to put
aside temporarily the expectations that he has of history, in the
same way as he must put aside his traditional expectations when
looking at the paintings of the Impressionists or the Cubists. I
hope the experience will modify his attitude to the French, and
to the past, but also that it will tell him something he did not
know about himself.

INTRODUCTION

ACCORDING to a public opinion poll, the French think of themselves as being, above all else, intelligent. All nations—as the same poll, carried further on an international scale, revealed—also consider themselves to be intelligent, but France was the country which placed intelligence highest, as the virtue it admired most. One of the aims of this book is to investigate this image, to assess the place that intelligence, or reason, or ideas have in French life, to explain how intellectuals came to be held in such exceptionally high esteem, and to show the consequences this has had. I hope this may serve to throw some light on the question of how the French differed from other nations in this period. But I believe the role of the intellectuals is something that particularly needs to be studied in France, as a basis for getting beyond the confusing and interminable conflicts of which its history seems to be composed. For not only have the intellectuals played a leading part in these conflicts, but they have also interpreted and labelled them in such a way as to influence all subsequent thought about them. It was they who formulated the issues which they claimed divided the country and defined the principles which were at stake. Their generalisations became accepted truths, to the extent that they shaped events, for new controversies were fitted into categories they had devised. They have bequeathed to historians a framework into which the events of the past can be conveniently slotted, but this inherited framework is not necessarily the only one that can be used. The reasons why it was evolved need to be examined more closely, and there seems to be room, at any rate, for another perspective.

Modern French history is usually interpreted in one of two ways. The more traditional approach is to show it as the unfolding of a struggle between revolution and reaction. In this view, France appears as fundamentally torn politically, religiously and ideologically. Instability, violence and unrelenting polemic are the result. An alternative approach is to regard these struggles as the superficial covering of social divisions and to show that power was concentrated, despite the victory of democracy, in the bourgeoisie, or even in a small section of it, composed of no more than a few hundred families. The triumph of this class is seen as the outcome of the Revolution and subsequent history consists in its efforts to consolidate its hold and in attempts by the masses to overthrow it. Both these interpretations involve stress, above all, on the factors which divided Frenchmen. In the former case, it is principles that are studied, and the different political ideas the country produced are judged to be crucial in explaining what happened. In the latter case, the inequalities of economic privilege, and their social consequences, are brought out to reveal the incompleteness of the Revolution and to show how far its principles were from being implemented in practice. A history which studies these conflicts can portray the past as some people of the time saw it. But it seems useful to ask also whether partisanship and prejudice did not distort the vision these people had, whether their parties were as disagreed as their leaders claimed, whether the reformers, while damning the past, did not silently cling to other parts of their heritage, and whether the animosities between social classes were as total as they sometimes appeared. The common beliefs, attitudes and values of Frenchmen, which often cut across ideological and class lines, are difficult to formulate, because little was said about them in the turmoil of political strife, but unspoken assumptions need to be taken into account if the divisions are to be seen in perspective, and if their limits and significance are to be assessed. It is helpful to know not only what Frenchmen quarrelled about, but also what place their quarrels had in their lives, beside those aspects of their existence on which they were agreed. The family is one example of a common institution which was largely unquestioned and which may have lain at the root of certain forms of behaviour which have been considered peculiarly French. At the same time, tensions within the family were probably as divisive as any political disagreements. This is a subject about which comparatively little has been written and on which new light is badly needed. My own contribution to it here must be regarded as tentative and exploratory. There seems to be scope for further investigation of the more permanent features of French society, to counterbalance the study of events, change, development, movements and fashions which have attracted rather more attention.[1]

I do not mean by this that I am seeking to define the immutable French soul, mind or character. But this is something many people talked about and I have tried to investigate why they came to believe that there was such a thing. The forces that lay behind the attempt to create it deserve study. To understand it, however, one must first get away from the nationalist perspective, which still unconsciously dominates much writing: one should not unquestioningly assume that France was one nation in this period, simply because the French Revolution proclaimed it to be so. French history is too often told from the point of view of the country's rulers and their preoccupation with their own power. France in this period was composed of a large variety of groups which had lives of their own. I have tried to describe the problems, ambitions, feuds and frustrations of some of these. They form an important part of this book.

It is true there was a strong movement to master this variety and to render it uniform. This created a struggle which was in many ways more fundamental than the better-known debates about monarchy and republic. Centralisation survived the Revolution as is well known, but so too did the resistance to it, which was far more vigorous than is often realised. The struggle was not only political, but also intellectual, cultural and social. One needs to examine not only the activities of the state in order to understand it, but also the spread of myths surrounding the state and the development of attitudes towards it. The makers of the myths—the intellectuals—deserve special attention, as much as the politicians.

It is customary nowadays to begin a history book with a preface of apology for its defects. This is not the result of modesty, and it is no mere convention. Historical writing is in a state of difficulty and uncertainty. History used to occupy a high place in the hierarchy of the moral sciences. Revolutionary youth used to flock enthusiastically to attend historical lectures, which were sometimes landmarks in national agitation. Historical

---

[1] This stress on *change* can be seen in the titles of some of the standard works in this period: *The Development of Modern France* by Sir Denis Brogan (1940); *L'Évolution de la troisième république* (1921) by Charles Seignobos; *Gloires et tragédies de la troisième république* by Maurice Baumont (1956).

study was a part of political life. This is no longer so. Though
still cultivated by some as a 'liberal education', history, following philosophy, has become largely an intellectual exercise or—
when it is readable—even just an entertainment. It is the social
sciences which have taken over its task of offering broad
generalisations and universal explanations. Historians on the
whole no longer claim to impart great truths of wide application,
or to be on the point of discovering them. Even the lively small
groups pioneering new approaches or tapping new sources have
strictly limited expectations.

This situation is perhaps the inevitable result of the ever-
growing ambition of the subject. There is no aspect of life which
it does not attempt to investigate. The movement to extend its
scope is not a new one. Voltaire, Macaulay and Michelet, for
example, all in turn protested against the concentration on
kings and parliaments. But the movement is today still something of a crusade, which shows how difficult it has been to
achieve its aims. Inadequate sources hold up progress, new
interests push back the horizon into an ever greater distance.
The variety of human activity cannot be compressed into a
single volume, and no individual can comprehend its totality.
No one writing a general history can hope to attain the goal he
sets himself.

However, there are now more historians than there have ever
been before; but paradoxically this has made it even more
difficult for anyone to form a full picture of the past. There is
now too much to be read. In order to write a general history of
France from 1848 to 1945, one should presumably be acquainted
with the books published in those years. I calculate that there
are about one million of them (roughly 10,000 appearing each
year). If one reads one book every day, for ten years, one can
sample only 3,650, and it would be an arbitrary sample. But
there are also periodicals and newspapers, of which at least
2,000 were in existence in 1865, nearly 8,000 in 1938, and 15,000
in the 1950s. The manuscript material, distributed between
national, provincial, ecclesiastical, business and private archives,
is, despite the ravages of time and neglect, even more bulky. In
addition to what the age itself produced, one needs to read
what modern historians have written about it. The Annual
Bibliography of the History of France lists 9,246 books and

articles as having been published in 1970 alone. A count made in 1969 revealed that there were 1,380 doctoral theses being written in French universities on history since 1789; 640 of them were about France. This says nothing of the considerably more numerous masters' theses, nor of the research in progress on French history in the universities of other countries. As higher education expands, their output is assuming alarming proportions. The number of doctorates in history awarded by the universities of the U.S.A. increased fourfold in the twenty years after 1945. No historian, however, can confine himself to reading simply about his own period or country; nor can he neglect new ideas being put forth in cognate subjects like sociology, economics, psychology, political science, literature, and their bibliography, in several languages, is even more daunting. No one can ever feel fully qualified or ready to write a general book.[1]

Research is being conducted in an increasingly thorough way but on ever narrower subjects. This specialisation is creating barriers of incomprehension between the different branches of history. New techniques, for example in economic history and historical demography, which are in some respects becoming branches of mathematics, demand a completely different training. This kind of detailed research, and these new methods, often yield highly original results, but the problem of communicating them is becoming difficult. The confusion is exacerbated by the fact that historical research seldom follows straight lines, with accumulative effects, towards clear objectives, as, say, in medicine it is possible to aim at curing a particular disease. The interests of every generation shift the focus and grand projects peter out inconclusively. New discoveries enter the textbooks very slowly, and are usually fitted into a traditional framework somehow, rather than radically altering it. It is very difficult for an individual to obtain an independent perspective over a really broad expanse of history. So old generalisations survive tenaciously even though the specialists have shown them to be false.

These are some of the reasons why historians apologise, as I

---

[1] List of French theses in progress, compiled by Professor J. B. Duroselle (unpublished, typewritten 1969); Boyd C. Shafer, *Historical Study in the West* (New York, 1968), 204.

do. But it seems to me that there is also another side to
these difficulties. History today is more vigorous, ingenious and
skilful than it has ever been. The vast new mass of material
available calls not for despair but for a new approach, different
from that which seemed suitable when historians expected to
have in their own libraries all the books they proposed to consider. Lord Acton, lecturing on the French Revolution, said
that 'in a few years, all will be known that ever can be known'.
He was mistaken, and history now appears as a subject in which
the full truth will never be known. The attempt to make history
a science was highly fruitful, but the benefits can be retained
without making this nineteenth-century ideal a shackle. Natural
scientists have in any case abandoned the illusions about
methodology which that ideal contained. History can continue
to learn from the natural and social sciences, but it does not
increase its prestige by claiming to be a branch of whatever is
currently most fashionable.

It has attractions and virtues of its own. It can turn its handi-
caps to good account. In an age of increasing specialisation, it
remains, despite its own internal difficulties, the least limited of
subjects. There is no aspect of life it cannot study. It produces
no final synthesis, but it does allow its students to make their
own. It leaves the fullest scope for each individual to develop
it in his own way. The contributors to Acton's *Cambridge Modern
History* were required to make sure that no one should know
where one had laid down his pen and another had taken it up.
This was acceptable when it was believed that the truth was
there to be discovered and summarised, but it is no longer so.
Historians admit that, however scrupulous they are, their
selection of the facts and their use of them are coloured by their
own personality. What they see in the past is partly the result
of their particular kind of eyesight, of the education and upbringing they have had, and of their personal interests and
prejudices. Except in certain statistical problems, it is unlikely
that any two people will see quite the same thing, or express
what they see in the same way. History is a subject which
requires them to use all the resources of their individuality,
imagination and sympathy in the appreciation of character and
events. To urge them to repress themselves into faceless and
mechanical anonymity is to make their task impossible. Tech-

nical competence is something they can acquire quite easily, but, unlike some scientists who apparently do their best work straight away in their twenties, historians benefit from wider experience and human qualities. One of their aims in being historians is indeed to broaden their contact with the world, however vicariously.

Historical study is a personal experience, and the subjective elements in it deserve to be valued, when so many other branches of knowledge are becoming largely technical. To admit that historians solve their problems of colour and light, that they create their compositions for reasons which are ultimately subjective, because these seem to them to be coherent and true, is not to admit a fault, but to assert that each individual historian can express himself in his work. Of course, the more careful and controlled his detail, the more likely he is to be convincing, but, since he uses literary style as his medium, he has the opportunity not only to prove a point, but to evoke the atmosphere of an age—to reconstitute it with a meaning and character which contemporaries might not have seen. Far from preaching that this or that brand of history—social, ideological, or statistical—is the right one, which all young men anxious to move with the times should pursue, I believe that the extremely varied way in which history is studied is the very source of its strength and will be of its continued popularity.

But I do not regard history as designed simply to give pleasure or to satisfy antiquarian curiosity. It is capable of being more than art or gossip. It is not a luxury, but an essential part of the constant process of re-assessment that every generation makes of itself, of the constant debate about what is worth keeping of the past and what is not. Detachment from present concerns is not in my view a necessary preliminary to the writing of 'scholarly' history. On the contrary, I believe historians can make a contribution to clearer thinking about present ideals, habits and institutions, in which the inherited element is always large.

I have, therefore, not written a chronological history of events, of which there are already several able ones. My method has been, rather, analytical, in the sense that I have tried to disentangle the different elements and aspects of French life, and to study each independently and in its inter-relationships.

I hope that in this way the generalisations traditionally made about France will as it were come loose, that it will be possible to see how they were invented, and by whom, and what they represent and what they conceal. My emphasis has been on understanding values, ambitions, human relationships and the forces which influenced thinking. This particular approach means I have left a lot out: my book has no pretensions to being comprehensive.

Volume two will look at the history of psychology and of fashions in behaviour to see how the individual and his emotional problems were viewed and how they were dealt with at different periods. It will examine the history of the provinces, to discover how far independent cultures survived the influence of Paris—which will help to clarify the significance of that influence. It will analyse relations with other countries, including the colonies, not from the point of view of diplomacy or governments,[1] but asking what Frenchmen knew about foreigners, how they treated them and how they evolved their sense of national identity in the process. I shall study the role of intellectuals, men of letters, teachers, the clergy and the army, analyse the influence they exerted and the kinds of outlook they propagated. I shall then try to show how these different forces interacted in the crisis which the First World War produced, how new solutions were unsuccessfully sought in the years that followed and how Vichy emerged as the tragic denouement of this civilisation. A general conclusion will summarise the argument of the book, in the light of the new perspectives created by developments since 1945. The footnotes are designed to indicate some of my sources; a fuller bibliography will be placed at the end of volume two.[2]

[1] This is studied in other volumes in this series; A. J. P. Taylor's *Struggle for Mastery in Europe 1848–1918* (Oxford 1954) has already been published.

[2] In the notes, place of publication is London for books in English and Paris for books in French, unless otherwise indicated. French money may be converted into British currency, up to 1914, at the rate of twenty-five francs to the pound: one franc equalled a little less than one shilling. After 1914 the exchange rate fluctuated between 40 and 70 francs 1919–23, collapsing in 1925 and 1926 to 87–245, steady at around 123 from 1927 to 1930, up to 80–90 in 1931–3, and 70–75 in 1935, then down to 74–106 in 1936, 105–52 in 1937 and 174–7 in 1939.

Part I

1. The Pretensions of the Bourgeoisie

THE bourgeois is a central figure in every modern history. In France more than anywhere else, because aristocracy and monarchy were defeated in the great Revolution, the bourgeois appeared manifestly supreme for a century and a half after it, to the extent that the two words have been combined into a single idea: *la France bourgeoise*. It is argued that it was in this period that the bourgeois attained self-confidence, ceased to aspire to enter the old hierarchy, and sought rather to replace it. He developed his own moral and economic doctrine and formed an original class with a spiritual unity.[1] At the same time he became an object of attack, satire and animosity, far more concerted than ever before. The Age of the Bourgeoisie is the setting in which the history of these years is usually placed. The notion has bred a large number of generalisations. The first stage in any study of France must be a clarification of its meaning and an assessment of its value as an instrument of explanation.

There are two ways of understanding the phrase *la France bourgeoise*. It means first of all the domination of bourgeois attitudes of mind. In this definition, the rise of the bourgeoisie can be traced, from the sixteenth century or earlier, not from the point of view of political or economic power, but in terms of the development of rules of conduct and ways of thought which gradually won increasing acceptance, in opposition to the ideals vaunted by the monarchy, the aristocracy and the Church. In this view what distinguished France after the Revolution was the prevalence of the bourgeois mentality, not just among the rich, but equally among artisans, shopkeepers and even peasants. The longevity of bourgeois domination—that

---

[1] Charles Morazé, *La France bourgeoise* (1946), 65. See also Régine Pernoud, *Histoire de la bourgeoisie en France* (1960-2); Elinor G. Barber, *The Bourgeoisie in 18th Century France* (Princeton, N.J., 1955); B. Groethüysen, *Les Origines de l'esprit bourgeois en France* (1927).

is to say, the rule of those who exemplified, practised or advocated bourgeois virtues most successfully—is explained by the masses' adhesion to and approval of those virtues. There were hard-fought struggles for success, but these disputes did not involve fundamental differences, and that is why regimes succeeded each other without transforming the structure of society. Only when the very rich tried to copy the old aristocracy and ceased to be the common man's ideal, did they meet with opposition and resistance. An attempt will be made here to define the bourgeoisie's values, to investigate how far these formed the basis of a consensus which held France together, and to analyse more closely the whole notion of consensus.

The second meaning of *la France bourgeoise* involves political analysis and economic determinism. After the monarchical and aristocratic *ancien régime*, it is argued, the Revolution gave political power to the bourgeoisie. The Declaration of the Rights of Man was only a pretence of democracy and equality. Though the seigneurial privileges were abolished, those of money were not. The bourgeoisie took the place of the aristocracy. They bought the confiscated national lands. They filled the parliamentary assemblies, even when universal suffrage nominally gave sovereignty to the masses. The equality of opportunity they preached was false since only the well-to-do could afford secondary education, which was the key to success. They devoted much of their energy to fighting the Church, which they claimed was imprisoning the people in mysticism and superstition, but there were those who said that this was only a way of consolidating their own leadership and distracting the masses from their social grievances. This theory has been refined by those who distinguish between the types of bourgeoisie which dominated in different periods. It is argued that each political regime based itself on a new 'rising class'. Thus Louis-Philippe was 'managed by the *grands bourgeois* for the profit of their class'. Napoleon III's reign was that of big business. The Third Republic was sustained by the middle bourgeoisie, the graduates of the scientific schools and universities.[1] However, the Marxists maintain that this apparent gradual democratisation is an illusion and that France has ultimately been controlled not by the bourgeoisie in general

[1] Charles Morazé, *La France bourgeoise* (1946), 149.

but by the financial magnates who held the purse strings in all
the major activities and achievements of the country. Building
on this, France has been exposed as dominated by 200
families. The royalists, incited by their hate of the Orleanists,
provided more social documentation for this phenomenon, by
showing how the families which came to the fore at the Revolution of 1789, clung to office through every subsequent regime,
changing their party labels to suit the prevailing fashions but
always accumulating new power by intermarriage, so that they
became veritable dynasties, successfully preventing the growth
of real democracy.[1] This view became particularly widespread
at the time of the Popular Front. Léon Blum held this group
responsible for his failure. Using the word bourgeoisie rather
loosely, he wrote: 'Despite all appearances to the contrary, it
is the bourgeoisie which has ruled France for the past century
and a half.' Even when the masses made their will felt in parliament, the bourgeoisie was able to resist. It controlled the local
assemblies, the upper ranks of the civil service, the press,
finance, the business world, and, under the Third Republic,
the Senate. 'The French bourgeoisie held power for all this time,
refusing to resign it or share it.' In 1940 the disastrous results
of their blindness and conservatism were revealed. They were
shown up as degenerate, incompetent, out of date, wedded to
traditions of routine, and with no reserves of energy or imagination to meet the crisis of that year.[2]

The succeeding chapters will investigate this interpretation
and review the facts which give it its strength. But before
studying the financial oligarchy, it is desirable to see how it
related to other sections of the bourgeoisie, and how much
cohesion this class had. It will be argued that the reason why
the people put up with the accumulation of so much power in
such few hands for so long, is to be found in the deep fragmentation of the bourgeoisie. It was the ability of these different small
worlds to coexist, preserving a great deal of mutual independence, that made the abuses of each one acceptable to the many
who were only marginally affected by them.

Nothing is more difficult to define than bourgeois, and it must
be accepted at the outset that the notion is necessarily a vague

[1] E. Beau de Loménie, *Les Responsabilités des dynasties bourgeoises* (1943).
[2] L. Blum, *A l'échelle humaine* (1945).

one. In 1950, when polls were held in France and the U.S.A. asking people what classes they belonged to, 5·4 per cent of the Americans said upper, 45·2 per cent said middle, 10·6 per cent working, 0·8 per cent farming, 4 per cent lower, 6·5 per cent other and 27·5 per cent gave no answer. But in France 7·9 per cent said they were bourgeois, 22·5 per cent middle, 27·1 per cent working, 13·7 per cent peasants, 7·5 per cent poor, 2·3 per cent other and 19 per cent no answer. As with their political parties, so with their social status, the French give more complicated answers. 32·3 per cent of the professional, business and higher administrative people questioned called themselves bourgeois, but 57·6 per cent claimed to be middle class and 5·3 per cent working class. Likewise, 5 per cent of the artisans and skilled workers thought they were bourgeois, 36·4 per cent middle class and 52·9 per cent working class.[1] The bourgeoisie is a peculiarly French category—as is the peasantry, for few American or British farmers deny membership of the larger working world simply because they live by agriculture. It is impossible to say how many people one is talking about when one discusses the bourgeoisie. Does one mean the electors of Louis-Philippe's 'bourgeois monarchy'—200,000 males? But one knows, from the way he was overthrown, how arbitrary this distinction was and how it excluded at least as many of comparable social rank. Does one mean those who had servants? There were about a million servants in 1900, but would the fall in their number paradoxically mean that the size of the bourgeoisie diminished in the twentieth century? Does one mean those who had some inherited capital or income? That gives about 15 per cent of the population, but one should bear in mind that the average value of inheritances was about sixteen times higher in Paris than in the Ariège in 1900 (but falling to three times in 1934) so that the significance of private income varied enormously in different regions and that its distribution changed rapidly in the twentieth century. Does one mean those who had enough capital to pay for their funerals? The figure in Paris in the 1840s was 17 per cent.

---

[1] Natalie Rogoff, 'Social Stratification in France and in the U.S.', *American Journal of Sociology*, 58 (1953), 347–57. Cf. N. Xydias, 'Classes sociales et conscience de classe à Vienne-en-France (Isère)' in *Trans. Second World Congress of Sociology* (London, 1954), 2. 246–51.

Perhaps the best-known attempt to explain the significance of the word was made in 1925 by Edmond Goblot, a professor of philosophy at Lyon. His analysis fits in with what four-fifths of the Frenchmen questioned in 1950 stated was the principal criterion which determined class: style of life. Goblot insists that it is not wealth that makes a man a bourgeois, but the way the wealth is acquired and the way it is spent. There are rich people who are not bourgeois, and there are poor ones who are accepted as belonging to the bourgeoisie. A bourgeois must spend his money to maintain a certain decorum in his clothes, his accommodation and his food. This does not require large sums. The bourgeois spent less money than the worker on food. What distinguished him was that he served his food differently, with a tablecloth laid symmetrically, and placed in a special room, not in the kitchen. He had to have a *salon*, furnished with a piano, paintings, candelabras, clocks and bibelots, in which to receive visitors and to show that he possessed a surplus of wealth, dedicated to cultured living, beyond the basic necessities. The rest of his house could be of Spartan simplicity and often was, because he had to spend his money on other things, to keep up his status. He had to pay for his children to go to secondary school, to enable them to take up professions to keep them bourgeois. If they became artisans, he would lose his self-respect. A bourgeois had to be able to perform his job in bourgeois costume, so that manual or dirty physical work was unacceptable. That is why there was such a sharp social distinction between the shopkeeper, who served customers himself, and the wholesaler, who by giving orders and never touching his goods could therefore claim to be a bourgeois. There were indeed wholesalers who refused to receive retailers in their homes.[1] All this implied that the bourgeois gave much effort to distinguishing himself from the masses. He cultivated *distinction*, which involved a special kind of politeness, laying stress on giving a good impression. He had to show taste, which meant knowing what was *correct*, and inclining therefore to conservatism and understatement. That is why for so long the bourgeois wore a black uniform, pointing out his precise rank only with details of cut and cloth. He did not aim to outdo other bourgeois but to keep up with them: moderation and the

[1] Cf. Hugues Le Roux, *Nos Fils* (1898), on his grandfather, 65–82.

traditional virtues were his guide. Do as others do: that was the level he worked up to. Do not be common: that was the barrier he had to maintain.

Education and the family were two of the principal concerns of the bourgeois and he spent a lot of his money on them. He had to equip his sons with the *baccalauréat* and his daughters with a dowry. He laid stress on the acquisition of *culture générale*, which distinguished him from mechanics and artisans; by the twentieth century he may have quickly forgotten his Latin but at least he could speak classical French.[1] He did not allow his wife to work, until 1914 at least, but used her to cultivate the domestic virtues of which he made himself the champion. He linked morality with chastity, fidelity and duty. Even when he asserted his independence against the Church, his quarrel with it was about politics, not about ethics.[2]

However, there are difficulties about this kind of definition of the bourgeoisie. One could buy oneself in or out of the class within a couple of generations. The distinction between bourgeois and noble was not absolutely clear. Those who had been bourgeois long enough, and were rich enough, married into the nobility, which gladly welcomed their hefty dowries. The richest industrialists and financiers—like Schneider, whose four daughters all married noblemen and whose grandson married an Orleans—were rapidly absorbed into the nobility. Those who could not wait made themselves noble by a do-it-yourself process: they just assumed titles, a process which became much easier once the republic was proclaimed. The number of nobles paradoxically rose after 1789. There were about three times as many people falsely parading titles in the twentieth century as there were genuine nobles. Two thousand claimed to have papal titles, but between 1831 and 1906 the pope granted only 300 titles. And it should be remembered that many of the genuine nobles had legally bought their titles before the Revolution, by purchasing state offices.[3] The bourgeoisie and

---

[1] Raoul de La Grasserie, *Des Parlers des différentes classes sociales. Études de psychologie et de sociologie linguistiques* (1909), distinguishes between bourgeois speech, *parler familier* which the bourgeois might speak at home, *parler populaire* of the masses, and criminal slang. Cf. my forthcoming study of this author.

[2] Edmond Goblot, *La Barrière et le niveau. Étude sociologique sur la bourgeoisie française* (1925).

[3] Vicomte de Marsay, *Du temps des privilèges* (1946), chapter 27; Jean de Belle-

the aristocracy had much in common; what differed now was
that movement between the classes was easier and more rapid.
The distinctions were less firm and therefore there was more
room for snobbish rejection. Noble exclusiveness was a matter
of show. It strongly resembled the *distinction* the bourgeoisie
cultivated. And the bourgeoisie adopted many of the ideals
associated with the aristocracy. Though they praised work,
their ideal was also to live off a private income, to have a house
in the country, and divide their time between it and the town
in exactly the same way as the aristocracy. Though they began
as revolutionaries—like the eighteenth-century nobility—many
of them, by the end of the nineteenth, had accepted Catholicism as a mark of respectability. Their attitude to commerce
was aristocratic. They adopted aristocratic attitudes towards
social status. The aristocracy for its part did not disdain to
work in the bourgeois civil service: the departments of finance
and justice and the army were particularly smart. The aristocracy joined the bourgeoisie in business and industry, particularly banks, insurance, railways, mines and steel, where the
boards of directors often contained between a third and a
quarter of noblemen.[1] The nobles went into agriculture in
a massive way after 1830, but many bourgeois also had farms.
Possibly the nobles claimed a peculiar quality and had as their
special ideal *prowess*—as opposed to bourgeois moderation.
They claimed this could not be acquired but could only be
inherited; but the bourgeoisie also laid great stress on family
qualities. Both were obsessed by making marriages of the
right kind, and their politeness differed no more than their
clothes. The argument therefore that the nineteenth-century
bourgeois cultivated ideals radically different from the aristocracy needs to be qualified. The nobles were former bourgeois and the bourgeoisie were moving up. They may have
differed before they reached the top, when they were
climbing, but they adopted many of the nobles' values when
they could.

fond, *La Ménagerie du Vatican* (1906); *Le Crapouillot* (1937), issue on 'Vraie et fausse
noblesse'; Woelmont de Brumagne, *La Noblesse francaise subsistante* (1928). See
below pp. 393 ff. for a discussion of the nobility.

[1] Jesse R. Pitts, 'The Bourgeois Family and French Economic Retardation'
(Ph.D. Harvard, unpublished thesis, 1957), 235 n.

In the same way the values of the bourgeoisie were shared by many of those beneath them in the social scale. The gradations were equally blurred here. The bourgeois was supposedly distinguished from the worker by his education, but this was a distinction made more definitely by the academic members of it: there were many members of the provincial bourgeoisie who managed their properties and held influential positions in business without having a *baccalauréat*. Likewise there were *bacheliers*, especially in towns, who were the sons of workers and small shopkeepers, but the possession of the supposedly distinctive bourgeois education did not make them bourgeois: many entered business or the civil service, but married into the class they came from and remained in it. The son of the *instituteur* often climbed up in the social hierarchy, but the relation of class and education was complex and not automatic. The *lycée* was not an exclusively bourgeois institution, and indeed some bourgeois refused to send their daughters to it because they would be contaminated by lower-class girls. The masses did not distinguish as clearly between secondary and primary education as did the professors, and among the illiterate, any sign of learning made a man a bourgeois. Supposedly, the bourgeoisie represented the triumph of merit but they were quick to entrench their privileges in their families with the same determination as the aristocracy. The passion for thrift and for property was shared by the peasants and the artisans. Only the factory worker refused this ideal, from despair, and he could be classified by the amount he drank, showing the degree of his despair.[1] The taste for culture was not a bourgeois prerogative: indeed it was precisely for his false interest and conservative philistinism that the bourgeois was attacked. Though the bourgeois went to the theatre, so did artisans, clerks and even some workers, and it was they who probably in even greater numbers flocked to the painting Salons. The bourgeois kept his wife at home and gave her a servant to do the housework; but the worker called his wife *la bourgeoise* precisely because she was often not a wage earner either. The dowry was a universal institution with all but paupers, until it was whittled away, from the bottom of the social scale upwards, by inflation and depression between the wars. After 1900 the dowry was no longer required of women

[1] D. Poulot, *Le Sublime* (1870).

who married officers. Officers used to have all sorts of compulsory aids to maintaining their status as an élite—they were forbidden to go to cheap cafés and restaurants, to take cheap seats in theatres or railways, their wives were forbidden to work. (A *lycée* headmistress who married a captain had to resign.) But as men from the ranks were increasingly given commissions (and after 1904 there were more of these than there were graduates of St. Cyr) the differences between the bourgeois officer and the ordinary soldier were more like the difference between a foreman and a worker. Many merchants with a working-class way of life had servants, though there was still the difference perhaps that the bourgeois's servant never took her meals at the same table. The workers began going on holiday to the country, some had houses in their place of origin, even if the seaside resorts divided themselves on a class basis. While at the top end the bourgeoisie aped the aristocracy, at the bottom end, and in certain circles, they imitated some working-class practices. Even before 1914, some began travelling third class, while prosperous shopkeepers with no pretence to gentility and who were not even parvenus travelled second or even first. Bourgeois students took on manual work when they could not afford their fees.[1]

Bourgeois values were thus not just bourgeois. Other classes could also claim at least some of them as their own. Had the aristocracy and the workers believed in radically different ways of life, there would have been far more conflict between the classes. But the bourgeoisie's moderation meant that they consciously or unconsciously represented the common denominator of the ambitions of their time. The phrase *la France bourgeoise* was thus a tautology in that to be a bourgeois meant to subscribe to the most general national aspirations. The worker was far from being always the enemy of these. The difficulties arose when in response to economic frictions, some of the bourgeoisie claimed to represent not the good life but the ruling class.

In the middle of the nineteenth century strong objections were voiced to the suggestion that France was divided into classes.[2] The Revolution, it was said, had abolished these. Gambetta refused to use the word class and spoke of *couches*

---

[1] There is a good critique of Goblot in M. L. Ferré, *Les Classes sociales dans la France contemporaine* (1936), published by the author.

[2] A. Vavasseur, *Qu'est-ce que la bourgeoisie?* (1897).

sociales.[1] Increasingly, bourgeois became a dirty word, used by different people to categorise their enemies: it meant the exploiter for the socialist, the master for the servant, the civilian for the soldier, the man of vulgar taste for the artist, the capitalist for the penniless.[2] The grandson of Henri Germain of the Crédit Lyonnais published his memoirs under the title *Bourgeoisie on Fire*. Maurice Boudet wrote a book in 1953 called *Appeal by the Bourgeoisie*, as though it had already been condemned.[3] In a reaction, leagues and societies were formed to defend the bourgeoisie as a class, menaced in particular by inflation.[4] Some urged that the communist menace could only be met if the bourgeoisie put aside its selfish preoccupations and resumed the leadership it had enjoyed in the Revolution.[5] Bishop Ancel of Lyon defended the bourgeoisie as a ruling class, anxious, and equipped by its culture and abilities, to rule. They were, he said, heirs to the victors of the Revolution but also to the *noblesse de robe*, they were distinguished by their ability to place the general good above their individual interests: 'it is magnificent', he wrote, 'to be a true bourgeois'.[6] There were protests against the accusation that the bourgeoisie had ruined the country, couched, for example, in these terms: 'We, the honest bourgeois, formed by solid traditions and nourished by knowledge and experience, we alone carry in our solid heads the salvation of civilisation, but we shall impose our law only by force of intellectual vigour and moral rectitude.' Such men rejected the definitions of the bourgeois as he who had a salon, or he who had capital, and argued that his most important quality was that he was accepted as one, and showed it by his *distinction*. They quoted a Gallup poll finding that 70 per cent of Frenchmen would prefer to live in the *belle époque* of the Third Republic as proof of the triumph of the bourgeois ideal and the continued desire of the French to be bourgeois.[7]

[1] For the meaning of this see Zeldin, *Politics and Anger*, chapter 7.

[2] Pierre Sanbert, *Notre Bourgeoisie* (Nancy, 1931); and cf. Jean V. Altier, *Les Origines de la satire antibourgeoise en France* (Geneva, 1966).

[3] André Germain, *La Bourgeoisie qui brûle* (1951); Maurice Boudet, *Bourgeoisie en appel* (1953); cf. Pierre Lucius, *Déchéances des bourgeoisies d'argent* (1936).

[4] R. Aron, *Inventaires III: classes moyennes* (1939), 287–340.

[5] Just Haristoy, *L'Heure de la bourgeoisie* (1937), 229.

[6] Alfred Ancel, *La Mentalité bourgeoise* (1950), 70.

[7] Felix Colmet Daâge, *La Classe bourgeoise. Ses origines, ses lois d'existence, son rôle social* (1959). Cf. Georges Hourdin, *Pour les valeurs bourgeoises* (1968).

A great deal of research is still needed to trace the changes that have occurred in the bourgeoisie and to throw light on its professional and regional variations. In some regions, for example, the bourgeoisie was keen on buying land, in others it was not. In some it isolated itself from the masses more than in others; in some there was more rapid social renewal than in others.[1] In primitive and poor districts the word had a special significance. Jules Simon recounts how in Brittany in the 1820s a retired naval foreman had married a peasant girl. She and her daughters, all dressed as peasants, worked manually on his farm, but nevertheless he was considered a bourgeois, because he always wore a bowler hat and frock-coat and never clogs. He read his newspaper, an occupation which took him all day. He was called *Monsieur* Frélaut. He kept the books of the *mairie* for a small salary (there was no schoolmaster then at Larmor) and he played his game of *boules* every afternoon with the other bourgeois of Larmor. His son was a bourgeois like him, destined for the priesthood. At noon dinner was served to M. Frélaut, in which his son participated during the holidays: a bourgeois dinner—meat or fish and vegetables. The messieurs were waited on by the mother and sisters, who sat down only when the men had finished, to eat pancakes, milk and sometimes a piece of pork fat. The father was an atheist, though all his family went to church and his son was studying for the priesthood. Here the Church was the best way to rise out of the peasantry and the seminaries were full of boys who gave up after a few years and took jobs as notaries, clerks or tutors with scarcely enough to live on but allowed to wear top hats and tattered frock coats and to be called 'monsieur'. A family that succeeded in getting a son into the priesthood considered itself almost ennobled and took on new airs. The priests and the bourgeois were the only ones in these remote areas who could speak French, even though the former often spoke it in a stilted and correct way like a foreign language.[2]

Because of the vagueness of the notion, the supremacy of bourgeois ideals cannot serve as a key to understanding the

---

[1] *La Bourgeoisie alsacienne* (Strasbourg, 1954, published by the Société savante d'Alsace). Abel Chatelian, *Les Horizons d'une géohistoire de la bourgeoisie lyonnaise* (Lyon, 1950, extract from the *Revue de Géographie de Lyon*).

[2] Jules Simon, *Premières Années* (1901), 39, 91, 319.

forces at work in French society, at least until a much more careful analysis of these ideals is undertaken. This will be attempted over the whole course of this book, by examining in turn different aspects of life and the values manifested in them. Meanwhile, the second problem posed at the beginning of this chapter, as to how far the bourgeoisie dominated France, in terms of economic, political and social activities, can perhaps best be approached by a few detailed case studies. Six occupations will now be investigated, to show how difficult it is to attribute influence or cohesion to them in any simple sense. The conflicts within each group, and the isolation of each group within society, meant that many separate worlds could coexist side by side. How they interacted and how they related to the rest of the country is a complex affair.

2. Doctors

THE care a nation takes of its health always reveals a lot about its attitudes to life. In France, the medical profession is particularly interesting, for there is a political dimension to its influence. Its rise to power in the state is one of the striking features of this century. There were 15 doctors in the Assembly of 1789, 26 in that of 1791, 40 in the Convention. About a dozen served in the smaller Restoration Chamber of Deputies and 28 in that of July. In 1848, 49 of the constituents were doctors, and in 1849, 34 of the legislators. There were 11 in Napoleon III's Corps Législatif of 251 members, 33 in the National Assembly of 1871, but by 1898 their number had risen to 72.[1] It may be argued from these figures that doctors gradually replaced the old landowning class and in some cases the clergy as leaders of public opinion and that in the Third Republic they reached the zenith of their prestige and influence. But to say this is to beg many questions: it is to assume that doctors were not also landowners, that their influence was an alternative and opposed to the old notable class, that the profession meant the same thing over 150 years, that the opportunities open to doctors were unchanging, and that their appearance in parliament always represented an acknowledgement of their influence, rather than that the doctors were seeking new fields in which to act, to compensate for difficulties they were experiencing in the exercise of their profession.

Medicine in France in this period was in fact in a state of confusion and division as total as that which afflicted politics. It is impossible to paint a picture of doctors as the products of a new science whose capacity and skill were gradually established, recognised and accepted. There was no one medical science, and the rivalry between the different theories was as merciless and disruptive as the cut-throat competition of commerce. In 1850 the medicine of cure by bleeding, purging and the administration of enemas was still in existence, for all the

[1] P. Trisca, *Les Médecins sociologues et hommes d'état* (1923).

discoveries of the capital cities, whose doctrines were slow to penetrate the countryside. The efforts of Voltaire's doctor Tronchin (1709–81) and his school to replace this by the use of fresh air, exercise, vegetarianism, water-drinking, breast-feeding and vaccination were slow to win acceptance. The enlightenment even saw a regression to the doctrine of vitalism— the belief that a mysterious vital element regulates the organs and fights death. This doctrine was taken up by the faculty of medicine of Montpellier and taught by it till the twentieth century—so that Paris and Montpellier taught medicine in radically different ways.[1] The training which the doctors prac-tising between 1850 and 1900 received preserved the strangest errors taught by men highly esteemed in the first half of the century. One of these, to take an example, was Broussais (1772–1838), a man of great eloquence, imposing presence, and unrelenting combativeness, who wielded great power in the medical world. He imagined that the cause of all diseases was inflammation, particularly in the intestines. He prescribed abundant blood-letting, leeches and severe diets. His starving patients, bled white, died like flies, but he was nevertheless made a professor at the faculty of Paris (1831). When towards the end of his career his star waned and his students turned elsewhere, he took up phrenology and his very popular lectures on this gave him a second lease of life. Equally influential but at a more popular level was F. V. Raspail (1794–1878), whose *Natural History of Health and Illness* (1843) and annual en-cyclopedias (1846–64) became best sellers as manuals of self-medication: he advocated camphor as the cure for all diseases.

Possibly the single most successful doctor of the nineteenth century was Philippe Ricord (1800–89), personal physician to Napoleon III and the national expert on syphilis. Born in Baltimore, the son of a bankrupt French shipowner, he rose to become Paris's busiest and possibly richest doctor. His house in the rue de Tournon contained five large salons for his patients to wait in: one for ordinary people, always crammed full and each given a number, one for women, who entered by a separate staircase, one for people with letters of recommendation, and a fourth for friends and doctors. All were decorated magnifi-cently with paintings and sculptures, for he was a great collector.

[1] F. Berard, *Doctrine médicale de Montpellier* (1819).

An enormous fifth reception salon had two Rubens, a Van Dyke, Géricaults, etc. His office contained on three walls a large library surmounted by a gallery of busts of the great physicians of all time, underneath it glass cases with Paris's best collection of surgical instruments and on the fourth wall portraits of his masters Dupuytren and Orfila, and one of himself by Couture. He was France's most decorated celebrity after Alexandre Dumas, with seventeen medals: he was popular not least for being a man of the world, indulgent to his patients and famous for his witticisms.[1] His *Treatise on Venereal Diseases* (1838) did rightly distinguish between gonorrhoea and syphilis, but he insisted that the latter was not contagious through secondary lesions: he continued to administer his incorrect doctrine to all the rich of Europe, despite the discoveries of the more obscure Joseph Rollet of Lyon (1856).

The visitor to Paris in 1848 would have found some 1,550 doctors there, 300 of them decorated with the legion of honour, offering every variety of cure. At least 50 per cent of them had published books to advocate their theories and many of them advertised in every available medium. Dr. Bachoni offered electro-physico-chemical treatments with no payment if no result. Dr. Barras offered a modification of the Broussais doctrine, replacing gastritis by gastralgia as the cause of all ills. Dr. Becquerel offered cures for stammering in conflict with those of Dr. Jourdan with whom he conducted public disputes. Dr. Belliol's name covered the walls of Paris and the small advertisement columns in the papers offering a 'new vegetal method'. Dr. Leuret, author of *The Moral Treatment of Madness* (1840), though refuted by Dr. Blanche and voted against by the Academy of Medicine, persisted in tying his mad patients to planks of wood and throwing cold water over them. Dr. Brièrre de Boismont wrote that the number of madmen was bound to increase with the progress of civilisation and profited from this by running an asylum for the middle class, at fees ranging from 8,000 to 12,000 francs a year.[2] Dr. Piorry invented 'plessimetrism', known alternatively as 'organographism', which used percussion to discover about internal organs, and wrote a book on *Common Sense Medicine* (1864), advocating less use of dangerous

---

[1] Paul Labarthe, *Nos Médecins contemporains* (1868), 44.
[2] See his article in *Annales d'Hygiène* (1839).

drugs, more curing by deep breathing and by spitting.[1] Dr.
Jean Giraudeau de Saint Gervais did not just cover the walls
of Paris with his name, but paid newspapers to praise him
and hacks to write books for him, and he had a permanent
column of advertisements in several papers. His *Manual of
Health, and Advice on the Art of Healing Oneself* was sold by the
thousand in grocer's shops.[2] All manner of healers adopted
scientific jargon and competed successfully against the teaching
of the faculties, but it was not a struggle of unqualified quacks
against learned professors. Phrenology (and also physiognomy
and cranioscopy), for example, had academicians and professors teaching it, and applying it to education, jurisprudence
and medicine. The Academy of Medicine treated old wives'
tales with respect: in 1846 a Breton girl, Angélique Cottin,
was reported to give electric shocks to those who touched her.
The Academy appointed a commission under Arago to report
on the case. In 1837 a member of the Academy established a
prize to encourage investigations of magnetic healing. The
'microscopists', 'pharmaco-chemists' and 'numerists' (applying
statistics to the study of disease) met with vigorous opposition.
The Academy did not disdain to discuss theoretical questions.
The doctors, far from ignoring the quacks and the theorists,
engaged in constant polemic with them, and the medical press
attacked and ridiculed every idea, new and old, and every
personality in the same slanderous and uninhibited way as the
political papers.[3] In the country, doctors had to fight the even
more powerful resistance of superstition and traditional remedies. A whole army of rival practitioners offered cheaper and
sometimes more acceptable treatment: the urine healer (who
prescribed medicines after examining the urine of the patient),
the *orviétan* merchant (the itinerant seller of drugs), the sorcerers,
the nuns, the priests, the old women, the midwives, the pharmacists. The peasants in any case had their own views about
diseases. They preferred annual purges to vaccination; they had
a firm belief in the hereditary nature of illnesses and thought
they could not catch (they would not have used that word in the

[1] Dr. Piorry, *La Médecine du bon sens* (1864).

[2] C. Sachaille de la Barre, *Les Médecins de Paris jugés par leurs œuvres ou statistique
scientifique et morale des médecins de Paris* (1845).

[3] Louis Peisse, *La Médecine et les médecins. Philosophie, doctrines, institutions, mœurs et
biographies médicales* (1857), 2 vols.

pre-microbe age) diseases their parents had not had; and they long persisted in calling in the doctor as a last resort—often too late—when all else had failed.[1]

In 1911 a doctor describing popular medicine in the Vendée reported that the doctrines of Broussais still had many fervent followers. Bone-setters still made a good living and died well-to-do, bequeathing their secrets to a chosen disciple on their deathbed. Magical and herbal cures, distributed by clairvoyantes, were much used; special trains were organised to take large crowds to holy places, where every disease was cured by miracles. Babies were given wine and eau-de-vie to make them strong. Madmen were considered to be the victims of curses and the Devil.[2] In 1953 an inquiry revealed that the competition of charlatans, especially in the countryside, remained very powerful.[3] The law made it very difficult to stop charlatans. If, for example, a doctor prescribed a remedy and the chemist who dispensed it decided to make it a speciality of his own, advertising it as 'recommended by Dr. X', nothing could be done to prevent him. Often these advertisements quoted recommendations from fictitious doctors, but the law again upheld their freedom. Thus in 1884 a doctor advertised artificial insemination saying that 'this operation which at first may seem immoral has not only been approved by the Academy of Medicine but has been the object of its felicitations and encouragement'—which was totally untrue. Another who sold 'uterine vacuum cleaners' claimed to have received medals for inventing it, but he was convicted for procuring abortions. At the turn of the century there were still doctors who prescribed superstitious remedies, like curing cancer by living on a boat on the Rhone and playing music during meals. The *Petit Méridional* of Montpellier contained advertisements by a doctor offering consultations by correspondence. This was fairly common: questionnaires were distributed for the prospective patient to fill in; when he had sent this in with a fee, he got back a prescription, often a very expensive one. It is true that Dr. Rey de Jougla, who, during the Second Empire, offered cures for all incurable diseases at

[1] Dr. Munaret, *Du Médecin des villes et du médecin de campagne. Mœurs et science* (1840, second edition).

[2] Dr. Boismoreau, *Coutumes médicales et superstitions populaires du bocage vendéen* (1911).

[3] Jean Éparvier, *Médecins de campagne: enquête* (1953), 23, 49, 64.

a flat rate of 16 francs was convicted for fraud, but it took a very long time to diminish the rivalry of the magnetisers and somnambulists, of whom in 1890 there were about 500 fully occupied in Paris alone. The faculty of medicine then voted to condemn them, but the government nevertheless allowed the foundation of a school to train them. In the 1890s, the courts were divided about them, some convicting them of illegal practice of medicine, but some (notably Angers) acquitting them. By a law of 1805 nuns and priests were allowed to give medical care, provided they signed no prescriptions and gave their advice free—but many women's orders did in fact distribute medicine and in Morbihan the success of their 150 illegal pharmacies was such that in the last twenty-five years of the century the number of doctors practising diminished by a third, driven out by their cheaper competition.

It is a mistake to think that science improved the health of the nation in gradual stages. The adoption of antiseptics by the French army was so slow that there was an actual regression in the efficiency of amputations: in the Napoleonic wars only about 2 per cent died after these operations but in the 1870 war the mortality was far higher, on occasions reaching 100 per cent.[1] The association of typhoid with impure water was established in 1854 but it was only in 1886 when the secretary of the Academy of Sciences lost three daughters from it that the idea was accepted, and in the 1890s deaths from typhoid were halved. There were, however, always areas of the country which resisted new remedies: smallpox continued to flourish because of objections to vaccination, especially in Brittany. The doctors were often their own worst enemies: it was not simply that they were unable to defend themselves against charlatans. The commission appointed by the ministry of justice in 1895 to find means to combat morphinomania 'which was invading all classes of society' blamed the spread of the addiction on the example set by doctors and pharmacists.[2]

Just as in politics the Action Française revealed reaction towards traditionalism in the period between the two world wars, so at the same time there was a similar return to the past

[1] P. M. M. Laignel-Lavastine, *Histoire générale de la médecine* (1949), 3. 9.
[2] Dr. P. Brouardel, *L'Exercice de la médecine et le charlatanisme* (1899), 106, 155, 249, 465–82.

in medical doctrines. Neo-Hippocratism was taken up by many distinguished doctors, professors and deans of faculty, culminating in the National Congress of Neo-Hippocratic Medicine in 1937, which was widely supported and reported. This doctrine stressed that the causes of many diseases remained unknown, that chemistry had its limits, that there should be a return to the clinical approach and to an appreciation of the individual temperament of each patient. Writing in 1945 on *Official and Heretical Medicine*, Alexis Carrel, the Nobel Prize winning biologist, described the differences which divided French medicine as inevitable reflections of differing conceptions of man and life. On the one hand there was official medicine, approved by the faculties and the state, but against it was independent medicine, often favoured by younger doctors starting their careers. It was not just the failure of the faculties to reform their educational methods. (The efforts of the powerful Charles Bouchard, professor at Paris from 1879 to 1912, co-operating with his friend Louis Liard, vice-rector of the Sorbonne, were defeated by the conservatism of the profession.) The variety of medical approaches in the nineteenth century crystallised in the twentieth into better-argued rival systems, often metaphysically based, and partially representing a reaction against physical-chemical science—not dissimilar to the reaction seen also in literature. Distinguished practitioners wrote in favour of reviving the study of 'humours'. Acupuncture was introduced in the 1920s and Soulié de Morant's book (1934) popularised it. Even medical astrology became respectable, rechristened cosmobiology. The first French Congress of Therapeutics in 1933 showed a new stress on nature cures. Above all, homoeopathy, which had first come to France with its inventor Samuel Hahnemann in 1835 and had won over about 150 doctors by 1914, increased its following to 567 doctors with orthodox qualifications by 1938, plus over 1,500 unqualified practitioners.[1] The homoeopaths were, it is true, bitterly divided themselves on the exact application of their doctrine: a modernising sect under Frotier-Bernoville modified the traditional teaching to make it fit with that of the Neo-Hippocratics. While Freud made some converts in the treatment of mental illness there were numerous alternatives to

[1] Laignel-Lavastine, 3. 576.

psycho-analysis. Desoille and Guillerey each developed different
cures using dreams, the former basing his theories on those of
his master Caslan the occultist. There was a long tradition of
experiment with hypnosis. Miraculous cures were seriously
defended. Whereas in 1904 and 1912 doctors who tried to
write theses about the religious cures of Lourdes were failed,
in 1930 Dr. Monnier successfully got a thesis on this subject
accepted. As early as 1879 doctors had formed a medical
authentication bureau at Lourdes, which Dr. Boissarie had run
very successfully from 1891 to 1917, opening their findings to all
the profession. Between the wars, scientifically inexplicable
phenomena, far from being discredited, became respectable.
In 1936 Dr. Delore called for the creation of a 'national institute for the authentication and scientific study of traditional and
empiric practices'.[1]

Doctors thus remained controversial figures throughout
these hundred years and did not automatically benefit from
the respect for men of science to which—rather theoretically—
it is assumed they must have been increasingly entitled. In 1833
Balzac did indeed write: 'Today the peasant prefers to listen to
the doctor who gives him a prescription to save his body than to
the priest who sermonises him about the salvation of his soul.'
But he also made the doctor say: 'I was a bourgeois and for
them [the peasants] a bourgeois is an enemy.'[2] A century later
a doctor writing his memoirs said the worker preferred the
schoolmaster to the doctor because the former was 'a man of
learning and only half a bourgeois, whereas the doctor is a complete bourgeois and often a clerical too'.[3] The position of the
doctors remained ambivalent. The question to ask about them
is not how they rose in the social scale, how they won status and
respect, for they were always a group of great diversity and
attitudes to them varied according to region and circumstance
almost as much as they changed with time. The important
point to realise is that for long the doctor's profession was not

---

[1] P. Delore, médecin des hôpitaux de Lyon, *Tendances de la médecine contemporaine.
La Médecine à la croisée des chemins* (1936), 164–89; Alexis Carrel (ed.), *Médecine
officielle et médecines hérétiques* (1945); A. L. J. Rouot, *Essai sur l'information médicale du
public* (Bordeaux, 1959) is a brief introduction to a subject that deserves further
investigation.

[2] H. de Balzac, *Le Médecin de campagne* (1832).

[3] Dr. Ch. Fiessinger, *Souvenirs d'un médecin de campagne* (1933), 96.

really a career. Only to a very limited extent was it a way of
rising in the world, partly because those who entered it needed
a lot of capital to obtain the education, and partly because it
seldom yielded high rewards. Charton's *Guide to Careers* of 1842
stressed the heavy expenses involved and the poor rewards:
'Some can obtain an honest living (from the exercise of medicine) but most will attain a mediocrity of position which is really
hardly encouraging.'[1] He thought 3,000 francs a year was as
much as the majority could expect to make. What he recommended the profession for was its independence. It allowed
a man to be his own master. This was one of its great attractions
when independence was a widespread ideal. The man who
invested a similar amount of money in setting up a business or
shop wanted to be his own master too, but very often he planned
to make more money quickly so as to buy state bonds and retire
to real independence on the interest. The doctor could not
usually expect to make money; he seldom retired; his training
was to a certain extent a sort of liberal education which enabled
him to give dignity and influence to a modest inherited wealth.
The doctors of humble origin—like Emile Combes—usually
needed to marry money and ideally to marry the daughter of
a doctor in practice. In the mid nineteenth century doctors
could not live off fees from the masses: they were kept in practice by the fees of the rich, who as it were subsidised the influence
doctors obtained by giving free or almost free treatment to the
poor. This is one of the reasons why the doctor appeared so
obviously as a bourgeois. But by no means all had the qualities
to attract rich patients. To succeed in the upper ranks of the
profession needed more than brains: 'nepotism, favoritism,
camaraderie are carried to the highest degree'.[2] This explains
why so many were forced to advertise, to offer cut prices and
quack, but attractive and guaranteed, cures. But the real way
to success became to find a part-time official appointment,
giving a prestige which attracted more clients and yielding a
small but fixed supplementary income (they were called 'fixes').
The plum appointments were of course physician to the bishop,
consultant at the local hospital, but prison doctor, police
surgeon, director of a thermal establishment were all valuable.
Above all the less successful became official doctors treating the

[1] Charton, 394. [2] Charton, 387.

poor of the commune, for which they often got a third or less of their very lowest normal fee, but at least the guarantee of some regular business. The development of these subsidiary occupations, the increase in the number of state and local authority bodies which employed doctors, the growth of mutual benefit societies which insured against illness, and the beginnings of a social security system gradually transformed the situation of many doctors, making them almost civil servants or officials— but of a somewhat *ancien régime* type—paid in small amounts from various sources.

It is difficult to discover how much the doctors earned at different times. There are certainly ample complaints about the inadequacies of their rewards, laments that there were too many of them chasing too few patients, who did not pay their bills, regrets that doctors did not have a uniform like the priest and the magistrate to improve their status, and descriptions of some who 'spoke Greek and Latin to men who hardly understood French' and lined their consulting rooms with books to heighten the impression of a mystic craft.[1] A doctor wrote a book in 1889 protesting against the ridiculous fee of one franc a head p.a. paid for working in the medical service for the indigent, objecting to doctors being pushed to the very bottom of the social ladder and ironically declaiming: 'We do not dispute the first rank to the magistrature, clergy or army. Nor do we wish to place ourselves on the same level as engineers, actors, painters, architects and sculptors. We ask only that we may occupy a middle rank, more or less: we would like for example to be classed between the solicitor and the photographer'—not so much for the respect as for financial reward.[2] It is interesting that he felt the magistrates and clergy looked upon him as a rival 'who penetrates the innermost secrets of families'.[3] In

[1] Dr. Munaret, *Du Médecin des villes et du médecin de campagne. Mœurs et science* (2nd edition 1840)—a curious collection of social information, interestingly in praise of the petty bourgeoisie.

[2] Dr. Victor Macrobius, *Malades, médecins et pharmaciens* (1889), 36.

[3] Dr. P. Brouardel, *Le Secret médical* (1887), 87. Certainly doctors were not insignificant intermediaries in the marriage market and they worried about how their oath of professional secrecy should affect their attitude in inquiries made to them in arranged marriages: should they reveal that their patients were afflicted with syphilis? Such was the atmosphere of secrecy among them that some even refused to issue certificates giving the cause of death—some even to issue death certificates at all.

1901 in an impressionistic but instructive survey of 'the intellectual proletariat', it was estimated that half a dozen doctors earned between two and three hundred thousand francs a year, about a hundred over 40,000, but about 80 per cent less than 8,000 francs. The majority of doctors, therefore, were 'proletariat' if they did not have private means. Many doctors in Paris tried to supplement their income by acting as 'beaters' for more famous colleagues, working for pharmacists to help sell expensive drugs, doing abortions etc. In the provinces half the doctors could not earn a decent living—but 'the inquisitorial habits of the countryside' did not allow interlopers to establish themselves easily. The less successful relied on making a good marriage, and so becoming farmers, industrialists or *rentiers*, according to the size of the dowry they obtained. 'The least favoured went into politics.'[1]

Le Concours Médical, a professional journal, estimated in 1881 that 12,000 francs was the minimum a doctor needed to live in the wealthier parts of France and asserted that the majority were far from earning this. 'They spend their patrimony. Fortunately sometimes a dowry re-establishes some sort of balance and allows them to educate their children.' One should not take their complaints too literally, for one Alsatian country doctor admitted to earning a modest income but added that it was as much as the combined salaries of the priest, the pastor and the rabbi.[2] A doctor writing to the paper at this time reported earning 11,000 a year, except that 35 to 40 per cent of his fees were never paid, so he got only some 7,000. This was a common complaint. There was an enormous amount of haggling over fees and the doctors contributed to it by varying their fees according to what they thought they could extract from their patients. Dr. Récamier, physician to Mme de Boigne, said in 1828 that the fee for a visit used to be 3 francs but he felt he must ask for 6. However, for her, he would reduce it to 4. Nevertheless, in the middle of the 1860s provincial doctors were still asking for only 1½ or 2 francs, and most of the consultations in their offices were free. The General Association of Doctors of France, founded in 1858, was opposed to uniformity or any central control, claiming that doctors could not be

---

[1] Henry Bérenger *et al.*, *Les Prolétaires intellectuels en France* (1901), 7–9.
[2] Dr. Georges Laffitte, *Le Médecin* (1936), xx.

expected to keep accounts and that they had no need for pensions. It argued that a doctor would lose prestige if he surrendered 'that arbitrary power which allows him, depending on the time, the place, the nature and the degree of the services rendered and a thousand other circumstances, to raise or to lower the price of his treatment'. In 1879 a more radical association, the Concours Médical, was founded to press for higher and more uniform fees: in 1897 it publicised Dr. Jeanne's tariff, as a model for adoption by local associations. But even this divided patients into three classes by wealth, and recommended flexibility between 1 and 10 francs a visit, depending on the patient's income; moreover it allowed many additions for extra time and care, and suggested the figures should be multiplied by ten for the 'highest masters of medicine'. In the same year the doctors of the Haute-Saône adopted a minimum tariff—on this same three-class basis—and the practice spread to other departments. The main benefit was to extract considerably more money from public authorities and insurance companies.[1] To get private patients to pay their bills, however, remained difficult: both the ethical code and the law made it almost impossible to force them. In some parts of France, e.g. Allier, doctors were customarily paid only after their patient's death, as a share in his inheritance, and it was normal everywhere to wait a long time for payment.

The elimination of competition by the unqualified and by charlatans was slow and never fully successful. For the first three-quarters of the nineteenth century, the main demand of the doctors was the abolition of the 'officers of health'. Until 1838 these were men, usually of humble origin, glorified medical orderlies, who obtained diplomas to practise medicine from specially instituted departmental committees with very low standards. After this date the faculties issued the diplomas and in 1854 the departmental commissions were abolished, so that the standard of education gradually rose. In the last decade of the July Monarchy almost as many diplomas were issued (2,850) as doctorates in medicine (3,045) but by 1869–78 the ratio fell to 1,014 officers against 5,344 doctors and by 1889–97 to 627 officers against 6,658 doctors. The idea had

[1] J. L. Cariage, *L'Exercice de la médecine en France à la fin du 19ᵉ siècle et au début du 20ᵉ siècle* (1965, privately printed).

been that in the poorer regions which had no fully qualified doctor, the officers of health would provide some medical services. In fact the officers found more lucrative employment in the richer areas, and large sections of the country continued to be underprivileged. In 1891 the poor department of Lozère had 24 doctors and only one officer; the Somme had 83 doctors and 141 officers, the Nord 353 doctors and 201 officers. The problem of the officers gradually died out: whereas in 1848 there were about 7,500 of them, in 1900 there were only 2,000 left. Instead foreign doctors became the new bogey: there were 541 in 1911, 750 in 1929, but even more threatening was the number of foreign medical students, who were particularly noticeable because they tended to concentrate in a few towns. In 1931 for example 76 per cent of the students at the Rouen medical school were foreign, at Tours 41 per cent.[1] Charlatans bought doctorates abroad, especially from the university of Philadelphia, which advertised them for sale at 500 francs.

In the country doctors often dealt with teeth as well, but in towns increasing competition came from a growing number of dentists. Dentistry required no qualifications: some practitioners were former mechanics and locksmiths. In 1890 France had only some 2,000 dentists (600 of them in Paris) as opposed to 4,000 in England and 15,000 in the U.S.A. The Americans' recognised superiority resulted in many of these coming to practise in France: Evans, dentist to Napoleon III, was one of the first and most famous. Many young Englishmen also found it useful to serve an apprenticeship in France, where there were no examinations: the enormous Dental Clinic of the Louvre was entirely manned by Englishmen. In 1892 a law was passed requiring qualifications for dentists and penalising the illegal practice of medicine in general. Hitherto the law had only allowed individuals to sue charlatans and they had to show that they had personally suffered damage. Now trade unions were allowed to bring charlatans to court. But their efforts seemed only to make the latter more famous. The herborists were spared by the new law (there were 300 of them in Paris, 50 in Marseille, and 50 more in other towns). Napoleon had established examinations for them, as a kind of junior health officer;

---

[1] Dr. Georges Laffitte, *Le Médecin. Sa Formation, son rôle dans la société moderne* (Bordeaux, 1936), 70.

a decree of 1854 had divided them into two classes, so con-
firming their status; and in 1892 the pressure from the doctors
to abolish them was unsuccessful because it would have been
extremely expensive to buy them out, their shops being worth
over 100,000 francs each when put up for sale.

As a result of all this competition and confusion, the nineteenth century did not see the rise in the number of doctors that
is often assumed to have occurred. On the contrary between
1847 and 1896 the number of doctors fell by some 3,500 and
the number of officers of health by nearly 5,000—though if one
counts all those who actually practised, the figures show
smaller diminution. The increase occurred only in the twentieth century, after the supposed zenith of medical influence.
The idea of medical influence needs to be analysed more carefully. The opportunities open to the upper ranks of the profession did gradually widen. At first it was men at the very top,
members of the Academy of Medicine, founded in 1820, who
were consulted by the government. Then in the Second Empire
onwards, specialised national and local committees were
officially established to deal with public hygiene, hospitals,
schools, etc., which gave some doctors a chance to become a
cross between notables and official advisers. Finally in 1930
the creation of the ministry of public health made it possible
for doctors to become senior civil servants and administrators
using public money. Meanwhile at the level of the mass of
doctors, important transformations were also occurring. It
became increasingly difficult to survive as a family doctor,
particularly if one tried to maintain a bourgeois standard of
living comparable with that of the more successful in the profession. More and more doctors took on part or full-time work
on a salaried basis and became workers in the sanitary industry
instead of independent professional men. They then began
forming trade unions, bargaining to improve their conditions
like other workers. Inevitably they could not unite completely.
Only in 1928 was a fusion achieved between the Union of
Medical Trade Unions and the Federation of Medical Trade
Unions. The Vichy regime organised the doctors into a corporation run by a state-controlled Order of Doctors, against which
organisations have developed to oppose its dictatorship. A
Federation of Salaried Doctors has also been founded, and

separate unions for general practitioners and specialists. The
latter represent an important new rift. In 1958 there were no
fewer than 14,680 specialists, i.e. one for every two general
practitioners: specialisation was institutionalised in 1930 when
the Social Insurance took the decision to reimburse specialist
treatment at higher rates. The divisions did not prevent the
doctors from looking more like a pressure group, fighting for
public funds, pursuing selfish interests. The myth of the doctors
as a solid phalanx of anticlericals and atheists also needs to be
exploded. In 1936 a book was published entitled *The Freemason
Doctors*, but the authors were able to produce few names to
support their accusation. Doctors have stood for parliament as

	Doctors in practice	Total doctors	Officers of health
1847		18,099	7,456
1866	11,254	16,822	5,568
1876		14,326	3,633
1886	11,995		2,794
1896	13,412	14,538	2,114
1906	18,211		
1911	20,113		
1921	20,364		
1931	25,410		200
1958	30,318	47,000	

members of almost every party. There were certainly not more
doctors in France than elsewhere. The impression visitors to
Paris got that there must be was fair enough, because (in 1931)
Paris did indeed have more doctors than any other city in
Europe. But France as a whole came seventeenth in the world
for the density of doctors, having one for every 1,578 inhabitants, compared to 1,183 in Great Britain, 1,280 in Germany,
1,326 in the U.S.A., and 788 in Austria. Proportionate to the
population, there were over three times fewer doctors in Mayenne than in Seine.[1]

The problems facing doctors, the way they made careers for
themselves, and the nature of their influence can be illuminated
by taking a few examples. Dr. Gabriel Maurange, born in

[1] Jacqueline Pincemin and Alain Laugier, 'Les Médecins', in *Revue Française
des Sciences Politiques* (Dec. 1959), 881–900; G. Laffitte, *Le Médecin* (Bordeaux,
1936), 31.

Bordeaux in 1865, had a clog maker as a grandfather and a railway clerk as a father; and his brother trained as a barrister,
though marriage turned him into a wine merchant. He failed
his *baccalauréat* in philosophy and so tried the one in science
instead, which he passed; he decided to enter medical school
rather than the Polytechnique partly because his mother had
died owing to neglect by her doctor. Bordeaux was still pretty
backward in medicine in the 1880s: sterilisation was adopted
only by accident, because the professor happened to see it used
on a visit to Paris for the *concours d'agrégation*. The system of
patronage, of the professor having a select band of disciples,
was in full vigour. When Maurange tried to write a thesis on a
mistaken diagnosis by his professor and to suggest a new cure for
peritonitis, the latter was furious and Maurange left for Paris.
It was easy enough qualifying but without a protector it was
almost impossible to establish oneself. The favourite students—
the *internes*—were given public posts to start them off; but the
vast majority barely knew their professors more than by sight
and as the number of students increased (they doubled between 1900 and 1935) they were lucky if they got that far.
Maurange was penniless but he knew that if he was to succeed
he must pretend that he was successful. He borrowed 500 francs.
He got smart bourgeois clothes on credit from a Jewish tailor. He
took a flat in the rue Littré for 650 francs and employed a *femme
de ménage*. He hired a carriage for 300 francs a month—a cheap
rate, because he used it only in the mornings; in the afternoons
it was let to rich old ladies. He spent his evenings talking to
young men in his own position: the eternal subject was how to
succeed. He was saved by the 'flu epidemic of 1889–90—he
helped the physician to the senate and earned 600 francs. The
south-west network assisted him: provincials nearly always
kept together in the capital and the successful among them
passed on patronage to the beginners. He asked his protector
to get him the *palmes académiques* from the senate: thus decorated,
he grew his beard, looked solemn, and ventured on a debt of
6,000 francs to set up consulting rooms. He made 5,000 francs
in his first year, but he also got to know some aristocratic
families. His name was passed round, and by his third year he
was up to 12,000 and in his fourth he had doubled that. He
found incredible ignorance among these aristocratic clients of

the most elementary principles of hygiene, limitless credulity in every kind of healer, absolute faith in all remedies which had the picture of a priest or nun on the label or simply the statement that they were manufactured in a convent or monastery. The aristocracy all had family doctors, but ignored their advice and kept them rather as a kind of retainer. The rich liked to call in second opinions. Maurange in the 1890s inaugurated the practice of seeing clients only by appointment and he did well. His father in Bordeaux, who from timidity had opposed his move to Paris, was now dazzled by his success and they were reconciled. Maurange's income increased as the social level of his clientele went up. He augmented it by starting a nurses' school but he made the mistake of having it undenominational: the religious issue brought discord: the protestants captured dominance, and he left, but rich enough now to give up all his part-time jobs. In 1908 he moved to a more fashionable address near the Madeleine. The war brought many foreign patients, particularly English and American ones, and he increasingly developed this lucrative side of his work. He obtained the title of Chevalier of the Legion of Honour, thanks to the actor Monnet-Sully of the Comédie Française, whose doctor he was and who was a friend of Clemenceau. The decoration brought a great increase in the demand for his services and the famous specialists began calling him *cher ami*.[1]

In the provinces success was achieved more gradually; several generations were often needed to build up influence, clientele and income. In Mende, capital of the Lozère (population about 6,000), the majority of medical practitioners in the eighteenth century were not doctors: the town had twenty-five surgeons, nine apothecaries and seventeen doctors—the surgeons receiving their education from privately owned schools. But after the Revolution surgeons were compelled to take degrees in medicine and faculties were opened for pharmacists. There was thus an upgrading and equalisation of the different categories. But there was not room in a small town for so many qualified people expecting to live at a fairly high standard: the number of doctors fell to eight or nine. The amount of money spent on medicine was concentrated into few channels and the 'notable' doctors of the nineteenth century

[1] Dr. Gabriel Maurange, *Livre de raison d'un médecin parisien 1815–1938* (1938).

were the result. Even then only one or two rose to this 'notable' level at any one time. The history of the unsuccessful doctors and those who dealt with the poor is undocumented: but their poverty was almost inevitable, since the 'notables' were shameless pluralists, monopolising so many of the official appointments open to doctors and then handing them down from father to son, that there were few pickings left for the majority. One such notable family was established during the Revolution by J. P. Barbut. He was the son of a peasant, but because he was sickly and had a malformed arm, he was sent to school. He was patronised by a doctor who helped him to qualify. He became a deputy, a justice of the peace, director of the Bagnols thermal waters, took up farming, wrote a book on the agriculture of the Lozère and became a member of the Superior Council of Agriculture—while continuing to minister to all classes. Medicine was thus only a part of a wider social activity. After his death, his practice was taken over by his son-in-law, Aristide Barbot, born in 1800, who practised from 1827 to 1861. This man, the son of a banker-barrister, had enough capital to spend 6,319 francs modernising his equipment in 1829–30; and he was able to have his sons educated in Paris. He lived comfortably, at the rate of about 2,500 francs a year. He subscribed to the *Journal de Médecine* to keep himself up to date; he improved his standing in the town by introducing Lennec's methods of auscultation and Morton and Jackson's anaesthesia with little delay. He accumulated the posts of prison doctor, member of the sanitary council, surgeon to the National Guard, member of the commission for public education and the *école normale*, and was elected municipal councillor. He hunted, played whist in a new club of which he was a founder member, went to the theatre, and gave dinners, above all, great family dinners: he had four brothers and sisters and sixteen cousins-german and his wife had fourteen cousins. He was a liberal; he kept all his jobs through every revolution. He married his elder daughter to a notary, his younger son became a notary, and his eldest succeeded him in his own practice (1857–98). This son married the daughter of a manufacturer, became mayor of the town, inherited his father's appointments, and collected even more, outdoing him also in the sumptuousness of his dinners—rivalry in which was one of the pastimes of the bourgeoisie. And he was succeeded by his son. The nineteenth century was a golden age for the pharmacists too—the number in Mende fell to one or two—and monopoly brought them great prosperity. Even so, one family after having produced five generations of pharmacists, brought up the next son to be a doctor—the inevitable social progression.[1]

Success in medicine was, to many doctors, only a means to an end. Their ideal of the good life, while including service to the community, also often involved activity in other spheres, and in particular the arts. French doctors were famous for their dedication to hobbies, and one can see the place these had in their lives if one looks at some of the leading luminaries. Hippolyte Hérard (1819–1913), president of the Academy of Medicine, gave as much effort to his piano playing to the point of almost having two careers: 'was not Aesculapius the son of Apollo?' Albert Robin (1847–1928), who became a member of the Academy of Medicine at forty, also ran the metallurgical factory he inherited from his father and was a reviewer for the *New York Herald* for many years, which did not stop him publishing over 400 articles in medical journals and being a consultant to the Tsar of Russia. He, by the way, had been cut off by his father when he originally refused to enter the family business, and he had worked his way through medical school on his own. Louis Brocq (1856–1928) was another who was cut off for refusing to be a barrister like his father and his brother, both of them *bâtonniers* of Agen. When he became famous as a doctor the father relented, reconciliation took place, and he spent his annual holidays at home in Agen. But Brocq's passion was collecting: he had paintings by Monet, Pissarro, Sisley, Renoir and Degas. Jean Hallé (1868–1951) came of a long line of painters going back to the seventeenth century, though some members of his family turned to medicine in the nineteenth. He was a family doctor in the Faubourg Saint Germain where his family had lived for 300 years. He painted, exhibited, travelled abroad and between his two country houses.[2] French doctors have long had a very flourishing painting society, with large

[1] Dr. Marcel Barbot, 'Médecins, chirurgiens, et apothicaires mendois des origines au 20ᵉ siècle' (1952, unpublished typescript).

[2] Édouard Rist, *Vingt-cinq portraits de médecins français 1900–50* (1955), lives of members of the Academy of Medicine.

exhibitions; they have been critics and patrons of the arts.[1] An extraordinarily large number of writers have been trained as doctors, and not a few of them have then used their knowledge to attack the profession they forsook or could not find a place in, for its powerlessness and credulity.[2]

Two tentative conclusions may be suggested. The prestige of science and the conquests of medicine placed the doctors in key positions in society, but, like the clergy, their knowledge and their medicine was challenged. Their exclusiveness produced a hostility or jealousy against them which was the counterpart to the anticlericalism which the clergy aroused. This is a factor which needs to be weighed in any discussion of the domination of the bourgeoisie. Each section of this class raised itself up by a monopoly which gave them power and enemies at the same time. Bourgeois society was riddled with a vast number of different anticlericalisms. In these many-sided conflicts, not everybody knew who was his worst enemy. Secondly, the doctors demonstrate, as the other occupations to be discussed will also, that the prestige of technical knowledge in any one subject was seldom accepted as being, by itself, an adequate mark of success. The ideal of general culture remained the final crowning of life. Hence the preoccupation with the arts and letters which was so common. It will be argued in due course that perhaps one ought to talk not of the domination of France by the bourgeoisie, nor even by money, but of the unacknowledged rule of the intellectuals.

A later chapter, dealing with psychology,[3] will discuss in greater detail the relationship of the doctors with the intellectuals. Doctors, and particularly those concerned with mental health, offered explanations of human behaviour and motivation which were not necessarily the same as those proposed by philosophers, or biographers, or novelists. This question, of the way different groups viewed emotion, nervousness, melancholy and other similar troubles, can yield important clues about both the compartmentalisation of French society and about the ideas that were generally accepted in it.

[1] Dr. Paul Labarthe, *Le Carnet du docteur au salon de peinture de 1874* (1874).

[2] Dr. François Salières, *Écrivains contre médecins* (1948); René Cruchet, *La Médecine et les médecins dans la littérature française* (Louisiana and Bordeaux, 1933).

[3] See Zeldin, *France 1848–1945*, vol. 2; Zeldin, *Anxiety and Hypocrisy* (forthcoming).

3. Notaries

ANOTHER occupation which was regarded as having a key position in social, political and economic life was that of notary. The traditional picture of the notary is of a stable, respectable, conservative and well-to-do man exercising a profound and acknowledged influence on the masses. It is true that the notaries were often mayors of their villages. Even today 200 of them still are. The notaries published many books and articles in praise of their profession and stressing their responsibilities as notables.[1] One from Besançon, for example, writing in Napoleon III's reign, ascribed their importance to their being not only public functionaries but also independent men who held their posts for life, and had paid for them. Their duties, he said, placed them on a par with the clergy, for they were present 'at the origin and end of all things in civil life, as the priest is in the religious order. It is the notary who in the marriage contract establishes the first bases and first links of the family; it is he whom the dying man summons to his bedside to confide his final wishes. As a guardian of every kind of interest, as a confidant of the most secret thoughts, as arbiter in most business deals, as an almost necessary intermediary in the movement of property and capital, he becomes the friend, the judge, the protector of families. The good he can do in these tasks can be readily understood: he can prevent divisions between relatives, he can diminish the demands of a greedy or discontented creditor, save an unfortunate debtor from complete ruin; protect minors, women and absentees in the inventory, accounting and division of bequests; in short, everywhere he represents law and justice.'[2]

There were about 40,000 notaries in the late eighteenth century, 13,900 in 1803, 10,300 in 1834, 9,765 in 1855, 8,910 in 1894, 8,164 in 1912, and 6,323, in 1969. These figures at once

[1] Good bibliography in Albert Amiaud, *Recherches bibliographiques sur le notariat français* (1881).

[2] Édouard Clerc, président de la chambre des notaires de Besançon, *Théorie du notariat pour servir aux examens de capacité* (3rd edition 1861), xxii.

reveal one of the main and constant problems of the profession: that it was <u>overcrowded</u> and that a large proportion was unable to get a decent living out of it. In the *ancien régime* there was an immense variety of notaries, royal and seigniorial, so that every little town had one and often more than one, and sometimes even villages had them.[1] Inevitably a lot were on the level of impecunious artisans; it was not unusual for their wives to be shopkeepers. An author writing in 1891 had personally known a Breton notary whose wife kept an inn next to her husband's office, to which his clients went for a drink before and after their business.[2] Until the eighteenth century, the notary's office was called a *boutique*; the first occasion the word *étude* was used was in 1736. In this period, the value of these practices was often low, since they were increasingly burdened by many kinds of taxation—even if they were exempt from many other taxes—and their profits were diminished by the creation of many new offices by the king. The top echelons had acquired compatibility of their profession with nobility, but the lowest were struggling for a bare living. In the cahiers of 1789, they demanded above all a reduction in their numbers, the prevention of competition between themselves and the suppression of rival professions. Napoleon met their wishes in part. He kept only the state notaries, and he divided these into three classes, the first with the right to practise within the jurisdiction of a court of appeal (about 4 per cent of them), the second within an *arrondissement* (about 13 per cent), and the third within a canton (the vast majority). They retained the ownership of their offices, with the right to sell them. They were <u>civil servants but received no salary, relying</u> entirely on fees. They thus kept a <u>great deal of independence</u>, but their plutocratic recruitment kept them in constant fear that their offices might be nationalised. There was frequent talk of buying them out and opening the profession to competition by examination —but it was calculated in the 1850s that this would require at least 800 million francs—as much as it cost to build a whole railway system.[3]

[1] Ludovic Langlois, *La Communauté des notaires de Tours de 1512 à 1791* (1911), 472.
[2] Jules Rouxel, *La Crise notariale. Étude économique et psychologique du notariat moderne* (1891), 20.
[3] A. Jeannest St. Hilaire, *Du Notariat et des offices* (1857), 115.

In order to become a notary one needed no diploma and even today the majority of notaries do not have a school leaving certificate (*baccalauréat*).[1] One usually served an apprenticeship[2] —but the 30,000 to 40,000 notaries' clerks very rarely became notaries, because the main qualification was the possession of 15,000 to 20,000 francs at the very least, in the mid nineteenth century, to buy the cheapest *étude*, and 40,000 francs upwards for most others, 100,000 francs for one in a departmental capital, 300,000 francs in a Paris suburb and up to 700,000 francs for the most lucrative of all in the centre of Paris.[3] In addition the purchaser had to give the state caution money varying according to the area he served, 1,800 to 5,200 francs for third-class notaries, 3,000 to 12,000 francs for second-class ones and 40,000 to 50,000 francs for the first class. The size of the town did not count in this reckoning of caution money: Roubaix with a population of 100,000 in the 1890s still required only 5,200 francs, because it was only the capital of a canton, but Nantes, with the same population, being a departmental capital, required 25,000 francs.[4] A notary's office was to some extent an investment. In 1870 it could be bought at ten years' purchase—but by 1890 it was down to seven or eight years.[5] Competition and crises made the returns less certain than might at first appear. After investing these large sums, notaries not infrequently went bankrupt. Since there was no serious control of their suitability or of their integrity, many absconded with their clients' funds. Until 1870 there was each year an average of a dozen scandals followed by loss of office. In 1875 there were 28 such scandals, in 1882 there were 31, in 1883 41, in 1884 55, in 1886 71, and in 1889 103. In the years 1880–6 62 million francs were embezzled or lost by notaries. In one canton in the Nord, in 1888, all five notaries took flight together, and in the same year four notaries in Nantes were simultaneously prosecuted. In the second half of the century, there was thus practically no canton in France which had not experienced a bankrupt or criminal notary. Hostile articles were written

[1] Paul Lefèvre, *Les Notaires* (1969).
[2] Lucien Genty, *La Basoche notariale. Origines et histoire du XIVe siècle à nos jours de la cléricature notariale* (1888).
[3] E. Charton, *Guide pour le choix d'un état* (1842), 464.
[4] Rouxel, 52.
[5] Cf. Charton with P. Jacquemart, *Professions et métiers* (1892), 708–10.

(following the lead of the President of the Court of Cassation in 1854) saying the notaries had a crime rate three times higher than the inhabitants of Paris, dangerous city though that was. More recently only in Paris have bankruptcies been successfully avoided: there have been none there for the past fifty years. It is the notaries of the south who are most prone to default. The two worst periods were the 1840s and 1880s—and each was followed by a campaign and legislation against them.[1]

The crises were the result of vicious circles: the attraction of the office put up the price beyond what it was worth and the bankruptcies brought discredit on the whole profession. Many towns, however agreeable physically, could not afford a notary. The prospect of an easy and prosperous existence was a mirage, produced by the few who had large inherited incomes. The average net earnings of a notary in the 1850s were estimated at between 2,000 and 3,000 francs.[2] The notaries pressed for the abolition of the least productive *études* and, as occasion offered, many were abolished—no fewer than 429 between 1895 and 1909. But in 1913—by which time prices and wages had risen considerably, there were still some offices yielding less than 2,000 francs a year gross, 1,572 yielding less than 5,000 francs gross, 2,760 5,000 to 10,000 francs, 2,880 10,000 to 30,000, and only about a thousand over 30,000—many of the Paris offices of course reaching far higher figures, over 100,000 francs.[3] The variation in the income of notaries was thus so great that some earned fifty times as much as others—which no doubt helped to confuse popular conceptions of the office. Some notaries were barely distinguishable from peasants—just capable of reading and writing and having no education beyond the primary school.[4] In 1970 this problem of the varied nature of the notaries had still not been solved. Though on average Paris notaries employed twenty-five clerks each, there were still 593 notaries who worked alone without any clerk at all, 'like veritable artisans', and there were several hundred offices up for sale unable to find purchasers. Though in 1934 a central

[1] Rouxel, 2–3.

[2] Jeannest, 155.

[3] Émile Bender, *La Réforme notariale* (1913), 143.

[4] Raoul de La Grasserie, *L'État actuel et la réforme du notariat en France* (1898), 159–60.

fund was at last established, on the basis of subscriptions from notaries, to guarantee the public against defaulters, and though in 1945 a slightly more vigorous system of education was introduced, the bankruptcies and embezzlements continue (in 1968 there were fourteen). The profession has set up a scheme to enable those without capital to borrow 50 per cent of the cost of their office—but the profession is still not democratised. The Armand-Rueff commission of 1959–60 was the latest in the long line of inquiries set up to see how change could be effected. This commission was somewhat more effective than that of 1909, before which the notaries refused to appear.

Balzac painted the notary as the model of respectability and reliability. 'When a notary has not got the immobile and gently rounded face you can recognise, if he does not offer to society the unlimited guarantee of his mediocrity, if he is not the polished steel cog that he ought to be, if there is left in him any suggestion that he is in the least bit an artist, capricious, passionate or a lover, he is lost.'[1] But it is very difficult to describe such a varied collection of people briefly with any accuracy; and in any case the role the notary played in the life of the country varied not only with his personal characteristics, but also with the region where he practised. Different provinces made use of his services in a far from uniform way. In the legal province of Grenoble (the area over which the court of appeal of Grenoble had jurisdiction) the notary was used in the 1850s to draw up only one legal document for every eleven inhabitants, but in Agen he made one for every six inhabitants. The notaries were likewise used almost twice as often, proportionately to the population, in Caen as in Orléans. This was not strictly related to the litigiousness of the different regions. Grenoble and Caen used their notaries about the same, but the former went to court almost twice as often as the latter, four times as often as Orléans, and five times as often as Angers. The geography of legal influence deserves its map beside that of the Church's influence.[2] It is not easy to explain it until much detailed research is done. But a factor of importance is the cost of the notarial act. At first there was no uniformity at all in the fees

[1] Raymond Herment, *Sous la poussière des panonceaux* (Nice, 1955), 275.

[2] A. Jeannest St. Hilaire, *Du Notariat et des offices* (1857), 346–7.

notaries charged; vigorous competition and undercutting were the rule. For long they resisted attempts to impose a uniform tariff: but gradually different provinces drew up minimum rates and it was only in 1945 that a national rate was agreed. Even so the way fees were calculated was very complicated and a notary had no trouble at all in juggling with the nomenclature of the services he had rendered to vary his bill. The drawing up of a power of attorney could cost (in 1900) either 9 francs or 26 francs, depending on how it was done.[1] The result was that a host of unqualified competitors mushroomed to offer alternatives. Every town began to see agencies set up in it— information bureaux, estate agents, debt collectors, legal advisory services, sometimes run in a hired room of an inn by a retired sergeant-major, a barrister or a land surveyor. Notaries' clerks wrote books advising people how to draw up legal documents without the intervention of notaries. The saving in money could certainly be enormous, even though the notaries argued that the subsequent lawsuits, due to ignorance of the law, cancelled these out, and that these amateur fees, being uncontrolled, often turned out to be expensive swindles. But a peasant dying in 1865 leaving a small field and a hovel worth 900 francs might pay as much as 458 francs in fees to the notary and other officials. He had strong temptations to go elsewhere—all the more so because in addition the state had a right to 208 francs in tax, and the notary was bound to levy it, while the amateurs were not.[2]

For the notaries were tax collectors as well as lawyers and indeed the variety of their functions was such that they exerted an influence—both moral and financial—which could justly be compared with that of the priests. In the country they worked on Sundays, doing much business with peasants coming in to church from the surrounding hamlets. Some even opened stalls in the market-place and were so busy they got the peasants to sign blank sheets of paper which they filled in later. Their textbooks enjoined them to use their skills to moralise and reconcile their clients, bolster paternal authority and filial piety, urge the unmarried to marry, but then to attend the wedding feasts with 'an imposing gravity' designed to extirpate the indecency that so frequently marred these celebrations.[1] As will be seen later, the notaries played a major role in altering the financial aspects of family life through the way they drew up marriage contracts—thus contributing to establishing new relations between husbands, wives, children and relatives. They modernised the law—in keeping with pressure from public opinion—while in these matters parliament usually set up committees which never reported. It is strange their legislative activities have been so little studied. The way they have modified parliamentary laws, and found means to soften or get round them altogether, has probably been even more significant than the jurisprudence of the courts, essential though knowledge of this is to understanding what really happened in France, as opposed to what the politicians said ought to happen. The notaries had a decisive influence on the economic development of the country, through their control of the small man's investments. It was to them that people traditionally took their savings—when they ventured to go beyond the stage of keeping their money under the mattress—for a return, it seems, of between $3\frac{1}{2}$ to 5 per cent. They were the intermediaries when people wished to borrow and they found lenders, usually on mortgage security. It has been estimated that in 1912 they arranged loans to the tune of 748 million francs, whereas the Crédit Foncier de France lent only 124 million.[2] Now the principle which guided them was not the object of the loan, but the reliability of security which could be obtained for it. It is known that they channelled the majority of small savings into mortgages and state bonds. Their education and training were usually inadequate to enable them to cope with the problems of industrialisation. Because companies tended to avoid using them as far as possible, so as to spare themselves the high cost of official notarial acts, they had fewer relations with industry than was desirable from the point of view of economic expansion.[3] In this they seem to have kept up with the times less than in family relations—but again this is a subject on which more research needs to be done.

[1] R..., notaire, *Le Notariat considéré dans ses rapports intimes et journaliers avec la morale* (1847), 104; A. J. Massé, *Le Parfait Notaire* (1807).

[2] Fernand Dubas, *Du Rôle actuel économique et social du notariat français* (Caen thesis, Mesnil, Eure, 1918), 60.

[3] André Desmazières, *L'Évolution du rôle du notaire dans la constitution des sociétés par actions* (1948).

Now every act the notary drew up involved the payment of dues to the state as well as fees to himself. On average he collected eight times as much money in taxes as in fees. He therefore stood in the ambiguous position of being partly a tax collector and partly an adviser to individuals on how to avoid paying taxes. The notary has to pay the taxes on the deeds he executes, whether the client pays them to him or not, but he gets no personal commission from the taxes. His interest is to multiply the number of deeds, rather than to increase the tax yield. Until 1918 he made free use of deposit safes in banks to defraud the treasury of death-duties. (A law of 1923 required a representative of the ministry of finance to be present at the opening of these safes after a death.) Because of his fiscal responsibilities, he has to use a language in the drawing up of deeds which meets with the approval of the stamp duty administration, so he does not readily find new solutions for new situations: the old formulae protected him best. It is only very recently that he has been working towards the use of clearer language—though conversely he is also losing his role of adviser and confessor and becoming more of a technician.[1] To prevent him running off with the money deposited with him, or using it for speculation, laws have been passed requiring him to deposit it with the Bank of France: this was worth 1,400 million to the state in 1935 but it is not clear that the laws were always followed. More successful were the voluntary agreements by which he drew up the mortgages for loans made by the Crédit Agricole, in return for which employment he deposited large sums from his clients with it.

The simple view of the notary as a representative of bourgeois law, order and domination is clearly a myth of wishful thinking created by the conservatives themselves. No doubt he did influence the peasants' lives. No doubt being 'less superior, less isolated than the magistrature, more independent than administrative civil servants', he could more easily communicate with the masses. His parish was small enough—each dealt on average with around 3,000 people. But as one notary said, 'The subtle cunning of the peasant, cleverly disguised under the pretence of

[1] Marcel Brisse, *Essai sur le rôle fiscal du notaire* (1937), 214–17; Charles Collet and André Oudard, *L'Évolution du notariat parisien au cours de l'époque contemporaine 1900–1960* (1961).

ingenuous ignorance and an attractive *bonhomie*, give him un-
doubted advantages in [his] incessant struggle against the
notary.'[1] The scenes that took place in his office were often
ritual pantomimes or market bargaining rather than confessions,
with the peasants lying and the notary using his experience to
discern the truth that honour or slyness refused to reveal.
Economically, each was often trying to make a profit out of the
other. The town notary, shielded behind his clerks, was a
dangerous official. The truly rural one was a force in local
rivalries whom the peasant might try to play off against the
mayor and the irate officials. It was no accident that the
notaries were persecuted at the Revolution more than any
other profession, some say more than the aristocracy—for they
were usurers.

The notaries moreover were at war not just with their clients
but with the magistracy too. Poor though some of them were,
they were nearly always richer than the ill-paid judges, and
they had invested their inheritances to make money out of the
law. They had an active business life, while the magistrates,
brought up on the classics and condemned to a retiring and
modest existence, compensated for their poverty by a pretence
of social superiority. But the magistrates had in theory certain
supervisory functions over them—in disputes they could fix
their fees—and they used their powers with an acrimony
inspired by a fierce and notorious jealousy. Thus, for example,
in cases of compulsory seizures or sales, the courts had the
option of ordering the sale to be held officially by the justice
of the peace or privately by a notary, and they consistently
deprived the notaries of business. The latter replied by inventing
a procedure during the Restoration inserting clauses in contracts
they drew up that, in the event of a sale being necessary, this
should be done privately by the notary. But the courts declared
these clauses invalid. And so the quarrel continued under
different guises. Finally the notaries were ill at ease with
the government. Their privileges were under constant threat
and the question of the reform of the notariat recurred again
and again in parliament. Because of their image as solid
conservatives, they had a reputation of being Orleanist—
but this seems to be another over-simple generalisation.

[1] Jeannest, 168.

It was said that many were Bonapartist because Napoleon reconstituted their order after the Revolution and enhanced their prestige by ordering voting registers to be kept in their *études*. Under Louis-Philippe they did not oppose the government, but were constantly attacked by it. In 1844 they were required to pay the *patente* like petty shopkeepers even though an *ordonnance* of 1843 forbade them to take part in business or industry. In 1841 a tax of 2 per cent was imposed in the transmission of their offices, but they were given no guarantee to the ownership of them and plans to reform them were discussed. The Court of Cassation in 1841 made an exception of notaries and allowed the state to sue them for arrears of taxation for thirty years. It also declared null and void any notary's act not made in the real presence of two notaries (when it was an accepted practice that the second one added his signature afterwards). But then the government of Napoleon III harassed them with interference in the pricing of their offices: the Third Republic tried repeatedly to control their activities more closely.

The role of notaries in society has thus varied considerably in different regions and at different times. Most recently the notaries have emerged as a pressure group, organised at last in a trade union. In 1934 a series of *conférences générales des notaires* were established as a 'melting-pot of ideas and a centre of intellectual activity'. These have urged notaries to take a larger part in the social, economic and political life of the nation.[1] This may mean that, at the ebb of their influence, the notaries are seeking to revive their power by turning themselves into some kind of intellectuals. But perhaps it shows also how the sources of influence change with time: perhaps their activities hold a less important place in daily life today, or perhaps the other forms of power they sometimes combined with their notarial profession—leadership in local affairs—are now more exposed to attack and questioning.

[1] Herment, 333.

4. The Rich

A COMMON generalisation about France is that it was controlled for most of this period by 200 families who held most of its wealth, ran its major industries, and bribed its politicians to do their bidding. Behind the façade of democracy stood a discreet oligarchy, most of whose names the public did not even know. This idea was particularly current in the 1930s. Daladier made it a political slogan. 'Two hundred families', he declared to the Radical Congress of 1934, 'are master of the French economy and in fact of French politics. The influence of two hundred families weighs on the fiscal system, on transport, on credit. The two hundred families place their delegates in political office. They interfere with public opinion, because they control the press.' The precise number of families and the precise date at which they acquired their influence varied in the accusations of different people. Daladier called it 'a new feudalism'. A contemporary of his, the Senator Lesaché, who went into greater detail in unveiling the oligarchy, claimed it had grown up only in the 1920s, and he put the figure variously at between 150 and 300.[1] But already in 1869 Georges Duchêne, a friend of Proudhon, had inveighed against the monopoly of power in the hands of '200 nabobs', adding that 'Antiquity does not contain any examples of an oligarchy so concentrated.'[2] The figure of 200 was always rather theoretical. It was suggested probably by the annual meeting of the shareholders of the Bank of France. Though the Bank had over 40,000 shareholders, under its Napoleonic statutes only the 200 with the largest number of shares could attend the meeting. They had subscribed only a small fraction of the Bank's capital, but they had complete control of it. They elected its fifteen regents, usually from among their own number. Members of the same few families were regents for generation after generation, accentuating the oligarchical nature of the control. Even the Governor of the Bank, though appointed

[1] Henry Coston, *Le Retour des 200 familles* (1960), 10–12.
[2] Georges Duchêne, *L'Empire industriel* (1869), 299.

by the state, had to own 100 shares. The state's nominees to the board of regents could be outvoted by the industrialists and financiers who formed the majority.

This arrangement epitomised, in the eyes of the radicals and socialists in particular, what went on in most large firms. Their boards of directors were composed of men who held only a small number of shares but enough to get themselves elected. The great mass of shareholders did not have the leisure to attend the company meetings, or else were specifically excluded by the statutes, or by the issue of non-voting shares. The banks offered to collect dividends for those of them who deposited their shares with them and in return obtained the voting rights of those shares. They were thus able to obtain a disproportionate number of directorships for their own nominees, and all the more so since they frequently demanded a seat on the board in return for relatively small loans. The directorships of the large firms in France thus came to be held by a narrow circle of men who usually did nothing else for their livings, and could afford not to, because they kept dividends down to a minimum but paid themselves enormous fees. Already under Napoleon III, Émile Péreire held nineteen directorships, his brother Isaac twelve, and his nephew Eugène nine. Together with other relatives the Péreire clan thus controlled fifty companies with a capital of five milliard francs.[1] Duchêne claimed that 183 individuals in this way controlled two-thirds of the share capital on the market in 1869. In the 1930s, Lederlin was a director of 63 companies, Ernest Cuvelette of 47, Ernest Mercier of 46; there were in all about 144 people, each of whom was a director of at least ten companies.[2] Since many of these were intermarried, family exclusiveness placed a further barrier between them and the masses. Baron Georges Brincard, for example, President of the Crédit Lyonnais, was the son-in-law of the founder of that leading bank, Henri Germain. He was related to the Gramont, Rothschild, Fabre-Luce, and Voguë families, all of whom had numerous representatives on many other boards. Then the Rothschilds were in turn related to the Fould, Heine and Lazard banking families. Schneider the metallurgist was related to Lebaudy the sugar refiner, Mame the Catholic

[1] G. Duchêne, *Études sur la féodalité française* (1867), 37.
[2] *Le Crapouillot* (Mar. 1936) issue on 'Les Deux Cent familles', 21–2.

publishers, Wendel the other great metallurgist, Cossè Brissac and Citroen. And so it went on. The opposition to these clans was inevitably exacerbated when they used their wealth to subsidise political causes (which was particularly noticeable in the inter-war period), when they bought up newspapers and gave directorships or shares to politicians they hoped to influence. Three presidents of the republic in the inter-war years —Doumer, Doumergue and Lebrun—had all been directors of leading companies.[1]

Another attack on the 200 families was made in 1910 by Francis Delaisi. He argued that only one-quarter of the national budget was spent on civil servants. About another quarter was paid in interest to the *rentiers*. The rest went to the state's contractors and suppliers of armaments and public works. Three-quarters of taxation was thus fed back to the rich. The oligarchy in charge of the Bank of France used the national wealth to support another clique, the republican party, as its tool in politics. The Crédit Foncier, which dispensed credit to farmers and had mortgages on one-fifth of the land of France, was also ruled by its 200 largest shareholders, paying $2\frac{1}{2}$ per cent to its petty-bourgeois investors but charging $4\frac{1}{2}$ per cent to its borrowers. The four large deposit banks paid $\frac{1}{2}$ per cent or 1 per cent to their 1,500,000 depositors, but charged 3 or 4 per cent to its most favoured borrowers; they diverted French savings into foreign stocks, for their private profit but with disastrous results for the French economy. The oligarchs were not anti-democratic, because they knew how to manipulate democracy. They spent money freely at elections, supporting radicals and independent socialists when it suited them. Briand's *Lanterne* was said to have been subsidised by Eugène Péreire and the Compagnie Transatlantique. When they did not put a deputy under an obligation to them at the time of his election, they were quick to offer him lucrative posts as 'legal adviser' to their companies. Thus Waldeck-Rousseau was paid (so said Delaisi) 100,000 francs a year by American insurance companies, in return for which they were allowed to drain France quietly of its savings. The Rente Foncière Company employed Millerand as its legal counsel, the Crédit Foncier and St. Gobain

[1] Jean Baumier, *Les Grandes Affaires françaises. Des 200 familles aux 200 managers* (1967).

employed Poincaré: and the latter after successfully defending St. Gobain in a lawsuit which might have sent to prison two of its directors, the Marquis de Vogüé and Thureau-Dangin (permanent secretary of the Académie Française), was elected to the Academy. The pettiest provincial lawyer-deputy could now count on jobs from two or three companies, to earn 40,000 francs a year: former ministers could expect ten times that sum. The financial oligarchy safeguarded itself by quickly adding to its boards any budding politician likely to hold or to return to office. With all these precautions it was able to ensure that the *rapporteurs* of all bills concerned with contracts would be favourable to them. The Senator Humbert, *rapporteur* of the war budget, received 12,000 francs a year from the firm of Darracq, which manufactured lorries for the army, and it even gave him a percentage commission on every order he obtained for it. Humbert confessed all this, to prove his honesty, when brought to trial on another matter. He produced his accounts which showed, he said, that he behaved as all other politicians did— and no one contradicted him. His expenses were 64,200 francs a year, and his parliamentary salary 15,000. He bridged the gap by being 'agent général' of the Darracq lorry factory, at 12,000 a year plus commission; and by earning a further 18,000 for running *Le Matin*, a newspaper where he could beat the patriotic drum, which would stimulate military contracts.

Of course the oligarchs also went into parliament themselves, but they discreetly formed an independent group, which though small, was able to throw its weight to the left or the right in a decisive manner. Aynard the banker, regent of the Bank of France, on the boards of the Aciéries de St. Étienne, the PLM railway and the Compagnie Générale de Navigation, and Joseph Reinach, Rothschild's nominee, were pointed out as the men who controlled this group and so the destinies of ministries. The permanence of their domination came from the fact that the rich subsidised both left and right. The Crédit Lyonnais and the large industrialists subsidised the Catholics, the Société Générale, the Jewish bankers and the Comité Mascuraud of smaller businessmen paid the freemasons. In so far as parties depended on newspapers, and newspapers could not survive without financial advertisements (since other forms of advertisement took a long time to develop), the press was in the pay of the oligarchs. Censorship might have been legally abolished, but there were things which the bankers forbade the press to mention. Thus Jean Dupuy, owner of the best-selling *Petit Parisien*, is said to have made a deal with Waldeck-Rousseau to drop his opposition to Dreyfus, in return for a seat in the cabinet. Bunau-Varilla, owner of *Le Matin*, is said to have obtained confiscated monastic property for his son-in-law at a ludicrously low price, in return for showing favourable neutrality to Combes. Clemenceau was thrown out of parliament for having incurred the wrath of the *Petit Journal*, until the Jewish bankers behind *L'Aurore* decided to bring him back. So democracy in France was a façade. There were, said Delaisi, about fifty-five people who, by their control of big business, were omnipotent over the country's life.[1]

The theory of the 200 families draws attention to relationships of great importance—on which more will be said later—but it was never based on an impartial scrutiny of history. Thus the number of people in the oligarchy was probably very much larger than 200. In 1922, for example, a list of the main companies in France contained 434 firms (covering mines, metal, transport, banks, public utilities, insurance and property) with about 4,000 directors. Of these about 520 were directors of three companies or more.[2] By 1953 there were 22,753 limited liability companies, but even if one puts aside all those with assets of less than three milliard francs, one is still left with almost 2,000 directors.[3] Industry was not sufficiently concentrated to give even this group of people a dominant role in the economy. In 1906 there were 215 industrial firms with over 1,000 workers; in 1931 there were 421; in 1936 296. There were also, at these three dates 412, 713, and 615 firms with between 500 and 1,000 workers.[4] In 1906 51 per cent of the industrial working class were employed by firms with less than fifty workers.[5] A study still needs to be made of the proportion

[1] Francis Delaisi, *La Démocratie et les financiers* (1910).

[2] Based on Annuaire Chaix, *Les Principales Sociétés par action* (1932).

[3] Nicole Delfortrie-Soubeyroux, *Les Dirigeants de l'industrie française* (1961), is an analysis of these 1964 directors.

[4] J. M. Jeanneney, *Forces et faiblesses de l'économie française* (1956), 259. The statistics do not give information about ownership and these firms may have been owned by a smaller number.

[5] A. Fontaine *et al.*, *La Concentration des entreprises* (1913), 59.

of the national product for which the large firms were responsible.

Some idea of just how many rich men there were in France can be obtained—very roughly—from the statistics of inheritances. In 1933 53·6 per cent of the people who died (354,147 out of 661,082) left nothing. Of those who did leave something, 52 per cent (185,473) left less than 10,000 francs. Another 119,774 left less than 50,000 francs. 25,808 left between 50,000 and 100,000 francs, and 14,838 left between 100,000 and 250,000. Now all those leaving between 10,000 and 250,000 francs together left only 6,606 million. But 1,512 people left over one million each, 4,203 million together, i.e. 30 per cent of all wealth left at death, and of these 1,512 162 account for 1,718 million. There were thus indeed 162 people dying in one year owning about 10 per cent of the wealth left in that year. This means that there was a very small minority of very rich people, but this minority must be numbered in several or many thousands (multiply 1,512 or even 162 by 20, if wealth changes hands every twenty years).[1] One may, to take it another way, look at the wealth left by people dying in 1900, before death-duties arrived to encourage fraudulent declarations. At that date, a mere 2 per cent of those who left any money accounted for over half of the total amount of money left. But in this year about two-thirds of all those dying left something, and 2 per cent of deaths produces well over 10,000 people a year.[2] 30 per cent of the total value of inheritances were left by 15 per cent of those leaving anything, so there was indeed a sizeable middle class. It may be that as the total value of property left increased in the course of this period—the value of successions rose from 2,700 million in 1850 to 7,200 in 1901—so the distance between the penniless and the rich increased. But there seems to be some disagreement about this. What a man leaves at his death does not give a full picture of his prosperity. Statistics have been brought forward to show that the distance between rich and poor has decreased because the poor are less poor than they used to be and there are fewer poor people. Colbert had an income 500 times that of a labourer, but few could claim the same today. The ratio between the income of a *conseiller*

[1] Augustin Hamon, *Les Maîtres de la France* (1936), 1. 21.
[2] P. Sorlin, *La Société française* (1969), 1. 131.

d'état and a labourer has fallen from 55 : 1 in 1800 to 18 : 1 in 1900 and 7 : 1 in 1960. Moreover, in 1800 75 per cent of the population was at the level of the labourer but in 1960 less than 10 per cent were. In terms of purchasing power, the rich have not got richer. The real purchasing power of a labourer has tripled or even quadrupled since 1830 but that of a middle-grade civil servant has barely changed. Men without qualifications have had their incomes raised to 80 per cent of those of qualified workers, as opposed to 50 per cent in 1800. Women are now only 20 per cent behind men.[1] In this period there was a radical transformation of the status of the poor. Until the early nineteenth century famine still descended on them whenever there was a bad harvest. Their standard of living was directly dependent on the weather, and the price of bread could fluctuate threefold in different years. But in 1850, for the first time, the price of a quintal of wheat fell to less than 100 hours of labourer's work, and 1856 was the last year in which it exceeded 200. 1891 was the last year in which it exceeded 100. By 1935 it had fallen to 50, by 1955 to 25, and by 1958 to 20.[2] Differences in wealth therefore meant different things at the two extremes of our period.

Altogether in 1900 the idle rich might have consisted of as many as half a million people. At any rate that number of adults declared themselves to be *rentiers* pursuing no other occupation; though of course a large proportion of these were probably more idle than rich. It should be remembered that in 1848 Louis-Philippe's electorate of the well-to-do had grown to nearly a quarter of a million. But a very significant change in the character of the rich took place in these fifty years, at least so far as the source of their income was concerned. In 1848 only about 5 per cent of money left at death was in shares, while 58 per cent was in land or houses. By 1900 31 per cent was in shares and only 45 per cent in land or houses. At the beginning of this period therefore the rich were above all landlords, drawing rent from houses or farms. These were considered the safest form of investment, assuring the greatest social prestige. As a result, the weight of the exploitation of the rich was felt by the masses in a very different way at these two dates. The

[1] Jean Fourastié, *Machinisme et bien être. Niveau de vie et genre de vie en France de 1700 à nos jours* (1962), 52.　　　　　　　　　　[2] Ibid., 65.

investor under Louis-Philippe liked to know personally exactly where he was putting his money. So he would buy a farm he could see, and a house whose tenants he would choose. He would lend substantial amounts of cash to individuals whose value he could assess. His money would extend his influence among a definite body of people: if he was rich enough he would build up a whole clan of dependants. This can be seen by looking at the distribution of wealth of men calling themselves 'proprietors' in the Paris of Louis-Philippe. They invested about 43 per cent of their wealth in land or houses (two-thirds of it in Paris, one-third in the provinces), they placed about 18 per cent in state bonds, safest after houses, and then they lent 15 per cent to individuals. They put only 3·7 per cent in company shares, and 4·5 per cent in the shares of the Bank of France. Retired members of the liberal professions, on average, lent 25 per cent of their wealth to individuals and put 53 per cent in land and houses. Those who were pure *rentiers* with no immovable property at all, lent 44 per cent of their wealth to individuals, put 33 per cent in state bonds but only 5 per cent in company shares. When, in the third quarter of the nineteenth century, the price of land began to fall, houses became even more popular as an alternative. Rents tripled in value between 1850 and 1913, as house building took on enormous proportions in the cities.

However, as prosperity increased under Napoleon III the rich began to have difficulty in knowing what to do with their money. That is why the speculation for which that reign is notorious could become so feverish. Not all the French were as frightened of taking risks as has been made out. A great many poured a lot of money into highly imaginative and even romantic industrial and financial schemes. Financial newspapers telling those with money to spare what to do with it sprang up on every side. In 1881 there were at least 228 of these (as against 95 political papers: who will dare conclude that the French must therefore have been more interested in money than politics?). In 1857 the largest circulation of a financial newspaper was 7,000; in 1880 there were several with nearly 100,000 readers each.[1] That is why Proudhon could castigate the

[1] Michael Palmer, 'The Press in the early Third Republic', D.Phil. thesis in preparation at St. Antony's College, Oxford.

plutocrats as speculators.[1] Nevertheless, though this press, for mercenary reasons, tried to sell every kind of share, it was only partly successful in turning the plutocrats into shareholders. The change did occur, as has been seen, but to a limited extent. The most respectable of the financial journalists counselled extreme caution. Paul Leroy-Beaulieu may be taken as the most influential of these: his work on *The Art of Investing and Managing One's Fortune* sold 33,000 copies in its first two years and was also serialised in the *Économiste Français*. He stressed forcefully that land had lost a quarter of its value between 1880 and 1900, and that its purchase could involve taxes of up to 10 per cent of the price. He thought that investment in houses was equally outdated, and should be left to experts. But he also vigorously dissuaded his readers from investing directly in industry. Industrial shares he classified as speculative. 'Recent disasters', he said menacingly, quoting the collapse of the Paris Omnibus Co. and the Say Sugar Refineries as examples, 'prove that industrial firms which are perfectly sound can in a few weeks or months and with no one suspecting it, be gravely compromised and sometimes even destroyed by the mistakes, optimism or fraud of their directors who appeared to merit every confidence.' Such shares, commendable though they were because they were often the instruments of the most recent progress, should be left to the great capitalists who could afford to take risks, though even they should confine themselves to industries of which they had some technical knowledge. To *pères de famille* Leroy-Beaulieu recommended state bonds and railways (French and foreign).[2] The figures do not all agree on exactly how far the French followed this advice, but it is certain in any case that by the turn of the century they were investing noticeably less in houses and lands. The anonymous shareholder replaced the personal usurer. It was this which encouraged the socialist outcry against the faceless plutocracy.

However, in the course of the inter-war period the French investor was changing once again. Bounding inflation forced a revision of traditional views. The collapse of many of the foreign countries into which they had poured so much money,

[1] P. J. Proudhon, *Manuel du spéculateur* (1856).
[2] P. Leroy-Beaulieu, *L'Art de placer et gérer sa fortune* (1908 edition), 83, 86, 203, etc.

most notably Russia and Austria, showed that state bonds were
far from being safest. So there was a return to land and houses
once more, slowly at first, but greatly speeded up by the
Second World War. According to one calculation, investment
in these rose from 37 per cent in 1908 to 43 per cent in 1934 to
54 per cent in 1949 and 60 per cent in 1953.[1] This change did
not entirely follow the rules of logic, for rent control introduced
after the First World War made houses less profitable, and
agriculture slumped. But after repeated disasters playing for
safety became the principal aim. This is shown for example by
the growing popularity of hoarding gold, even though, again,
this was not financially speaking the most profitable way of
using one's money. Such was the popularity of the gold louis
(far easier to hoard than the bulky ingot), that it carried a
premium of 40 per cent. But it did have the important attraction that it could most easily escape death-duties. The be-
wilderment of the French investor in the middle of the twentieth
century may be seen from an inquiry carried out into savings
habits in 1953. 24 per cent of Frenchmen thought that gold was
the safest investment (but only 3 per cent of Belgians, who in
general gave very different answers). The habit of saving had
not quite been destroyed by inflation. 58 per cent of the
bourgeois questioned and 34 per cent of the workers said they
believed in saving. However, by now they were equally
disillusioned with state bonds, and the Belgians proved to be
three times more willing to subscribe to them than the French.
72 per cent believed that investment in land, houses, gold,
jewelry and pictures was the most secure: only 16 per cent
stood up for shares. A mere 8 per cent followed the stock
market. Only 11 per cent had inherited shares. But this does
show roughly the considerable number of people involved in
the global category of the faceless plutocracy.[2] It had clearly
become a plutocracy on the defensive, which is perhaps why
it became so aggressive politically in the inter-war years. It
is not surprising that a guide to investment published in
1935 should be entitled *The Art of Managing and Protecting one's
Fortune*.[3]

[1] Paul Cornut, *Répartition de la fortune privée en France* (1963), chapter 29.
[2] Roger Truptil, *L'Art de gérer sa fortune* (1957), 50–93.
[3] Constantin Piron, *L'Art de gérer et de défendre sa fortune* (1935).

5. Industrialists

THE reality behind the myth of the 200 families is complicated. It deserves to be looked at in greater detail. It would be useful also to study it in the light of another general accusation made about French industrialists, which in many ways contradicts it. This is the family firm theory of David Landes. He has argued that the average French entrepreneur was a small businessman acting for himself or at most on behalf of a handful of partners, and that this was not only true in 1875 but, despite some exceptions, was still so at the end of the century. These small businessmen were essentially conservatives, disliking the new and the unknown, slow to modernise their equipment, doggedly self-sufficient financially. With rare exceptions, firms were organised on a family basis, obtaining finance from family or close friends only and very seldom on the open market. They were seen not as a method of producing goods with a view to obtaining indefinite wealth and power, but as 'a sort of fief that maintained and enhanced the position of the family, just as the produce of the manor and the men at arms it could muster were the material basis of medieval status'. Business was thus seen only as a means, not as an end in itself, engaged in for the preservation more than the creation of riches. Caution therefore had to be its watchword, and rapid expansion was never sought. Such firms could exist side by side with the few modern companies which were established because their ethos was partially accepted by the latter also, who preferred to raise their prices rather than eliminate these inefficient competitors.[1] This picture of France as a country of small firms is of course supported by the global statistics, though the statistics conceal almost as much as they reveal.

Landes has been mainly concerned with explaining the weakness of the French economy, the slow rate of its industrial

[1] D. Landes, 'French Entrepreneurship and Industrial Growth in the Nineteenth Century', *Journal of Economic History*, 9 (1949), 45–61. See also his masterly general economic history, *The Unbound Prometheus* (1969), which gives further references.

growth in the nineteenth century, and its loss of the hegemony
it held under Napoleon I. This is a debate which has proved
somewhat inconclusive. Those who have attacked Landes
have not produced any generally accepted alternative explanation. Perhaps a simple explanation is not to be looked
for. There is even doubt as to whether there is anything to
explain, in that, now that France has resumed its industrial
expansion, some are arguing that the backwardness was only
a temporary lull, or even that there never was any backwardness. If production figures are studied on a *per capita* basis,
France does not lag much behind its rivals. What happened
was simply that the populations of different countries increased
at different times.[1] Besides, Germany was also a country of small
family firms and the statistics of the size of its firms are almost
identical with those of France. In Russia, as in France, business
and industry were looked down upon as contemptible, but that
did not prevent an annual rate of industrial growth in the
1890s of about 9 per cent.[2] Others are now claiming that the
decisive factor in French economic development was the backwardness of agriculture, rather than of industry. Shortage of
factory labour and a static home market are said to have held
up industrialisation more than lack of capital, natural resources
or ambition on the part of entrepreneurs. The economists are
still disagreed, pending the publication of a giant quantitative
analysis of all the available statistics being undertaken by a team
under Jan Marczewski. It might be most profitable at this stage
therefore to examine the different sectors of the economy to see
who did run them and what little can be said about their
methods and their mentalities.[3]

The industry which fits David Landes's description most
easily is that of textiles, which, in the mid nineteenth century,
was of course France's largest industry and at the end of this
period was the fourth largest in the world, after Britain, U.S.A.,

[1] Rondo Cameron, 'L'Économie française, passé, présent, avenir', *Annales* (Sept.–
Oct. 1970), 1418–33; id., 'Profit, croissance et stagnation en France au xixᵉ
siècle', *Économie appliquée* (1957), 409–44; id., 'Economic Growth and Stagnation
in France 1815–1914', *Journal of Modern History* (1958), 1–13.

[2] Alexander Gerschenkron, *Economic Backwardness in Historical Perspective* (Cambridge, Mass., 1962), 62.

[3] C. Kindleberger, *Economic Growth in France and Britain 1851–1950* (1964), is an
excellent guide to the controversies. See the *Cahiers de l'Institut de Science Économique
appliquée* for J. Marczewski's *Histoire quantitative de l'économie française* (in progress).

and India. Concentration made little progress. In 1950 only 9·5 per cent of the weaving factories had over 500 looms, 35 per cent had less than 100, 22 per cent had between 101 and 300. In spinning, the five largest firms had only 17 per cent of the spindles, seventeen other firms had 25 per cent of them, but 55 per cent were shared by no fewer than 138 firms. Family control of small units was the rule, but there was great variety among them. In the Second Empire, several different types of manufacturer could be distinguished. The most famous names in the industry were those of Alsace and the Nord, like Dolfuss in Mulhouse and Motte in Roubaix, which had built up a network of firms, related by marriage, and surviving throughout this century in the same families. Their members dominated the politics or social welfare of their towns, and sometimes won seats in parliament. But they were of course far from controlling anything like even a third of the total production of the country; and they did not present a united front, or exhibit a uniform conduct, in the face of either crisis or prosperity. The large firms of the Nord came to be the archetype of the conservative family business. Their practice was not to expand the size of their units, but rather to endow each new generation with its own small units. Thus a younger son would be married off to the daughter of a rival, and the two parents would combine to set them up with a factory of their own, to which they gave both their surnames, hyphened. The ideal seemed to be to give each member of the family economic independence, perhaps as an unconscious counterpoise to the closeness of their family ties. No member would be allowed to go bankrupt, the family would always rescue him and set him up again; but industrially they worked separately. Cut-throat competition obviously had no place in such an arrangement. These manufacturers concentrated on maximising profits, not production. Borrowing from outside the family was avoided. The ploughing back of profits (*autofinance*) was the normal way to expand, though of course expansion was limited by the need to set up younger sons on their own and pay dowries to daughters. What expanded therefore was the family rather than the firm. These leading families tended to have many children (which does not make them typical of France). Thus when in 1940 Mme Pollet-Motte died, she left 1,257 descendants, nephews and nieces. But her particular (hyphenated) firm was not especially large. If there was not enough money to set up all the children, then some went into the Church. Pious Catholicism, active social work and a conscientious paternalism characterised these textile families.

The memoirs left by some of the northern textile manufacturers are much more about their families than about their firms. They stress the activity of their women in their businesses, and not only by the introduction of a proportion of the initial capital and by joining the name of their father's to that of their husband's firm. 'One should not fail to recognise', wrote one of them, 'the important role the women [of the nineteenth century] played in the home which they animated with their permanent presence. They had absolute control—that goes without saying —of the running of the house, but at a time when the business or the workshop and the home were built as one, they participated in the professional duties of their husbands at the same time as they gave a great deal of attention to the education of their children. It was on this close collaboration of the head of the firm and his wife that the astonishingly rapid rise of industry in Roubaix-Tourcoing in the early nineteenth century was built.' The historian of the Motte-Clarisse family (of whom there were 1,622 alive in this single branch in 1952) finds 'the family spirit' evident from the very first extant letter in its archives. Parents expected and obtained obedience. 'Believe in my affection', wrote a father to his daughter in 1869, 'as I believe in your submission and your assiduity in your duties.' Children were asked to pray for the dead members of their dynasty, as for the living. All were required to attend weekly family dinners which were raised almost to the status of religious ceremonies or as one Motte called them 'compulsory festivals'. Madame Motte-Bredart's Sunday lunches began with a sung grace and the litanies of the Virgin were recited before the dessert. Mutual aid among members of this family was the practical consequence of their close-knit life. It was the closeness, the secrecy and the exclusiveness that stimulated accusations of oligarchy. But these families were not entirely self-sufficient. Though they nearly always went into the business, lack of ability or inclination sometimes meant that they could not run them on their own. They often delegated a great deal of power to managers, who, in many cases, were then married into the families. There are not infrequent cases of new firms being set up for young men in association with foremen who had proved their worth.

Prudence characterised their economic policy. One Motte went on a pilgrimage in 1836 'to obtain illumination from the Holy Ghost so that we should never undertake anything in business above our strength, lest we should be troubled by hazardous speculations'. His wife's favourite saying was 'Economy is the first profit'. The rule against borrowing was sometimes written into their articles of association. They carried this into their private lives, where simplicity and austerity were severely practised and sentimentality rigorously excluded. One twentieth-century magnate, who was brought up in this textile world, recalls the bedroom of his parents furnished 'worse than a hotel for commercial travellers'. They rose early, worked hours as long as those they imposed on their employees, and very often thought of little besides their work. On the whole, they avoided higher education and they were stauncher patrons of the Church than of the arts.[1]

However, these generalisations about the notables in textiles ignore many exceptions. From time to time these families threw up individuals who were innovators, who broke with tradition (within limits), and who brought about expansion and modernisation. Alfred Motte, for example, born in 1852, and set up in business by his relatives, proceeded to establish at least four other firms. He was a veritable industrial impresario, but he concealed his work behind the traditional façade of family firms. Each of his new companies was set up in association with a manager, who was in charge of its daily running while Motte gave general supervision. Motte broke with the habit of specialising in only one branch of textiles; he was a great believer in industrial enterprise and in the legitimacy of competition and natural selection between firms. Family firms, that is to say, could be vigorous as well as defensive. The well-known textile firms of Alsace, in contrast to those of the north, often were. Their Protestantism set them even further apart from the

---

[1] Fernand Motte, *Souvenirs personnels d'un demi-siècle de vie et de pensée 1886–1942* (Lille, 1943, privately printed); Gaston Motte, *Les Motte, étude de la descendance Motte-Clarisse 1750–1950* (Roubaix, 1952, privately printed); Gérard Hannezo, 'Histoire d'une famille du Nord: les Barrois' (stencilled, about 1964).

rest of society. They were among the few supporters of free trade. This was not simply because they were optimistic but because as specialists in printing cloth they worked much more for the export market. Jules Siegfried, father of the famous writer, was among the most colourful and enterprising of these Alsatians. He became a millionaire at twenty-nine by seeing that the American Civil War would cut off France's supply of cotton: he went to India and imported from there. His activity as a cotton merchant took on an international scale. He travelled widely and sent his sons on world tours. He admired the U.S.A. and Britain as exponents of industrial initiative and he despised civil servants who were content with fixed salaries, engineers whom he thought of as pure theorists, and professors, for he had no use for books or culture. When his son André showed academic inclinations, he urged him to become Director of the School of Political Sciences, not simply its employee, for he understood only the success that brought power. His motto was 'to live is to act'—and he had it engraved even on his cuff-links. But it is interesting to see why he did not become a Rockefeller. He confined himself to cotton, a branch of industry where he felt he knew what he was doing. There were limits to his ambition. At forty-four he retired from business, giving his firm to his younger brother and devoting himself to politics and social work. He refused to marry 'well' and preferred the daughter of a Protestant pastor who turned him further in the direction of public service. He left his children to make their own way in the world, as he had done.[1]

However, these textile dynasties formed only a small proportion of the employers in this industry. The bulk, in the middle of the nineteenth century, were merchant-manufacturers still using artisan labour and just beginning to turn to mechanised weaving in factories. Such men had yet to establish themselves: they had often begun as dyers, or cloth merchants in small towns. Few rose very fast, for the self-made man was an exception in textiles. They did not set the pace: their humble origins made them continue to see their future in small, regional, if not purely local, terms. They preserved the mentality of the retailer. It is true that there were a few manufacturers, found in particular in Normandy, who did not look on textiles as an end

[1] A. Siegfried, *Jules Siegfried 1836–1922* (1946).

in itself, nor as a profession, but simply as a means of making money and rising in the social scale. Pouyer-Quertier, who became minister of finance under Thiers, was such a man. Born in 1820, the son of a small manufacturer and farmer, he had early seen the possibilities opened up by new machinery. He visited England and brought back ideas on modernisation. In 1859 he bought a bankrupt firm on the outskirts of Rouen, and made it the largest cotton-spinning factory in Normandy. His income reached 1,800,000 francs a year. But he used his wealth to go into parliament and become a politician. The textile dynasties by contrast never placed politics before their traditional family activity.

The variety of the textile employers was strikingly revealed in the 1860s when a severe crisis coincided with the shock produced by the free trade treaty with England. The well-established firms of the east, which had adequate capital, proved perfectly capable of withstanding competition. Some rising and enterprising firms in Roubaix, Armentières and Reims seized the opportunity to mechanise their factories and to form larger units. It was Normandy, which was the largest cotton-weaving area in France, but also the most backward, with artisan organisation and little capital, that was hit most severely. The effect of the crisis of the 1860s was to complete the transformation of the textile industry and to destroy hand weaving. Vigorous expansion coincided with catastrophic collapses. The expansion did not cease even after protection was re-established. The consumption of cotton textiles increased by 270 per cent between 1869 and 1913 and exports increased more than sixfold between 1867 and 1896, even if it was, to a considerable extent, to the protected colonial markets.[1] Concentration continued in the industry, so that whereas there were eighteen cotton firms in Alsace in 1861 there were only eight in 1910.[2] But these changes did not exceed certain limits. There was a levelling off in the twentieth century. Between 1900 and 1950 textile production fell by 10 per cent, as compared with an increase of 51 per cent in the rest of Europe. In the 1950s 240 plants were withdrawn from production but there were still nearly 2,000 left and only 255 had more than 200 employees.

[1] H. Sée, Histoire économique (1951), 2. 302.
[2] Kindleberger, 174 n.

The concentration affected ownership much more than production units. But even new-style magnates like Marcel Boussac (b. 1891), who by 1950 had sixty-five factories employing over 10,000 workers in all branches of textiles, from the import of raw cotton to the retail sale of his own products, with the firm of Christian Dior as one of his satellites, was still only responsible for 10 per cent of French cotton production.[1] The textile industry could not be labelled as congenitally backward. In the economic renaissance of the Fifth Republic, the disadvantages of price compared to other Common Market countries (30 per cent higher than the U.S.) were wiped out by a 50 per cent increase in productivity. But the family structure of the industry survived.[2]

The textile industrialists seemed a threat to democracy largely because their family organisation let very few facts about their firms escape to the public. Secrecy in business reached its maximum here. But it is clear from the statistics that this impenetrable world was a fragmented one. It is clear also from the history of employers' organisations that the textile owners were poor recruits and disliked regimentation by a union. They formed only ineffective alliances and gave little support to the employers' movement in general. The only exceptions were the woollen manufacturers—a small minority —who between the wars developed a keenness for corporatism.

The situation was very different in iron and steel. It is from this industry that the most numerous examples of concentrated control by the 200 families were given. Concentration indeed started early here. Under the July Monarchy there were about 1,000 iron foundries, but by the end of the century that number had been reduced by three-quarters. (In 1960 it was down to 140.) However already in 1828 the ten largest accounted for 39 per cent of the capital and were responsible for 22 per cent of production. By 1869 they had doubled their share of production to 55 per cent with de Wendel's firms alone producing 11·2 per cent of the total.[3] This was as concentrated as any industry became in France. Moreover, these iron

---

[1] Jacques Boudet, *Le Monde des affaires* (1952), 644–6.

[2] John Sheahan, *Promotion and Control of Industry in Post-War France* (Cambridge, Mass., 1963), 139. C. Fohlen, *L'Industrie textile au temps du second empire* (1956).

[3] Six articles by B. Gille (some of them under the pseudonym of J. B. Silly) on concentration in *Revue d'Histoire de la Sidérurgie* (1962, 1963, and 1965).

masters got together very early to form a pressure group. After various attempts under Louis-Philippe, they formed the Comité des Forges in 1864, which has been the most stable and powerful employers' organisation ever since. The secrecy with which it conducted its affairs gave rise to many legends. No serious history of its activities has been written. There can be no doubt, however, that it busied itself pressing for customs protection and for industrial clauses to be added to French loans to foreign countries, so that these would buy their equipment from France. It organised an employers' boycott of Millerand's *Conseils du Travail* and an insurance fund to enable them to resist strikes. In the 1914–18 war its power received official sanction and stimulus when the government virtually surrendered its control of the distribution of war contracts involving iron and steel to it and made it the official organ for the purchase of iron and steel abroad. Immediately vigorous attacks were launched on it for alleged profiteering, favouritism in the distribution process, and above all for a supposed deal with the government for its factories in German occupied territories to be spared from bombing. A parliamentary commission under Viollette's presidency was set up after the peace to investigate, but never reported. Instead, the members of the Comité des Forges were enriched by having the newly acquired mines and factories of Lorraine, once more French, distributed among them. Now the marketing agreements by the iron masters, begun as early as 1876 in the Comptoir de Longwy and multiplied since then, were accused of being dangerous cartels. In the 1930s the drastic drop in demand for iron and steel at a time when French output had reached record levels produced a tightening of unity among the firms and their ability to hold prices at higher levels, relative to other commodities, was taken as proof of their acting contrary to the public interest. Their open association with the political parties of the right and their public admission of financial participation in the elections of 1924, made their destruction an essential aim of the left. Iron and steel was scheduled for nationalisation, and would have been taken over but for the chaos of the early years of the Fourth Republic and the withdrawal of the Communists from the government in 1947. They used their escape to participate whole-heartedly in the Monnet plan and to combine into larger units, with enormous new plants. As a result the French iron and steel industry has a greater degree of concentration than either England or Germany. The four leading companies by 1960 accounted for 57 per cent of total output, with each one being responsible for between 12 and 14 per cent.

The power of the iron masters should not be exaggerated, important though it was. Their escape from nationalisation was due to luck, not to any resistance they put up. Though they controlled a crucial sector of the economy, in terms of their contribution to the national product, or of their capital, they were not as dominant as they seemed. In 1847 iron and steel were responsible for a contribution to the national product of 1·1 per cent (as against the textile industry's 17·9 per cent) and in 1910 2·2 per cent (as against textiles' 16·5 per cent). Even together with all the metallurgical industries it added up to less than one-third of the textiles industry.[1] The capital of Le Creusot in 1881 was about one-twelfth of that of the PLM railway and less than that of Paris's water and bus companies. Even in 1964 the largest iron and steel firm came only eighth among the top firms in France, in terms of capital.[2] The members of the Comité des Forges, moreover, were not as united as they might have appeared. This body experienced difficulties immediately after it was founded, with a rival Comité des Forges de Champagne being founded against it.[3] Its disputes were so severe that in 1877 it decided to stop discussing questions of manufacture, commerce and protection, with the result that it became little more than a social club. It was reactivated after 1890 and in 1904 appointed an energetic full-time secretary, Robert Pinot, who held the office for twenty-two years. Pinot was a disciple of Le Play. He had written admiring articles on the mutual benefit societies of Swiss watch-makers: he had been private secretary to the Bonapartist-royalist politician, Baron Mackau, and also deputy director of the Musée Social, until sacked by its founder the comte de Chambrun (who believed that study could solve the social question) for being too authoritarian. Pinot made the voice of

[1] M. Pinson, 'La Sidérurgie française' in *Cahiers de l'I.S.E.A.* (Feb. 1965), 11–12.

[2] B. Gille, 'Esquisse d'une histoire du syndicalisme patronal dans l'industrie sidérurgique française', *Revue d'Histoire de la Sidérurgie*, 5 (1964), 209–49.

[3] J. B. Silly, 'Les plus grands sociétés métallurgiques en 1881', *Revue d'Histoire de la Sidérurgie*, 6 (1965), 255–72. Cf. *Entreprise*, 31 Oct. 1964.

the Comité des Forges heard loudly; he appeared before every parliamentary commission; he set up a Society for Economic Study and Information in 1920, with fifteen full-time researchers, as a nominally independent publicity office. However, he had his difficulties. It was a dissident group among the employers who started the attack on the Comité des Forges which led to the Viollette investigation. The relations between the makers of iron products and their major consumers, like the railways, were far from uniformly cordial, and on several occasions led to the formation of splinter organisations. Pinot himself gave only lukewarm support to the Confederation of French Employers, fearing that if the decisions were reached by a majority, his own industries would easily be outvoted, as he put it, by quarries, leather goods and hotels.[1] The iron masters' cartels were never as powerful as the German ones. Their agreements were often broken, there were no penalties imposed on members, and they had only small staffs compared to their German counterparts. The concentration in the iron industry, though impressive by French standards, was, before the 1950s, below German levels. Thus in 1913 there were in the principal iron-smelting areas of Lorraine, Nord and Pas de Calais, nine firms producing 15 per cent of output, seven producing 38 per cent, four producing 33 per cent, and one (Wendel) producing 9 per cent; that is to say, twelve firms producing 80 per cent. By contrast Germany had seven firms responsible for 88 per cent of its production.[2] There was much controversy as to whether the iron masters used their power in a Malthusian way to limit production and keep up prices. The evidence is far from complete. It is clear that the large producers of the centre had increasing difficulties with raw materials in the nineteenth century. So as to be able to import these at minimal cost, they began building works on the coast. Le Creusot, founded in Saône-et-Loire originally because of its proximity to both ore- and coal-mines, found itself obliged to import from Algeria. However, the discovery of the Thomas process, and of the immensely rich iron deposits of the Briey region in the 1880s, led to a rise in production from 2·5 million metric tons in 1873–7 and 4·99 million in 1898–1902 to 14·4 million in

[1] André François-Poncet, *La Vie et l'œuvre de Robert Pinot* (1927).
[2] N. J. G. Pounds and W. N. Parker, *Coal and Steel in Western Europe* (1957), 309.

1910–12.[1] In the inter-war years the industry's performance
compared favourably with the rest of Europe. But two features
seem to distinguish it. First, competition within it was not ruth-
less enough to eliminate inefficient equipment or to stimulate technological improvements. French units of production
were considerably smaller than Germany's. Whereas the U.S.A.
had in 1927 demonstrated the vast increase in productivity
possible through the adoption of wide strip mills and had by
1939 installed twenty-eight of these, with Britain then having
two and Germany one, France got round to installing one only
in the late 1940s. Secondly, the French iron and steel firms
avoided distributing more than a fraction of their profits to
their shareholders, and instead built up enormous reserves.
Thus the Société de Commentry, Fourchambault and Decaze-
ville never distributed a dividend greater than 60 francs per
share between 1854 and 1914, when its net profits were over
200 francs per share in twenty-four of these years and over 300
in seven years. Similarly the Société des Forges de St. Étienne
distributed on average 90 francs per share in dividends between
1869 and 1914, when its profits were 300 francs. The Aciéries de
Longwy had a capital of 30 million francs in 1914 but had
built up reserves of 35 million, after providing for depreciation.
The iron industry, because of the connections of its directors,
was in a particularly favourable position to raise money from
the public, but it preferred to pay for a great deal of its equipment by *autofinance*. The complaints that it also kept prices
unnecessarily high have been investigated in only one instance
and proved unjustified. The price of rails fell from 3,200 (on an
hours-of-work index) in 1828 to 2,100 in 1838 to 800 in 1882
and 250 in 1960.[2]

However, the iron masters' strength came also from the fact
that they were not simply that. They had a stake in many other
branches of the economy. In the nineteenth century the
majority of iron masters were nobles. Iron was the one respectable industry. The bourgeoisie did own foundries particularly
in the north and east but seldom worked them personally and
rather used them as investments. The nobles were active

[1] Comité des Forges, *La Sidérurgie française (1864–1914)* (about 1920), 64.
[2] J. P. Courthéoux, 'Les Pouvoirs économiques et sociaux dans un secteur
industriel: la sidérurgie', *Revue d'Histoire Économique et Sociale* (1960), 339–76.

themselves, however; Helvetius, Lamartine's father and many presidents of *parlements* were among the varied types who managed their own factories.[1] This tradition of part-time supervision never quite vanished. After the Revolution the iron masters went into politics in surprisingly large numbers. Under the July Monarchy the richest men in fourteen departments were iron masters and they enjoyed proportionate political influence. The large firms all had their representatives in parliament. Eugène Schneider, under the Second Empire, while building up his family firm's fortunes at a fast rate, did not grudge the time to be president of the legislature (1865–70), an almost full-time occupation for three or four months of the year at least. His son-in-law became a minister of MacMahon and his grandsons followed him in parliament. It is curious that some of the Wendels do not seem to have derived adequate satisfaction from their iron making, however brilliantly successful they were. Thus Ignace de Wendel (1741–95), founder (with William Wilkinson) of Le Creusot, committed suicide, expressing the hope that his children would not be as unhappy as he had been. His son François (1778–1825) had no interest in iron, and wanted to be a sailor, but both his career and his firm were ruined by the Revolution and he decided to revive the firm in order to 'establish my fortune on a solid basis and to leave a good reputation to my children, as the best of all inheritances.' But he also went into politics and desperately wanted a peerage as a reward from it. His will began 'I, the undersigned, François de Wendel, former pupil of the royal navy, officer in the regiment of hussars and cavalry, and today, *against my will*, iron master and owner of several firms which have prospered despite and against all...'He left four million francs, but considered himself a failure because he had not been a sailor, had shown only mediocre talent as a deputy in parliament, and had not solved all his industrial problems. His eldest son preferred to be a farmer. But his younger son went to the Polytechnic and with the help of another polytechnician, who married his daughter, the scientific progress of the firm was assured. In the next generation a nephew François de Curel, despite his literary tastes, was sent to the École Centrale. He joined the firm but wrote plays and novels and became a member of the French Academy. Another

[1] B. Gille, *Les Origines de la grande industrie métallurgique en France* (1947), 161.

François (1874–1949) while running the firm was also an active parliamentarian in the inter-war years, and vice-president of the Fédération républicaine. He was one of those who bought the newspaper *Le Temps* as a political instrument.[1] The iron masters were successful in obtaining influential office on several occasions. For example, Guillain, president of the Comité des Forges was a minister in Dupuy's cabinet of 1898. In 1957 it was calculated that fifteen of the directors of metallurgical companies had been or were ministers and fifty-four had been or were members of parliament.[2]

There were thus striking differences between textile manufacturers and ironmasters, and, in addition, neither were homogeneous groups. Other branches of industry would reveal still further variety. The secretiveness of these men has made it difficult to get to know them, but almost every new piece of research is bringing out their diversity, complexity, and, more often than hostile novelists have been willing to allow, considerable stores of individuality.

[1] René Sédillot, *La Maison de Wendel de 1704 à nos jours* (1958, privately printed), 122, 164, 247, 274; B. Gille, 'La Psychologie d'un maître de forges', *Revue d'Histoire de la Sidérurgie*, 6 (1965), 61–72.

[2] See further J. Vial, *L'Industrialisation de la sidérurgie française 1814–64* (1967), 1. 170–85, 199. For an interesting biography of a nineteenth-century iron master, see G. Thuillier, *Georges Dufaud et les débuts du grand capitalisme dans la métallurgie en Nivernais au 19e siecle* (1959). Carol Kent's thesis on Camille Cavallier and Pont-à-Mousson (Oxford D. Phil. 1972), based on the firm's archives, is a valuable critique of David Landes's Theory.

6. Bankers

MORE than any other group, the bankers were accused of being the ultimate repository of power, the decisive oligarchy. 'The bankers', wrote Stendhal, 'are at the heart of the state. The bourgeoisie has replaced the faubourg St Germain and the bankers are the nobility of the bourgeois class.' Marx, in claiming that the monarchy of July was the instrument of the rich, made the qualification that it was the financial aristocracy, rather than the industrialists, who ran the country. Since then a large number of books have been written on the Rule of Money, backed, on occasion, by anti-Semitic attacks as in Toussenel's book on *The Jews, Kings of our Time*.[1] The sense of a small and closed circle controlling vast wealth was heightened by the notion of La Haute Banque—a term first used under the Restoration. The Rothschilds were the most famous of this group, but they became important only in the course of the first half of the century, when they rapidly outstripped a large number of rivals. The Haute Banque was not the united body it appeared to be. It consisted first of all of a number of Protestant banks originating for the most part in the eighteenth century, founded by Swiss Huguenots returning to their country of origin. Mallet Frères, founded in about 1713, is the oldest Paris bank surviving under its original name. Members of it have sat as regents of the Bank of France, which they helped to found, uninterruptedly from 1800 to 1936. It had interests in the PLM Railway, of which Charles Mallet was president, the Ottoman Bank, the Bank of Syria and Lebanon, the Banque Franco-Serbe, the Phoenix and National insurance companies, the Havre Docks, the Ateliers de la Loire, the Wolfram mines of Tonkin and Lesieur-Afrique. The Hottinguer Bank had a similar spread, though specialising in mines and metallurgy; the Mirabaud Bank in mines and food (Nicolas wine, Glacières de Paris); the Vernes and Neuflize Banks in a wide variety. The Jews joined this select circle in the nineteenth

[1] A. Toussenel, *Histoire de la féodalité financière* (1847).

century. Adolphe d'Eichtal was the first Jew to become a regent
of the Bank of France 1839–49; Alphonse de Rothschild
followed in 1855; Fould became finance minister of Napoleon
III and left a powerful political and industrial dynasty; his
bank amalgamated with another Jewish one, Heine.[1] There
was a great deal of intermarriage in these families, though their
members were also eagerly sought as husbands or wives by the
old aristocracy; but their community of interest should not
be exaggerated. Under Louis-Philippe there was a distinct
division between the older firms, who lived in the rue faubourg
St. Honoré and tended to be centre conservatives, and the new
ones, who inclined more to the left and lived in the rue de la
Chaussée d'Antin. Their wealth likewise was not as enormous
as people believed. The Mallet bank in 1823 had only one
million francs capital: André and Lottier (the predecessors of
Neuflize) only four million in 1848. It was probably Rothschild's phenomenally rapid rise, from the enormous profits he
made from state loans after Waterloo, that created the Midas
legend.

The magnates of finance must however be seen in a fuller
context. The magnates did not eliminate the lesser bankers and
money-lenders whose hold on people was often more direct. In
1866 there were 8,080 people in banking of whom 2,649 were
employers; and in addition there were 2,556 employers and
3,674 employed in 'credit establishments'. In these vague
statistics, it is not possible to distinguish the exact nature of the
services they performed. But the notable fact is that, as in so
many other branches of French life, the small man continued
to coexist with those of national importance. In 1896 there
were no fewer than 7,931 *patrons* and 30,484 employees in
banking (one-quarter of whom worked in firms of over 500
employees and one-quarter in firms of 50 to 500). In 1921 the
employees rose to 120,673 and in 1931 to 160,139. But even
after the increased concentration and the rise of monster institutions with several hundred branches, and even after the
elimination of simple money-lenders, there were in 1936 no
fewer than 2,100 banks. It was calculated that in 1936 there
were probably over 10,000 bank branches, which meant one for

[1] The Fould family, though originally Jewish, was converted to Protestantism in
the early nineteenth century.

every 1,000 households and one for every 200 traders and firms (*patentés*). Another calculation, made in 1954 and eliminating minor bankers more drastically, arrived at 268 deposit banks (6 large national firms, 82 Paris banks, 22 regional banks and 158 local banks), 38 investment banks, 19 specialised finance institutions, 27 foreign banks and 22 miscellaneous banks.[1] Now in 1937 the four largest banks received only 46 per cent of bank deposits, though if one added the eleven next largest, together they received 73 per cent of deposits. This left a quarter of deposits in the 184 other banks—and these calculations take into account only banks publishing their accounts.

The history of this mass of small banks is even more obscure than that of the large ones, but they clearly had an important place in provincial life. They survived because they provided a personal service and because they could assess their risks more accurately through personal knowledge of their clients. They frequently remained in the same family for many generations. The bank of Tardeaux Frères, founded in Limoges in 1809, has been handed down from father to son ever since. It has built up a faithful clientele in the local porcelain and shoe industries, and also among the farmers of the four surrounding departments, where it has built up thirteen branches and sixty-five part-time offices. The large provincial towns all had numerous well-established banks—Marseille as many as thirty. Alsace was another region with many strong local banks. The Crédit du Nord was so successful in the northern departments that it became larger than two of the six national banks.[2] At the very time when they might have been ruined by the competition of the large deposit banks, they were given a new lease of life by some of the Paris investment banks. The Banque de Paris et des Pays Bas, for example, which had no network of branches, used to collaborate with the Crédit Lyonnais for the sale of new shares in the provinces, but, being anxious not to be too dependent on one firm, it began using regional banks to place these investments for it instead. The regional banks were also able to perform services which the Parisian ones neglected. Thus the Charpenay Bank, established in Grenoble in 1864, worked in

[1] J. S. E. Wilson, *French Banking Structure and Credit* (1957).
[2] 1954 balance-sheet totals, in milliard francs: Crédit Lyonnais 493, Société Générale 415, B.N.C.I. 359, Caisse nationale d'escompte 359.

close touch with local industry. The son of the founder was trained at the School of Waters and Forests and his son-in-law as an engineer. These men could understand the new hydro-electric industry. They increased their capital in the early twentieth century with contributions from a score of local industrialists. By 1931 they had 1,957 shareholders, 9,135 current accounts, and seventeen branches. In that year they went bankrupt. But in the course of its existence the bank had lent 66 million francs to electricity firms, 83 to electro-metallurgical ones, 180 to papermakers and 63 to glovemakers—the major local industries.[1] This kind of industrial financing meant that the control of the economy continued in many aspects to be decentralised. Of course it involved risks, and in the catastrophic years 1929-37 670 small banks collapsed. However, French businessmen have continued the practice of using several banks simultaneously (which is not normal in England) and this has kept the latter's numbers up.

These small banks should not be looked at as valiant survivors of a better world, in the way the artisans were. It was due to very clear deficiencies in the traditional banking facilities that the large deposit banks won their mass support. Though in due course these large institutions were seen as a menace to freedom, they at first presented themselves as liberating the country from the stranglehold of the small money-lender. Louis Reybaud in his best-selling novel *Jérôme Paturot in Search of a Social Position* (1843) described his hero's attempts to get a loan from one of these men. The banker sent him to a subordinate, who received him with 'the contempt, the calculated coldness, the arrogance and the mistrust of a man who has a lot of money: all usurers are alike'. After some discussion, the loan was granted but on severe terms: interest 5 per cent, commission 0.5 per cent, renewable quarterly, i.e. 2 per cent p.a., fees and commission for the notary drawing up the security documents 2 per cent, stamp duties 2 per cent, which made a total of 11 per cent. The tyranny of usurers is seldom written about in histories of the nineteenth century, but it was certainly more severe, in many respects, than the taxation and controls of governments and the oppression of nobles or churchmen. Interest rates were high. Some nascent industries are known to

[1] G. Charpenay, *Les Banques régionalistes* (1939).

have paid between 10 and 15 per cent and even over 20 per cent, which was why *autofinance* became so widespread.

Most bankers were, to begin with, traders as well. The Seillière Bank (founded in 1800) which financed Le Creusot, and which has remained, under its changed title Veuve Demachy et Cie, bankers to the Wendels, was only part of a wider economic activity by its founder, who was also a draper in the Vosges, an iron master in the Ardennes and supplier of military equipment to the Algiers expedition of 1830. The Hottinguer Bank was for long also the principal importer of cotton into France; Rothschilds had a virtual monopoly of the importation of tea. Conversely Worms et Cie were for long France's principal coal merchants before adding an investment bank which is most probably the largest in Paris. The Haute Banque tended to confine itself to a small number of clients, and to live off the profits of a few large firms: the Seillière Bank (which had only thirty clients) off Le Creusot and the Wendels, the Périer Bank off Anzin. On a humbler level, the dozen bankers of Nevers were nearly all products of the local pottery industry. Those of Lyon—more numerous still—were silk merchants; those of Nantes shipowners. At an even more rudimentary stage, the money-lenders of the countryside included notaries and *trésoriers généraux*—state officials who did more private than public business. These small men had a massive amount of business, because they specialised in mortgages on land, long considered the safest of investments, and involving some 500 million francs each year in the 1840s, at a time when the Bank of France was discounting only about 150 million francs of commercial paper. These two figures are not truly comparable, since the Bank of France refused to give credit beyond three months, and it required three signatures on the paper it discounted.

The great problem of industry therefore was to get long-term credit. But there was strong prejudice against the very notion of this. Thiers in 1840, giving vent, as he so often did, to the common opinion of the ordinary middle-class man, declaimed against industry being given credit too easily or over too long a period: that would be to 'make it possible for all sorts of incapable men, men with neither ability nor money, to start up businesses; they would spin cotton and weave cloth blindly,

without measure; they would burden the markets with a mass
of products and would compete against old-established traders
and these mushroom men would thus ruin men who have been
in business for forty or fifty years'.[1] The Chamber of Commerce
of Amiens wrote in the same way in 1836: 'To offer industry too
much capital would be an inducement to it to give its production a dangerous expansion. . . . Our own capital can suffice for
our needs.'[2] Since the days of Law, bank was almost a dirty
word—banks were the cause of economic crises—and many
banks preferred to call themselves *caisses*. Before 1848, France's
banking structure was characterised by dispersion of resources,
narrowness of activity, and ignorance of financial methods and
the rules of credit. These features have been held responsible
for the slow rate of industrialisation in the nineteenth century,
and the explosion in economic activity which occurred under
Napoleon III may be related to the discovery of new methods of
utilising savings.

The real pioneer in these was Jacques Laffitte, the self-made
notary's clerk who rose to be Louis-Philippe's banker and
prime minister. In 1837 he succeeded in persuading the leading
financiers, industrialists and merchants to subscribe 50 million
francs to found a giant company designed to stimulate industry
by offering to buy shares in new and promising ventures.
Under the Second Empire two Jews from Bordeaux, Émile and
Isaac Péreire, cousins of Olinde Rodrigues, who had been Saint-
Simon's secretary, developed this idea on a larger scale. Their
Crédit Mobilier, founded with the support of the Fould Bank
and of Napoleon III's special patronage, played an important
part in financing the rapid railway building of this reign, in
founding the Compagnie Générale Transatlantique, the Paris
Omnibus Co., insurance companies, and in fusing the six com-
peting gas works of Paris. It handled the finances of sixteen
firms with a combined capital of one billion francs, equal to
one-fifth of the value of all stocks quoted on the Paris bourse.
It set up an active branch in Madrid and negotiated to expand
into several other countries. It helped to found, with a government subsidy, the Crédit Foncier. But it was faced with the

---

[1] Quoted by G. Palmade, *Capitalisme et capitalistes français au 19ᵉ siècle* (1961),
71.
[2] B. Gille, *La Banque et le crédit en France de 1815 à 1848* (1959), 371.

implacable hostility and rivalry of the Rothschilds, so that
when it got into difficulties in the late 1860s, it was
destroyed.

The Péreires were the most brilliant of a large number of
financiers who rose to shake the traditional world of banking,
which looked on them as speculators. National deposit banks
were another innovation in the Second Empire. The Crédit
Lyonnais was founded in 1863 by Henri Germain (1824–
1905), the son of a Lyon silk manufacturer. He personally
had only 100,000 francs capital, plus an income of 16,160
francs; he married the daughter of another silk merchant
who brought him a dowry of 760,000 francs. However, he
subscribed only 2,150 out of the 40,000 shares of his company:
over 300 bankers and leaders of the silk and metal industries
provided the rest. In the space of eighteen years he increased the
capital twentyfold and had 109 branches. He managed the
firm himself for over forty years. This was indeed the case of a
financier enjoying control of millions in excess of his personal
wealth. The bank carefully concealed the fact that in its first
eighteen years it made annual profits of 24 per cent. It gave away
only 9.52 per cent in dividends. 14.7 per cent went to reserves or
to the directors, so that the latter got about 20 per cent a year
return on their money. Still Germain had spotted that there was
a vast amount of money lying idle in Lyon. He offered free current
accounts to businessmen, and deposit accounts at 3 per cent. At
first he lent almost one-third of his available capital to industry,
but these turned out to be disastrous investments and the
Krach of 1882 convinced him that industry was too risky.
Henceforth he confined himself to dealing in insurance, property, public utilities and foreign state loans. 'Industrial
enterprises', Germain told his shareholders, 'even those which
are most carefully studied and even those which are administered most wisely, involve risks which we consider incompatible
with the security indispensable to the employment of the funds
of a deposit bank.'[1] The attraction of state loans was overwhelming, for, in the years 1871–4 alone, the Crédit Lyonnais
made a profit of no less than 25 million francs simply from
selling French government *rentes*.[2] It took over only one local

[1] G. Piron and M. Byé, *Traité d'économie politique*, vol. 4, *Le Crédit* (n.d.), 131.

[2] Jean Bouvier, *Le Crédit Lyonnais de 1863 à 1882* (1961).

bank in the course of its rise to be the largest deposit bank in France: it preferred to set up branches in its systematic search for new business. Its most rapid expansion took place between 1921 and 1931 when about a 1,000 new offices—all over the country—were opened.

Other banks soon followed, though they pursued slightly different paths. The Société Générale was originally started in 1864 as a ripost by the established banks against the upstart Crédit Mobilier: nineteen French firms and thirteen English ones subscribed over 80 per cent of its shares. It was thus at first an investment bank as well as a deposit bank, and it made profits several times those of the Crédit Lyonnais, but it took risks which caused it heavy losses, and after 1900 it concentrated simply on deposit banking and began opening up local branches on as massive a scale as the Crédit Lyonnais. The Crédit Industriel et Commercial, founded in 1859 on the model of an English joint stock bank, has by contrast avoided expanding into the provinces in the same way, but at an early stage took the decision to co-operate with local people to set up regional banks in which it invested, for example, Lyon (1865), Bordeaux (1880), etc., the Banque Dupont (established 1819 and powerful in the north), and in the 1930s the smaller banks which were in difficulties. The Comptoir National d'Escompte goes back to as early as 1848, and in 1870 it was the leading bank in France, but it was soon outdistanced by the Crédit Lyonnais and the Société Générale, and then suffered a severe blow when it backed the Société des Métaux with whom it shared several directors. The collapse of this speculation in 1889 caused the director of the bank to commit suicide—after which it became even more conservative than the Crédit Lyonnais. The Banque Nationale pour le Commerce et l'Industrie, on the other hand, dates only from 1931, when it was formed to replace another bank founded in 1913 forced into liquidation, but an immediate rapid expansion of branches brought it quickly into the big four. Though the banks have been unusually cautious in their attitude towards industry, it would be wrong to regard them as being uniformly timid. It has been claimed, for example, that after the era of Henri Germain, when caution was the rule, the early twentieth century showed a new outlook, dominated by Louis Dorizon, who in 1896 became director general of the Société Générale and who was much more interested in industrial development. He co-operated with Noetzlin, head of the Banque de Paris et des Pays Bas, in a programme of active investment. But in 1913 he was voted out of office by his frightened directors.[1]

By the time of the Popular Front, the presence of these large banks, with their mushrooming branches, was being increasingly felt. Paradoxically, however, just when public opinion became most hostile to their power, they were in fact suffering a rapid decline. Government and semi-public institutions were expanding very fast a good while before nationalisation. The Caisse des Dépôts was founded in 1816 for limited purposes, chiefly to look after moneys involved in legal disputes. Then, however, it was used to manage various other state funds—particularly the national savings bank and after 1930 the national insurance scheme. As a result it controlled deposits in 1939 considerably larger than all the private credit banks put together. The state savings bank (Caisse d'Épargne) expanded enormously in the inter-war years, after the abolition of a limit on the amount that could be deposited. Since it paid interest of between $2\frac{3}{4}$ and $3\frac{1}{4}$ per cent (in contrast to the $\frac{1}{2}$ per cent or $\frac{3}{4}$ per cent paid by the deposit banks), and the savings were withdrawable on demand (in Paris, and with a couple of days' notice in the provinces), there was a massive transfer of funds to it, and in 1938 its deposits amounted to 63 milliard francs, against 67 milliard in the main 132 banks publishing accounts. The state achieved these results partly by refusing to pay salaries to its civil servants (except senior ones) direct into banks, and insisting on using *chèques postales* instead. These state services did not appeal to a new class. In 1937 50 per cent of accounts in the Caisse d'Epargne were held by 'proprietors, *rentiers* and persons exercising no profession', another 15 per cent were civil servants and employees, and a further 9 per cent soldiers and sailors. Only 2·77 per cent were industrial workers. Investment in the inter-war period also became state sponsored on an enormous scale. Various national institutions were established to give loans to different sectors of the economy: the Crédit agricole (1920), Crédit national (1919), Crédit popu-

---

[1] R. Girault, 'Pour un portrait nouveau de l'homme d'affaires français vers 1914', *Revue d'Histoire Moderne et Contemporaine*, 16 (1969), 329–49.

laire (1917), and the H.B.M.[1] (cheap housing subsidies, dating back to 1894 but made active only after the war). The vast resources coming in to the Caisse des Dépôts were used for large public works programmes. Between 1913 and 1936 the banks increased their deposits by only 26 per cent, while prices rose fivefold. The rush away from the banks can be seen in the figures for one year in the great depression: in 1931 they lost 16 milliards of deposits, but deposits in the Caisse d'Épargne increased by ten milliards. The nationalisation of the banks thus followed a massive withdrawal of confidence.[2]

The relationship of the rich, the industrialists and the bankers to the rest of the population has been excessively simplified in the theories holding that it was a relationship of domination. Many detailed studies will be needed on individual firms and magnates before conclusions on this subject can be attempted. The state of knowledge on them is still rather rudimentary; serious company histories have only just begun to be published.[3] But modern research seems to be moving towards a view of the economy as far more fragmented and with far more autonomous pockets than the old generalisations suggest.

[1] Habitations à bon marché.

[2] Henry Laufenberger, *Les Banques françaises* (1940), 43, 77–80, 168; Robert Bigo, *Les Banques françaises au cours du 19ᵉ siècle* (1947); J. J. Laurendon, *Psychoanalyse des banques* (n.d., about 1963).

[3] See F. Braudel and E. Labrousse, *Histoire économique et sociale de la France*, tome 3, vol. 1 (1976), especially the chapters by Maurice Lévy-Leboyer, pp. 347–467. See also the latter's *Les Banques européennes et l'industrialisation* (1964).

7. The Ambitions of Ordinary Men

THE ambitions of people who never became very rich, who founded no dynasty or long-lasting company, and who lived in the middle and lower ranks of the business world, are difficult to write about, because they are seldom recorded. But the character of a society is greatly influenced by the form the ambitions of such men take, and by the extent to which they are satisfied or frustrated. Discussions of France's economic development have tended to move rather above this humbler level. Large industries and family concerns have attracted attention, and they can obviously be identified and investigated most readily. The firm which mushrooms from the invention of a clever man and is then sold to either a stranger with a different name, or, as seems to have happened very often, to a foreman or other associate within the firm, may be equally prosperous but its fortunes are far harder to follow. In the family firm, expansion is said to have been subordinated to the interests of the family. Persistence in producing the same things, at a moderate level, for a traditional market, and the setting up of small firms for younger sons and other relatives, was one way of interpreting this family interest. But it seems that there was an alternative which was possibly more frequently followed and that was to sell up as soon as one had made a reasonable amount of money—just as one had reached prosperity—and to retire on the proceeds, give oneself up to horticultural or literary hobbies, and finance the rise in the world of one's children by educating them for the liberal professions. Smaller firms, which were neither family firms nor joint stock companies, were by far the most numerous.

The discussion so far has been about how industrialists behaved. Another problem is why more people did not go into industry. It is well known that in France there were strong traditions which led parents to send their children into the civil service, or alternatively the liberal professions, and that these careers, once embarked on, were frequently passed on from father to son. Why did more people not become engineers and scientists? The answer is to be found partly in how people viewed ambition. If one examines the guides to careers, one can get some insight—however limited—into how contemporaries saw the job market at any one time. The advice of these books is of course biased and it may be argued that, in so far as they are sometimes concerned to urge people to enter certain careers, their advice has the weakness of all exhortations by moralists. There is no way of telling whether people actually listened to them. However, it is possible to compare what they said with what other sections of the community thought about the same problems from other angles. The exhortations of psychologists and doctors who were not concerned with economic growth are particularly instructive. It is possible that people were more willing to follow advice when they thought it would also benefit their health, so it is interesting to see how the doctors reinforced current economic prejudices. For all its inevitable limitations the history of attitudes to success is an important subject.

The guide to the choice of a career by Edouard Charton, published in 1842, is a good way of understanding contemporary opinion on the subject. Charton was a remarkable man with experience and contacts in many walks of life. Trained as a barrister, he was one of the most successful editors of the century, with an uncanny ability for spotting what the public wanted. He founded and ran the *Magasin Pittoresque* (1833), *L'Illustration* (1843), *Le Tour du Monde* (1860), three of the best-selling journals of popularized knowledge of this period. He was a Saint-Simonian in his youth, attaché at the ministry of justice 1840–8 (where he wrote the biographies of criminals condemned to death in these years, for the edification of Louis-Philippe), secretary-general at the ministry of education in 1848, prefect in 1870, deputy in 1871, senator in 1876, and president of the *Gauche républicaine* in the senate. His career makes him an enlightened, indeed advanced, bourgeois with an exceptional concern for the education of the masses, so that his opinions may be taken as being even a little ahead of his time.

Charton contrasts the situation during the July Monarchy with that prevailing during the *ancien régime*. In the latter people were kept out of a large number of activities by the accident of birth, and it was less easy to rise or fall in one's status. In addition *esprit de famille* opposed a barrier to individual desires and ambitions. 'A son looked upon it as a matter of honour, more than he would today, to uphold the reputation that his ancestors had acquired in their employment or trade.' Birth, law, custom and paternal authority combined to limit people's horizons and left little scope for uncertainty about their careers. But by the mid nineteenth century freedom of choice was, theoretically, unlimited. *Esprit de famille* had weakened. 'Parents and children were often separated by differences in education, opinion or beliefs and physically by the results of centralisation, which draws all young ambition to the large cities.' However, even a Saint-Simonian like Charton thinks that there were still a great number of advantages to be obtained from following in one's father's profession, so that 'one cannot be too perturbed to see them so often ignored or disdained'. The son who follows this 'most simple and most natural course' is spared a painful and long uncertainty; he can be taught his trade by his father and inherit his clients and relations, confidence and esteem. Charton recommends a break with this tradition only in special circumstances, as when the profession requires special gifts which are totally lacking in the son, or when it is dying out, or when there are too many brothers. That is, only negative reasons and insurmountable obstacles should make men move out of traditional occupations. Charton insists that if this has to be done, the alternative chosen should be one where the son will find help from relatives or other protectors. Clearly patronage was still a factor of the utmost importance. But perhaps the most interesting of Charton's recommendations is that people should not set their targets too high. They should seek jobs which 'lead to *l'aisance*, comfort rather than riches, to esteem more than to admiration, to a normal development of the faculties, to an increase of intelligence and morality rather than the satisfaction of the passions'. The jobs which can bring riches may quite likely prove disastrous and lead to poverty, just as those for which admiration and glory is the highest reward for a few, can bring shame and ridicule on the many who fail. If one pushes oneself too hard one will use oneself up rapidly. 'The best way to make one's life a happy one is to make it useful, modest, simple and not too busy (*peu affairée*). This is a truth that the sages and poets have repeated since the beginning of time.' The ideal for a young man who had a little money should be to aim not to compromise it, rather than to try to double it, to find an honourable and peaceful position in the world which occupies and develops his intelligence, and which leads him by a slow but sure path to public esteem.

It is true this had to be reconciled with the practice of most parents who sought for their sons 'a profession which seems to be placed in public esteem a little above that which they themselves exercise. In this they only yield to the sentiment which leads us to give our children a higher and higher position, in accordance with the supposition that happiness is proportionate to the elevation of social rank.' Charton thus recognises that upward social mobility had increasingly replaced acceptance of one's inherited station, but he saw these aspirations as fraught with dangers and urged moderation and prudence. Drive and ambition were not for him the way to success, and money should not be the goal. He constantly lays stress on 'public esteem' as the most rewarding aim and no profession which was either not respectable in itself or which had unrespectable practitioners should be considered, however much money might be earned. Thus a solicitor usually made more money than a barrister, except in the very top ranks, but his job was definitely 'less tempting'. Dentists and some pharmacists were highly prosperous but 'vain pride' kept people away from these professions. Financial middlemen had the reputation of being gamblers and the danger of being polluted by their 'immorality' was held against working with them. To win public esteem one must be prudent: the respected banker was the circumspect one, who lent money very timidly. The architect could only expect work if he 'won the confidence of the well-to-do and kept it by a severe morality'. Some concession, it is true, had to be made to those who thirsted for glory. Glory was a noble ambition, but parents were right to be hesitant to allow their children to become, for example, artists, whose reward was glory. Though artists had 'never been so honoured, encouraged and highly paid', quite exceptional talents were required, and besides the admiration of the crowds was a mixed blessing. 'The respected man is happier than he who is admired and the most desirable life is the most simple one.'

What the doctors had to say about ambition from the point of view of health was enough to put anyone off it. Descuret, in his work on *The Medicine of the Passions* (1842), was clear that excessive ambition revealed itself in immediate and dangerous clinical symptoms. The ambitious man 'becomes pale, his brow grows furrowed, his eyes withdraw into their sockets, his glance becomes unsteady and worried, his cheek-bones become prominent, his temples hollow, and his hair falls out or grows white with time. He is nearly always out of breath, he suffers from palpitations of the heart and from cruel insomnia. His pulse is normally feverish, his breath burning, and his digestion imperfect, with acute or chronic inflammation of the bowels. He is frequently killed by cancer of the stomach or the liver, by apoplexy, or by an organic affection of the heart. But the most usual end of this passion [of ambition] is melancholy and above all ambitious monomania.' The madhouses were full of unsuccessful ambitious people who imagined they were generals, popes or God. Every political revolution produced an overcrowding of the asylums: the middle-class ones were particularly full. The trouble with ambition was that it offended the basic rule of hygiene of the day: prudence. Dr. Descuret, basing himself on twenty-three years of practice in Paris, commented that ambition was 'much more common than one thinks; it is creeping into all ranks, all conditions, and even affecting children'. It was particularly common among bilious, bilious-sanguine and melancholic people, who sought jobs above their talents, going beyond the boundaries of emulation, which was the acceptable desire to distinguish oneself among one's equals. The cure for ambition was a country life, with long walks, hunting, light food to re-establish the digestion, massage, warm baths and varied but not tiring reading. The patient's pride should be humiliated, obstacles raised against his desires; he should be removed from large towns, especially the court and the company of parvenus, he should be given friends who were happy with their lot, 'undesirous either by modesty or circumspection, of raising themselves to a higher state. By their habitual company (for all is contagious among men) he will end up by being convinced that glory and happiness cannot be allied on earth and that most ambitious people are simply unhappy slaves who have painfully ascended the difficult path of life to arrive at death with more noise but also with more misfortunes than other men.' Dr. Descuret is firm: 'An ambitious man is a sick man.' The illness is most difficult to cure when it affects a statesman brutally disgraced without any recompense which might salve his vanity. Death or consumptive fever frequently follows. The physician, in the latter case, 'can only console and suggest religion as the best remedy'. Dr. Descuret is a good representative of the middle class, but his recommendations usefully remind one that a good half of this class at the very least was conservative and viewed social mobility with alarm. Ambition, he said, was inevitably stimulated by constitutional and representative government, which based itself on the 'pride of the middle classes' and he was worried that this 'pride had since been communicated to the lower ranks'.[1] The notion that doctors were usually radical is of course a myth.

Another doctor, Bergeret, writing in 1878 on *The Passions and Their Dangers and Inconveniences for Individuals, the Family and Society*, begins with 150 pages against the passion for wealth (before going on to the passion for debauchery). This passion, he says, caused men to work too hard, and it killed them 'by an excessive tension of the brain'. It led them to embark on all sorts of hazardous enterprises and all sorts of jobs: few succeeded and most became ill from overwork, starvation or infection. It was reasonable for brilliant boys to go to the city, but it was blind vanity to try to rise above one's station without exceptional gifts. 'Ambition is the ruin of man.'[2] As late as 1914, Dr. A. Culerre, curiously combining traditional prejudices and modern ideas in his study of *Nervous Children*, said that, though no job necessarily produced nervous troubles, it was wise to avoid those which require excessively hard work. So business, politics, journalism and art were all to be avoided because of the worries and disappointments they brought. The liberal professions were much more desirable. They allowed a regular and ordered life which 'favoured the equilibrium of physiological functions', and left plenty of time to relax. And for those who

[1] Dr. J. B. F. Descuret, *La Médecine des passions ou les passions considérées dans leurs rapports avec les maladies, les lois et la religion* (1841), 9, 572–91.

[2] L. F. L. Bergeret, *Les Passions, dangers et inconvénients pour les individus, la famille et la société. Hygiène morale et sociale* (1878), 25–9.

were predisposed to nervous disorders, the military life was best, because of the discipline it imposed.[1]

By 1908 a best-selling writer on how to succeed in life was saying that the French must modify their habits of stagnation and follow the lead of the U.S.A. if they were to keep their rank in the world, for supremacy which was formerly won by arms was now to be obtained by business, commerce and industry as much as, if not more than, arts and letters. He quotes Carnegie and a new magazine *Commerce et Industrie* which had been established to adapt for France the advice of the American *Selling Magazine*. Ambition is no longer condemned, action and energy are what is needed. 'To work to earn money', the reader is assured, 'cannot dishonour you, if you use honest means.' However, even he does not propose that the American example should be followed completely. The millionaire is not the ideal. 'In recommending my reader to make money, I do not urge him to amass enormous sums. On the contrary, I want to tell him that while he should as quickly as possible free himself from the servitude engendered by poverty, it should not be just to fall into another servitude, that of money, which is as tyrannic.' His aim should be absolute independence, well-being and comfort. He should simply free himself from the need to worry about survival, so as to be able to use his time as he pleases, to go on holiday, to surround himself with fine art, good furniture and books. In other words, the old French ideal really survived beneath the new phraseology. In France, he says, there was no need to make money with the same unflagging dedication as there was in America. 'A Frenchman has a right to some pleasures, to vacations, to the charms of restful conversation and it is in this way, in this manner more conforming to our traditions, our tastes and our education, that I want to envisage the successful man.' He quotes doctors who have written books against *Haste* and against *Overwork*;[2] and he ends up recommending too much prudence in preference to temerity.[3]

In the light of these common prejudices, it is easier to

[1] Dr. A. Culerre, *Les Enfants nerveux* (1914), 291–2.

[2] Dr. Toulouse, *Comment conserver la santé* (1914); Dr. Pierrot, *Travail et surménage* (1911).

[3] Silvain Rondès, *L'Homme qui réussit. Sa Mentalité. Ses Méthodes* (1908), 70–85, 183–94.

understand why more able people did not go into industry. Charton pays the usual lip-service to industry's importance and even predicts that it would in the future hold out good career prospects, but it is clear that these were prospects at a humble level. 'The career of science', he says, 'as a profession is open only to a small number of people and it needs the unison of fortunate circumstances to rise in it with success.' By that he means there were a few openings in the university: he looked on science as an academic subject. He felt he could unconditionally advise only the sons of scientists to become scientists. They might hope to get their fathers' jobs 'almost by right, provided they are more or less worthy. To maintain a name is easier than to make one.' Unless one was in this category, 'it would not be prudent for a young man without fortune to try and earn a living by studying natural history, unless he has extraordinary gifts. He is unlikely to get even one of the jobs yielding a modest comfort and he will probably never emerge from a state close to poverty.' Applied scientists were not much sought after either. 'Disastrous examples would not be difficult to cite to prove how one must be on guard against modifications which experience has not sufficiently sanctioned. So the sort of aversion felt by many industrialists for men of science is not a complete error.' The rewards in industry were not high: one would start at only 1,500 or 2,000 francs and rise to only 6,000. All industries were risky. The best advice one could give to a man who took it into his head to go into industry was at least to beware of mushroom firms, basing themselves on the caprice of a fashion or on hazardous speculation. It would be wiser to seek a job with lower pay but more security. Charton says that it was 'quite rare for families having wealth or even a competency to destine their children for the vague functions and the chancy career of civil engineer'. There was the École Centrale which trained young people who could aspire to a modest existence; and it was a good thing for producing educated industrialists and able foremen. 'But for the big projects being planned or executed the country possesses a sufficient number of engineers and it will be rare for private industry to choose, for the management of these works, men who have only too easily assumed the title of civil engineer.' The right course for one who wanted to supervise great engineering feats was to go to the Polytechnic,

serve the state in the Ponts et Chaussées for a few years, and
then leave for private industry, which would pay him three or
four times his state salary. The engineers were thus a small élite,
controlled by the state.

Charton's advice to a man determined to make money
quickly, despite all the moral pressures against such a course,
was to enter retail trade. 'There are few jobs ensuring the
highest profits which are more certain, more regular and, let
us admit it, more considerable. It is not rare to see grocers,
bakers and other merchants of this type retire after fifteen
years at it, if not with a fortune, at least comfortably off.' Early
retirement is assumed to be the aim, to enable people to live the
good life—which money-making was not. Commerce, said
Charton, was difficult to engage in with dignity—but esteem
for it was growing, particularly in the upper ranks of 'high
commerce', which required economic and geographic knowledge. (The esteem was for the knowledge.) Of course, the
higher one went, the riskier it became. It was only the modest
shop that Charton advised. One can see therefore that this work
by an influential publicist, summarising contemporary opinion,
positively turned young people away from economic expansion,
and almost from economic activities; at best he found in small
commerce the most advisable way of making money, but he was
careful not to lead anyone astray into wanting too much money.[1]

Charton had a son, born in 1840, just two years before his
book was published. It is interesting to discover that he became
an engineer, after graduating from the École Centrale des Arts
et Métiers. Was he just asserting his independence of his father?
In 1880 this son produced a third edition of his father's careers
guide and it contains the answer. He thought that an engineer
enjoyed great respect because of the magnitude of the achievements of his profession in the nineteenth century, in railway
building and public works, but even he recommended the profession with reservations. First of all, he thought one was born
an engineer, as one was born an artist. It required exceptional
gifts. His article on the profession contains a long digression on

[1] E. Charton, *Guide pour le choix d'un état ou dictionnaire des professions* (1842). For
confirmation of Charton's views see J. H. Donnard, *Balzac, les réalités économiques et
sociales dans la comédie humaine* (1961), 277, quoting Chaptal, and the press of the
July Monarchy.

Leonardo da Vinci, showing how art and science were one, and he ends by recommending James Watt as an 'extremely erudite man of letters'. Jules Charton obviously thought of himself as something of an artist or writer: he was defending his choice of profession not in terms of its own standards but more as a branch of the traditionally admired arts. Secondly, he warns that, though a graduate of the Polytechnic had an assured future if he became an engineer, others graduating from less smart technical schools had to start in inferior manual jobs and had to spend ten or fifteen years before they obtained the rank of engineer. Though an engineer, he agrees with his father that commerce is preferable as a career to industry. In commerce he says the risks are limited, a merchant can lose only the goods he has; but in industry the risks are unlimited, a manufacturer may lose all his capital. 'Every progress inevitably brings risk': machines are suddenly put out of date, so the manufacturer needs not just capital to start his factory but at least as much again in reserve. Only large companies have any real chance in metallurgy, which is subject to constant crises. Mining is made perilous by the frequency of accidents. Openings in the textile industry he does not consider even worth discussing.[1]

In 1892 another voluminous guide to careers appeared, edited by an Inspector-General of Technical Education, Paul Jacquemart. His job almost required him to urge people away from the classical liberal professions, but it is highly significant that he too does not push them into industry, but, rather, into commerce. Again he pays lip-service to the engineers 'whose name has baptized the century', but he does not advise anyone to try to establish great industrial complexes. The aim is still to 'establish oneself on one's own account'. He discourages men away from metallurgy where this ideal is almost unattainable. He points out that industrial chemists normally earned considerably less than foremen; and that an engineer who went into the railways would have to start at the bottom, driving engines. There was clearly an important obstacle to industrial expansion so long as management and technologists were isolated and very differently rewarded. There also appeared to

[1] E. Charton, *Dictionnaire des professions* (3rd edition 1880 in collaboration with Paul Laffitte and Jules Charton), 152, 286, 328–30.

be some discrediting of the engineering profession by the recurrence of economic crises, in the same way as politicians were discredited by scandals and ministerial crises. The engineer's profession was a noble one, he said, but only when properly understood. 'The engineer must impose a brake (*frein*) on the exaggerations of the time. He must resist the mad crazes, he must refuse to work in hazardous projects and speculative developments.' Jacquemart gives very little space to engineering, three and a half pages out of over 1,000. By contrast he is enthusiastic about commerce. Most of the lavishly rewarded directors of the great department stores of Paris, he says, started with no money at all. Such was the pressure to get into commerce that in many shops young people worked without pay (as they once had in the civil service, but no longer). People were realising that the liberal professions were overcrowded, that commerce, while being 'less brilliant in appearance', was much more remunerative. So the old aristocratic contempt for it was disappearing and it was now recognised as one of the vital forces of the country. So many people wanted to be bank clerks that the job could only be obtained through patronage and only a very modest salary could be hoped for. The tables were turned, and Jacquemart was writing now about commerce as people had previously written about the traditionally respectable occupations. He quotes the large sums men were now willing to pay to set up as bakers—25,000 to 40,000 francs and over 100,000 in Paris, and even more as keepers of cafés and restaurants: some cafés in Paris were sold at over one million francs. Travelling salesmen were no longer the contemptible starvelings described by Balzac: their moral level had gone up a lot and they behaved as though they were well brought up. It was the exception now, noted Jacquemart, for sons to follow their fathers' professions. 'Everybody is impatient to move out of his sphere and has pretensions to rising.'[1]

The preference for commerce rather than industry was strengthened by the closed nature of the large and the family firm. 'Since large firms are the thing of the future', wrote another career guide, 'young men, even if they are rich, will risk a lot if they establish themselves as entrepreneurs or manufacturers.

[1] Paul Jacquemart, *Professions et métiers. Guide pratique pour le choix d'une carrière à l'usage des familles et de la jeunesse* (1892), 326, 524-7, 776.

Of factories and firms of middle or small size, none can succeed except those which are passed on from father to son, or which are maintained by money and an old clientele. Young men will do better therefore to enter as partners into already large businesses. If they have the means, they ought not to start on their own before they are forty, after having ensured by their experience and relations and the confidence they have inspired in their work, the nucleus of a clientele willing to support a new business. It is not an easy thing.' There was thus little encouragement to the young to make their fortunes quickly in industry, to stake all on manufacturing a new product.[1]

By the end of the century, with the expansion of education, it was becoming clear that the direction of ambitions would have to be altered, since the mass production of *bacheliers* was assuming excessive proportions. The suggestions of the politicians were mainly negative and not persuasive since they were hardly following the advice they were giving and since they appealed as much to patriotism as to self-interest. Méline preached a return to the land, an abandonment of the towns and large-scale industry, and a revival of farming and artisan activities.[2] Gabriel Hanotaux thought that though everybody should have the opportunity to go to school till they were fifteen, they should be stopped from staying on unless they were likely to be Pico de la Mirandolas and urged to go, not into the over-crowded civil service, but into anything else—the colonies, agriculture, industry, commerce.[3] There was an accentuation of propaganda in favour of the colonies.[4] Even professors of literature began to think there was need for more practical activities, but it is interesting that one of them, who wrote on *Prejudices of Yesterday and Careers of Today* (1908), suggested only horizontal movement into other jobs of the same social level rather than trying to use the less crowded and new professions to raise oneself to a higher class. The job a man took should depend on his family and friendships. 'The humble live and develop with the aid of the humble and the rich live and develop through the rich.' Though boys should seek jobs

[1] Paul Bastien, *Les Carrières commerciales, industrielles et agricoles* (1906), 203.
[2] J. Méline, *Le Retour à la terre* (1905).
[3] Gabriel Hanotaux, *Du Choix d'une carrière* (1904).
[4] Lt. Col. Péroz, *Hors des chemins battus* (1908).

different from their fathers', the peasant's son should naturally try only to become a mechanic, the middle-class child to fill the middle grades in industry, and it was the aristocracy which would provide its leaders. This professor's realism may well have been justified to a large extent. He certainly made no attempt to change old prejudices by advancing totally new criteria. He hoped the new careers would acquire respectability by assuming the values of the old ones. It is generally thought, he said, that the liberal professions are not pursued for individual profit but from concern for the social interest and that is why they are rewarded with honoraria rather than wages, whereas economic careers are supposed to aim only at personal interest. This distinction, he said, should be ended. Industry did have social aims and the boys he urged to enter it should stress them by limiting their profits, by acquiring culture and by practising *mœurs* which would make them similar to the liberal professions.[1] The transitions were very gradual. When Andrew Carnegie's *World of Business* was translated, it was used to bridge the gap between the old morality of duty and the pursuit of riches.[2]

A work on *The Best Professions to Make a Fortune In After the War* (1916) is another vigorous attack on going into the civil service and liberal professions. It recommends commerce and industry as the careers of the future, 'even if they seem more modest'. But there are reservations. The author stresses that most of these desirable jobs have to be obtained through influence and patronage. Thus of engineers he says that the engineering schools find jobs for their graduates in the firms of their older alumni but that these did not have enough vacancies. 'To get a job oneself as an engineer, one needs relations, patronage and luck. It is an excellent profession for those who manage to find a nook in it.' It was the same with chemists: jobs were obtained through influence. It is interesting also that though industry is now acceptable (but still limited by the old-boy network), the financial professions—which were essential to the expansion of industry—were decried as dangerous and to be avoided. The

[1] Gaston Valran, *Préjugés d'autrefois et carrières d'aujourd'hui* (Toulouse and Paris, 1908), 135, 356.
[2] A. Berlan, *Du Choix d'une carrière par Gabriel Hanotaux et l'empire des affaires par Andrew Carnegie* (Saint-Quentin, 1904)—by a journalist.

prospect of many vacancies after the war 'which had ravaged the élite of the nation' was the only real source of optimism for the young man with no friends in high places.[1]

The compendious *Guide Carus* on careers for young people, published in the 1930s, still showed that entry into industry was difficult. The war had greatly increased the number of engineers and the crisis after it meant that there was little hope of high salaries. Things were improving and jobs could be obtained by engineers without great difficulty though they were seldom advertised. But the graduate still had to start at the bottom, as an engine driver or as a draughtsman or even in purely manual work; he would get a salary below that of a skilled worker. Chemists could not be confident about rising very high. Until recently, it says, it was very rare to see a man who had no capital, but only a degree from the School of Chemistry, become a director. 'Formerly and sometimes even today people say there are too many chemists being produced by the schools. It is true that the chemists are barely beginning to win a place in the sun; they have had many prejudices to conquer; and they will need to triumph over many others, apart from the mistrust and jealousies to be surmounted.' There was no career structure for them: the chief chemist in a factory would be assisted by subordinates with only an elementary education. The jobs which were presented as being most attractive in this period, and which were reported to be most sought after, were ones in commerce. Careers in commerce could more easily be reconciled with traditional values and the style of life they allowed was more like that of the old bureaucrats. People were interested in commerce now because it was 'a clean profession, exercised in a distinguished and elegant milieu. Men of taste appreciate the careful grooming, the distinguished manners, work in the company of colleagues from good society, courteous relations with a selected clientele, a pleasant atmophere in a shop arranged and decorated with art. The life was hard and busy, but enlivened by a reflection of grace and distinction.' The qualities required were good taste, love of order, elegance in elocution, that is, the qualities of a gentleman with discretion and moderate culture. It offered security, a fixed

[1] Jean Liévin, *Les Meilleures Professions pour faire fortune après la guerre* (1916), 19, 25.

salary with bonuses, and good prospects of reaching high rewards. The uncertainties of business in the mid nineteenth century were no longer frightening in the service of great department stores. Accountants were becoming valued professional people. In the large industrial firms, it was the commercial jobs which were most sought after. The commercial and administrative sections nearly all worked only a five day week, while the factories continued all day Saturday and some involved night work. There was little attraction in being exiled as an engineer to some bleak industrial area, isolated from the society and pleasures which even medium towns could provide.[1]

All this suggests that there was an additional reason for the special form France's industrial expansion took, which has not hitherto been studied, and which is to be found in the history of ambition and prestige. The civil service and the liberal professions had an attraction which survived tenaciously. When the pressure for public office and clients became too severe and the rewards too limited by comparison with other careers, it was to commerce if not to industry that the new generation's interests were channelled. There was a gap in the career structure of industry which prevented it from recruiting able men with high ambitions, unless they happened to be in that world already, or to stumble on some invention or fortuitous opportunity. It was difficult for a man to move from the middle to the upper ranks of industry; there were few openings for graduates in the middle ranks, where instead industrialists preferred to employ workers who had proved themselves, but who would not expect to rise to the top. The large family firms kept their opportunities open mainly to those who married into them. It was not just that the bankers would not finance new ventures: it was also that people hesitated to ask them for loans, because they did not believe in the idea of a new venture.

The career books were right in what they said about the opportunities open to engineers.[2] In 1955 it was calculated that industry offered proportionately to the number of people it

[1] Guide général pour la jeunesse Carus (1934), 213, 478–81, 503–4, 521–3, 527, 571, 667.
[2] There is no history of the engineering profession. M. Thepot is writing one for the period 1815–48. Cf. J. Petot, Histoire de l'administration des ponts et chaussées 1599–1815 (1958). Mr. John Weiss's Harvard thesis promises to throw light on the educational background.

employed the lowest number of managerial posts. Only 2·85 per cent of its employees came in this upper category. In the older industries the figure was lower still—1 per cent in the coal-mines, 2·1 per cent in textiles, and it was only in a few new industries that the proportion was noticeably higher: 4·7 per cent in chemicals and 6·8 per cent in petrol. But commerce was more attractive even than this. It had 7·5 per cent as managers, banking and insurance together had 9·2 per cent (certain branches of insurance had as much as 20 per cent). Significantly the most attractive of all was still the civil service with 14 per cent (16 per cent in the state administration). An engineer who went into the service of the state would therefore do well, and it is not surprising that the graduates of the Polytechnic who went into private business were mainly the ones who came out bottom of their class. Taking as a sample the graduates of the Polytechnic who graduated in 1929, 1938, and 1950, one sees that only 4 per cent of the top twenty but 80 per cent of the bottom twenty went straight into private industry. The path increasingly followed by the brightest graduates was to work for a while in the civil service and then to use the double prestige of their school and their government connections to move straight into top posts in the private sector. The view that France was moving towards a technocracy is misleading. There was no real break from the rule of the civil service: the most powerful technocrats were still civil servants, except that they took over private business also. The very top managerial posts were reserved for such men.

A survey of upper management in the metallurgical and mining industry undertaken in 1956 showed that 46 per cent of the Polytechnic graduates were in this rank, but only 31 per cent of the graduates of the less prestigious École Centrale were in it. The graduates of Arts et Métiers and of the local engineering schools could seldom rise above the lower management ranks, in much the same way as it was difficult for workers to rise above the rank of foremen. The engineers thus had a very different future before them, depending on their origins. The upper-class ones tended to move from firm to firm and to end up in Paris. The lower ones often stayed all their lives in the same firm working their way up to the rank of department head. The man without an engineering degree who wanted to make

his way in industry very seldom got to the very top of large
firms. The idea of management by amateurs was not accepted
by them. The non-scientist could become head of sales, finance,
administration or personnel, but in France these never became
top management posts, having far less power and prestige than
in the U.S.A.: they were the dead end of a career, representing
the upper level a middle manager could reach. It was the
production managers who got the most promotion: the Polytechnic engineer after a spell in the provincial factories of the
firm could expect to make a jump straight into a controlling
position in Paris, above the other departmental heads with
longer service. Prospects in family firms were less bright. Really
able engineers could hardly be attracted to them since the ceiling of promotion was limited by the directing posts being
reserved for members of the family. Only occasionally was
a Polytechnic or a Centrale graduate imported to boost such
a firm—and it was sometimes done by marrying him into the
family. More often however there was a prejudice in family
firms, particularly in the nineteenth century, against employing
anyone with a formal and advanced scientific education. The
more highly qualified an engineer, the more theoretical his
training was. The Polytechnic graduate spent 75 per cent of his
time in theoretical work. There were too few of them to manage
anything more than a small number of large firms in a few
industries. In the remaining ones, it was customary for the
self-made or family-firm industrialist to disparage the *esprit
ingénieur*, by which was meant the neglect of the commercial
and practical side of things.[1] These firms preferred to employ
the humbler product of the local arts and crafts school, who had
spent 60 per cent of his training on practical work, and who
was only a glorified mechanic with no pretensions to rising very
high. Even this graduate had to fight hard to win a position of
minor influence, because his degree gave him little advantage
over the self-taught. It was estimated in 1962 that half the occu-
pants of managerial positions in industry as a whole had no
higher education at all, and many considerations—of experience,
influence and family—were involved in their recruitment.

The ambition to become a captain of industry from humble
beginnings was therefore not a realistic one in this period. The

[1] Hugues Le Roux, *Nos Fils: que feront-ils?* (1898), 127.

man who stood the best chance was the Polytechnic graduate, but, as is known, he usually came from good middle- or upper-class stock and he needed to make himself acceptable to the financial giants who controlled the large companies. This sort of person seldom attempted to establish his own empire. Many certainly did found their own firms, but very few seem to have reached any size. The obituaries of the Society of Civil Engineers are highly suggestive in this respect. They show that the engineers with no special family connections very often used their talents in two ways, neither of which contributed much to economic expansion in France. A certain number seem to have deserved the accusations of impracticality. Their education gave them a taste for pure science and they became part-time professors and writers. Others went abroad. It is striking to see the number of French engineers considerable parts of whose careers were spent in South America, Spain, Egypt, Indo-China, etc. French talent, like French capital, was exported to assist the industrialisation of other countries. The decorations they received and listed in their annuals included many from colonial and foreign governments and more of them appear to have been decorated by the ministry of education than by the Legion of Honour.[1] The career of Octave de Rochefort, son of the pamphleteer Henry Rochefort, can illustrate this. After graduating as an engineer from the École Centrale in 1884, he went off to manage a forest in Algeria for two years, was an engineer in Argentina, 1887 to 1880, and then entered the coal-mining industry in the U.S.A. There he became interested in typewriters: he returned to found a factory of these in 1896, producing also calculating machines, Braille machines and transformers—but all, it seems, without any great fortune resulting.[2] In the

[1] François Jacquin, *Les Cadres de l'industrie et du commerce* (1955), particularly interesting for a survey of the Renault factory managers; David Granick, *The European Executive* (1962), an illuminating comparative study of Britain, France, Germany, Belgium, and the U.S.A. The individual lives of engineers deserve study.

Statistics are not easy to acquire, and further research is needed. For obituaries see *Mémoires et compte rendu des travaux de la Société des ingénieurs civils de France* (1898), 418–28; (Nov. 1910), 501–19; (Jan. 1912), 17; (May 1912), 634 etc. For the engineers' literary activities see F. Divisia, *Exposés d'économique: Vol. 1: L'Apport des ingénieurs français aux sciences économiques* (1951).

[2] Henry Junger, *Dictionnaire biographique des grands négociants et industriels* (1895), vol. 9 of Henry Carnoy's series of dictionaries, 101.

twentieth century, the engineers found a third and different outlet for their frustrations: they saw themselves as social conciliators, intermediaries between employers and workers. Many tended towards social catholicism.[1]

One of the explanations of the rush into commerce is probably that until the Revolution commerce was regulated. To be a merchant was almost as privileged as to be a noble or a state official. The merchants had long fought vigorously to keep poachers out of their domain. The small shopkeeper of the twentieth century who tried to make as much profit as he could, who considered his clientele to belong to him and to owe him a living, was heir to the mentality of the *ancien régime* merchants who regarded their monopoly as a kind of *rente* paid by the public. The doctrine of the Church, that the needs of the seller should determine the price of his goods, that he ought to charge as much as was necessary to enable him to live decently, contributed to this attitude. It is true merchants were not esteemed by other classes but within their own they were certainly envied by those beneath them.

It is frequent in developing countries for the tertiary (commercial and administrative) sector of the economy to expand only after the primary (agricultural) sector has declined and the secondary (industrial) sector has grown. In France, the most rapidly expanding sector of the economy in the nineteenth century was however the tertiary one:

	1856	1876	1896	1906	1926	1931	1936	1946
Primary	51·7	48·8	44·8	42·7	38·3	35·6	35·5	36·0
Secondary	26·8	27·3	28·6	29·2	32·8	33·3	30·5	29·5
Tertiary	21·4	23·9	26·3	28·1	28·9	31·1	33·9	34·5

The table shows that it increased, in the forty years 1856–96, twice as much as the industrial sector. Another calculation, dividing the total population according to the occupation of the head of the family, gets the following even more striking results, in millions (though the 1856 figures seem very doubtful):

[1] Georges Lamirand, *Le Rôle social de l'ingénieur* (1923, new edition 1937); see also Marcel Barbier, *Le Problème français de la formation des ingénieurs, d'après quelques écrits récents* (1955).

	Total population	Agriculture	Industry	Commerce and transport	Liberal professions and civil service	Proprietors and *rentiers*	Without profession or profession unknown
1856	36·178	19	10·47	1·732	1·67	1·758	1·484
1876	36·9	18·969	9·275	3·89	1·96	2·153	0·704
1891	38·13	17·436	9·532	5·161	2·530	2·170	1·304

It is probable that the number drawing their income from commerce doubled, while those dependent on industry rose by only 50 per cent. However, in the twentieth century the commercial population increased by only a very moderate amount (from 1·88 million active population to 2·16 in 1946). It was only after the Second World War that the rapid rise was resumed, producing an increase as much as 34 per cent in eight years, but then the increase was related to an industrial explosion, whereas in the nineteenth century it was not. Commercial opportunities in the nineteenth century were multiplied by increasing prosperity in all forms of activity, added to the continued dispersion of the population, so that far more retail outlets were preserved than would have been normal in other industrialising nations. In 1954 37 per cent of the French population still lived in communes of under 2,000 inhabitants (compared with 18·5 per cent in Germany and 7 per cent in Italy). 40 per cent of the German population lived in towns of over 50,000, 30 per cent of Italians, but only 23 per cent of Frenchmen.[1] The way commercial activity increased may be judged best on a local scale. In the Forez, which contained the industrial town of St. Étienne, but also covered a large agricultural area, the number of fairs doubled in the nineteenth century, from 307 in 1809 to 713 in 1909, and this increase came mainly after 1870. In addition to these fairs, as against the 21 weekly markets in 1818, there were 90 in 1909. The number of wine shops doubled likewise, rising from 4,051 in 1857 to 8,738 in 1908.[2]

[1] Jean Fourastié, *Migrations professionnelles 1900–1955* (Institut National d'Études démographiques, travaux et documents, cahier no. 31, 1957), 157; Claude Quin, *Physionomie et perspectives d'évolution de l'appareil commercial français 1950–1970* (1964), 47. J. C. Toutain, *La Population de la France de 1700 à 1959* (1963), 146.

[2] L. J. Gras, *Histoire du commerce local et des industries qui s'y rattachent dans la région stéphanoise et forézienne* (St. Étienne, 1910), 398–400, 407, 423.

In Paris, the number of retail grocers probably doubled almost exactly in the short space of twenty-five years, 1856–79.[1]

Now a certain amount of the commercial expansion did take place in the form of more modern and larger units. By 1940 the co-operatives had 9,000 shops and 2·75 million members and had between 13 and 14 per cent of the commercial turnover; but 60 per cent of these co-op shops were to the north of a line from Cherbourg to Geneva. Chain stores are said to have begun in 1866 when four wholesalers of Reims began selling directly to the public; in the 1880s chain stores selling shoes appeared, then wine, milk, clothes and books. By 1940 there were 23,000 chain stores dealing in food alone—accounting for a quarter of the national turnover, but having grown almost entirely through self-financing and without any assistance from the banks. The large department stores were born under the Second Empire, again self-financed. The single-price shop, so successful in the U.S.A. well before the First World War, reached France in 1927 (or 1929). But in 1931 there were still only some 100 retail shops with over 500 employees, whereas there were approximately half a million tiny shops: 91 per cent of retail outlets employed three or fewer assistants. In addition there were those who ministered to the 200,000 fairs and markets in the country.[2]

These small merchants occupied a distinctive role in French society. Gabriel Hanotaux praised them as representing the most democratic of French careers, where it was easiest to start with a little and make a fortune, where there was the greatest independence, and where every man had a good chance of succeeding.[3] Parliament seemed to support this view when it repeatedly imposed heavy discriminatory taxes on chain and department stores, in an attempt to halt their progress. Any shop with over 200 employees had to pay a tax equivalent to about a fifth of the wages it paid to any employee above that number.[4] Special taxes were imposed on retail shops with turnovers

[1] Firmin Didot, *Annuaire Almanach du commerce* (1856 and 1879), lists of *épiciers en détail*.

[2] Centre d'Information inter-professionnelles, *Le Commerce: documents* (1943).

[3] Victor Ray, *Pour faire fortune, par un ancien commerçant* (Moulins, 1922), 8; A. Demonceaux, *Le Choix d'une carrière commerciale, industrielle ou financière. Guide pratique des parents et de la jeunesse* (3rd edition, n.d., about 1920).

[4] Law of 28 Apr. 1893. See Yves Guyot, *Le Commerce et les commerçants* (1909), 203.

above a million francs (and 91·9 per cent of retailers had turn-overs below half a million), and double *patente* was imposed on chain stores. In 1935 expansion of retail trade by travelling vans was forbidden (*camions bazars*); in 1936 the creation of new *prix unique* shops and of new shoe shops was forbidden.[1] It should not be thought that parliament was simply yielding to a pressure group. French society would have been far less mobile without these small shopkeepers, however much the cost of living might have been reduced by their disappearance. It was not dynasties of shopkeepers that they established. A retailer who had made a fortune, said the Chartons in 1880, would make his son follow after him only very unwillingly and as a last resort: he would do his best to make him enter the liberal professions.[2] The visitor to Paris who absented himself for twenty years would find very few of the same shops, owned by the same people, still active. The ideal was to make money quickly—which partly explains the high prices charged—and then to retire to live off one's capital. The idea that retailers did make a great deal of money was of course partly a myth.[3] Some 40 per cent of small businesses normally went bankrupt (at the end of the nineteenth century) but it will never be possible to discover much about the finances of the retailer. Of those who did go bankrupt 90 per cent kept no accounts. One of the great attractions of retail trade resulted from precisely this. It was easier to avoid taxation. It has been officially calculated by the French government in 1955 that the joint-stock companies were concealing 19–25 per cent of their net profits, smaller individual enterprises and partnerships between 42 and 48 per cent, but that artisans and shopkeepers far out-distanced them.[4] The large store had to open its books to the tax inspector: the small shopkeeper simply made a declaration. Being a shopkeeper was to a certain extent a tax dodge, a way of making money at the expense of the state. The history of shopkeeping is indeed a history of a struggle to escape state control. The controls of the *ancien régime*—though partially abolished by the ending of the corporations—nevertheless

---

[1] Gaston Defossé, *Le Commerce intérieur* (1944), 175.
[2] E. Charton, 3rd edition, 152.
[3] Marcel Porte, *Entrepreneurs et profits industriels* (1901), 183.
[4] *Les Informations industrielles et commerciales*, no. 546 (7 Oct. 1955).

continued in a multitude of other restrictions. One of the lesser-known achievements of Napoleon III was to introduce greater liberty for shopkeepers, and in particular to end the limitations on bakers' and butchers' shops. However, every town had its own regulations and taxes and the shopkeeper had to be an adept at circumventing the law. That is why the radicals liked him. He incarnated resistance to authority, individualism and the right to better oneself. Commerce provided a means of rising in the world as important as education, though it has been less talked about by politicians and historians, because it was not institutionalised by legislation. It was as it were the back-stairs way up, for the civil code enshrined secrecy in commercial activities as a legal principle. The passion for secrecy made trade all the more hazardous. It restricted the rise of credit-checking firms and agencies supplying commercial information.[1] Commerce had some of the elements of guerrilla warfare. It was warfare, one should add, against the wholesaler as well as against the state, so that the shopkeeper was doubly the *small* man.[2] Far from diminishing with the rise of the large stores, the number of people setting up as shopkeepers on their own continued to increase.

The heroes of commerce were more democratic figures than those of industry. The ones who particularly caught the popular imagination—because the extent of their activities raised them out of this normally secretive world—were the founders of the large department stores of Paris. They came from humble origins: Boucicaut (1810–77), the founder of the *Bon Marché*, was the son of a hatter; he began as a pedlar before coming to Paris. Chauchard (1821–1909), the founder of the *Louvre*, was the son of a restaurant keeper; he worked his way up from being an assistant at a small shop, the *Pauvre Diable*. Cognacq (1839–1928) of the *Samaritaine* was a shop assistant from the age of twelve. All spent their early years in poverty. Boucicaut was the real pioneer in introducing new methods: fixed prices, low profit margins, commissions on sales for the staff, clearance sales at regular intervals and an elaborate social security system for all the employees. Chauchard was more of a social climber

[1] Maurice Mayer, *Le Secret des affaires commerciales* (1900), 276.
[2] Roger Picard, *Distribution et consommation, les cahiers du redressement français*, no. 11 (1927).

and political dealer: he appears to have got help from the financier Périer to found his shop in 1855, which catered for the rich with sumptuous salons and luxurious décor. His relations with the radical politicians remain obscure, except that he secured from them the exceptionally high decoration of Grand Officer of the Legion of Honour in 1906 and he left a lot of money to Georges Leygues. Cognacq started his first shop with his own savings of 5,000 francs and lost all. He took up peddling on the Pont Neuf, saved up another 5,000, and rented a small boutique nearby, the original site of the Samaritaine, in 1870. Two years later he married Louise Jay, a chief assistant in the dress department of the Bon Marché, who had saved up 20,000. This shows how quickly capital could be accumulated in commerce. The couple never borrowed a *sou* all their lives, and confined their advertising to sending out catalogues. The values and methods of shopkeepers were incarnated in this store. Each of the ninety sections was a separate shop, with the seller getting only a nominal retaining salary (300–1,200 francs a year in 1933), and relying on his 3 per cent commission, which could produce an income comparing favourably with any profession. Both Boucicaut and Cognacq introduced participation in profits for the staff (rising with rank). They and Chauchard all gave vast sums to charity and became leading philanthropists. In the case of Cognacq, it was said that his motive was a violent hate of the state and a determination to pay nothing in death-duties. None of them had children. Boucicaut and Cognacq both had very active wives, making their firms very much the husband-and-wife teams so common in retail trade. Mme Boucicaut ran the Bon Marché on her own as a widow with great success. After they had made their fortunes, Cognacq and Chauchard went in for collecting paintings, which they bequeathed respectively to the city of Paris and the Louvre Museum. Their collections were enormous and very valuable, but it is not clear that either of them was really interested in painting. Cognacq really loved the theatre, where declamation recalled to him his own successes as pedlar on the Pont Neuf. Louise Cognacq reconciled herself to his expenditure on art by saying she preferred 'for the sake of his health' that the money should go to art dealers rather than a mistress. Cognacq was in any case too short-sighted really to enjoy his pictures.[1] He was totally uninterested in politics but religiously read all the commercial advertisements in the papers. He occasionally travelled, because he found it improved his appetite. He sometimes went to the Opéra Comique, because music put him into a particularly relaxing sleep. But though the principles on which he built his fortune were commercial, and though he hated the state, in the organisation of his shop he followed the bureaucratic and hierarchic methods of the state with almost identical over-staffing and elaborate form filling. The Samaritaine was no anarchist federation of communes. Regulations governed every detail of behaviour, from prohibiting the wearing of silk stockings and *décolleté* dresses by the assistants, to the requirement that each of the 8,000 employees should always sit in the same place at the free lunch. 'Conformism was his law. Any initiative frightened him; his strength came from his inertia, systematically opposed to all audacity.'[2]

The world of commerce was infinitely varied not only because of the enormous differences in wealth between the extremes, but also because, particularly at the humbler levels, different practices and mentalities survived in different regions. Educational qualifications, at least until 1914, counted for little. The École Supérieure de Commerce de Paris founded in 1820 by some wholesalers to raise the level of 'citizens so contemptuously called merchants', bought in 1830 by Adolphe Blanqui, brother of the revolutionary, run by him as a profit-making concern, taken over eventually by the Chamber of Commerce, was principally patronised by well-to-do pupils, with families already in business.[3] Between the wars a few schools for salesmen (one of them modelled on Mrs. Prince's establishment in Boston, which trained people for Filene's Store and which was subsequently absorbed into Simmons College) and a few courses using Harvard Business School graduates were introduced, but they had little impact. Correspondence courses to obtain minimal qualifications were more popular.[4]

[1] Francis Jourdain, *Né en '76* (1951), 255–69, describes the relations of his father, the painter, with Cognacq, who was his best client.

[2] Fernand Laudet, *La Samaritaine* (1933); and Jourdain, 267.

[3] Alfred Renouard, *Histoire de l'école supérieure de commerce de Paris* (1898, 3rd edition, expanded, 1920).

[4] Daniel Briod, *La Science de la vente et sa place dans l'enseignement commercial* (1929).

Whether these modernised merchants made more money than the old-fashioned ones is not clear. What is known is that in the country as a whole commercial properties increased in value in the first half of the twentieth century more than any other form of investment, and they were the only form of investment which did not suffer from two world wars. The regional variations in profitability were, it is true, very great but they have not yet been analysed. They do not seem to be immediately related to local agricultural or industrial growth, and the enormous prosperity of the shopkeepers of the Aude and Vaucluse, for example, far in excess of neighbouring departments like the Var and Hérault and of rich ones like the Nord, has still to be explained.[1] But it may be that this accumulation of commercial wealth provided the same sort of basis for the economic expansion of the 1950s as the similar merchant prosperity in eighteenth-century England did for the Industrial Revolution which, partly for that reason, occurred so much earlier here.

[1] Paul Cornut, *Répartition de la fortune privée en France* (1963), 247–75. In Paris between 1900 and 1924, the value of retail businesses increased eightfold in money terms, or nearly twice in real terms. Restaurants and hotels went up in value fifteen times, grocery shops and *crémeries* ten times, butchers' shops eight times, bakeries six times and fruiterers four times. In the country as a whole, the number of retail businesses rose from 198,000 to 226,000 in the period 1901 to 1912; in these years, between 5 and 6 per cent of businesses changed hands every year. A. Bonnefoy, *L'Achat et la vente des fonds de commerce dans l'économie moderne* (1924); *Recherches statistiques sur la Ville de Paris* (1860), vol. 6, 630–1; E. Clementel and M. de Toro, *Larousse commercial* (1930), 607; Diane de Luppé, *Le Commerce de vin dans le département de la Seine de 1851 a 1860 d'après le fonds des faillites du tribunal de commerce de la Seine* (unpublished thesis in the library of the Paris faculty of law, 1968).

8. Bureaucrats

THE civil service is another of the professions where expansion is usually equated with the increase in the power of the bourgeoisie. There is a great deal of truth in this. However, increase in numbers and functions did not automatically involve an increase in influence or status. On the contrary, if one examines why people went into the civil service and what exactly individuals were able to do when they were in it, one sees that membership of it gave an ambiguous position in society, which altered in the course of the century, which varied profoundly with one's place in the hierarchy, and which by 1940 was subject to much hostility.

France was one of the pioneers of bureaucracy in Europe. In the seventeenth and eighteenth centuries the number of civil service jobs exploded to enormous proportions. The reason was partly that the king needed money and rather than obtain it from parliament, as in England, he preserved his absolutism by selling offices. These offices gave some exemption from taxation, the higher ones even brought a debased nobility with them, and all acquired prestige. State jobs became an investment, in which moderate return on capital was compensated for by social advantages. The French acquired the habit of putting their money into state offices, and into land, rather than industry. Low but secure yields were accepted as the correct ambition for sensible men, and a modest style of living for those who rose in this way was consecrated as a social norm. The Revolution ended the sale of offices—except in a few cases—but it did not alter the investment habits of the country, or the social status attached to public employment. A certain amount of merit was now needed to enter the civil service, but education, which was the principal proof of merit, still had to be bought. The myth of equality of opportunity heightened the status of those who rose in the hierarchy. The Revolution made the civil service more than an investment; it turned it into something of a lottery into which everybody in theory had the right to enter; and the hunger for its prizes became all the more frantic.

In 1842, in his Guide to the Professions, Charton gave some interesting reasons to explain, as he put it, why 'a career in the public service is very much sought after by those whom birth or education places in the upper and middle classes'. It was an alternative preferable to industry and the liberal professions, where the chance of failure or disaster was considerable. It was a safe career, but it also led to high stakes because the salaries of senior posts were large by any standards. However, it required only moderate amounts of capital to be laid out, smaller than were required in other professions.[1] The civil service was thus approached by men with much the same attitude as if they were thinking of buying property. The problem is to discover just what kind of advantages went with the investment and how attitudes to it developed. Certainly its attractions made themselves felt in all classes during the nineteenth century. Parliamentary government meant that the patronage necessary to obtain an introduction into it was much more widely available to anyone willing to make a bargain with a deputy in return for his vote. The spread of education gave more and more people a chance to obtain the basic qualifications.

France had the reputation of having the highest number of civil service posts in Europe at the beginning of our period and it maintained that reputation by quadrupling the number in the hundred years covered by this book. When in 1848 the government was asked to publish a list of all its employees it refused, saying the task would be too great and it would require fifty volumes. Accurate statistics were never a strong point before 1945 and the exact number of civil servants is not definitely established. But roughly speaking it seems that in 1848 there were about a quarter of a million, in 1914 half a million, and in 1945 one million. The real distinction between France and comparable countries is not in the number of public servants but in the number employed by the central government. Britain in 1950 had 687,000 civil servants, but it had in addition 1,500,000 local government employees, whereas France had only 370,000 of these. The U.S.A. seems to have more public servants of various kinds than France. Between the wars it was calculated

[1] E. Charton, *Guide pour le choix d'un état* (1842), 261.

that a city like Bordeaux had one public servant to every eighty-
two inhabitants, but this was not much different from Newark,
N.J., with 1:86 and was an average between Seattle's 1:52 and
Dayton's 1:157.[1]

What was an even more radical difference was the place that
the civil service had in French life. The civil service fulfilled two
important functions, apparently contradictory. On the one
hand it continued to serve as a major avenue for social mobility,
but on the other hand the families it helped to raise in the social
scale very often did not move out to make their way at a
higher level in the world of business or industry, but stayed on in
the service. Thus the bureaucracy as it expanded its activities
became, to a certain extent, an enormous, constantly growing
clan of families. While the test of merit was still increasingly
applied, the civil servants almost formed a hereditary class, with
considerable cohesion of outlook and values. They were not
quite a corporation, but they had a lot in common with the
rivals they were displacing, the clergy.

Detailed studies of the state's employees are still in progress—
the sociology of bureaucracy is now a budding subject in France.
There is one statistical analysis which, though it deals with
the post-1945 period, is very illuminating and its conclusions
will probably be found to be true of the pre-war years with due
modifications to allow for the increased democratisation of
education. The administrative grades of the civil service were
in the 1960s filled for the most part by men of upper-class
origin. Thus only 15·2 per cent of civil servants of humble
birth reached this grade, 19·3 per cent of those of middle birth,
but 65 per cent of those from the upper class. Only 12 per cent
of all civil servants were born in Paris but 39·1 per cent of the
administrative grade were. Only 23·3 per cent of this upper
grade had no other member of their family in the civil service.
In cases where they had a father who had been a civil servant, 87·3 per cent of these also had other relatives who
were civil servants and 47·6 per cent had not only a father but
also a grandfather or father-in-law plus other collaterals who
were civil servants too. What is particularly striking is the
limited movement in the upper class of French society between

[1] W. R. Sharp, *The French Civil Service, Bureaucracy in Transition* (New York, 1931),
418; F. Ridley and J. Blondel, *Public Administration in France* (2nd edition 1969), 29.

those who serve the state and those who do not. Thus only 9 per cent of sons of upper-class fathers went into the civil service when their fathers were employed in the private sector, but 57 per cent went in when their fathers were in public employment. There is an even stronger dynastic tradition in the lower ranks: 44 per cent of sons of private *employés* (clerks) go into the civil service but 82 per cent of sons of public ones. The closed nature of the recruitment of the state becomes all the more pronounced when it is seen that certain parts of the country are far more involved than others. Broadly, the south of France sends far more of its children to the civil service than the north. Over 5 per cent of the natives of Corsica obtain state employment, over 3 per cent of those of departments like Hérault, Aude, Ariège, Hautes-Pyrénées, Pyrénées-Orientales, Haute-Garonne, Lot-et-Garonne, Lot, Corrèze, Lozère, and the three Alpine departments.[1] Moreover, men born in small towns of 10,000 to 20,000 inhabitants—which often owe their importance mainly to their administrative function and which have proportionately a far larger number of civil servants, occupying the most prestigious roles in the towns—enter the civil service almost twice as much as those born in large cities (where the attractions of commerce and industry are overwhelming) or isolated rural villages.[2] It would be an exaggeration to say that one part of the country makes money while another part governs, but public opinion polls about the civil service reveal far less hostility to it in the south than in the north.[3]

The nature of the civil service has changed since the Revolution so that few generalisations apply equally to the whole period. In many cases, however, the changes were deceptive, and the traditions of the past were maintained under the new forms. But what did not happen was simply the opening of the careers to the talents.

One radical transformation in this period was the disappearance of large salaries. At the end of the July Monarchy, the rewards for those who reached the top were outstanding and placed

---

[1] Michel Crozier, *Petits Fonctionnaires au travail* (1955), shows that in a survey of 3,500 clerical workers, 33 per cent were daughters of civil servants and 40 per cent came from the south-west.

[2] A. Darbel and D. Schnapper, *Les Agents du système administratif* (1969), 22, 61, 70, 75, 91, 95.

[3] Bernard Gournay, *L'Administration* (1964), 83–4.

them among the richest men in the country. Four ambassadors were paid over 150,000 francs a year, 102 civil servants earned over 20,000 francs, and 1,009 over 10,000 francs. At the other end, junior officials earned derisory sums for what was very similar work; but work was not what they were really paid for. This was still a spoils system. There were 277 prefects and sub-prefects: two of them got over 60,000 but 228 got around 3,000 francs. Salaries varied greatly between the different ministries. The finances paid best: the director in charge of indirect taxation in a department got between 7,200 and 12,000 francs. The learned careers were paid worst. The engineer-in-chief, controlling the roads and bridges of a department, got only 4,500 to 5,000 and the rector of an academy, with several departments under him, got only 6,000 to 7,200 francs. Accordingly France's financial administration was the largest item in its budget: 89 million went to pay the salaries of financial officials, as against only 62 million for the army, 26 for the navy, 30 for religion, 15 for justice, 7·6 for the ministry of the interior, about 5 each for the foreign office, public works and education, 1·7 for agriculture and commerce, plus 11 million for central administration. This gives some idea of the distribution of the spoils available. But salaries were not the only rewards to be had. Some jobs were still paid in medieval fashion entirely from fees levied from the public—not just the notaries, but also the conservators of mortgages and the clerks of courts. Some obtained fees as supplements to their salaries: professors of faculties got a share of enrolment, examination and certificate fees; employees of the financial administration got bonuses for increasing revenue collected; those capturing contraband or discovering tax frauds got a share of seizures, fines and confiscations. The salaries of some, e.g. those working in the chancelleries of consulates and in some financial jobs, were variable. The chief tax-collectors had the privilege of delegating their duties, so that a *receveur particulier des finances*, earning between 15,000 and 20,000 francs (side by side with and covering the same area as a sub-prefect earning 3,000 to 4,000), would often appoint a substitute at 1,800 or 2,000.[1] By the end of our period these variations had been largely ironed out and in 1946, when a uniform salary structure was worked out, the discrepancy

[1] Pierre Legendre, *L'Administration du 18e siècle à nos jours* (1968), 179.

between the best paid and the worst paid was no longer in a ratio of 150 to one but had been reduced to eleven to one (or eight to one after taxation). Mediocrity replaced splendour and economy took the place of largesse as the hallmarks of the public servant. The civil service ceased to be a path to riches.

On the other hand it had also been a part-time occupation for gentlemen who bought themselves in, and whose income came only in part from their salaries. Equally drastic therefore was the disappearance of private incomes as a necessary adjunct to many state jobs. Almost all the better jobs in the state service had required the young entrant to spend one or two years, and sometimes longer, working unpaid, learning his duties and winning favour. In some branches, e.g. the inspection of finance, candidates wishing to be deputy inspectors had to have a guarantee from their parents of a private income of 2,000 francs to last so long as they held that rank. In other posts parents had to promise to maintain their sons for at least two years while, e.g. they held the post of supernumerary in the department of direct taxation. When the son finally obtained a paid post, many jobs in the financial service required the deposit of caution money—equal to three times the salary received as a *percepteur* and, when promoted to be *receveur particulier*, equal to five times the salary. In the foreign service, until 1894, candidates had to have a private income of 6,000 francs. The civil service could hardly be said to be open to all the talents until, at the very least, it paid its young recruits a living wage. In the judicial service, the rank of entry, *juge suppléant*, ceased to be unpaid only in 1910. However, even after this, the cost of education necessary to enter the civil service remained an obstacle to democratic recruitment. For the best jobs, the École Libre des Sciences politiques held a virtual monopoly in the preparation of candidates for the ministries of finance and foreign affairs, and as it was a fee-paying institution, recruits to these ministries remained well-to-do. When therefore the peasant stared at a poster announcing a competition for admission to the civil service, with the democratic phrase 'The emperor (or the republic) invites all to apply', he was not taken in. The civil service still retained strong elements of a caste.

The introduction of impartial examinations as a method of entry was slow to take effect. The supposedly democratic competitions (*concours*) set up by the Revolution were generally decided by criteria of patronage and nepotism. When candidates were actually tested, the examinations were usually so perfunctory as to be purely symbolic. It was only in 1872–4 that an attempt was made to introduce serious examinations and they were regularly used after that for many jobs, but it seems that it was only at the turn of the century that they were fully established as normal. However, it should not be thought that this ended the matter and brought about impartial admission on merit. The civil service took the sort of recruits its conservative heads thought it needed. The *concours* often continued to test only a restricted range of qualities; success was sometimes determined by the relation of the candidate with a *patron*, whose teaching he was required to regurgitate. Recruitment to the colonial service, for example, was for a time reactionary because it drew mainly from the École Coloniale which was run by the Comité de l'Afrique française, and which admitted only people with the same mentality as the financial oligarchy interested in the colonies. The patronage system was thus transformed or modified rather than completely abolished. The early years of the Third Republic, when the stress on merit was trumpeted most loudly, were also years in which the 'abuse of recommendations was pushed to unheard of extremes': Léon Say, when minister of finance, likened the pressures on him for jobs to those prevalent in the *ancien régime*.[1] Millerand said he received 150 letters a day asking for jobs and between the wars the under-secretary of the Post Office was still receiving 100,000 letters a year from politicians and other influential personages recommending people for employment, promotion or transfer. A magistrate seeking promotion got thirty-eight deputies and senators to write to the minister of justice to support him, as was made public in a particular case in 1930. A crisis occurred at the turn of the century, when the passions produced by anticlericalism caused Combes to defend favouritism publicly and somewhat tactlessly. As a result, in 1905 every civil servant was given the right to see his file if he was threatened with a disciplinary penalty, with transfer against his will or with the postponement of advancement due to him

---

[1] Quoted by Vicomte d'Avenel, 'L'Extension du fonctionnarisme depuis 1870', *Revue des Deux Mondes* (1 Mar. 1888), 95.

by seniority. This transformed the annual reports of superiors about their juniors which were once a mine of information about every aspect of the man's life, into a purely formal and meaningless routine, and it made promotion by seniority an almost inflexibly applied rule.

Judges and university and secondary teachers had won their security in the 1880s, primary teachers were protected by laws of 1880 and 1919, but some departments were slower to win legislation, and for them the Conseil d'État served as an appeal court. Every year after 1919 about 1,500 cases of wrongful dismissal or failure to get promotion were brought before it—but a case often took four years to decide and if the government refused to implement the Conseil's decision, another four years would be necessary to force it. By the 1930s the trade unions were satisfied that they had eliminated favouritism, in so far as was possible. Deputies still continued to write to ministers recommending their constituents, and the ministers replied that they would submit their letters to the appropriate authorities who would see that justice was done. The deputies could send this reply to the constituent and in this way everybody was more or less satisfied.[1] However, examinations did not make the civil service into a coherent institution, all of whose branches recruited from the same source. Admission inevitably remained something of a mystery, affected by the accidents of social connections, when not only each university organised its competitions separately, but within each, different departments worked at recruitment totally independently. In 1927, for example, ten different bodies within the ministry of finance were offering jobs without any co-operation and there were 1,200 different competitions annually. Even if favouritism was eliminated, the individual eccentricities and traditions of each department could more easily survive in this fragmentary system.

A subtle change came about when civil servants who had been political nominees attempted to turn their jobs into lifetime careers. For long politics played a significant part in many appointments. Until 1870 civil servants were required to take an oath of loyalty to the regime in power. Each revolution therefore produced sweeping dismissals and the introduction of

[1] Sharp, 73.

partisans of the new government. This situation altered for
two reasons. On the one hand governments found it difficult to
find tens of thousands of suitable civil servants in the aftermath
of each revolution; inevitably many experienced men had
to be allowed to stay on. With time the political complexion
of their offices became diluted, and political appointments
tended to be confined to a smaller number of posts. However,
more important was the pressure from the civil servants themselves to obtain security. Once in office, even the political ones
adopted the airs of disinterested public service: even Napoleon
III's prefects, the principal instruments of his repressive
policies, tried to cultivate detachment and to look on themselves as professional administrators.[1] They began protesting
against senior positions of command being allocated arbitrarily
to men with no experience. The political opposition in every
regime found the centralisation of the civil service a good way
of reducing the government's power. The obsession with pensions completed the transformation. It was only gradually that
the prospect of a pension became a major attraction of public
employment. Originally only the army had a satisfactory retirement scheme, giving pensions of a respectable size (4,000 francs
for a lieutenant-general, 1,200 for a captain) after thirty years'
service (twenty-five in the navy). The clergy never got any
pensions at all, and the *percepteurs des contributions indirectes*, whose
posts were considered not so much salaried jobs as purchased
contracts, got nothing either. Others were paid under the law of
1790, which aimed to produce half pay after thirty years of
service, though it is not clear that it always reached that figure.
The law had in fact provided for the state to pay only one sixth
of the top salary earned after thirty years of service to a selected
and small number of civil servants. It also allowed 5 per cent
of salaries to be paid into a fund to supplement this, but the
fund proved inadequate. The state began subsidising it, but the
arrangements of the fund remained complicated and different
for each ministry.[2] Only in 1853 did the state unify the pension
system and start paying pensions to civil servants directly itself,
as it did to the army, except that it still retained the 5 per cent

[1] See B. le Clère and Vincent Wright, *Les Préfets du second empire* (1973).
[2] Vivien, 'Études administratives: Les fonctionnaires publics', *Revue des Deux
Mondes* (15 Oct. 1845), 215–70.

employee's contribution.[1] Inevitably once this happened it became much more difficult to dismiss anybody and deprive him
of his accumulating investment. In this way the civil servants
won back something of the *ancien régime* character of their
occupations, when they enjoyed a right to their salaries irrespective of whether they were performing a useful function. The
state in fact encouraged them to maintain the ancient obsession
with status and hierarchy, by developing a system of promotion
with so many different grades and sub-categories, that ambitions could both be satisfied by tiny increases in salary and
controlled by a rigid scale through which every career had to
proceed. The centralising doctrine, that salaries had to be linked
with a hierarchy of towns, so that promotions usually involved
transfers, meant that internal jealousies, rivalries and frustrations played a major role in the life of the civil servant, and made
his world more and more a private one.[2]

These changes inevitably affected the prestige of the civil
service. The more comfortable and secure the civil servants
made themselves, the more they cut themselves off from the
world of politics, the more they shut out merit and opted for
seniority, the more they lost their place of leadership in society.
The functions of the majority of them were in any case ceasing
to be administrative and supervisory. The great increase in their
numbers in the period 1850–1900 was due above all to the
recruitment of 80,000 new primary-school teachers and 50,000
new postmen, both inferior and poorly paid grades, so that the
average level of the civil service sank accordingly. Most civil
servants were not grand. Their salaries ceased to be impressive
and in 1901 articles were published lamenting their fate as a
new proletariat. The average salary in 1900 was only 1,490
francs, hardly equal to that of a good labourer.[3] At this period
only a thousand civil servants were earning over 15,000 francs
a year, and the highest salary was only 35,000. But the department stores of Paris by themselves were paying over 250 of their
employees salaries of 20,000 to 25,000, equal to that of most
prefects, and in business many could hope to earn 50,000,

[1] H. Blerzy, 'Le Fonctionnarisme dans l'état', *Revue des Deux Mondes* (15 Sept.
1871), 444–59.
[2] Cf. A. Granveau, *Analyse philosophique des usages* (1865), 25–7.
[3] Bérenger, *Le Prolétariat intellectuel* (1901), 63.

100,000, or more.[1] After the Great War, the situation of the civil servants grew drastically worse, as their salaries totally failed to keep up with inflation. In 1927, when the cost of living had risen five fold since 1914, the salaries of most of them had gone up between only two and three times in the upper ranks and between four and five times in the lower ranks. The senior men thus received yet another blow. Their humiliation was likened to that of the half-pay officers of the Napoleonic armies dashed down from their glory after 1815. Resignations flowed in at unprecedented levels. In 1920–6, out of a total of ninety inspectors of finance, seventy-four resigned; there were eighty resignations a year in the senior grades of the department of direct taxation, as opposed to twenty a year before the war. The number of candidates for admission fell so that it became difficult to recruit at all, even though standards were noticeably lowered. Thus before 1914 48 per cent of the candidates for the *enregistrement* were successful, in 1920–6 64 per cent were. There used to be about four candidates for every post of inspector in this department, there were now barely enough to fill the vacancies. The ministry of labour used to get 150 candidates for each examination to fill four or five posts, in 1927 it got thirty. Those who had maintained their status by supplementing honorific but poorly paid posts with their private incomes found their investments had lost most of their value. Magistrates were reported travelling in third-class railway carriages. Schoolmasters were compelled to take on second jobs. Engineers, who could double their salaries before the war by going into private industry, now had little choice, when the real value of their state salaries fell by half.[2] It remained possible to fill the lowest ranks, but men from poorer social and educational backgrounds had to be accepted higher up. Many jobs were now reserved for victims of the war and for their widows— 100 per cent of all concierge and copyist jobs, 75 per cent of mail carriers, 100 per cent of customs officials. This was one way of employing these people usefully instead of paying them pensions, but it conflicted with the principle of merit and it

[1] Vicomte d'Avenel, 'Fonctionnaires de l'état et des administrations privées', *Revue des Deux Mondes* (15 July 1906), 391–413.

[2] 'La Crise des cadres de la nation', *L'Europe Nouvelle* (26 Mar. 1927), special issue.

accentuated the image of shabbiness and mediocrity that the civil service increasingly assumed.

In 1927 a member of the Institute wrote: 'Today the élite no longer wants to serve the state.' This was a situation which had already begun at the end of the nineteenth century, he said. Till then, the civil service gave great honour and social rank. 'Thirty years ago, in provincial towns, social rank did not depend on wealth or personal value but on the job a man had and the family background to which he was linked by birth or marriage.' These considerations put men in 'good society'. Service in the state not only gave social rank but it also had a matrimonial value. But now this was no longer the case. Security of tenure meant officials no longer had power; they could not hire and fire as private industrialists could; automatic promotion meant there were no sanctions against the inefficient and no proofs of merit or even of influence.[1]

There was another reason why there were fewer applicants for each job. By 1945 there were twice as many jobs as there had been in 1914. Most of these were inevitably in the lower grades. The image of the civil servant changed, to become more drab and depressed. The old distinction between the highly paid and the men on starvation salaries was replaced by another, since hardly any were highly paid any more. There were now those who spent all their lives in the service and those who used it for their own purposes before they moved on. Because much of this increase in numbers occurred at a time of economic depression, the status of the civil service was doubly damaged. Those who entered it appeared to be taking refuge from the world, to be seeking security above all else, sacrificing income and hope. The isolation of these lower grades from the rest of the country was accentuated. On the other hand, in the upper echelons more and more graduates of the *grandes écoles* abandoned public service to go into industry and business. Young men of good family became inspectors of finance only as a preparation for careers with large companies. A low job in the civil service led nowhere. One at the top—provided one had the right family background or political connections— opened the doors of high finance. The links between business

[1] H. Truchy, 'L'Élite et la fonction publique', *Revue Politique et Parlementaire* (10 Dec. 1927), 339–48.

and the upper civil service grew much stronger, as more of the latter were drawn into the former, and as the leaders of both were increasingly graduates of the *grandes écoles*. The old dividing lines now became blurred. The idea of serving the state lost its quasi-military character when the mass of civil servants joined trade unions and argued their rights against the state, just like ordinary workers fighting capitalism. The distinction between private and public service became less important in the top ranks when both were monopolised by the same people. Success had to be redefined by new criteria. A peasant could still get his son to become an *instituteur*, who could in turn get his son to become a secondary-school master, and his son might well rise to be a university professor and even a member of the Institute. This was a frequent path of social promotion. But after his hard climb the professor would find himself confronted by financiers and businessmen who moved in and out of the best-paid posts with a facility he had never known. He would then realise that the holding of high office by itself gave only a limited status. When the state lost its arbitrary powers, a fact which had always been true became more obvious, that the great civil servants of the past owed their status to several different factors which they had succeeded in combining—money, family, unpaid local office, learning, membership of influential society, landownership. Without these, the new self-made civil servant, with only a pension between himself and the world, felt himself surrounded by forces almost as powerful as the state, but much more elusive: and there was a strong temptation to make his peace with them.

In the late nineteenth century, civil servants were supposed to be loyal adherents of republicanism, freemasons and laic opponents of clericalism. They were not as loyal as the myth required them to be, but they had at least to be discreet about their conservative family traditions. By the mid twentieth century this had changed. The upper ranks of the civil service contained a larger proportion of practising Catholics than was normal in the social class from which they came—in the 1960s as many as 40 per cent attended church regularly.[1] The *instituteurs* were perhaps the most steadfastly loyal anticlericals, but the secondary teachers always included many believers, and

[1] Darbel and Schnapper, 94.

even the Sorbonne, for long a citadel of the left wing, has in the last decade fallen too. In less political ministries conservatism was always respectable, partly because civil servants, when appointed by a revolutionary regime, usually tried to reconquer the social prestige their predecessors had enjoyed, but which they as new-comers did not immediately obtain, and this meant gaining acceptance in the salons of the upper class. The Bonapartists succeeded to some extent in this social climbing, and to a certain extent the opportunist republicans too, though often the civil servants had to form social circles of their own. This isolation, which diminished in the inter-war period at the top levels, persisted longer at lower levels. It was noticeable that civil servants rising in the hierarchy, and coming from poorer social backgrounds, tended to adopt the conservative habits of their superiors—e.g. religious practice—to make themselves acceptable, even though men of upper class origin could get by easily enough without religion.

As the rewards of the civil service became less certain, so some of its members exaggerated their pretensions and tried to bolster their role with the help of ideology and formalism. Bureaucracy was increasingly seen as anti-democratic and opposed as a survival of the *ancien régime*. The complaints grew louder just when the civil servants became increasingly insecure: against the magistrates who made up for their absurdly low salaries by wearing fancy dress, treating those who appeared before them with authoritarian aloofness, and living a withdrawn social life; against the resurrection of the feudal mentality in which the world was divided into 'administrators' and the public, who were called 'the administered', or even 'subjects'. There were attacks against the superiority complex of the civil servants who looked upon themselves as heirs of the nobles of the *robe* keeping the public at a distance, rather than being there to serve them. As taxation increased and the matters in which the state interfered widened, so these complaints became more bitter.[1] The new tensions can be illustrated from the way the civil servants defended themselves: 'The civil servants', wrote one of them in 1911, 'are objects of rancour but whether they know it or not, they do not care. They are conscious of their strength. They are aware that three-quarters of

[1] B. Gournay, *L'Administration* (1964), 82–5.

the French look upon them with envy and this certitude of superiority is the balm that heals the wounds inflicted on their pride. A civil servant is responsible only to his chiefs. Therefore, what distinguishes him at the outset is a perfect tranquillity of mind, due to the absence of all worries other than the very legitimate ones of promotion.'[1] Another author, writing in 1901, rationalised the civil servant's immobility into a virtue, making him an indispensable arbiter in a disorganised society. 'All the time, the civil servant is opposing to the passing and thought-less caprices of the elected powers the obstacle of his traditions and his sage delays.' He is unlike the businessman, whose fortune is built on the unstable foundations of speculative capital, 'too often lacking a scientific patrimony or a moral culture, without hereditary cohesion, without a common fund of ideas or beliefs'. The business world could be called an aristocracy only through 'poverty of language': the true aristoc-racy of modern France was supplied by the civil service, recruited from all classes, and so in close contact with them, endowed with a 'uniformity of preparatory education and then of work and intellectual development, which give it a solid and rich common basis'.[2]

The irony of the situation was that it was becoming increas-ingly difficult for the civil servant to make decisions. It is often maintained that since the ministers of the Third Republic stayed in office for so short a time, real power was exercised by the civil servants. The conquest of the French empire, for example, does indeed seem to a considerable extent to have been organised by them; until 1946 parliament had limited power over the colonies. In the foreign office men like Philippe Berthelot, its secretary general, exercised great influence over successive ministers.[3] The senior civil servant's power was prob-ably smaller in internal departments. The education ministry placed distinguished scholars at the head of its various sections. Octave Gréard and Louis Liard, for example, exercised enor-mous and still unchronicled influence on the educational system.[4] But in some technical ministries power was not given

[1] Anon., *Les Fonctionnaires* (3rd edition 1911), 19.
[2] René Favarielle, 'Le Fonctionnarisme', *Revue de Paris* (15 Sept. 1901), 405–7. On the bureaucratic mentality, see André Moufflet, *M. Le Bureau et son âme* (1933).
[3] Auguste Bréal, *Philippe Berthelot* (1937).
[4] W. Bruneau is writing a doctoral thesis on Louis Liard.

to the technical experts. Thus in the ministry of public works, the central administration was staffed by some 230 people most of whom had no technical knowledge: they had reached their position by slow promotion from the rank of *expéditionnaire*, for which only a primary education was required. These superior clerks ruled the engineers. What was worse, the ministry was rigidly divided into *directions* with no real co-ordination between them, so that if anyone succeeded in getting a policy adopted, he might find it negated by the work of another *direction*. This was particularly true in transport: railways, roads, and canals were constructed independently (after 1876) so that each built up artificial traffic, distributing subsidies to enable it to compete with the other forms of communication. Each territorial department had an engineer in charge—an area determined irrespective of the amount of work available, and sometimes far too big—but the engineer was subordinate to the prefect and was unable to make contracts himself. The national roads were under his jurisdiction but the departmental and local ones under the prefect's. Fishing in canals was under the control of the ministry of justice, but under the ministry of agriculture in other waters, while the ministry of public works had to ensure the upkeep of waterways. The decision to rebuild a little bridge could take years of negotiation and correspondence. It is true that the ministry of public works could point to the building of France's railway network as its great achievement, but the great financial scandals involved should not be forgotten. Certainly the engineers felt they were fettered by clerks and politicians, that their talents were not properly used, decisions were never made by those most competent, with the result that there was no real responsibility, since no one knew who had taken the decision.[1]

In those areas of state activity where civil servants were principally employed in routine tasks, which did not necessarily call for initiative or the formulation of new policies—for example, in its industrial activities or in tax collection—the power of the senior civil servants was drastically reduced when security of tenure and promotion by seniority were established. The director of a state factory was transformed into a kind of

[1] Henri Chardon, *Les Travaux publics. Essai sur le fonctionnement de nos administrations* (1904), 27, 357.

judge. Every act was foreseen in regulations, so that the director's function was only to keep peace and order, to proclaim the law. Since he no longer had an outlet for proving himself, he very often engaged in secondary activities such as teaching or consultancy and he made up for the prosaic nature of his duties by being an artist or a writer. He sought his identity therefore outside the service. In it, his task was to keep himself from being submerged: he had to ensure that the new and young technical experts should not challenge his own prestige by being given too much freedom to change things. As an alternative to withdrawing into the world of culture, the director could play out a theatrical role of being a busy and important man, constantly making weighty decisions, even though the decisions were always the same one. But one factor for effective decision making was totally lacking. The hierarchical structure made communication between different grades almost impossible. Some civil servants were befogged by being called 'collaborators' and 'dear colleagues' by their superiors, but the different grades (on the whole) came from different worlds, with independent recruiting systems; every man knew how far he could go. To protect his own small freedom of action, he had to hedge himself with impenetrable barriers of regulations which made genuine co-operation or exchange of ideas very difficult.[1]

Still, for all the ambiguities and insecurities in the position of the civil servant, the goodwill, if not the assistance, of the state was needed for the accomplishment of a great number of things, and the civil servant remained powerful, if only from his nuisance value, as an intermediary. He had perhaps ceased to be the master of the country, as he once may have appeared to be, but he made a significant contribution to the formation of those who were its masters. He was, however, too much on the defensive to use his prestige effectively. As Viollet Le Duc noted in 1863: 'If a project appears from which new ideas might emerge, it is submitted for examination to persons who are by conviction or rather by lack of conviction enemies of all innovation.'[2] It is not a simple matter to define the relation

---

[1] Michel Crozier, *Le Phénomène bureaucratique* (1963).

[2] Quoted in Pierre Legendre, *Histoire de l'administration de 1750 à nos jours* (1968), 526. Cf. Jules Ferry's attacks on the Eaux et Forêts in Pierre Soudet, *L'Administration vue par les siens et par d'autres* (1960), 42.

between the civil service and change in this century. The civil
service had become a sort of Frankenstein.

The picture which these chapters on the bourgeoisie have
been attempting to build up is one which does not support the
view of this class as unified, coherent or self-conscious. The
internal conflicts and contradictory interests within it appear
as a major characteristic of it. These were conflicts of which
Marx himself was very much aware, though he believed that
they were 'intermediate and transitional', doomed to disappear.
It is unfortunate that he never wrote the fifty-second chapter of
Capital, which breaks off just when he was about to discuss this
subject, because as a result rather simplified versions of his
theory of class have been applied to this century, ignoring the
fact that his theory was heuristic rather than descriptive of
conditions in his day. If the bourgeoisie did have the means of
material production in its control—a proposition which needs
qualification—it was by no means clear that it also controlled
the means of intellectual production. The subtle relationship
between these two will need more detailed analysis. Meanwhile,
the next two chapters will investigate further the question of
how far the development of new forms of production was
creating a polarised confrontation of classes.

9. Peasants

The Myth of the Peasant Democracy

THE peasants could theoretically have been masters of France. When universal manhood suffrage was proclaimed in 1848, they constituted well over half the population and in 1939 they were still by far the largest single class. However, they did not make use of their power. It is important to understand why. The history of the peasantry cannot be written simply in terms of the issues which parliaments debated or of the parties into which these were divided. These bourgeois preoccupations certainly affected the peasants, but the main reason why the peasants did not throw their weight more decisively was that they were fighting other battles, largely unchronicled by the literate classes, but far more important to them. It is with these battles that this chapter will be concerned.

In 1850 the economist Adolphe Blanqui, brother of the revolutionary, went on a tour of the French countryside and came back astounded by it. 'The economic fact', he wrote, 'which is today most worthy of attention in France, and which stands out in the most striking way, is the difference in the condition and well-being which distinguishes the inhabitants of the towns from those of the countryside . . . One would think one was seeing two different peoples, living, though on the same soil, lives so distinct that they seem foreigners to each other, even though they are united by the links of the most domineering centralisation that has ever existed.'[1] Blanqui was far from being the only man to write about the peasants almost as though they were a different species. Karl Marx, at the same time, compared the peasants of France to a sack of potatoes, each with individual characteristics but all of the same kind: he made no attempt to investigate them further. The peasants are not studied in Balzac's universal portrait of French society.

[1] A. Blanqui, 'Tableau des populations rurales de la France en 1850', *Journal des Économistes*, 28 (1851), 9.

Though he called one of his novels *Les Paysans* and devoted several volumes ostensibly to painting scenes of rural life, Balzac could not describe the peasants, because he was full of contempt for them. They were savages, like Fenimore Cooper's Red Indians, and he was concerned with them only as subjects for his schemes to improve them. The peasants indeed were the objects of denigration, far more sweeping than the artists ever bestowed on the bourgeois. Léon Cladel, himself just escaped from a remote village in Tarn-et-Garonne, enamoured of the sophistication of Paris but guilty and uneasy in its literary world, hurled insults back at them, as 'quadrupeds on two feet . . . Greedy, envious, hypocritical, crafty, cynical, cowardly and brutal, the peasant is the same everywhere, north and south.' He exclaimed with horror that these ignorant rustics should have so much power 'to order new dragonnades, to re-establish the inquisition', to back a new *coup d'état*.

People risen from their ranks often attacked them most vigorously, seeing education and peasantry as extreme opposites representing respectively civilisation and barbarism. The peasants did after all speak not only a different dialect, but sometimes even a different language. The peasants' silences were always a mystery to those who did not share their preoccupations. A country priest, in a book about them published in 1885, confessed: 'I would love the peasants, if the peasant did not disgust me . . . [The peasant] is the least romantic, the least idealistic of men. Plunged into reality, he is the opposite of the dilettante and will never give thirty *sous* for even the most magnificent landscape painting . . . He is original sin, surviving and visible in all its brutal *naïveté* . . . The peasant loves nothing nor anybody but for the use he can make of it.' He never gives presents. He never goes for an idle stroll. He gives his arm to his wife the day of their marriage for the first and last time. He is as uperstitious animal, believing in witches like the Romans and the Gauls. Nothing will move him from his opinions. But the minute he reaches market, he ceases to be a Christian or a man: he is at war with everybody and will spare nothing, however sacred, to get the highest price he can for his goods.[1] This was more or less the picture that Zola painted in his *Earth*, perhaps the first novel to have a peasant as its central character. For

[1] Joseph Roux, *Pensées* (1885).

Zola, the peasant was above all concerned with the acquisition of land, to which he was attached with an animal passion: he represented simplicity and ferocity, greed and conservatism. Jules Renard entitled his novel of the peasantry *Our Savage Brothers* and it was much praised for its accuracy.[1]

While some saw the peasant either as the raw clay from which civilisation had to be fashioned, or as an obstacle to the spread of enlightenment, others, who wished to change society as it had developed, saw in him the repository of unsullied virtues. The romantics, the Catholic revivalists, the believers in a conservative and hierarchic order, all held him up as a model of a human unspoilt by progress. George Sand wrote books about him or rather books about how she would have liked him to be, inaugurating a whole genre of rustic novels. She, however, did more than just idealise him, even if she did admit that she believed that 'in the rural life there are fewer causes of corruption than elsewhere'. She really wanted to understand the peasant, but she honestly confessed that she had failed: 'I cannot form a clear idea of his emotions,' she wrote, 'and it is this that torments me.' Two painters of her generation attempted the same thing: Millet (the son of a peasant and himself a former shepherd) and Courbet showed them weighed down by their labours.[2] Napoleon III inaugurated his reign with an inquiry into popular poetry forgotten 'because of a thoughtless contempt by our rather too worldly literature'.[3] Folklore societies were formed. Vincent d'Indy (a church organist) incorporated peasant tunes into his music for the bourgeoisie. The revivers of regional literature made dialect respectable. Eugène Le Roy wrote powerful novels about the peasants of his native Périgord, suggesting that the spark of revolution lay hidden among them. His *Jacquou le Croquant* (1904) described a *jacquerie* led by an orphaned agricultural labourer (based, for its details, on the sacking of Marshal Bugeaud's château, not all that long before).[4] But Le Roy, the son of a farm manager and a washerwoman, had climbed out of the peasant ranks to become a tax collector. Émile Guillaumin is

[1] E. Zola, *La Terre* (1887); Jules Renard, *Nos Frères farouches* (1908).
[2] Millet, *Paysanne assise, Paysan greffant un arbre, Femme faisant paître sa vache*; G. Courbet, *Casseurs de pierre*.
[3] See J. Antran, *La Vie rurale* (1856).
[4] Cf. M. Ballot, *Eugène Le Roy, écrivain rustique* (1949).

perhaps more significant because he always remained a peasant, never had more than a primary education, and wrote his books after a full day's work as a sharecropper. His *Life of a Simple Man* is the first genuine autobiography of a peasant. He decided to write it after reading *Jacquou le Croquant*. Two publishers rejected it and he only got it printed eventually on a shared cost basis. Guillaumin was the first defender of the peasants who did not idealise them or try to put heroic qualities into them. He consciously attempted to explain them to the townsmen who wondered whether they had brains or hearts. He admitted that the peasants were indifferent to the charms of nature, but thought that they gave the impression of lacking sensibility because they suffered from a punctilious modesty which prevented them from saying what they thought or complaining about their troubles. He wanted the peasants to get rid of their inferiority complex, their submissive attitude, their mistrust of novelty, their self-sufficiency, their envy, their *naïveté* and rapacity, their absorption with buying land, and so their inability to live in better domestic conditions and to enjoy leisure. He deplored submission to authority and the blind acceptance of traditions inherited from one's father. His book might therefore have been almost as much an indictment of his class as Zola's imaginative exercise, had it not inspired sympathy and interest instead of the horror that Zola produced. Though it made peasants human, they were still a separate world.[1]

All these points of view, favourable and derogatory, come together in one generalisation which is too often taken, rather naïvely, as the explanation of why the peasant made so little use of his political power. This is that the peasant was basically conservative, or at least resigned to his lot. Innovation, it is argued, has no place in the countryside. All creativity comes from the towns. The peasant will accept change only when it ceases to be new, when he can do so without causing a scandal in the village. There must be scandal if he gives the impression that he thinks he is cleverer than his father, for in his kind of society, prestige is to a great extent obtained from conformity

[1] R. Mathé, *Émile Guillaumin* (1966), a good biography. For more emotional, conservative portrayals of peasants, see R. Bazin, *La Terre qui meurt* (1899). For a good analysis of the literature, P. Vernois, *Le Roman rustique (1860–1925)* (1962).

with traditions (so that the son of a nonconformist would be expected to be one too). A peasant's prestige comes also from the reputation his family has acquired over several generations: therefore he cannot take a step without involving them; the whole weight of grandparents and female pressure is on him. Likewise the peasant will prefer to own eight thin cows, giving little milk, to five good ones, because prestige counts as much in his eyes as purely economic considerations. He often prefers to eke out a miserable living from an arid plot he owns himself, to the comfort and high wages he might earn working on an efficient farm. The peasant will thus always rouse the despair of agronomists who cannot get him to adopt their scientific methods. The peasant, for example, may not consider himself a true peasant if he does not produce his own bread, whatever his soil is best suited for. Self-sufficiency is his ideal, which may also imply independence of the wider world intellectually as well as materially.[1]

These generalisations about the innate conservatism of the peasant need to be interpreted carefully in the context of French history. The observance of traditional routines, agricultural and social, should not obscure the fact that conflict was part of those routines, and that the pressures involved in preserving them add up to a situation which is far from being one of stagnation. The peasants were neither satisfied nor contented. They were constantly trying to improve their lot, to enlarge their farms, to raise their status. Their world was torn by deep divisions, and by animosities both of interest and of pride. Their lives were absorbed as much by these as by the business of earning their living. It seems more accurate to see their world held together by tension than by a pastoral sleepiness. If that is so, their conservatism may be seen as more the product of insecurity than of innate sluggishness. The constant attempt to anchor themselves more firmly to their own plot of soil was a result of the same feeling, for the peasants of France were, despite the outward impression, perhaps the most insecure part of the nation. They had freed themselves from feudal ties but they had not succeeded in winning true independence. How

[1] Henri Mendras, *Les Transformations du métier d'agriculteur dans la France contemporaine* (1967), is an interesting study of the problems of change since the Second World War.

many of them could call themselves their own masters in the full sense? Debt was their great scourge; but they had to get into debt to round off their farms; and the sharecroppers and tenants likewise were nearly always in debt to their masters. In other countries this sometimes institutionalised into 'debt peonage' which was one remove from slavery. In France it could survive hidden under the mask of liberal rhetoric, because these peasants were no longer dependent simply on one noble class. They were indebted to one another, which made their relationships more complicated and more strained. Lucien Fabre, in a vigorous novel about them written between the wars, talked of 'the implacable subjection resulting from the fear the peasant is in, of not being able to pay his rent, his tax, his debts incurred for the purchase of machines, the ironwork for his cattle, his stock of seeds and of plants, the visits of the veterinary, the renewal of his farmyard livestock, the stud fees, and so many other things . . . He saw the bailiff at his heels whenever a hailstorm threatened or when the frosts of May killed the fruits in flower . . .' He owed money to the tax collector, the notary, the shopkeepers, the usurers, the landlord and a host more.[1] In such conditions the peasant could not afford to experiment. The real change in peasant attitudes could begin only after the First World War—when inflation cancelled their debts—and after the Second, when social security and tenants' rights came to compensate for the permanent uncertainties of the climate.

The supposed general conservatism of the peasant must also be reconciled with the readiness of a sizeable section of the peasantry to vote left wing, to engage in strikes, riots and revolutions, to leave the land, to emigrate seasonally or permanently to the towns. These various forms of protest occurred in different degrees in different parts of the country. Their regional distribution is explained by the immense diversity of economic and social conditions prevalent in France. Though the peasants may have appeared to townsmen uniformly as barbarians, there were enormous variations in their organisation and relationships. Indeed it has been claimed that France contained more than one 'agrarian civilisation', with varying social organisation and farming methods, but there has been

[1] Lucien Fabre, *Le Tarramagnou* (1925), 61.

some dispute as to just how many of these civilisations there were. The basic distinction is between regions of open-field farming common in the north and regions of enclosure in the

MAP. 1. The contrast of village and isolated peasants (1950s). Based on Fauvet and Mendras: *Les Paysans et la Politique* (1958), 29

west and south. The former involved communal control of agriculture, and was often accompanied by the agglomeration of the peasants in large villages, while the latter allowed their dispersal in hamlets and farms. Patterns of settlement are very distinct in Artois and Picardy where in about 90 per cent of the communes, the majority of the peasants live in villages, while in Brittany or the Massif Central only 30 or 40 per cent do. However, one needs to distinguish again between different forms of enclosure: that of the south, where it represented individualism and produced an irregular variety of crops, and that in the west, where it was the result of a collective attempt to add some grain to a system based principally on cattle raising. It was once argued that racial characteristics, Roman or German, survived in this way; then it was thought that it was the physical nature of the soil, and the distribution of water, which determined these variations. But increasingly historical investigation of the way the rural landscape has been formed has stressed different traditions in the way the land has been won for agriculture from waste and woodland, and has shown the different degrees of collectivism and co-operation shown by the peasantry. No simple division emerges, however, for the same sort of villages did not always produce the same kind of agricultural development: the large rural agglomerations of the south were individualistic while those of the north were collectivist. The collectivist traditions moreover decayed at different speeds in different areas: in the Caux and Thiérache for example there was enclosure in the seventeenth and eighteenth centuries, but for different reasons from those affecting the Vendée. The liberty of the south inevitably produced even more variations. But the different ways the peasants had acquired the land and conquered the soil in each particular area meant that they had traditions, problems and enemies of great variety. The north and the south of France were shown to be profoundly different, though further study revealed that this simple division required numerous qualifications.[1] However, it was made clear that peasants living in villages had very different attitudes to those living in lonely farms or hamlets. In the scattered type of settlement, the farmers were separated from the rest of the population. They lived on isolated farms, at best in hamlets with other farmers. The local artisans, the doctor, the shop, the church

[1] M. Bloch, *Les Caractères originaux de l'histoire rurale française* (1931), but see the modifications to his ideas in vol. 2 published in 1956; R. Dion, *Essai sur la formation du paysage rural français* (Tours, 1934); and E. Juillard *et al.*, *Structures agraires et paysages ruraux: un quart de siècle de recherches françaises* (Nancy, 1957).

would be situated largely apart from them in villages, to which
the elderly and the widowed would also retire. Agriculture and
its services were thus, to a considerable extent, separated and
sometimes at war.

The sense of community depended also on the way the
land was worked. The common generalisation that the peasants
were innately individualistic and independent is another bourgeois myth. It is important to remember that though individual
peasant property had developed before the Revolution, ownership did not imply complete liberty to work the land as one
pleased. When the strips and plots were tiny, it was essential
to co-operate in sowing and reaping. No man could reach his
plot without going through those of his neighbours. After the
harvest all had a right to pasture their animals freely in the
fields.[1] The Revolution gave the rural population total independence, just as it allowed all men to practise whatever trade
they pleased, but this legal right sometimes remained rather
theoretical. The position in the nineteenth century was that the
old community spirit was breaking up but it was not dead.[2]
This was the source of one of the most bitter—though again
largely unchronicled—fights which absorbed the peasants. A
study of the Vendée plains has shown the survival of collective
harvests, collective fruit picking, common pasture, gleaning
and raking, well into the nineteenth century. Owners could not
go into their own fields until a public proclamation allowed
them, nor could they remove their wheat-sheaves till the
opening of the paths was announced. The mayor and the
municipal council went out into the vineyards to decide when
the vine should be picked. One by one, villages abandoned
these controls. In this region the collapse finally occurred only
in the period 1870–1900, though one isolated commune,
Petosse, kept its common pasture traditions till 1957. As the
records of the commune of Le Langon put it in 1898, 'owners
are anxious to enjoy full property of their lands'. The problem
of how to acquire this full property was an important and
absorbing one. And since there was often much dispute about
who had the right to what, and cases of the rich usurping or

---

[1] O. Leclerc-Thouin, *L'Agriculture de l'ouest de la France* (1843), 43.
[2] On this, see A. Soboul, 'La Communauté rurale', *Revue de Synthèse* (1957),
283–307.

buying these rights, to the detriment of the poor, one of the first things the poor peasants did in 1848, when authority broke down, was to rush into formerly common lands, to reclaim their ancient rights. There were powerful pressures, working both ways, for and against their preservation.[1]

At the beginning of this period nearly five million hectares, i.e. about 9 per cent of French soil, was common land, owned and managed collectively by the communes; by the end of it, the figure was still as much as 8 per cent. There were about 1,700,000 hectares of forests and 2,800,000 of pasture and waste; only 150,000 were arable. The mountainous regions had a far higher proportion of their land in common. In 1863 Hautes-Alpes had 51 per cent of its territory in common, Hautes-Pyrénées 43 per cent, and Savoie 42 per cent. Nine departments had between 21 and 30 per cent of their territory in common and another 21 departments between 10 and 19 per cent.[2] Corsica in the 1950s still had 28 per cent of its territory in common: the area had declined only 10 per cent in the course of the twentieth century and only 7 per cent in the nineteenth. Some Corsican villages have as much as 67 per cent of their land in common.[3] In such regions the inhabitants depended for some of their livelihood, and sometimes almost completely, on the right to use the commons. The attitude of revolutions and governments to these commons had been ambivalent. In 1792 a law had ordered the division of these lands among the inhabitants but in 1793 another law repealed this. The agronomists thought common ownership was an obstacle to progress.

---

[1] Jacqueline Moguelet, 'Les Pratiques communautaires dans la plaine vendéenne au 19ᵉ siècle', *Annales* (July–Aug. 1963), 666–76. On forest rights, see Henri Evrard, *Notes historiques sur les biens communaux du canton de Varennes-en-Argonne* (Paris thesis, Bar-le-Duc, 1912), and Michel Duval, *La Révolution et les droits d'usage dans les forêts de l'ancienne Bretagne* (Rennes, 1954). In general, A. Soboul, 'Survivance féodales dans la société rurale au 19ᵉ siècle, *Annales* (Sept.–Oct. 1968), 965–86; and for the situation in the east of France at the turn of the century, G. Eugène Simon, 'Les Biens communaux', *La Nouvelle Revue*, 88 (1894), 699–719, with graphic details about individual villages.

[2] J. de Crisenoy, 'Statistique des biens communaux et des sections de communes', *Revue Générale d'Administration* (1887), 257–75; R. Graffin, *Les Biens communaux* (1899); Edmond Cleray, *De la mise en valeur des biens communaux* (1900), appendix. 4,855,000 hectares in 1863, 4,316,000 hectares in 1877.

[3] Janine Pomponi, 'La Vie rurale de deux communes corses: Serra di Scopamene et Sotta' (Aix, Travaux et mémoires de la faculté de lettres, vol. 26, 1962, stencilled), 60, 100.

The rich wanted to buy and enclose. The poor were generally opposed to division because paradoxically they had most to lose by it. Even if the land was distributed equally and freely among the inhabitants of the village, each would get a plot so small or of such poor quality that it would be of little value to him; it was usually more advantageous to the poor to have the right to pasture their few animals on the wastelands: this could make all the difference to their survival. A struggle was thus set up between the rich and the poor, the individualists and the conservatives, over these commons, quite apart from the quarrels which went on as to how the commons should be managed or farmed. In many cases, the individualists won, even if by a roundabout route, and a fully capitalist economy would be introduced into the village. Thus, for example, in 1851 the village of Caire du Cheylade in Cantal sold off two mountains it owned in common and with the proceeds bought state bonds. In the 1930s every family was still drawing a share of the interest from these bonds, but by then worth only the derisory sum of 45 francs. This village, situated in a mountainous region, had exceptionally vast commons, so it also decided to divide another part of them equally among the inhabitants, giving each a small plot. Many of the plots of course were situated in highly inconvenient positions. A rich man came along, bought these tiny bits up, and created enormous private grazings for himself. Within a few years the village found itself noticeably poorer than it had been.[1] In parts of Alsace there were very sizeable commons; some villages had no local taxes, because their income from the forests they owned sufficed to pay their expenses. Financial crises might lead them to sell, which could upset their whole economy and bring about general ruin. Alternatively, when there were influential 'village cocks' able to get their way, the commons would be leased out, nothing would remain of the community organisation except the notional rent. In other parts, however, villages distributed commons to the inhabitants in plots which could not be sublet. If they were badly worked, they reverted to the village. If there were not enough plots, a waiting list was established. Living in such a village thus carried with it the right to enjoy an

[1] A. Durand, *La Vie rurale dans les massifs volcaniques des Dores, du Cézallier, du Cantal et de l'Aubrac* (Aurillac, 1946), 146.

allotment. Some sense of community spirit could thus survive, but it could also be eroded as these rights became more like private property.[1]

It is possible to study the effect of these common possessions in the mountains of the southern Jura. This area lies at the junction of the northern *langue d'œil*, with its open-field villages and larger farms, and the south, with its smallholders, combining pasture and vine. One cannot simply contrast one with the other. Quite small areas have developed in different ways. In the poor communes, with no commons or forests, the peasants, with their excessively small and dispersed plots, and their low milk yields, have found no means of escaping from their stagnation. They have supplemented their bare livelihoods by taking orphaned and abandoned children from the Assistance Publique, which means they have more than their fair share of idiots and subnormal people. By contrast, in other areas the habit of managing the commons together has stimulated the growth of milk co-operatives, which are the basis of the Gruyère industry. But not all peasants have accepted co-operation with equal enthusiasm. Those who sold their milk to intermediaries have remained isolated from the consequences of the greatly expanded markets and they have been co-operators only from necessity. The most dynamic peasants in fact have been those whose vines were destroyed by phylloxera, who were forced into modern milking methods, and who have supplemented their earnings by polyculture. It would be far too simplistic to link the various traditions of common ownership and common agriculture with the willingness which some modernising peasants showed, in the second half of the twentieth century, to abandon their individualism. On the contrary, those who had common rights were often highly conservative. But co-operation was far from being alien to the traditions of the peasantry.[2]

The notion that a man could do as he pleased with his property, though proclaimed by parliament, was not accepted by the courts. The Civil Code had introduced a strong element of Roman law into its provisions on private property but this was gradually reversed. The first breach occurred in 1855, in a

[1] E. Julliard, *La Vie rurale dans la plaine de Basse-Alsace* (1953), 224–9.
[2] R. Lebeau, *La Vie rurale dans les montagnes du Jura méridional* (Lyon, 1955).

celebrated case which came before the court of Colmar. An owner had built a false chimney solely to spoil the view of his neighbour. The court ordered him to destroy the chimney. Lawyers protested that this decision was contrary to the Civil Code, but in 1887 the Court of Cassation expanded it into the general principle that owners must not cause a nuisance to their neighbours: it decided in favour of people protesting against the smoke emitted by railway engines passing by their land. The great enemy of the rights of the individual proprietor was Duguit, who wrote many books, and influenced a whole group of pupils, in favour of the new idea that property was not a right but a social function, that society allowed men to enjoy property provided this was subordinated to the social interest.[1] He claimed that the individualism of the Civil Code was based on an unreal, abstract view of man, who was naturally good, whereas law ought to be concerned with protecting the weak. At the same time therefore as the old community of the country-side was collapsing, the law courts and the legislators under solidarist influence bolstered it up in new ways.[2]

The republicans like to claim that it was the Revolution of 1789 which had brought equality to France, by expropriating the nobility and Church and creating a nation of small peasant proprietors. The Civil Code's prescription that land must be divided equally between children is supposed to have given every man a birthright. Michelet contrasted aristocratic England, owned by 32,000 rich men who got others to work for them, with democratic France, where the land was shared out between 15 or 20 million peasants who cultivated it themselves.[3] These figures were quite mythical and were made no truer by the fact that a Republican League of Small Property, presided over by Paul Deschanel, existed to propagate the myth.

The equal division of property among children was by no

---

[1] L. Duguit, *Les Transformations générales du droit privé depuis le code Napoléon* (1912); G. Pirou, 'Duguit et l'économie politique', *Revue d'Économie Politique* (1933).

[2] Gaston Morin, *La Révolte du droit contre le code* (1945). Outside agriculture, this movement revealed itself in restrictions on employment of women and children, provisions for confiscation of land for public utility schemes, leasehold reform, and the protection of tenants (1926, 1927, and 1933). During the First and Second World Wars farmers were obliged to work their lands, which could be leased to someone else if they were abandoned.

[3] J. Michelet, *Le Peuple* (1844; ed. L. Refort, 1946), 32.

means a universal demand of the peasantry. There were, it is true, some who said that the arbitrary whims of tyrannical fathers should be restrained, but others pointed out the much more keenly felt difficulty, that division could not work satisfactorily on poor lands and small estates. Equal division might destroy the nobility but it would also ruin smallholders, by fragmenting their lands into plots too tiny to provide a living and so it would turn proprietors into labourers. In Roman law, a father could dispose freely of two-thirds of his property if he had four children or fewer. This law prevailed in eight southern provinces, and in restricted form in seven others. But already before the Revolution considerable areas of France, ruled by customary law, had division of property among children as a normal practice. The Civil Code thus did not introduce a radically new system of inheritance. Its main effect was to limit the rights of fathers in the south. The Civil Code was in fact a compromise. It gave fathers with one child the right to dispose freely of half their property, to those with two children the right to dispose freely of one third and to those with three the right to dispose freely of one quarter. From the legal point of view, it did not change matters much in the north, and not that drastically in the south. In actual practice, in the way the Civil Code was worked, it made even less difference, because it was frequently not applied, and traditional customs survived despite it. The agricultural inquiry of 1866, which, among other things, investigated inheritance, revealed that the bourgeoisie on the whole accepted the Civil Code's principle of equal division but that the peasants did not. The latter were keen to leave the father with a larger share of his property to dispose of as he saw fit. Groups of small owners even got together to petition the senate for this reform.

By the time of the Second Empire, equal division was almost universal in the north-east of France, where custom favoured it, but even here this did not mean that the agricultural holdings were always split up. The larger and richer holdings allowed arrangements to be made among the heirs so that the profitability of the farms should not be damaged. One son would run the farm, and pay his brothers and sisters their share in money, from his profits, or he could rent their share from them. On the Breton coast, where alternative employment at sea or in market gardening meant that land did not have to provide a whole living, property was divided equally, and the little plots served as subsidiary allotments; but in the interior of Finistère and Morbihan, the poor isolated farmers could not allow this and farms were passed on whole to one son only. In the Côtes du Nord, uneconomic division was avoided by the heirs living together as a community, and the girls being prevented from marrying. Despite the Revolution and the Code, there were farms in Mayenne, of 20–40 hectares (50–100 acres) which had never been divided from time immemorial. The Bretons, like the Irish, had large families but postponed marriage as late as possible. The Normans sometimes solved the same problem by having fewer legitimate children but more illegitimate ones. In the centre of France the custom of migrating to large towns until retirement similarly encouraged the maintenance of the family farm as a working unit. The demand for greater testamentary freedom was particularly strong here. In the Nièvre, girls sometimes renounced their share of their inheritance on getting married, and various schemes were used to favour the eldest son. Notaries often helped by getting the children to accept a low valuation of the parents' estate. Of course, such stratagems did not always work, or not for long. Frequently they were disputed by the next generation and lawsuits dragged on for many years. Certain areas were notorious for the mercilessness with which heirs demanded their fair share against such ploys. In the eastern Pyrénées even the houses were divided up among them. In the Haute-Saône there was particularly active litigation.

The sociologist Le Play drew attention to the conflict between custom and law in his monograph of a Pyrenean family, which had owned 18 hectares for four centuries, passed on from father to eldest son. After the Revolution the property was nominally divided, but the eldest son received the *quotité disponible* (the share the father could bequeath freely) and took over the farm. He gradually paid off his brothers and sisters, though some helped by not marrying, living with him, and bequeathing their share to his eldest son. In 1836 the owner died leaving eight children and a farm worth 17,368 francs. The eldest was a girl. Her husband, in keeping with tradition, took her name and the farm. She got 4,342 francs as her free share (*préciput*), plus a one-eighth share in the remainder. Two siblings did not marry and bequeathed their shares back to her eldest; the others were bought out. But when she died in 1864, an uncle challenged the original settlement and, though he lost, the legal costs were heavy. His lawsuit encouraged the idea that the traditional system existed at the expense of younger children. Not the Civil Code, but this kind of local experience, is what brought about change. Only in the next generation did the husbands of two sisters demand the payment of their share immediately. This forced the sale of part of the farm, which ceased to be a viable unit and in 1882 it was all finally sold.

An interesting study of the decline of the family spirit could be made from the records of inheritance. Ideally, it was agreed in the father's old age that one son (in some regions this son would be called the eldest, whatever he was in fact) should have the *quotité disponible* and the farm; in return he looked after the parents, who now retired, and he paid the other children a fixed sum over many years (which was often less than their true share). The division parents made could easily be disputed by rebellious children. The value of the property at the time of death, rather than at the time of the division, was what counted, so the whole settlement could be called into question if the decision was made before death. No generalisation is possible, in the present state of knowledge, about the progress of fragmentation of property as a result of the Code. It is certain that the number of parcels of land increased. In 1826 10·29 million parcels were counted, in 1881 14·29 million. In the process the average size of each parcel fell from 4·48 to 3·5 hectares, and by 1884 74 per cent of these parcels were of 2 hectares or less, but it cannot be said with what uniformity over the country as a whole. It was not a gradual and progressive movement. Property was certainly divided and subdivided in inheritance and France was notorious for the tiny plots into which the land was fragmented. But it was not inheritance alone that was responsible. The consequence of the Civil Code's provisions about inheritance was not to liberate the peasants in any simple way. They did increase equality of inheritance, but they also burdened the peasantry with a tyranny possibly as oppressive as that of the patriarchal father.

Mortgages were frequently necessary to carry out the division, to pay some heirs in land and some in money. Mortgages were often necessary to make farms fragmented by division into viable units. A large proportion of the spare cash of the peasantry was absorbed in healing the wounds of inheritance. A whole army of speculators, usurers and agents grew up to profit from the increasing freedom. In the mid nineteenth century they were known as 'the black bands'; these specialised in buying up large farms and selling them off in small bits. The peasantry bought on mortgage as much as it could. So its savings went into land purchase, rather than into modernisation. Legal fees and taxation on inheritance and sale were one of its major expenses.[1]

The paralysing effects of the struggle for the land were strikingly seen in the great Revolution. The bourgeoisie, much more than the peasantry, were the victors of this Revolution and it is important to understand why. The Constituent Assembly, controlled by the bourgeoisie, carefully distinguished between feudal dues classified as unjust and those which represented land rent. It abolished only the former, and decreed that the latter should be bought out with compensation. It was only in 1793 that all feudal rights were abolished. That was because the peasants refused to buy them out and simply ceased to pay these dues. But why did the peasants not also divide up the lands of the nobility and clergy, indeed all land, among themselves, by taking the law into their hands in the same way? The answer is that on this point their interests varied and they were not united. Already in 1789 about 30 to 40 per cent of France was owned by peasants, so there was a first division between those peasants who owned land and those who did not. Equal partition was not so attractive to those who already enjoyed a privileged position. Moreover, most of the land owned by the wealthier classes was rented out, under various forms of tenure, to peasants. These (tenant farmers and sharecroppers) were fighting their way up the social scale by acquiring these tenancies. They would lose if all the land was divided equally between all peasants, including the vast multitude of landless labourers. This conflict between the

[1] Alexandre de Brandt, *Droit et coutumes des populations rurales de la France en matière successionale* (1901).

various categories of peasants made it impossible for the whole
body to act with unison.[1]

The French Revolution therefore did not create a peasant
democracy. Nevertheless, a myth persisted that the land of
France was owned (as Michelet said) by 20 million peasants.
Michelet got this figure from out of his own head. He could not
have got it from anywhere else, because the number of landowners was unknown in his day, and remained unknown
throughout this period. The statistics the government collected
were incapable of revealing the facts, because they were compiled from taxation returns made for other purposes.[2] All that
was known was that the land was divided into an enormous
number of separate plots paying separate tax. In 1826, as has
been seen, there were about 10 million of them; and by 1875
there were 14 million. It did not follow that there were as many
landowners, and certainly not that there were as many peasants
working their own fields. For (taking the figures for the year
1882, at the zenith of agricultural prosperity) 38·2 per cent of
these plots were under 1 hectare (2½ acres) in extent. Another
32·9 per cent were between 1 and 5 hectares. Together these
small plots covered only 13·5 per cent of the 45 million hectares
in private ownership. About a quarter of the plots (26·4 per
cent) were between 5 and 40 hectares in extent, but they
covered only 31·5 per cent of the land. A mere 2·5 per cent of
the plots, however (those over 40 hectares), covered 45 per cent
of the land. It could be argued therefore that almost half of
France was owned by large owners. Though France was nothing
like England, where in the 1870s about 2,184 landowners
with over 5,000 acres each owned half the land of the United
Kingdom, there were at any rate some 49,243 plots in France
of over 100 hectares (250 acres) covering one quarter of the
country. These large farms were concentrated in certain
regions: three departments had over 50 per cent of their
territory covered by them,[3] and another eleven 40 to 50 per

---

[1] G. Lefebvre, 'La Place de la révolution dans l'histoire agraire de la France',
Annales d'Histoire economique et sociale, 1 (1929), 506–23.

[2] The only way to establish the proportion of property owners is to study the
question commune by commune, using the *cadastre* and the population census at
this level, where every name is given. This is now beginning to be done by regional
historians.

[3] Hautes-Alpes, Cher, Bouches du Rhône.

cent of their territory.[1] By contrast there were four departments
where large farms covered under 6 per cent of the territory,[2]
another eleven with 6 to 10 per cent, and a further twenty-
six with 10 to 20 per cent. These large estates, however, were
not necessarily the most prosperous, because almost half their
extent was uncultivated. The large landowners had only 40
per cent of arable land, and only 31 per cent of vineland, but
68 per cent of forests.[3] Many of France's *richest* farmers did not
fall into this category, with its wide expanses of deserted land.
In dealing with large property in France, it is necessary to be
clear what one is talking about, and to take into consideration
not just acreage, but the income derived from it and the way it
was farmed.

Some of the most illuminating work on this subject has been
done by Philippe Vigier, who studied the landownership of
some 600 communes in six departments of the south-east as it
existed in the mid nineteenth century. Vigier showed that
statistics on a departmental level—let alone a national one—
are highly unreliable as guides to the real nature of landownership. The south-east is, by and large, a region of small
peasant proprietorship. But if one looks at this at the level
of the commune one sees at least six different types of such
proprietorship. Thus the commune of Aiguilles in the Hautes-
Alpes had in 1851 745 inhabitants of whom 458 were owner-
cultivators. On the face of it this looks like a peasant democracy.
But over three-quarters of the commune consisted of wood and
pasture owned by the commune, so that each proprietor had
private ownership on average of less than 2 hectares. This was
quite inadequate for them to live off. Only a dozen or so could
in fact get a full living from the land. The vast majority got
a little from using the commons, but they had to absent themselves in seasonal migration to keep themselves. Another commune Saint-Julien-en-Quint (Drôme) was of the same size.
Its lands were also divided between many proprietors—302.
But two-thirds of the land was owned by about sixty-six people
and there were in particular four landowners with substantially

---

[1] Alpes-Maritimes, Landes, Hautes-Pyrénées, Nièvre, Pyrénées-Orientales,
Corse, Allier, Basses-Alpes, Loir-et-Cher, Indre, Var.

[2] Charente-Inférieure, Rhône, Seine, Tarn-et-Garonne.

[3] Flour de Saint-Genis, *La Propriété rurale en France* (1902), 83.

more land than the average. The majority of the peasant proprietors, here as at Aiguilles, depended on seasonal migration and artisan activities; but the unequal distribution of the land created a different social hierarchy, which was all the more significant in that these small owners had bought their plots over several centuries, in a silent struggle which gradually deprived the nobles of their once dominant holdings. By contrast, the larger farms of Donzère (Drôme) had been created over the years by rich men, employing sharecroppers, who had reclaimed the river banks previously flooded. These farms yielded a much higher income than others in the region. In purely numerical terms, there were 438 small owners in this commune. But they owned only 27 per cent of the land, while eleven rich ones owned 39 per cent. Ostensibly this was a village of small owners, but in reality these were dependent on the rich for employment and it was with their labour that the rich made their high incomes. The different relationships created by landownership are shown again by La Frette (Isère) where there were forty-six middle-sized owners with between 5 and 30 hectares, one rich man with 113 hectares, but 570 smallholders with 56 per cent of the land. But the land was poor, unirrigated and worth very little. The middle owners ran their farms with little outside labour and so had little influence. The bourgeoisie did not consider it worth buying land here. So the small owners were able to run the village themselves, and their dependence was on each other. But they could hardly be said to be living off the land; they had to engage in numerous activities to survive. Valensole (Basses-Alpes) again had 442 smallholders, but they were concentrated in the *bourg* and the surrounding area, which was divided into tiny plots, worked very intensely. Beyond this, however, twenty-seven large owners held 41 per cent of the land and employed 667 labourers and servants so that two distinct societies coexisted, one in the *bourg* and a different one in the countryside around it. Bourdeaux (Drôme) provides a further variation: its larger farms yielded less than half the income of those of Donzère but even so they were worth over twice as much as the smallholdings.[1] Thus a small proprietor was not necessarily a peasant and could be prin-

[1] P. Vigier, *Essai sur la répartition de la propriété foncière dans la région alpine. Son évolution des origines du cadastre à la fin du second empire* (1963).

cipally an artisan, or subsidiarily a labourer; and his property
in a great number of cases was far from giving him independence. Conversely one did not need an enormous acreage to
enjoy dominant influence in a village.

The statistics of 1862 conveniently break up the agricultural
population to show tenurial relationships. At that date there
were 57,639 proprietors who cultivated their land through
a farm manager. There were 1,754,934 proprietors who cultivated their land themselves and cultivated nothing but their
own land. But there were even more landowners who could
not survive simply on their own lands. 648,836 proprietors
also cultivated other people's land as tenant farmers; 203,860
cultivated other people's lands as sharecroppers, and 1,134,490
worked for others as labourers. All these categories add up to
3,799,759 proprietors. There were, however, almost as many
people on the land who were not proprietors: 3,553,091 in all.
Of these, 386,533 were tenant farmers, 201,527 were sharecroppers, 869,254 labourers, and 2,095,777 farm employees of
different kinds (638,129 female servants, 584,320 male servants,
353,184 general farm workers, 219,753 shepherds, 122,803
cowherds, 110,801 carters, 66,787 foremen). This means that
about half the population on the land owned some land, but
only half of these (i.e. a quarter of the total agricultural population) had enough land to live off.[1] Moreover, though the
people farming their own land were in a majority (to the
extent of three-quarters), the acreage they covered was
only half that of the country. Almost one-half of the land was
worked by tenant and share farmers, who on average had
farms two and a half times as large as the owner-occupiers (11
hectares, as against 4·37 hectares). Moreover, these tenants
were particularly concentrated in the north of France, so that
in some regions tenants predominated.[2] Sharecroppers likewise occupied large areas of the south-west and centre. The
conclusion is that France was not a country of small peasant
proprietors, but of small, middle and large owners, each
covering about one-third of the country in total acreage, but
distributed unevenly over the different regions, so that the land
was worked in an enormous variety of ways. France had no

[1] A. de Foville, *Le Morcellement* (1885), 77-8.
[2] See map, p. 161.

latifundia to compare with Spain or with the Duke of Sutherland's 50,000 hectares, but it had nearly everything else.

This varied agricultural world was split up by an exceptionally fragmented social structure. Political equality was balanced by an elaborate hierarchy. Any one of these three million odd proprietors could not expect to marry the daughter of any other. Elaborate investigations of his precise standing would first be necessary and when it came to detail, any one man would find that there were not all that many girls who would acknowledge him as a suitable match. The limits of equality were revealed very forcefully in the marriage market. Thus proprietors were distinguished not just by an infinite variation of wealth, but by the kind of land they owned, how long their family had owned it, the type of house they had, how many animals they possessed, how much cash they had, and how much, given the size of their family, they could afford to spend on a dowry. A proprietor would consider himself superior to a sharecropper, and even labourers distinguished themselves according to their parentage. A brief survey of these various gradations may be helpful.

In the most fertile regions of France, the richest and most successful farmers were not landowners, but tenant farmers. The land here was bought up to a considerable extent—around Paris to the extent of 30 to 40 per cent—by city dwellers, as investments.[1] The ownership of the land was still very much fragmented. In Seine-et-Marne there were in 1942 no fewer than 150,000 properties. But tenants rented them and farmed them in large units. In this department there were only 7,930 farms. 50 per cent of the cultivated area was in farms of over 100 hectares. The trend here has been the opposite of that in other regions, where direct owner-farming has increased. In Seine-et-Marne tenants farmed 24 per cent of the farms in 1892, but 57 per cent in 1946. The size of farms increased accordingly: in 1892 only 35 per cent were over 100 hectares, in 1929 50 per cent were, in 1946 53 per cent. When workers talk of the 'patron' here, they mean the tenant farmer, not the landlord. The tenants indeed developed into a group of some originality. In the first half of the century, an ordinary peasant

[1] For city investment in land see Henri Elhaï, *Recherches sur la propriété foncière des citadins en Haute-Normandie* (C.N.R.S., 1965).

could still hope to become one of them by gradually increasing
the acreage he rented. A case is recorded of a farmer who began
in 1880 with a mere 20 hectares rented and only 2,000 francs of
equipment. Three years later he had made enough to rent a
farm of 60 hectares, obtaining a loan of 7,000 francs for his
equipment from the landowner. In 1887 he moved again into
a farm of 100 hectares. In 1890 he bought his farmhouse for
4,000 francs, and over the next twenty years also acquired 120
hectares around it, as well as an additional farm of 80 hectares.
By 1910 therefore he owned 200 hectares and rented 260.[1]
However, the amount of capital required for the intensive,
market-oriented farming that flourished here increased rapidly.
If 1840 is taken as a base line, the capitalisation is estimated to
have doubled by 1870, trebled by 1900, and quadrupled by
1940. Profits of course were much higher than in the subsistence farming regions: they were as high as 20 per cent in the
first half of the nineteenth century, and around 15 per cent
after 1860—enough to make possible the tripling of capital in
a generation. After the crisis of 1880, they fell to 10 per cent,
and 8 to 10 per cent has been the level they have remained at
since then—except for the really bad years of 1928–41. The
result of this high profitability has been that dynasties of tenant
farmers have grown up, not dissimilar to those of the textile
industrialists of the north. In the Soissonnais, the Ferté family
had, by the 1950s, acquired no less than 5,300 hectares in
seventeen farms, or, if their sons-in-law are included, 7,800
hectares in twenty-five farms. The Leroux family had 2,700
hectares in ten farms, and there were many more. In 1839 the
Agricultural Society of Senlis, composed of landowners,
opposed the admission of tenant farmers to its membership.
But in 1859 the Bonapartist prefect of Seine-et-Marne talked
of the tenant farmers as a 'caste', with 2,350 members 'of the
first order, to whom the salons of the prefecture are open'. In
1840 the amount of capital represented by ownership was about
six times that of the capital normally invested in running a
farm. By 1870 the ratio was often down to 1:4 and by 1900 to
1:3 or even 1:2. The tenants became more and more men of
considerable substance. Around 1850 they began to stop feeding

[1] Eugène Creveaux, 'Les Cultivateurs du Laonnais', *La Science Sociale*, 87 (Nov.
1911), 33–5.

their workers. By the turn of the century they had turned into gentleman farmers, on a par with industrialists, no longer educated simply at primary school, but sending their children to the *lycée* or the church school and then to agricultural colleges and to travel abroad. They lived in increasingly comfortable houses. In the 1930s they had tennis-courts and powerful cars and some even private aeroplanes. Jules Benard, of an old and increasingly wealthy family of this kind, president of the Agricultural Society of Meaux, even rose to become a regent of the Bank of France, though he was quite exceptional. Some of these families were old, like the Ferté, who had been in the same farm at Terny since 1580. But there were also professional farmers from other regions—notably the Flemish—who immigrated with capital accumulated elsewhere to seize the opportunities here—like the Cuypers who in under fifty years (over three generations) accumulated six farms of over 300 hectares each. 11 per cent of farms of over 400 hectares in the region south of Paris, between the Seine and the Oise, were run by people from Flanders. The new men were more vigorous in their methods, and not much different from city speculators; it was they who were the pioneers of new ideas. They took pride in their achievements—as the older families took pride in their ancestors. One, who tripled the size of his farm in forty years, put up an obelisk in his courtyard to commemorate the fact.

The tenant farmers became mayors of their communes in many cases and after 1850 their influence was certainly more widely felt than that of the aristocracy. The landowners in these areas included some of the richest people in France. Jewish and Protestant bankers liked to invest here. Half a dozen Rothschilds owned between them over 10,000 hectares near Armainvilliers and Chantilly, Péreire owned 3,000 hectares. Baron Hottinguer owned the Château de Guermantes. Three branches of the aristocratic Grammont family owned 1,700 hectares and noble names were sprinkled over the countryside: Mackau, Moustier, Ségur, Bertier de Sauvigny. But to the local inhabitants by the turn of the century these were frequently just names and their estates were concealed and isolated behind high walls. These landowners were usually barely a part of the local economy. The tenant farmers, being

too busy with agriculture, seldom ventured into national politics, so landlords like Broglie, Haussonville and Lafayette were
able to enjoy the parliamentary seats. The power of the tenants
penetrated instead into the local sugar industry—the indispensable adjunct of the beet farming which was one of the pillars
of their prosperity. The profits from sugar refining were a
valuable complement to those of agriculture: in the Second
Empire the refineries often paid dividends of 50 to 60 per cent;
that of Puisieux, near Laon, founded in 1865, paid a 100 per
cent dividend in its first year. The tenants widened their influence by allowing some relatives to become notaries, judges
and civil servants locally, but they were proud that their
wealth allowed them to set up nearly all their children with
farms of their own. They acquired even greater stability as a
class by a tacit code which forbade competition between them:
they refused to rent land which had formerly been let to a
neighbour of equal status, they did not compete in the wages
they paid, and would not employ labourers sacked by their
neighbours. Such ties made it possible for them to form co-
operatives, though it took them a long time to get round to this,
and it was the pressure of the crisis of the 1930s and the organisation of the wheat market in 1936 that drove them into it. But
once they discovered the benefits of co-operatives, they put
them to good use, and so distinguished themselves still further
from the small proprietors who toyed with co-operatives so
timidly, though they needed them even more. By then of course
these tenant farmers were living a different kind of life, in a
different class, from the rest of the peasantry and from the
traditional owner of middle-sized farms. The latter still worked
with their labourers, and often ate with them; it was not impossible for a good worker to marry one of their daughters and
to succeed to her family's farm. The large tenant farmers by
contrast treated their labourers in much the same way as
industrial employers did, and all the more so since the labourers
were migrants, and (particularly after 1919) foreigners. However, the exclusiveness of tenant farmers should not be exaggerated. 'His physical appearance', wrote an observer as late as
1953, 'without being that of a peasant is nevertheless definitely
of a man of the land. Among his workers and neighbours, it
would often be impossible to pick him out, except perhaps by

his more austere mien . . . He is capable of discussing general ideas, but he is still prudent, mistrustful and not really interested in other people's point of view.'[1]

In other regions, the accumulation of wealth by a peasant did not usually involve the same change of status. At the turn of the century in Lot-et-Garonne, for example, there were, within a radius of 20 kilometres, over a hundred farms yielding good profits, but none of them over 35 hectares. The owners possessed between 50,000 and 200,000 francs in capital; some were reputed to be millionaires; but they worked in the fields themselves, wore the same clothes and sat at the same tables as the men they employed. Less than a tenth of them had been landowners for more than four generations. Their grandfathers or great-grandfathers had been farmhands or share-croppers. They had saved up say a thousand francs by the time they were twenty-five, had married wives who brought them half as much again in dowry, and within seven or eight years had collected three or four thousand francs, enough to buy land, on mortgage, for 5,000 francs. They went on working as labourers so as to pay off their debt and to buy cattle. They grew rich by constant hard work, by spending only the very minimum and turning practically all their earnings into capital, by marrying into families of the same origin and with the same ambitions, by being careful to use only well-tried agricultural methods, and by limiting the size of their families.[2]

Next in the social hierarchy was the peasant who succeeded in keeping his farm at the same size, providing for his children with his profits. Le Play made famous a particularly remarkable example of this kind in Béarn in the mid nineteenth century, remarkable because this peasant had maintained the patriarchal structure of his family. It was in the commune of Lavedan (Hautes-Pyrénées), in mountains covered by snow for half the year and intensely hot in the summer. There were 1,376 inhabitants, 473 of them artisans or merchant families, 172 wood-

[1] Philippe Bernard, *Économie et sociologie de la Seine-et-Marne 1850–1950* (1953); Pierre Brunet, *Structure agraire et économie rurale des plateaux tertiaires entre la Seine et l'Oise* (Caen, 1960); Michel Philipponneau, *La Vie rurale de la banlieu parisienne* (1956); J. P. Moreau, *La Vie rurale dans le sud-est du bassin parisien* (1958).

[2] G. Maydieu, 'Notes pour servir à une monographie du paysan proprietaire du Lot-et-Garonne', *Revue d'économie politique*, 9 (1895), 159–64.

cutters, 173 living mainly from renting their houses to tourists, 102 following liberal professions (it is not clear which), 372 peasants working exclusively on lands they owned themselves, and 84 working partly for themselves and partly for others. The family of Melouga owned 8 cows and 3 to 5 heifers, who provided them with two-thirds of their income, and 90 goats and 55 sheep who provided the rest of it. They had little land, and their animals got about 40 per cent of their food from pasturing on the village commons. The family made their own clothes and clogs, grew their own food, had their own honey. In winter they made objects in wood which they sold to outsiders. The cash from their milk and cheese they used to accumulate savings to pay dowries and constitute trousseaux; this meant they had to save on average 600 francs a year, since they usually had between eight and ten children. Their way of life seemed exactly proportioned to earning this surplus, which made it possible for the main family house and farm to remain intact through the generations.

The way a peasant had to resort to industry in order to buy land, and the way he was thus able to reach a very decent standard of living, can be seen from the biography of the peasant-soapmaker of Basse-Provence, written in 1859. This man was then aged 51. He lived in a village between Aix and Marseille, one-third of which was owned by a nobleman, with the doctor and the notary having the only other sizeable farms. No peasant owned more than 20 hectares here; the soil was arid and unirrigated and most people had to have subsidiary occupations. The subject of the biography had as a result of inheritance and a lifetime of saving built up a fortune worth nearly 25,000 francs (£1,000), invested in a house and 6 hectares. However, he still could not quite afford to live on his land. He spent most of his time in Marseille, in a soap factory, where he was lodged free and where he had risen to be a charge hand. Only two-thirds of his land was worked to provide food for the family. His wife ran the farm and some of his eight children helped but the work was mainly done by a labourer they employed. It was the man's intention to retire soon and work the land himself. (His father had also been a soapmaker-peasant like him, who had saved enough to go back to the land

¹ F. Le Play, *Les Ouvriers européens* (2nd edition 1877–9), 4. 445 ff.

at the age of 39; sixteen years later, at the age of 55 he had decided to retire from farming and to divide his land among his four children, on condition that they each paid him a pension.) Our man had thus begun with one and a half hectares, plus a quarter of a house. While he lived in the soap factory, he sent his wife back to the village, to live in this quarter of a house and to work as a dressmaker (which their daughter did too, as soon as she was old enough). With their combined savings they were able to buy up the whole of the house and farm from his three siblings, for between them they had a cash annual income of some 2,000 francs (£80). In addition the daughter had saved up a trousseau worth 900 francs (including ten dresses and twenty pairs of stockings). They had a dressmaker's workshop, a kitchen of 20 square metres, and two bedrooms, five beds (for ten persons), twenty-five chairs, a variety of tables and dresses, three religious statues, four pious pictures, three prayer books, two books of French grammar, one book of old pious legends, one catechism. He had two Sunday suits, three pairs of work trousers, four coloured flannel waistcoats and one woollen one, six calico shirts, three ties, three pairs of stockings, three pairs of shoes, two pairs of underpants, two aprons, two grey felt hats and one cap. His wife's clothing included three cotton dresses, eighteen blouses, three jackets, six skirts, six kerchiefs, six pairs of stockings, two pairs of shoes, two corsets, three aprons, eight bonnets and one large brimmed black felt hat. He and his wife spoke Provençal for they knew little French, though their children knew it well. They were all piously Catholic.[1]

That there was often no clear distinction between a peasant and a worker can be seen from the history of a certain Victor living at Blaumont (Marne) between Reims and Chalons. Born of poor parents in the Vosges, he started life by emigrating to the Champagne, as a pedlar of haberdashery, but falling ill, he lost the little he possessed, and so for ten years he was a wandering labourer, seldom staying in the same job for more than a few months, and developing habits which led to frequent dismissals. He seduced a girl of 16, who had served an apprenticeship as a dressmaker and who came from a rather better

[1] A. Focillon, Monograph (Feb. 1859), in Le Play, Les Ouvriers européens (2nd edition 1877), 4. 390 ff.

family, of proprietors and gardeners. When a child was born, they married against her father's wishes, but he was unable to support her, so she went back with her child to her parents, while he continued to wander about in search of work. He was heavily in debt and nearly always drunk. His wife persuaded her father to help him settle. At this time, in the early 1840s, a canal was being built in the district. They decided to set up a hostel for the navvies. Her father lent them some money to get a house. The prospect of being able to buy the house stimulated Victor to hard work: they soon repaid the loan, became owners of the house, and by 1854 had also bought a garden and a field. This land required only a few days to till, so he continued to be a labourer, in agriculture in the autumn, and in road mending in the spring; having established a reputation as a good worker, he could find employment easily, despite his insolence when drunk. Access to common rights played a great part in his ascent. The village wasteland could be used only by sheep, so only the rich could profit from it. But the highways were open to all, and from the ditches beside them his wife collected grass for her rabbits. Their ultimate ambition was to buy a cow, which could be brought here to pasture or scavenge more profitably. Meanwhile they built their fortune on the collection of manure from the highway. The wife got up early in the morning to get the dung left by the carthorses on the main road from Chalons to Reims and by hard work she could collect a cubic metre in a week, which could be sold for $5\frac{1}{2}$ francs. In 1847, in the economic crisis, when the canal building stopped and the family had no other resource, it lived off this manure collecting. Even when they were better off, they still collected a cubic metre each month, but they used it on the garden and field: the younger daughter, aged 13, was in charge of this task. When the biography was written this family owned 360 ares (36,000 square metres) worth 1,220 francs. They had fifteen rabbits (eight of which they sold each year, and ate five themselves), one pig, which they bought in the spring and killed off in December. Their house had an earthen floor, and all their furniture and clothes were valued at only 779 francs. This Victor nevertheless knew how to take life philosophically. His two recreations were tobacco and the cabaret, on which he spent 36 francs and 26 francs respectively a year, out of a total expenditure of a thousand francs. This enabled him sometimes to spend whole days playing cards and drinking, though his increasing pride in his house and garden was now keeping him at home more. The narrow margin of his pleasures, however, can be seen from the fact that he had decided to destroy his dog when the law of 1855 imposed a tax of a few francs on dogs.[1] He could not recall this loss without deep emotion.[2]

Before the Revolution the most common form of tenancy was sharecropping, *métayage*. In 1760 it was estimated that four-sevenths of France was cultivated by sharecroppers; and in the 1830s still the proportion was believed to be between a half and a third. However, rent tenancy quickly replaced it in the course of the nineteenth century. In 1862 there were only about 400,000 sharecroppers (as against a million tenant farmers); in 1882 they were down to 320,000 and in 1929 to 200,000. Nevertheless their presence continued to be felt more than these figures suggest because they were concentrated in certain regions, notably the centre and south-west. The poverty to be found there was thus accentuated by a particularly old-fashioned, and frequently oppressive, form of tenure. The department of Gers had thirteen times more sharecroppers than tenant farmers, and twenty-one other departments had more of the former than the latter (in 1892): there were virtually none in the north and east. No generalisation is possible about what sharecropping implied in detail, because it differed so much from place to place, being based on ancient local customs. In 1913 the average size of a *métairie* was 50 to 60 hectares, but it varied from 2 hectares in the Var to over 100 on average in the Cher. The status of a sharecropper varied according to many criteria. Basically, sharecropping involved a division of the produce of a farm between owner and *métayer*—very frequently on a fifty-fifty basis, but sometimes, as in the Landes, with the *métayer* getting two-thirds or three-quarters. The *métayer* provided the labour; the owner provided the land, and nearly always also the working capital, the cattle, machines and fertilisers, because a *métayer* was essentially poor: if he had

[1] The law of 2 May 1855 required communes to raise a tax of between one and ten francs on dogs in order to pay for their public works. Every dog-owner was required to make a declaration stating the number of dogs he had and 'the purpose for which they are kept'.

[2] F. Le Play, *Les Ouvriers européens* (1877), 5. 323 ff.

capital he would buy land or be a tenant farmer. But in some
richer areas, the *métayer* provided the machines and the other

MAP 2. Tenants and sharecroppers in 1892. Based on Flour de Saint-Genis: *La
Propriéte rurale en France* (1902), 192

capital was supplied equally by both parties. The really important difference between cash tenancy and sharecropping was
that in the direction of the farming the sharecropper had to
follow the detailed instructions of the landowner—though in the

twentieth century this control diminished in some areas. In 1940 in the Limousin, there were still *métayers* who had worked the same land for three centuries—an almost feudal relic—but another characteristic of sharecropping was that the lease was usually verbal and short, so that it was virtually tenancy at will. The owner was in this way assured of getting at least a certain amount of produce, whereas a cash tenant was more liable to fall in debt to him. The owner also had in the *métayer* a kind of retainer: in addition to half the crops, he also frequently required quasi-feudal services (still known as *corvées*) like free carting, or domestic help from the wife.

A *Practical Treatise on Sharecropping* of 1882 said: 'The first duty of a *métayer* is to obey.'[1] Between 1880 and 1914 there was an aristocratic revival of sharecropping, which was praised as the ideal form of co-operation between capital and labour and the best way to ensure the moralising of the peasantry and the preservation of the authority of the upper classes: the number of *métayers* increased significantly between the 1882 and the 1892 censuses. Quite a lot of books have been written in praise of sharecropping, urging wider adoption of it, as a solution for social conflicts. The agronomist Gasparin even claimed that the egalitarian spirit of the French was in part due to the long existence of sharecropping. The system did indeed often give an industrious but penniless labourer the opportunity to have his own farm, to enjoy a certain amount of independence in his working habits, even to employ others sometimes, and conceivably also to save enough to buy a small plot of his own. In practice, however, the *métayer* was usually too poor to do justice to the land, and the owner too mean to spend on improving it, since he had to bear the whole cost of improvements but received back only half the profits. The progressive farmers of the north condemned the system as an 'association, on poor land, of slow work and timid capital'.

There were areas where *métayers* were submissive or respectful, though more recently the paternalism has increasingly died out. But in other areas sharecropping was the source of fierce antagonism which in 1908 even erupted into a revolt in the Bourbonnais, where the system was exacerbated by the owners using hated intermediaries—*fermiers-généraux*—to manage their

[1] A. de Tourdonnet, *Traité pratique du métayage* (1882), 207.

estates for them. The tensions and the human side of the system were poignantly described by a *métayer* of this region, Emile Guillaumin, in his *Life of a Simple Man* (1904). This masterpiece of peasant literature tells the story, clearly based on personal experience, of a sharecropper born in 1823, and the son of a sharecropper too. He had begun life as a goatherd at seven years of age, when he was punished if he came back with his charges earlier than eight or nine in the evening. At nine years he was promoted to look after the pigs; on fair days he would have the privilege of accompanying his father to the local town to sell them, but he would have to wait in the cold with them while his father went to a tavern to get drunk. Until the age of seventeen, he never possessed even the smallest coin of money. His first real contact with the outside world was military service. Every mother tried to save the 500 francs which could insure her child against call up (the insurer providing a substitute, as was still possible then). The mother of Tiennon (the hero of this book) managed to do this for her two eldest sons, but she had seven children and could not for him. Feeling that his parents had let him down, he left home and became a labourer. To go into the service of others, rather than helping one's father, was something of a betrayal, a rebellion, when it was not forced by need. Still, he went to the local fair with an ear of corn in his hat, and he was hired for a wage of 90 francs a year. But he was a labourer by his own free will, and he felt he could not marry an ordinary servant girl; he preferred to be bold and propose to a girl who had a dowry of 300 francs, and he was accepted when he obtained the same sum from his own father to balance it. After a few years more as a labourer, his father-in-law found him a *métairie* and he was able to enjoy the independence of his own farm, though on hard terms. He had to go straight into debt to his landlord to the extent of 1,000 francs, to buy his half share of the cattle, and he was charged 5 per cent interest on this: so he got considerably less than 50 per cent of the produce. He had to be very subservient to his landowner, who could never remember his name, who called him 'Thing', and who said to him 'Obey and work: I ask nothing else of you. And never bother me with requests for repairs: I do none, on principle.' In compensation, the landlord sometimes summoned him to the château and gave him a vast chunk of pork to eat in the kitchen, as a special treat. But Tiennon also had to be subservient to the landlord's manager and the latter's mistress, who pestered his wife with requests for menial services. Pathetic scenes took place which made him exclaim: 'We are still slaves.' He had to work very hard to get a living, sleeping only five or six hours a day, rising at four in the morning. Nevertheless, as 'head of a farm, I felt myself to be something of a king. Responsibility often weighed heavily on me, but I was proud to sit at the head of the table, near the loaf from which I cut large pieces at the beginning of every meal; and proud also to have, in the winter evenings, the chair by the fire, the place of honour.' After twenty years, he was able to repay the 1,000 francs and save 4,000 francs, including what he had inherited from his father-in-law. But he invested it at 5 per cent with a banker, who defaulted. He was back where he had started. Then, when he was fifty-five, his landowner demanded an increase of rent (for he paid a small rent—the *impôt colonique*—as well as sharing his produce). He refused and was given notice. All the effort he had put into improving his farm was wasted. His brother, who had played for higher stakes, and had used his 8,000 francs savings to buy a small farm of his own costing 15,000 francs, had been unable to make his mortgage payments and had also lost all. Old age held out only the prospect of failing health and tense relations with the children who had to support them.

The Revolution and the Civil Code had done very little for the *métayers*. A law of 1889 which purported at last to give them some protection in effect simply perpetuated 'local usages'. Bills to improve their lot were introduced in vain. The Popular Front's efforts (in a bill of 7 July 1937) to produce collective bargaining and a codification of customs were abortive. Their final emancipation came only in 1945 and 1946 when they were given the option of converting their contracts on demand into cash tenancies, so that in 1955 there were only 72,000 *métayers* left.[1] At the same time cash tenants were given first option to buy their farms if the landlord wished to sell; in

[1] L. Durousseau-Dugontier, *L'Évolution du métayage en France* (Poitiers thesis, Tulle, 1905), Pierre Laborderie-Boulou, *Le Métayage, particulièrement en Périgord* (Bordeaux thesis, 1905); P. Rouveroux, *Le Métayage* (1934); J. Dudez, *Le Métayage* (Bordeaux thesis, 1938), G. Pirou, *Traité d'économie politique*, vol. 1, part 2 (1941), 104–12.

any case they could not be evicted, since they were also given the right to renew their tenancies. A new age therefore started in 1945, when it was no longer the man who owned the land, but he who cultivated it, who became its effective master.

The wine-growing peasants were a very special case, economically and socially distinct, and with a reputation for having a different kind of mentality. Their history may help to explain this. Before the eighteenth century wine drinking was not a popular activity; and the wine produced till then was of a different kind. Until the sixteenth century indeed inns were forbidden to sell wine to locals: they provided it only to travellers. Peasants seldom drank wine, which was reserved for the bourgeoisie; at most they could hope for *piquette* (produced by running water over the residue left after the wine is made). Wine was generally produced by the upper classes for their own consumption, and that is why so many of the vineyards belonged to the nobility, to the Church and increasingly to the manufacturers and merchants of Bordeaux, Lyon and Dijon, and why the major wine areas are near important towns. The Parisian region was once a major wine-producing region; only around 1850–60 were the remnants of the vines there finally replaced by vegetables. However, in the course of the eighteenth century, the workers in the growing towns began demanding wine, and so a new kind of production developed to cater for their tastes. This was cheap wine, known as *gamay* as opposed to the fine *pinot*; its characteristic was that its yield was high, even if its quality was poor; and the people who produced it were the peasants who were gradually buying up the land in tiny bits from the upper classes. The first conflict of the wine-growing peasants was with the bourgeoisie and with the Church, whose lands they coveted and who, because of their resources, were able to produce a superior kind of wine, selling at a much higher price. Later, at the end of the nineteenth century, the peasants' main enemy were the mass-producing capitalists of the south, who beat the peasants at their own game by churning out vast quantities of *vin ordinaire* far more cheaply than any small peasant could. The winegrowers therefore had good grounds for being at war with the rich.

But, secondly, they also had a long tradition of conflict with

the state and the municipal authorities, because these had
replied to this new kind of catering for the poor drinker of the
towns by imposing increasingly heavy taxes on wines. Cheap
wine sometimes had to pay twice its value in tax by the end
of the *ancien régime*. This became a burning issue between the
masses and the government. So in 1791 the duties paid on wine
entering the towns were abolished; but the loss of revenue was
such that they were re-established in 1798 under the name of
octroi. Town workers used to go to the suburbs outside Paris to
escape it, and incredibly large numbers of wine shops sprouted
in this desolate area. In the nineteenth century, the winegrower
therefore continued to feel himself victimised by government
taxation; he was at war with the civil service which collected
it; and in very many cases he became a smuggler. Of course,
different regions produced different situations: the Beaujolais
region for example could afford to expand its production of
cheap wine because it had the right to send its wines to Lyon
cheaply; Mâcon by contrast had to pay tariffs four times
higher and so found it necessary to specialise in fine wines; and
again Orléans produced vinegar rather than fine wines not
because of the nature of its soil but because the latter were
destroyed by government policy. The result of this heavy taxation was that cheap wine did not cost very much less than good
wine: the peasants who produced it therefore concentrated on
quantity rather than quality, often harvesting three times as
many grapes from their land, and selling these at half the price
of the high-class vineyards. It was on this basis that they prospered, and it was under this pressure that skilled wine making
suffered in the nineteenth century. By 1875, good wine was
thus in a state of crisis. Fraud and competition made public
sales difficult and the best wine production came to be concentrated in the private bourgeois châteaux.

The area devoted to wine growing continued to increase
throughout the Second Empire. The railways opened up wide
markets; the 1860 treaty facilitated exports. Wine became one
of the major speculations of the period (indeed one of its major
industries, for it came second only to textiles): all classes invested
in it, from the small peasant to the stockbroker (like, e.g.,
Gaston Bazille, father of the impressionist); industrialists even
closed their factories and bought vineyards instead. Then, at

the height of this prosperity the phylloxera disease struck, with catastrophic results. Nearly all the vineyards had to be up-rooted. It required vast capital, as much as 5,000 francs a hectare, to replant with American roots and then a good deal of experiment, since the earliest grafts produced a wine with a 'foxy' smell (the English word was used, *vins foxés*). The distribution of wine growing was altered: several northern areas almost gave it up; but the south on the other hand greatly expanded its acreage. It planted new vines with high yields, suitable for mass production; and it also transformed the pattern of ownership, for here large capitalists moved in. While production was low, prices remained high, so the induce-ment to replant was strong. However, no sooner had the re-establishment of the vines been effected, than over-production occurred, and this has remained the chronic problem of the winegrowers ever since. It is true that the consumption of wine in France increased from 51 litres a head in 1848 to 77 litres in 1872 to 103 litres in 1904 and 136 litres in 1926. But during the phylloxera crisis the government had en-couraged Algeria to plant vines, and it had allowed Spanish and Italian imports. In addition fraudulent wine had flooded the market to the extent of about 40 per cent of the genuine product, as was revealed by the tripling of the amount of sugar used by the winemakers. It was in these years too that the vine-yards of California and South America expanded. Between 1870 and 1900, also, beet-alcohol production rose threefold. The winemakers emerged from their crisis into a very competitive world. There was so much wine, it hardly ever paid. Five disastrous years out of seven in 1900–7 brought the south not only to near bankruptcy, but actually to revolt. Parliament hastily passed ineffective laws, but the situation was finally saved by higher prices after 1912, and then by enormous pro-fiteering during the war. The peasants used their new-found wealth to pay off their debts, and favourable harvests from 1920 to 1929 restored their prosperity. But then once again over-production brought prices tumbling down and the 1930s were among the worst years the winegrowers had experienced. The Algerians, expecting a law to be passed to limit their produc-tion, increased their vineyards from 221,000 hectares in 1928 to 400,000 in 1935. There followed a remarkable revolution of a new kind. In 1907 the winegrowers had simply demanded that the government should find some solution to their problem: they themselves had none to offer; but in the 1930s they harnessed the power of the government to enforce a unique state control on their industry. Law after law was introduced to limit production, to forbid new planting, to offer tax abatements to those who destroyed their vineyards and to arrange for the buying up of surplus crops and their transformation into alcohol. The winegrowers made the nation subsidise them. The peculiarity of these laws was that they were a triumph for the small peasant: the controls were directed above all at the capitalist mass-producers. However, they were not effective in the long term. The 1939–45 war again brought profits; it was followed by a further period of overproduction, and in 1953 there was further legislation. But because of the vast electoral power of the peasant winegrowers, no fundamental transformation of land use was possible. From the rational economic point of view, what was needed was not a freezing of productivity, but the allocation of the land to those crops best suited to it and most in demand. Wine should be sent back to the hills where nothing else would grow, but where it flourished, and the plains should be used for the production of meat and milk. But there were too many emotional satisfactions and too many interests involved.

The world of wine was torn between the producers of quality and the producers of quantity, between the capitalists who treated their investment as they would any industry, and the peasants for whom winegrowing was a way of life, between the specialised small owner, the polycultural amateur, and the labourer who worked on someone else's large farm. The struggles between them had an element of tragedy, because the mass of small winegrowers were essentially gamblers, who lost much more often than they won. Some studies of individual budgets have shown how their lives were a series of hopes deceived and of accumulated debts, but with the occasional marvellous harvest which cancelled it all out and allowed them to start again. The small peasant seldom made a good living from his vines. This is partly why he had a reputation as a Red. The winegrowers certainly often voted left wing. But their opposition to the state, the tax official, the capitalist, the favoured owners of the fine brands, the wholesale merchant and the usurers, did not take them beyond radicalism: their ideal was very definitely property and independence, by individual effort. The workers might vote socialist or communist on the large estates, but the small owners had reservations. When they surrendered part of their independence to form co-operatives, as they had to, it was in the spirit of solidarity and mutuality, not of co-operative labour. Each still tilled his own plot, though the co-operative could exercise great influence on the kind of grapes that were grown and when they were harvested. The radicalism of these small winegrowers involved independence in another way too. They were not genuine peasants. They lived almost in an urban culture, in villages of a thousand or more. They had very little to do in the early summer; they could almost have holidays in July, August and October too. They frequently visited the near-by towns which the wine merchants made prosperous and whose entertainment and shopping they enjoyed. They dressed differently from the peasant immediately after work, particularly the young ones, who habitually went out in the village in the evenings. Except in winter, the men, both young and old, met in the village square to chat while waiting for their evening meal, playing different versions of bowls, or sitting on the terraces of the cafés. The married women and spinsters spent long hours sitting on chairs outside their houses, gossiping interminably. On Sunday afternoons, there were balls for the young. This active social life put a premium on discussion. These men developed a taste for general ideas. They were seldom pious, but they loved the feasts of the Church and celebrated baptisms and communions with vigour. But they were far from prosperous. Their standard of living was below the average for their class. Not only socially, but economically also, wine growing stood between agriculture and industry. In the south, it was often an alternative to industry. Until the 1930s, wine growing had as important an influence on density of population as industry. Apart from Brittany, all areas with over seventy inhabitants per square kilometre were either industrial or winegrowing: the vineyards of the Bordelais and Languedoc could compare with the textile regions of the Vosges and Caux. Textiles and viticulture had in fact been alternative supplements for rural areas which agriculture did not keep fully busy. That part of France which did not produce wine had domestic looms instead. When the peasants on the borderline found it unprofitable to make wine, they turned to lace making, which as it were marked the frontier.[1]

At the bottom of the peasants' social scale were the labourers: nearly 3 million of them in 1848, $2\frac{1}{2}$ million in 1892, $1\frac{1}{2}$ million in 1929, 1 million in 1946. This was the group on which the socialists and particularly the communists placed great hopes for new recruits, but with little success. Their wages, it is true, were probably even lower than those of town workers, particularly when seasonal unemployment is taken into consideration. They might find lodgings more cheaply, but these again were often worse in quality than the town slums about which the pious reformers were so indignant. They frequently had to supplement their earnings with domestic industries, which were among the worst paid in the country. However, there was little possibility of organising them nationally. Many of them worked isolated on farms where they might be the only labourer employed. Their standard of living was low, but in some areas not much lower than that of their employers. For a good many, being a labourer was only a stage in life, from which they hoped to escape, either to proprietorship or to the towns. Even this class was highly varied. Just before the Second World War, those in the Vienne, Cher, Saône-et-Loire were receiving wages almost twice as high as those in Dordogne and Lot-et-Garonne, for example. Their conditions of employment and lodging varied enormously. In the 1950s, when sociologists interrogated them about their ambitions, it emerged that they very often did not consider themselves part of the working class even when they migrated to the towns; for many their ultimate goal was to set themselves up independently on their own.[2]

[1] Roger Dion, *Histoire de la vigne et du vin en France des origines au 19ᵉ siècle* (1959), a massive, masterly study; Armand Perrin, *La Civilisation de la vigne* (1938); Robert Laurent, *Les Vignerons de la Côte d'Or au 19ᵉ siècle* (1957), an excellent thesis; Gaston Galtier, *Le Vignoble du Languedoc méditerranéen et du Roussillon. Étude comparative d'un vignoble de masse* (Montepellier, 1960, 3 vols.), full of interesting information; C. K. Warner, *The Winegrowers of France and the Government since 1875* (New York, 1960), valuable for the legislative side; for a comprehensive early survey, Dr. J. Guyot, *Études des vignobles de France* (1868, 3 vols.); for biographical monographs, Paul Descamps, *La Science sociale* (June 1907), and *Les Ouvriers des deux mondes*, 2nd series, vol. 3, no. 166.

[2] Françoise Langlois, *Les Salariés agricoles en France* (1962), 9, and annexe XI;

The Duping of the Peasants

Thus the peasants cannot be regarded as the solid ballast that kept France stable over these hundred years. They were, as has been seen, too much in a state of turmoil and internal rivalry. Their conflicts were no less absorbing to them because they did not fit simply into a clash of capitalist–worker, and because the peasants' ambitions, in seeking land, were seldom to rise into the bourgeoisie. But the conflicts were all the more frantic because they took place at a time when the society they knew was collapsing. It was shaken and indeed transformed by what was the peasant counterpart to the industrial strike, but without leaders and without dramatic incidents. It manifested itself silently, in millions of individual peasants leaving the land and migrating to the towns. This could have enriched the peasants who remained; it could have transformed agriculture into an efficient industry unburdened by an excessive, tradition-bound labour force; but in effect, in these years, it only served to reveal that agriculture was no longer the backbone of the country. Those who remained were deserted, not liberated. Rural depopulation became a neurotic worry instead of a sign of increasing opportunity.

During the Second Empire the countryside was inhabited more densely than it had ever been, and in certain regions to a degree which was unequalled in Western Europe. When the population fell, this fact was ignored; the abnormality of the position in 1850 was forgotten and only the vast number leaving the land was noticed. At the same time, the total population of France ceased to increase so that the losses from the land were not made good by a higher birth-rate. The proportion of the nation engaged in agriculture fell from 61 per cent in 1851 to 53 per cent in 1861 to 45 per cent in 1891 and 32·5 per cent in 1931–46. This drastic drop still left France with far more peasants than most other western countries: in 1939 Britain had only 5·7 per cent, Belgium 17 per cent, Germany 29 per cent.[1] The rural depopulation continued rapidly after the Second

A. Souchon, *La Crise de la main d' œuvre agricole en France* (1914); Alain Touraine, 'Les Ouvriers d'origine agricole', in *Sociologie du travail* (July–Sept. 1960), 230–45.

[1] These international statistics, not always fully comparable, are quoted in P. L. Yates, *Food Production in Western Europe* (1940), 19.

World War: the agricultural population fell between 1946 and 1960 from 32·5 per cent to 20 per cent.[1]

The emigration was of different kinds. In the nineteenth century it appears to have taken place with particular rapidity at certain periods: in 1861–5, when about 650,000 people left the land, in 1875–81, when the most intense emigration ever recorded took place with 840,000 people leaving, and in 1896–1901 when another 650,000 left. Each of these waves was a response to a particular crisis, but they were all largely migrations of poverty, of people who were marginal to rural society, or for whom the countryside could find no room. Previously some of those who could not earn a living off the land became rural artisans, or labourers, but these jobs were vanishing under pressure from industry, from the crisis in agriculture, and because the leasing or partition of commons made it more difficult to survive in the traditional ways. In the twentieth century this kind of massive departure occurred only once again, in 1936–8 when perhaps a third of a million people left the land after the urban workers won their important advantages under the Popular Front. However, for the rest of this century the emigration seems to have been steadier, with roughly the same numbers leaving each year in a regular trickle. Now, moreover, the departures were less of the poorest inhabitants as of the young and the adventurous, positively seeking a better life. Whereas before 1914 migrants usually went to the local small towns and reached the cities only over several generations, now they moved directly to the cities. After 1945 there were again new forms of migration, so it is not possible to describe this movement with blanket generalisations. Individual villages responded to the challenges with extraordinary variety; some showed great adaptability while others collapsed with traumatic rapidity.[2] There is need for more investigation of these unspoken disputes and ambitions, asking the sort of questions that modern social psychologists can pose. In one study of Brittany in the 1950s, it was found that 42 per cent of those who migrated in that

[1] P. Barral, *Les Agrariens français de Méline à Pisani* (1968), 19, 217, has useful tables.

[2] P. Clement and P. Vieille, 'L'Exode rurale', in *Études de comptabilité nationale* published by the Ministry of Finance (Apr. 1960), 57–130, which includes a full bibliography on this subject; P. Pinchemel, *Structures agraires et dépopulation rurale dans les campagnes picardes de 1836 à 1936* (1957).

period had made their decision to do so, or at least had considered it, before the age of 14, and another 35 per cent between the ages of 14 and 17. This suggests, for migration of this particular kind, a class of peasants who knew from an early age that there was no room for them on the land. It was not necessarily frustrated or unsuccessful people who went to the towns; perhaps often the middle ranks did so most, because the ablest children, if they were not drawn away by scholarships, could generally find a place in their local society and the most stupid could not move.[1]

The landless naturally had most inducement to leave. The land was drained of labourers, with catastrophic results particularly for the small bourgeois farmers so prevalent, for example, in the south-west. They could retaliate by importing Spaniards, Italians, Poles or other foreigners, which transformed rural society in one way. Or they might be forced to abandon farming, letting out their land and using their houses as summer holiday houses, while seeking careers in the cities; and rural society was transformed in another way.[2] The social structure of the countryside was simplified. Though modern communications did bring the peasant closer to the towns in some respects, they also had the effect of isolating him from them even more in other respects, by drawing the non-agricultural professions to the towns. The nation was thus divided more sharply into those who tilled the soil and those who drew their incomes from the city. The decline of domestic industries meant that the peasant became more of a specialist. He was no longer additionally an artisan in winter, or a building worker in slack periods.

The peasant world was almost constantly in crisis throughout these hundred years and in some very fundamental ways. It should not be forgotten that the trials of 1846–50 were among the most severe that European agriculture had ever experienced. The prosperity of the Second Empire attracted even more people into landownership but increased production was not matched by increased efficiency. Prosperity did not mean that agriculture increased its share of the national income: on the contrary in 1890 the 45 per cent of the population which was in

[1] André Levesque, *Le Problème psychologique des migrations rurales* (1958), 186.
[2] Dr. A. Labat, *L' Âme paysanne* (1939).

it drew only between 30 and 35 per cent of the national income.[1]
Improved communications opened new markets but also made
possible the competition of American, Balkan and Russian
wheat; they stimulated production but they also brought about
catastrophic falls in prices. The price of wheat fell by one-third
in the 1880s and 1890s, as compared with the Second Empire.
The price of land, which, taking 1821 as 100, had risen to 255
in 1851, 366 in 1879, fell to 279 in 1894. The phylloxera crisis
wiped out another of the cash crops on which many farmers
depended: in 1875 a record 84 million hectolitres of wine were
produced, but in 1879 only 25 million, and it was fifteen years
before production exceeded even half the high figure of 1875.
Prices rose because of the shortage, but the total income from
wine was still less than half that earned under the Second
Empire. Moreover, it required enormous capital to replant with
new roots.[2]

The answer of the government was to introduce protection,
as early as 1881, which was gradually widened and finally
consolidated in Meline's tariff law of 1892. This had three
results. First, 'agriculture was saved', as the supporters of protection put it. That is to say, agriculture was able to go on much
as before, to preserve subsistence and unspecialised methods
and to keep a higher proportion of labour on the land than
would otherwise have been possible. France was able to remain
a land of peasants. Agricultural prices did fall, but not as much
as in other countries, England for example. By the turn of the
century they were back to remunerative levels, the crisis was
over, and in the years just before the 1914 war they even
reached new peaks. So protection appeared to be justified; and
it was preserved as a basic creed of the republic. The level of
tariffs on foodstuffs in France was the highest in Western Europe,
about 29 per cent, equalled only by Austria–Hungary, compared to 22 per cent in Italy and Germany, 15 per cent in
Switzerland and 24 per cent in Sweden.[3]

A second effect of protection, however, was to save the
peasants from the need to modernise. A crucial sixty years were

[1] Cf. M. Latil, L'Évolution du revenu agricole (1954), 10–40.

[2] Cf. P. Caziot, La Valeur de la terre en France (1914), 7–9; D. Zolla, La Crise
agricole (1904).

[3] M. Tracy, Agriculture in Western Europe, Crisis and Adaptation since 1880 (1964),
31; H. Liepmann, Tariff Levels (1938), 413.

allowed to pass in which the problem of adapting them to industrial society was purposely neglected. That is why, when the issue was at last faced after 1950, it produced such violent reactions and why a 'peasant revolution' took place in the 1960s. As Méline saw it, protection should be part of a more general agricultural programme, in which increased capital investment and improved technical education should increase profitability. He passed laws to encourage agricultural credit societies, on mutualist lines, and in 1897 gave them state backing; but these remained small and never developed into a significant factor in the economy. As late as 1883, an inquiry revealed that a sizeable minority of members of agricultural societies believed that 'borrowing at whatever interest is disastrous for the farmer and the small peasant: in 80 per cent of cases, it leads to ruin . . . It is less important to give loans than to show how to do without them.'[1] Technical education was likewise spurned, as being too theoretical. Colleges were established but were allowed to wallow in penury. The National Agronomic Institute, founded in 1848, abolished by Napoleon III, was re-established by the Third Republic, but it produced only 26 graduates in 1876 and 87 in 1913. About 80 other colleges of a lower level were founded, and some 250 peripatetic professors were sent out to teach new methods. But this was a tiny force with which to tackle the problem of peasant ignorance, and it reached about 1 per cent of the agricultural population. The primary schools were the only places where the peasants did receive education, but these were generally run by schoolmasters who believed that the aim of the bright boy should be to escape from the land. What was missing was an intermediate college, where practical training could be provided, and this gap was not filled in these years.[2]

Instead, and this was the third consequence of protection, the peasants were encouraged to believe that it was to the state that they should turn to improve their lot. They were not unique in this, but they were perhaps unique in the way they got the state to believe also that they were particularly deserving of state aid. They succeeded in obtaining very significant

[1] Société Nationale d'Agriculture de France, *Enquête sur le crédit agricole* (1884), 1. 315, 319, quoted by P. Barral, 90.
[2] R. Chatelain, *L'Agriculture française et la formation professionnelle* (1953).

exemptions from taxation. In the 1890s a remarkable campaign for lower taxes on peasants, which a newspaper, *La Démocratie rurale*, organised and for which it collected a million signatures, was successful in winning important concessions. The peasants grew used to the idea that they should be subsidised by the rest of the nation. By 1963, seven-eighths of them paid no income tax; the state was devoting about 10 per cent of its budget to subsidising them; and the whole of Europe indeed contributed financially to maintaining their inefficiency.[1] But they were of course duped. The state got its own back by skimping on the services it provided for them, as will be seen. The peasants thought they were succeeding in preserving their independence, in being left alone, but they were in fact left behind. The paradox of the peasants' position in France is that they were idealised, subsidised and even feared as a great electoral force, but all the same they were unable to use their power, and they remained among the poorest people in the country.[2]

There were areas, however, where the peasants did seize the opportunities presented by the changing demands on agriculture. Farming in different areas developed very differently in the course of these hundred years. One can see this most strikingly if one compares Brittany with the region of the Garonne.[3] Around 1848, the Garonne was a reasonably prosperous agricultural region while Brittany was one of the poorest. The Garonne cultivated 68 per cent of its land, while Brittany cultivated only 57 per cent and allowed almost a third to lie waste. The Garonne derived its prosperity from its highly marketable wheat (to which it devoted twice as much land as Brittany), from its good quality wine and from its maize, with which it could feed a vast flock of poultry. Brittany by contrast was backward, isolated, its land lacking in lime and phosphate, so that enormous areas had to be left fallow for 40 to 60 years to enable them to recover from agriculture. Its inhabitants lived in primitive squalor, while those of the Garonne enjoyed a high standard of living, with white bread and wine. However,

[1] Daniel Chabanol, *Le Paysan, prolétaire ou P.G.D.* (1969), 11.

[2] M. Augé-Laribé, *La Politique agricole de la France de 1880 à 1940* (1950).

[3] Brittany: Côtes-du-Nord, Finistère, Ille-et-Vilaine, Morbihan, Loire-Inférieure. Garonne: Haute-Garonne, Gers, Lot, Tarn-et-Garonne, Lot-et-Garonne, Dordogne.

the changes of these hundred years completely altered this picture. By 1939 their positions were almost reversed. Production fell in the Garonne and rose dramatically in Brittany. The area of cultivated land in the Garonne fell to 65 per cent, while that of Brittany rose to 74 per cent. The wastelands of Brittany were brought under the plough and fertilised; its agricultural territory increased by one third, half of which was added to arable but half to pasture, for Brittany turned to the production of meat and milk for which there was an increasingly profitable market. The Garonne's concentration on wheat was disastrous, both because it exhausted the land and because the great depression hit hardest in the south-west. Wheat ceased to be profitable in small-scale farming. In addition the vineyards, destroyed by phylloxera, were reconstituted in great haste with plants of a quality inferior to that previously used but with much higher yields, for these new plants flourished particularly well in the liberally irrigated plains of the Garonne. The acreage devoted to vines fell by almost a half, but the total production was kept constant. However, in this production of *vin ordinaire* the south was able to beat it with even higher yields. In 1882 the Garonne produced 16 per cent of France's wine, and the south 28 per cent. By 1930–9, however, it was producing only 9 per cent and the south 51 per cent, for southern wine was always cheap, whereas Garonne wine was neither particularly cheap nor, any longer, good, and its yield was only 24 hectolitres per hectare compared with the south's 50 hectolitres per hectare. The Garonne made the mistake, that is, of not following the Loire valley, which reconstituted its vineyards with the distinctive Muscadet, capable of finding a good market. Brittany's wine production meanwhile doubled, its cider production tripled. In the production of food for the towns, Brittany's pastures were well placed, but the Garonne's vegetables and fruit had to compete with the climatically more favoured south and Algeria. Another of the traditional occupations of the Garonne, sheep farming, likewise ceased to be profitable with cheaper importation from abroad, and of its flock of over 2 million sheep in 1840 only 600,000 remained in 1939. The Garonne had naturally good communications but in addition it had early been favoured with roads and canals, of which it had twice as much as Brittany. By 1939, however, Brittany was no longer impenetrable: it had three times as much railway as the Garonne and five-sixths as much road. As a result, the population of the Garonne fell by 24 per cent, while that of Brittany rose by 14 per cent (1841–1936).[1]

The British or American tourist, disembarking at Cherbourg, nowadays sees a region totally different in appearance from what it was a hundred years ago. He may see the ruins of great barns, relics of the days when wheat was grown, and of cottages for labourers, who have likewise vanished. The region is now devoted to pasture, to the extent of as much as 95 per cent in the Cotentin, but there was practically no pasture in the time of Napoleon I. The land was then given over to buckwheat (the principal food of the people), wheat (their principal market product), rye, oats, barley and fallow. But between 1830 and 1930 the price of a cow increased sixfold, that of milk threefold. Wheat on the other hand became a little cheaper. Formerly the porous lands which were easy to cultivate, and on which roads could be built, were the really valuable ones. Now it is the heavy lands, turned over to pasture, and penetrated by the railways, which are most sought after. What was once a poor region is now one of the most profitable in France.[2]

The transformations which have occurred can be seen in more intimate detail by looking at the history of the village of Morette, in the Dauphiné, which happens to have been written by one of its inhabitants. After escaping to get higher education, the author decided to go back to the land. He shows how in 1806 his village had 398 inhabitants (in 81 families). In 1851 it had 528 and this was the highest ever. By 1901 the figure was down again to 402, by 1911 it was 326, by 1922, 232. It remained around this figure for the inter-war years; in 1946 it was down to 204. This decline was due principally to emigration, but also to a fall in the birthrate due to the ageing of the population. It is manifested physically in the ruins of abandoned farmhouses, undulating fields which had clearly once grown vines, and dis-

[1] Jean Chombart de Lauwe, *Bretagne et pays de la Garonne: évolution agricole comparée depuis un siècle* (1946). A. Armengaud, 'De quelques idées fausses concernant le pays de la Garonne vers 1840', *Revue d'histoire moderne et contemporaine* (Jan.–Mar. 1960), shows that the sharper contrast presented by Chombart de Lauwe needs to be toned down.

[2] Cf. Charles Vezin, *L'Évolution de l'agriculture de la Manche en un siècle, 1830–1930* (Paris thesis, printed at Saint-Lô, 1931).

used reservoirs in which hemp had once been steeped. The 113
hectares of arable land in 1827 were increased to 132 by 1862,
but by 1935 they were down to 45. The vines which covered
220 hectares in 1827 and 205 in 1862 were down to 65 hectares
in 1935. Undistinguished, they could not compete with the
cheaper products of the south, but a specialised crop like wal-
nuts had become highly profitable and 61 hectares were now
planted with it: and the return on this was four or five times
greater than that on wine or wheat. The pasture had risen from
35 hectares in 1862 to 216 in 1935; the 96 oxen of 1862 had
almost completely vanished, and had been replaced by cows.
Not only was the face of the countryside transformed, but also
the type of inhabitant. In 1851 the village had 1 lace maker,
2 wheelwrights, 2 tailors, 2 farriers, 1 clog maker, 1 hemp
comber, 3 weavers and 9 other textile workers, 7 carpenters,
1 mason, 6 sawyers, 3 drapers and 1 pork butcher. By 1896,
however, there were only 5 artisans left: a cobbler, a wheel-
wright, a dressmaker, a carpenter and a mason. After 1914 this
number was reduced to simply the mason and the carpenter
and they were absent from the village all day, since they found
their work largely outside it. The few small grocery shops fared
better; they survived because they were often part-time
occupations, run by wives, and now the motor car allowed
them to deliver over a larger area.

The old isolation was over. In 1848 the village had been
almost completely self-sufficient. The peasants built their
houses themselves out of wattle and daub, from local clay and
timber brought from the local woods. They clothed themselves
without spending any money: the weaver made them cloth from
hemp which they gave him and they wore clogs. They fed themselves on their own rye or black bread, cheese, chestnuts,
potatoes, beans and cabbages, pork but hardly ever beef or
lamb. They made their own oil and vinegar, and lit their homes
at night with a special oil they manufactured from nuts. Their
agricultural tools were nearly all wooden. When in 1849 the
municipal council attempted to break out from this isolation and
decided to subscribe to a newspaper for the mayor, the prefect
refused them permission to do it. These physical aspects of the
peasant's life changed soon after. A study of the possessions
of villagers, carried out by the Museum of Popular Arts and

Traditions, on the basis of notaries' inventories drawn up after death, showed that the break came around 1850–60. The furniture of the peasant of 1850 was hardly any different from what it had been in the eighteenth century.[1] By 1914, however, the houses in this village had stone or brick bases and window frames, they had concrete instead of earthen floors, they had plaster on their walls and manufactured tiles on their roofs. They were more spacious, with more furniture; chairs replaced benches. Shoes replaced clogs, clothes were made from varying materials, by tailors. Coffee arrived around 1860, though at first it was taken only on New Year's Day, but in time replaced bread dipped in eau-de-vie as the normal breakfast. In 1860 butcher's meat was not eaten, but it was gradually introduced together with such things as rice, macaroni and sugar. In 1908 the first telephone arrived—a public one, installed at the request of the municipal council; in 1910 the first bicycle was bought and quickly became a popular form of transport. In 1903 the primary-school master got a grant of 25 francs to open a library. His role in the village became increasingly important. He gained ground over the *curé* as people went to church less; an insolent answer by a girl who was refused absolution for refusing to give up dancing became famous and a sort of anticlerical war-cry; and after 1914 the village had no *curé* at all. By 1914 the peasants lived no longer in their village but in a whole region, drawing more and more of their services from outside. The travelling *charcutier* got himself a telephone (the only private person to have one). The peasants met together in 1897 to form a mutual insurance society; in 1914 they affiliated themselves to a trade union specialising in supplying fertilisers at wholesale prices; in 1929 they combined to raise a loan to buy a threshing machine; after 1936 they sold their milk to a firm that came round in a lorry to collect it; the nut growers formed a co-operative to sell their produce at higher prices. The young women followed the Parisian fashions. Newspapers were everywhere, though almost no one in 1939 had yet seen a cinema. The effect of all these changes was to produce peasants who in some ways were more peasant than they had ever been

[1] Suzanne Tardieu, 'L'Équipement de la maison', *Revue de synthèse* (July–Sept. 1957), 347–63. This article draws attention to 14,000 monographic descriptions compiled between 1941 and 1946, still awaiting analysis.

before—working the land and owning more of it, since there
were fewer of them to share it—but they were in other ways
peasants of a new kind. One might try to assess in what ways
their attitudes became really different.[1]

One way to investigate this question is to see what the
peasants did with their savings. A study of their wills and post-
mortem inventories in the Vaucluse shows that by 1938 6 per
cent of them had bank accounts, 13 per cent were members of
co-operatives. In 1900 21 per cent had put some money into
the national savings banks, by 1938 37 per cent of them had;
and this was the most popular kind of investment. Most interesting of all, however, is that in 1900 already 7 per cent of their
wealth was in shares and by 1938 29 per cent of it. Even the
very poorest peasants, who never invested in shares before 1914,
put money into them after the war. The increasingly commercial character of Vaucluse agriculture had drawn the peasants
into the capitalist system.[1]

The degree to which this took place is difficult to measure.
There have been those who have argued that by 1939 the
peasants were split into two groups, those who had adopted
modern methods and produced their goods for the market, and
those who had remained faithful to subsistence farming. This is
a useful half-truth. There is no doubt that the farming of the
northern plains bore little resemblance to the traditional polyculture of the Massif Central. It is useful to be reminded that,
from whatever angle one looks at the peasants, one never sees
a homogeneous group. However, the facts about their attitude
to modernisation require more careful scrutiny. The enormous
variation in the wealth of peasants in different regions in 1848
is well known. Now in the course of the second half of the century these variations were to a certain extent equalised. The
example given, of Brittany and the Garonne, shows how one
formerly desolate province improved dramatically. But though

[1] Joseph Garavel, *Les Paysans de la Morette: un siècle de vie rurale dans une commune du
Dauphiné* (1948). For another interesting village study, see Patrick Higonnet,
Pont-de-Montvert: Social Structure and Politics in a French Village (Cambridge, Mass.,
1971), which contains many stimulating ideas.

[2] Claude Mesliand, 'La Fortune paysanne dans le Vaucluse, 1900–1938',
Annales (1967), 88–136. It should be stressed that this region was exceptionally
commercial, and peasant investments would probably be different in the Centre of
France for example.

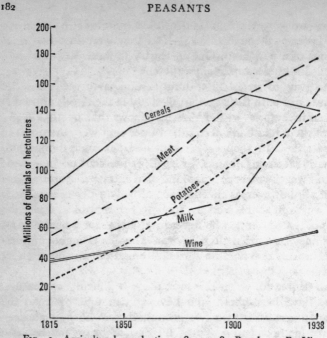

FIG. 1. Agricultural production 1815–1938. Based on P. Viau:
L'Agriculture dans l'économie (1967), 29

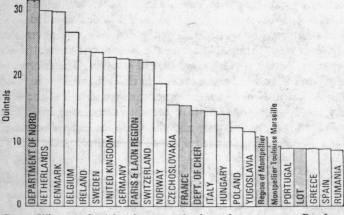

FIG. 2. Wheat productivity. Average quintals per hectare 1930–9. Based on
M. Cépède: *Agriculture et Alimentation en France durant la IIe guerre mondiale*
(1961), 24

the crisis in agriculture presented opportunities, as for example
for the Charentes, which changed from mediocre wine to good
dairy, it also took a toll of victims unable to meet the challenges.
In the course of the twentieth century, the regional disparities
increased once again. Thus between 1892 and 1939 the yield
of wheat per hectare over the whole of France rose from 12·6
to 15·4 quintals, but in fourteen departments it fell, and in
another eight it remained static. The result was that in some
cases modernisation widened the gap between the regions. Thus
in 1954–5, the productivity of agriculture in the department of
Aisne was 820,000 francs per worker, but in Creuse it was only
between 300,000 and 350,000. In Aisne 36 kilograms of fertilisers were used, in Creuse 2·1. Figures of national averages are
highly misleading. The graph opposite shows that agricultural
production rose until 1892, remained static till 1939, and then
rose again after the war. But if one looks at the statistics by
department, one sees that while between 1852 and 1892 the
national increase was from 100 to 185, in some departments it
rose very much more, e.g. in Ille-et-Vilaine to 294, Mayenne
296, Creuse 320, and in some appreciably less, e.g. Nord 113
and Var 105. Again over the period 1892–1955, the figure for
France as a whole was 98, but it was 46 in Saône-et-Loire, 48 in
Vosges, and 260 in Pyrénées-Orientales. The Paris and northern plains developed most rapidly in the first half of the nineteenth century; in the second half of the century less favoured
regions follow suit, eliminating fallow and waste. Mechanisation
started in the north in the 1860s, but elsewhere only after the
1890s. The static market after 1892, however, meant that the
differences between regions increased once more after that date
and became almost as great in 1939 as they had been in 1848.[1]

Nor should it be thought that the traditional peasant was
necessarily less well off than the modernising one. Laurence
Wylie, in his highly instructive study of the village of Chanzeaux, showed that the traditionalist probably did produce
only half of what he could do by more modern methods, and
he may have spent two months cutting down a hedge which
a bulldozer would have dealt with in a day, but nevertheless he
could end up with more money than the moderniser, if he had

[1] Jean Pantard, *Les Disparités régionales dans la croissance de l'agriculture française*
(1965), 20, 43, 60.

a farm of the right size. He had no real inducement to modernise, because he earned an adequate living, obtained satisfaction from his slower pace of work and from the freedom it gave him to pause and waste time talking to passing friends. His young neighbour, who had gone in for modernisation, was by contrast always on the run, and yet he was not making all that much money out of it, because his farm was not really large enough.[1] The structure of property and of farm areas did not develop enough to make modernisation possible, except in certain regions. It has been calculated that 15 hectares is the very minimum necessary for a farm to yield any profit at all, and those under this size survived because they used cheap family labour.[2] Nevertheless such small farms did survive in great numbers as this table shows:

Percentage of farms in *1892*, in *1929* and in *1955* having

		1892	*1929*	*1955*
1 hectare or less		39	25	6
1–5 hectares		32	29	29
5–10	,,	14	18	21
10–20	,,		15	24
20–50	,,	15	10	16
50–100	,,		2	3
Over 100	,,		1	1

The tiny plots have almost vanished. There were fewer small farms, but not very many fewer: in 1892 three-quarters of farms were under 10 hectares, in 1929 68 per cent were of this size and in 1955 56 per cent. In 1929 only 29 per cent and in 1955 only 26 per cent of French agricultural land was in farms of over 50 hectares.[3]

The extent of the modernisation of agriculture should not be exaggerated. In 1948–9 an able agronomist, René Dumont, toured the country making detailed investigations into just how far progress had gone, and his *Travels in France*, not unworthy of comparison with Arthur Young's, revealed very forcefully how strong the obstacles to change were. For example, he went to the village of Saint-Chaffrey (Hautes-Alpes)

[1] L. Wylie, *Chanzeaux. A Village in Anjou* (Cambridge, Mass., 1966), 130–1. See also another excellent book by him, *Village in the Vaucluse* (1961).
[2] J. Chombard de Lauwe, *Les Possibilités de la petite entreprise dans l'agriculture* (1954).
[3] Barral, 224, 303.

and compared the reports on it made by an inquiry of 1857 with what he saw himself. The village was still divided into the same tiny plots. Agriculture was still mainly the concern of the women and children, for the men sought employment in various occupations in the surrounding region, as they had done a hundred years before. Yet the number of hours spent on extracting food from the soil was very high. This was genuinely primitive agriculture; barley and fallow alternated in some parts, as they had done in the middle ages. In the Queyras valley there was no additional employment to be had, so agriculture was the main activity, but it produced only just enough to feed the farmers and their animals; this was pure subsistence farming, with the surplus grain of good years never being sold, but hoarded to meet the deficits of bad years. North of Carcassonne he found perfectly ordinary vines being cultivated on terraces which required ten times more labour than vines planted in the plains. He witnessed the valiant efforts of the Nantes region to grow fruit and vegetables for export, in which they had long experience from the time of Louis-Philippe when they first planted William pears to sell in England. These had been ruined by American competition; peaches, melons and strawberries had replaced them, only to be ruined in turn by the cheaper produce of the Midi. They had then changed to tomatoes and celery, but they were less efficient, because less artificial, than the Dutch. Modern methods had not been adopted whole-heartedly enough for them to be successful on the international market. In Cavaillon (Vaucluse) he did find some very go-ahead market gardeners, climatically more favoured, constantly and successfully adapting their produce to the needs of the towns, but next door to them there were still peasants who maintained subsistence ideals and planted their market produce only as a side line. Near Wassy (Haute-Marne), the agricultural revolution had not taken place in 1929, when three-quarters of the soil was still left to fallow. The inhabitants survived only through incredibly hard work: the mortality and rapid ageing of peasants in this situation was a grim reminder of what was once common to most of the country. In Saint-Hilaire-des-Landes he found a family proud of having built its own house, as peasants regularly did in Eastern Europe, but particularly proud because theirs had two storeys, a feat formerly considered unattainable by any except the inhabitants of châteaux and cities: they felt they had, by this construction, raised themselves on the social ladder. Nearby, a *métayer* had refused to take advantage of the law of 1946 allowing him to transform his sharecropping contract into a cash tenancy, 'for fear of displeasing his landlord'. The provisions of other laws for the improvement of rented farm dwellings were similarly ignored: 'Social progress here', commented Dumont, 'almost needs to be *imposed* on those who would benefit from it.' In Elven (Morbihan), the changes which had occurred elsewhere in the eighteenth and nineteenth centuries were still continuing. The population had continued to grow until 1926, and to make room, the wastelands had been nibbled at steadily till then, but the soil was poor, and did not repay the enormous trouble taken over it. Subsistence farming was practised, but it fed the population only in good years. Most of the village was owned by a nobleman, so there was practically no land to buy. Prices were so high, because of the competition, that the bourgeoisie did not try to invest in land here. In 1938, when the rich plains of the Soissonnais cost less than 6,000 francs a hectare, the land at Elven, among the poorest in France, was selling at between 8,000 and 9,000 francs. Even in more prosperous Normandy, Dumont saw how the change to meat and milk production was carried out unscientifically. The French lagged way behind Denmark and Holland in productivity, for on the whole they preferred to go only half-way to modernisation, adopting extensive pasture, rather than intensive fodder. In Normandy this system simply used more labour than was necessary (and it was adopted perhaps in order to leave enough employment for the surviving peasants); but in the south pasture was disastrous, because it was often unusable in winter and dried out in summer.[1]

The inferiority of French agriculture, by comparison with other western countries, thus continued throughout these hundred years. In the 1850s, Léonce de Lavergne had pointed out how far it was behind England. At that period, he wrote, the 'most striking feature in English agriculture, as compared to ours, consists in the number and quality of its sheep'. England had about the same total number as France but living on one

[1] René Dumont, *Voyages en France d'un agronome* (2nd edition 1956).

third of the acreage; they were far larger, because meat was
their primary aim, whereas wool was what they were kept for
in France. Nevertheless the two countries produced roughly the
same amount of wool, while England produced almost three
times as much meat. France was inferior not only to England,
but also to Scotland, and was judged just equal with Ireland.
Again, France had 10 million cattle and the U.K. 8 million,
which proportionately to the acreage gave England a considerable lead. France still used its cattle a great deal for
labour, while England was interested mainly in milk and meat.
Even cheese, said Lavergne, was superior in England (the cult
of French cheese is more recent).[1] England produced twice as
much milk as France. 'The art of rearing cattle for butcher-meat
only is scarcely known in France.' England also had more
horses and pigs. France was superior only in poultry, producing
about eight times in value as much as England; this partly
made up for what France lacked in butcher-meat. France of
course was the largest producer of wheat in Western Europe,
but the concentration on this was exhausting its soil and its
yields were appreciably below England's.[2]

In 1939, French prices for wheat were 45 per cent higher
than England's, because of low yields, small-scale farming and
inadequate use of fertilisers. Where machinery was used, it was
largely in harvesting, rather than in cultivation, and in the
south ploughing by oxen, or even cows, still continued. The
milk yield in France was the lowest in Western Europe, largely
because of inadequate feeding: France used less oil cake than

[1] France imported more cheese than it exported: in 1909–13 49 million lbs. as
against 32 million exported. But the French (in the 1920s) were consuming three
times as much cheese as the Americans, who, however, ate almost twice as much
butter. See T. R. Pirtle, *History of the Dairy Industry* (Chicago, Ill., 1926). For the
growth of industrialised cheese making, under the control of the cheese merchants,
see G. Tellier, *L'Industrie fromagère de Roquefort* (Albi, 1926). But, at least in the
1950s, Roquefort was a small industry. Out of a total production of 375,000 tons
of cheese in 1951, Gruyère and Emmenthal accounted for 90,000 tons, Camembert
for 85,000 tons, but no other one kind produced more than 20,000. O.E.C.D.,
Organisation and Structure of the Milk Markets in O.E.C.D. Member Countries (1963),
274. Margarine, invented by a Frenchman in 1869, was used in France before
1939 mainly to adulterate butter. J. H. van Stuyvenberg, *Margarine: An Economic,
Social and Scientific History 1869–1969* (Liverpool, 1969), 319.

[2] Léonce de Lavergne, *The Rural Economy of England, Scotland and Ireland* (English
translation, 1855). Cf. W. King, Earl of Lovelace, *Review of the Agricultural Statistics
of France* (1848).

Denmark, although it had five times as many cows. Most of
its milk was produced in very small herds; only 0·4 per cent
of cows had their milk yield recorded, even though state subsidies were available for recording societies. About one-fifth of
the dairy herd was believed to suffer from tuberculosis; some
claimed the proportion was much larger. Breeding was difficult
because of the enormous variety of breeds, so that in the
Pyrenees there was almost a different breed in every valley.
Much progress had been made in Normandy and the Charentes,
but these areas were still backward by European standards.
Poultry keeping was still where it had been a hundred years
before: in the Côte-d'Or the yield per hen was estimated at
only 60 eggs per annum, of which about half were laid in the
three months of February, March and April. France was the
only country in Western Europe (except Italy, not included
in these comparisons) whose livestock still provided less than
half of its total agricultural output. France had maintained
a balance between its agricultural activities, but at the expense
of being unable to compete in the world markets. Its backwardness should not, however, be exaggerated. The standard
of living of the German peasant was roughly the same; in the
large areas of poor soil he had to work longer hours to achieve
it; his diet was less varied; he seldom had a car; though on the
other hand his housing was definitely better than his French
counterpart's: there was no sleeping in cowsheds.[1]

Peasants in all industrialising countries had cause for complaint. The share of the national revenue which they received
fell everywhere in the twentieth century. Thus in the U.S.A.
it fell from 20 to 7½ per cent between 1900 and 1960. In France,
over the same period, it fell from 35 to 12 per cent, but it was no
consolation that this was an international phenomenon. In
France, the peasants felt the losses more, because their numbers had fallen less than elsewhere. The peasants were conscious that they had to produce more and more goods in order
to buy the same amount of industrial goods; their efforts to be
like other men, to enjoy the same standard of living, were constantly thwarted. Thus in 1955 agricultural products had only
two-thirds of the purchasing power they had had in 1914 and
half of that of 1865–75. Between 1945 and 1958 production

[1] P. L. Yates, *Food Production in Western Europe* (1940).

increased by 25 per cent, but the peasant's income rose only 4 per cent, while the income of the rest of the country rose by 46 per cent. This agricultural income was moreover very unequally distributed, because 56 per cent of farms enjoyed less than 20 per cent of it, while a mere 8 per cent had a third of it. In 1956 the annual average expenditure of all French households was 253,800 francs, but that of agricultural households was only 194,000 francs while rural households not in agriculture spent 216,000 and urban households 283,800. In the centre and west of France agricultural expenditure was as low as 182,000. The peasants were thus forced to spend 10 per cent less on food, 28 per cent less on clothes and 50 per cent less on culture and leisure than their urban counterparts. In 1960 only 16 per cent of secondary-school pupils had peasants as parents, as against 21 per cent who had workers. Only 55 per cent of rural communes had running water (in some departments only 20 to 30 per cent); only 2 per cent had baths or showers, as against 15 per cent in the towns. The peasants suffered more from tuberculosis, but they had only half the doctors the towns had.[1]

It can now be asked whether these diminishing returns, this record of failure in the economic rat race, and the awareness of falling status produced a sense of unity or class consciousness among the peasants. The answer seems to be definitely that it did not. All students of rural conditions are agreed that the divisions among the peasantry not only remained but even multiplied; and indeed they have proposed a large number of different classifications. At the time of the Second World War the peasants were certainly still very much differentiated by the way they lived, by the kind of houses they occupied, and by their patterns of settlement in hamlets, villages or *bourgs*. They had different attitudes according to the type of their economy: the polycultural peasant of the Garonne, the cattle farmer of Normandy, the winegrower of the Hérault, the market gardener of Roussillon, the mountain peasant of the Pyrenees or the Cantal, the wheat farmer of the Beauce were different types with different problems. Some were still subsistence farmers, others were not. A map has been produced, showing the extent of 'autoconsumption' of wheat, which gives some indication of the

[1] Jean Maynaud, *La Révolte paysanne* (1963), 17–37, 88.

survival of the former class. No one has properly discovered just how much of this autoconsumption there was, though an economist has produced a figure of about 23 per cent of total production for 1938.[1] Maps can also show the striking regional variations in the use of credit, fertilisers and machinery. Again owners, tenant farmers, sharecroppers and labourers were not easy to unite; and each of these, moreover, had different relations with other classes. In the west they often accepted nobles as mayors (but not always). In some regions the peasants were democratic, in others they combined this with acceptance of the Church, in some they were divided by the religious issue; in some areas they accepted traditional hierarchies, in others they were dominated by the rivalries of clans and clienteles, and in still others the capitalist invasion placed them in situations not unlike those of industrial workers. The peasants have never all voted for the same political party.[2] When the scientific analysis of voting behaviour made possible detailed study of their politics, it was found, in 1956, that about 20 per cent of them voted moderate, 17 per cent communist, 14 per cent socialist, 12 per cent M.R.P. and 14 per cent Poujadist—which was not very different from the way the towns voted. The claim, which Halbwachs made in 1939, that the peasants found their unity in one thing, their hostility to the towns, cannot be accepted, at least in this simple form.[3]

The peasants were particularly slow in finding a voice to express their grievances. The people who spoke in the name of agriculture in the nineteenth century were not peasants. Méline was from an industrial region; and the vast majority of ministers of agriculture were barristers and doctors. The Society of French Farmers, founded in 1868 by a professor of the National Agronomic Institute was presided over in turn by Drouyn de Lhuys, formerly Napoleon III's foreign minister, by the marquis Élie de Dampierre, who had large estates in the south-west, and by the marquis de Voguë, who combined this task with the presidency of the Suez Canal Company, St. Gobain and the French Red Cross. It was a powerful pressure group but it

[1] André de Cambiaire, *L'Autoconsommation agricole en France* (1952), 178.
[2] For further details see Zeldin, *Politics and Anger*, chapter 1.
[3] Cf. H. Mendras, 'Diversité des sociétés rurales françaises' in J. Fauvet and H. Mendras, *Les Paysans et la politique dans la France contemporaine* (1958), 23–35.

acted above all in the interests of the large farmers. It encouraged the formation of trade unions among the peasants, but it successfully kept these absorbed in purely commercial activities, notably the purchase of fertilisers. It did a good deal to prolong the influence of the nobles in the provinces, particularly where the nobles decided to opt out of politics and try this new approach. This was one reason why the agricultural trade union movement flourished in Finistère, but not in the neighbouring Côtes-du-Nord, for in the latter the nobles continued to pursue the parliamentary seats. The Society of Farmers was powerful enough to incite Gambetta to found a rival National Society for the Encouragement of Agriculture, designed to unite the smaller farmers and to be an instrument for the spread of republican doctrine. Thus the animosities of politics were exacerbated by new frictions at the professional level. When other unions, co-operatives and mutual insurance societies were established, under a variety of stimuli, they were immediately infiltrated if not taken over by the government or the politicians. Laws were passed, amid much rhetoric, instituting subsidies and credit banks to assist the peasants, but these benefits were distributed on strict principles of favouritism. Local politicians, particularly senators, became secretaries of the co-operatives and mutual organisations in their constituencies so as to bolster their electoral hold. The peasants, of course, were not keen on paying their subscriptions, and in any case the law made it difficult for their organisations to build up funds. None of these groups therefore became a real danger to the state.[1]

However, they were important in laying the foundations for some forms of common action. The peasants had long traditions of mutual assistance, and in some regions even of organised co-operation in farming. The nineteenth century was in some ways a gap, a period in which these traditions were suppressed while the peasants struggled for ownership of the land; but towards the end of it there was some revival of the co-operation. By 1941, 57 per cent of fertilisers used in France were bought through peasant co-operatives. This did not mean all that much, since so little fertiliser was used. The new dairy industry was perhaps the most ready to adopt co-operation. In Charente-Inférieure, 80 per cent of dairymen belonged to some

[1] Comte de Rocquigny, *Les Syndicats agricoles et leur œuvre* (1900).

form of marketing organisation in 1937. But by 1952, over the country as a whole, only 20 per cent of milk producers were co-operators. At the same time, 12 per cent of winegrowers were co-operators.[1] In 1910 there were about 110 co-operatives for the sharing of agricultural equipment, by 1920 500, by 1939 2,090 and 13,000 in 1967. The statistics, of doubtful reliability, which the leaders of these organisations proudly quoted, are not particularly impressive. Co-operation was definitely a minority movement, affecting mainly specialised growers and certain regions. Moreover, closer scrutiny of the way the co-operatives worked reveals that the idealism of the leaders was not very widely shared. It was a common practice to sell to the co-operatives products of inferior quality and reserve the best and most profitable part of the harvest for the merchants. The amount of co-operation in some cases was fairly limited: in the manufacture of Gruyère cheese, for example, some co-operatives were simply formed to buy equipment, which they then rented out to an individual who did all the cheese making and selling for his own profit; others manufactured collectively, but allowed each member to sell his own share; only some both manufactured and sold for the common benefit. Since many of these peasant organisations were led by conservatives, their aim was seldom to be revolutionary, to abolish the normal channels of commerce: rather they acted as watchdogs on the merchants and stepped in only when these failed. In sparsely populated regions co-operatives were often more expensive to run than private enterprise, because they continued to maintain numerous small uneconomic depots. In most cases the peasants were unwilling to assume the leadership of these co-operatives, because they had no leisure, or did not think it worth while to spare the time. The organisation was therefore in the hands of bureaucrats, nobles or clergymen; the central staff ran the services; and the peasants rejected any collective discipline. For example, they refused to stagger their sales of grain, preferring to make the best bargains they could. The return to collective agriculture was very slight indeed.[2]

[1] Producing 22 per cent of all *vin ordinaire* in France, 42 per cent of *qualité supérieure*, and 25 per cent of *appellation contrôlée*.

[2] André Hirschfeld, *La Coopération agricole en France* (1957); Jacob Baker *et al.*, *Report of the Inquiry on Cooperative Enterprise in Europe* (Washington D.C., 1937), 144–7; P. Boisseau, *Les Agriculteurs et l'entraide* (1968), 35; *André Cramois, Coopératives*

There were occasions when the peasants expressed their wrath or their resentments in spontaneous outbursts. The recapturing in 1848 of pastures and forests once held in common, the demonstrations and refusals to pay tax by the wine-growers in 1907 are examples. But there were also, after 1890, instances of protest with a certain amount of organisation. The impoverished woodcutters of the Centre formed 170 trade unions by the First World War and waged several strikes with some success, against the merchants who kept them on the very margin of survival.[1] The gardeners and labourers of the Paris region and the workers of the vineyards in the south formed unions which had much in common with industrial ones. The sharecroppers of Bourbonnais sprouted a few remarkable leaders of their own, organised themselves in protest against the more vexatious aspects of their leases, and even elected a deputy to parliament, though he was a primary-school master.[2] These were all, however, limited and local efforts, mainly affecting marginal groups. More significant was the penetration into the leadership of the general agricultural trade union movement, between the wars, of a 'new bourgeois peasantry', farmers with secondary education. The Church also played an important part in the democratisation of peasant organisations. Abbé Trochu, though frowned on by the hierarchy, founded and ran a highly successful newspaper in Rennes, *L'Ouest-Éclair*, between 1899 and 1930, in the name of Christian Democracy. This paper became the daily with the largest circulation in the west, and was backed up by half a dozen weeklies. Assisted by three other priests, Mancel, Geffriaud and Crublet, he stimulated the formation of some 200 unions, at the village level, with subsidiary youth groups, which effectively challenged the older unions run by the aristocrats. Brittany, partly as a result of

agricoles. Pourquoi et comment le paysan français est devenu coopérateur (n.d., about 1948); International Cooperative Alliance, *Cooperation in the European Market Economies* (1967), for comparative statistics see appendix; Susanne D. Berger, *Peasants against Politics. Rural Organisation in Finistère* (Harvard Ph.D. thesis, 1966), a stimulating, critical investigation based on fieldwork.

[1] M. Roblin, *Les Bûcherons de la Nièvre* (Paris thesis, 1903); R. Braque, 'Aux origines du syndicalisme dans les milieux ruraux de centre', in *Le Mouvement social* (Jan–Mar. 1963), 79–116; and René Bazin, *Le Blé qui lève* (1907).

[2] L. Lamoureux, *Les Syndicats agricoles* (1914); A. Hodée, *Les Jardiniers* (1928); G. Rister, *Le Travailleur agricole français* (1923); Y. Tavernier, *Le Syndicalisme paysan* (1969).

this, was to become one of the strongest bastions of peasant agitation. On a national level, the Catholic Agricultural Youth movement (J.A.C.), founded in 1929, did a great deal to transform the attitudes of the new generation. René Colson, a peasant from the Haute-Marne who was its secretary general from 1942 to 1948, created a new style of forward-looking organisation, which was to bear fruit in the 1960s: his influence has been likened to that which Pelloutier had on the urban workers at the turn of the century.[1]

It was not the peasants themselves who formed the first peasant party. The *Parti agraire et paysan français* (so called to show that it stood both for the proprietors and the labourers) was founded in 1928 by a colourful schoolmaster, Fleurant, who preferred to call himself Agricola, assisted by two barristers. They were said to have obtained financial support from the richest wheat merchant in France, Louis-Dreyfus. They certainly had the backing of advertisers, whose announcements, incorporated into the film shows they held at the end of their public meetings, were a profitable source of revenue. They did not rival the traditional agricultural unions, even though they quarrelled with them about tactics. In the elections of 1936 they won eight seats, but then withered away in internal dissensions. They showed what could be done if the peasant flag was raised, but were too conservative and compromising to make a real impact on the peasant world. More significant was the *Défense Paysanne*. This was not the creation of a peasant either. Henri d'Halluin, who preferred to call himself Dorgères, was a journalist and the son of a butcher. As editor of a small farmers' newspaper at Rennes, he had specialised in discovering mistakes in the *cadastre* and obtaining tax reductions for his readers. He began holding public meetings to protest against more general grievances, at first on Sundays and then more frequently, until in 1936 he and his associates were organising as many as 400 a month. His enormous vitality—he was in his early thirties— and his gift for attracting publicity won him a sizeable following. He claimed that by 1939 his various newspapers had 410,000 subscribers, mainly in the west and north. He organised these

[1] Gordon Wright, *Rural Revolution in France* (1964), is an excellent history of peasant movements since 1930. Cf. Paul Delourme, *Trente-Cinq Ans de politique religieuse* (1936).

followers in an unusually effective way. He knew how to use large crowds of peasants to put pressure on the state. He told them to bring their pitchforks with them and to distinguish themselves with green shirts; and he was not afraid of violence. He came to employ no less than sixty people to help him in his organisation, and most of these were genuine peasants, like, for example, François Coire, who had been an agricultural labourer, but who had the prestige of having won the Military Medal during the war, when he was twice promoted sergeant and twice demoted for his *mauvaise tête*. In 1936 Dorgères united with Agricola to form the Peasant Front, which waged battles against the strikers of the towns. The achievement Dorgères claimed for himself, and with which he explained his success, was that he created a new peasant pride, destroying the inferiority complex that had been almost universal among the peasantry; but in any case he certainly contributed to the formation of a belief among some of the peasants that they had the ability to get their complaints listened to by agitation, demonstration and on occasion violent pressure. It cannot be conceded that he made them feel really integrated in the state, because the state was the great enemy for him, together with the large capitalist trusts. He had no sophisticated programme, though he wrote able books expounding his doctrine. Pétain, whom he hailed as the 'Peasant Marshal', astutely appointed him director of peasant propaganda. Dorgères was disappointed with Vichy, but was nevertheless convicted of collaboration after the war. He then founded an advertising agency, whose profits enabled him, at the age of 55, to buy a newspaper and start a new movement. He ended up in alliance with Poujade.[1]

The Vichy regime made it possible for the peasants to take the really decisive step. The corporatist theory, which several peasant leaders, and notably Louis Salleron, had taken up as the cure for their troubles, was now officially adopted and a law was passed setting up a Peasant Corporation to institution- alise peasant unity. Every village was required to form a single syndicate, and to elect representatives to regional and national

[1] Henri Dorgères, *Au XXe siècle, dix ans de Jacquerie* (1959), interesting memoirs, id., *Haut les fourches* (1935), and *Révolution paysanne* (1943); J. M. Royer, 'De Dorgères à Poujade', in J. Fauvet and H. Mendras, *Les Paysans et la politique* (1958), 149–206.

committees. This had a very important effect on peasant politics. 'Peasants of France', said Caziot, the farmer and expert on land values whom Pétain chose as his minister of agriculture, 'you used to be masters of your land, but your power too often stopped at the boundaries of your farms. You will now have control over your own profession and you will be able to act over a much vaster area, in a position of equality with the other professions. So the inferiority complex, which you always feel, and which placed agriculture below other occupations, will disappear.'[1] How far this was achieved is debatable. But the compulsory merger of the rival unions which had divided villages was in many cases permanent. Though animosities were not ended, the possibility of united action was at last appreciated. The peasants were also forced to elect 30,000 syndics, and these were to provide much of the leadership which was active after the war. The idea that the peasants themselves must carry out their own revolution came to have real meaning. Vichy's Peasant Corporation was unsuccessful in many ways, but it was more successful than its other corporations because it was the most democratic. It has a significant place in peasant history.[2]

In 1945, however, power still eluded the peasants, as it had done in 1848. National politics, indeed, was still foreign to many of them. They were often passionately interested in municipal affairs, but party labels did not always mean the same thing to them as to the rest of the nation. To look at election results to discover what they thought is to beg the question. The peasants had not discovered how to implement their demands, partly because they were still so divided and unclear about them, and partly also because their practical concerns could only with difficulty be inserted into the party programmes overladen with ideological commitments. Few of them got elected to parliament. In 1889, out of a chamber of 576 deputies, there was not a single working peasant, though 131 large landowners, 10 medium-sized owners, 3 veterinaries, 1 agronomist and some thirty barristers and businessmen with

---

[1] P. Caziot in *La Vie de la France sous l'occupation 1940–4* (1957), i, 264.

[2] L. Salleron, *La Corporation paysanne* (1943) and *Naissance de l'état corporatif* (1942); Michel Cépède, *Agriculture et alimentation en France durant la deuxième guerre mondiale* (1961).

sizeable rural properties meant that the agricultural interest had about 30 per cent of the seats. By 1910 that figure had fallen to 18 per cent, and after 1924 it was as low as 11 to 13 per cent. By then the number of large landowners in parliament declined but they were replaced mainly by well-to-do medium ones.[1] The peasants did not step into the nobles' shoes. Their world was still a separate one.

[1] J. Fauvet and H. Mendras, 215.

10. Workers

The Worker and the Law

THE proletariat, in this period, were frequently talked of as outcasts of society, 'the dangerous classes', the pariahs. The limits on their freedom were very considerable. Investigators of their conditions were still saying in the early twentieth century that, 'without exaggeration', the rights of employers over them were 'heavier than those the feudal lords had over their serfs in the Middle Ages'.[1] Their legal position deserves to be examined, before one looks at how they themselves coped with their situation.

The French Revolution had done little for the worker.[2] He was given the right to practise any trade he pleased—the corporations were abolished—but subject to important and humiliating restrictions. He had to possess a *livret*—a certificate bearing his name, description and place of employment. He was forbidden to change his job until his master certified he was free of debt and obligations to him. Since it was very common for workers to receive loans in hard times from their employers, they could be effectively prevented from changing jobs by unscrupulous masters. If the employer agreed to the worker leaving, he could inscribe the amount owed to him in the *livret*, and the next employer was required to refund that sum to him in instalments, by withholding a proportion of the man's wages. The *livret* had to be held only by industrial workers, not by self-employed artisans nor by peasants, and was thus doubly discriminatory. It had its origins in the *ancien régime*, which had used something similar, as the decree of 1781 stated, 'to maintain subordination among workers in manufacturing districts'. Napoleon had required every worker, on leaving his job, to have his *livret* signed by the employer and

---

[1] D. Poulot, *Le Sublime* (1870); Léon and Maurice Bonneff, *La Vie tragique des travailleurs. Enquêtes sur la condition économique et morale des ouvriers et ouvrières d'industrie* (n.d., about 1908), 29.

[2] Roger Picard, *Les Cahiers de 1789 au point de vue industriel et commercial* (Paris thesis, 1910).

also by the mayor, who would insert in it the town to which
the worker stated he was moving. It thus served as a sort of
passport and a worker found that without one he would be
liable to imprisonment as a vagabond. But Napoleon failed to
match these sanctions on recalcitrant workers by penalties for
employers who ignored the law and in practice many employers
did not bother. (Some on the other hand took it upon themselves to inscribe comments about the worker in the *livret*,
which could damage his chances of future employment.)

In 1845 a bill was introduced to impose sanctions and make
it really effective, and in 1854 a law was finally passed to
reinvigorate the institution. Employers were instructed to
insist on *livrets*; all industrial workers, working in factories or at
home for an employer, and for the first time women too, were
required to have them. In Paris a police ordinance in addition
required employers to have the *livret* of every worker they took
on stamped with a visa by the police within twenty-four hours.
Nevertheless once again the law was only partially enforced—
mainly in large factories employing itinerant labour—but the
politically conscious workers protested violently against it,
as a *loi d'exception*. The mason-deputy Nadaud said they had
one foot chained to the police, and the other to the capitalist.
The liberal empire in 1870 proposed to abolish the whole
system, but fell before it could do so. It was only in 1890 that
the law finally ceased to look upon the industrial worker as a
dangerous person, needing careful surveillance.[1]

The workers were not deceived by the myth propagated by
the bourgeoisie that the Civil Code was egalitarian. Thiers
declared that the Civil Code was impossible to improve—at
most he could suggest only a few stylistic changes. Troplong,
First President of the Cour de Cassation, and author of the
leading commentary on the Civil Code (in 28 volumes, 1833–
58) 'justly named Troplong', revealingly declared himself
satisfied with it because he considered that democracy existed
when men have an equal right to the protection of the law 'in

[1] Alexandre Plantier, *Le Livret des ouvriers* (Paris thesis, 1900). The Second
Republic in 1851 limited the master's privileged position as creditor to 30 francs, and
the instalments repayable to 10 per cent of the wage. Despite its abolition in 1890,
the *livret* was reported to have survived in certain parts of the Nord nearly
twenty years later. L. and M. Bonneff, *La Vie tragique des travailleurs* (n.d., about
1908), 23–8.

conditions of inequality which they have created for themselves by the legitimate exercise of their natural powers'. The Civil Code certainly confirmed these inequalities. It had a narrow view of citizenship, which it confused with the possession of property, and so it made the penniless worker almost an outlaw. It was principally concerned not with making men equal but with protecting property. It contained numerous articles about contracts of sale, exchange and lease; it had as many as thirty-one articles about the legal position of rented livestock, but only two articles on the worker and his relations with his employers; and both of these were taken over from the *ancien régime*. The first stated that the services of a worker or servant could be engaged only for a definite period or task—a banal repetition of the abolition of serfdom. The second (article 1781) stated that in a dispute about wages, the word of the master was to be preferred to that of the worker in the absence of written records—just as article 1716 stated that in a dispute about rent, the word of the landlord was to be preferred to that of the tenant. The republican Garnier-Pagès might expostulate in 1847 against Guizot's 'detestable theory that there are different classes, the bourgeoisie and the poor class' and he might insist that 'there are no longer any classes . . . in France, there are only French citizens'. This was not true, even after 1848 when the masses were officially made citizens. Article 1781, as a result of repeated protests by the workers, was repealed in 1868. The workers, however, continued to complain that not only were they treated as inferiors on the few occasions they were mentioned in the Civil Code, but that even worse they were ignored by it. The law protected the bourgeoisie's property against thieves, but it did not protect workers against exploiters of their labour. 'We wish to cease to be helots in a nation of sybarites.'[1]

The Conseils de Prud'hommes, established by Napoleon to

---

[1] E. Glasson, 'Le Code Civil et la question ouvrière' in *Séances et Travaux de l'Académie des Sciences morales et politiques*, 25 (1886), 843–95; Albert Tissier, 'Le Code Civil et les classes ouvrières' in *Le Code Civil, Livre du Centenaire* published by the Société d'Études législatives (1904), 1. 73 ff.; Pierre Lavigne, *Le Travail dans les constitutions françaises 1789–1945* (1948); G. and H. Bourgin, *Les Patrons, les ouvriers et l'état: le régime de l'industrie en France de 1814 à 1830* (1912–41). Cf. Daphne Simon, 'Master and Servant' in John Saville, *Democracy and the Labour Movement* (1954).

reconcile minor disputes between master and man, were likewise for long weighted against the worker. The members of
these conciliation tribunals were elected, partly by the employers and partly by workers of the town in which they functioned; but the employers were given a majority of seats, and
the only workers who had the vote were the *patentés*, a small
minority. The dissatisfied worker who appealed to them was
thus appealing to his superiors, not his equals. Even so these
courts were popular, because they were extremely cheap (a
case could cost between 30 centimes and 1 franc 75) and no
lawyers were involved. Founded originally in 1806 to settle
small day-to-day disputes in the Lyon silk industry about the
quality of work done and the rates of payment—matters which
required technical knowledge not possessed by ordinary judges
—they were gradually extended to some other industries,
mainly textiles and metals, and to other towns:

	Number of Conseils de Prud'hommes	Number of cases dealt with by them
1830	53	11,000
1848	71	18,000
1852	83	40,000
1870	109	30,000
1892	146	52,000

During the Second Republic they had been very busy because
for a few years the workers obtained the majority of the seats.
A law of 27 May 1848 gave the vote to all workers, not just
patentés, and allocated to their representatives the same number
of seats as to the employers. This was an obviously necessary
reform. But the law carried the workers' victory too far, for it
classified foremen and *chefs d'atelier* (artisans employing a few
others) as employers and so greatly reduced the representation
of the larger factory owner. Napoleon III reclassified these men
as workers in 1853 and angered the workers even more by
arrogating to the administration the right to appoint the president and vice-president of the councils—who were in effect
invariably chosen from among the wealthiest employers. When
the Third Republic in 1880 gave up this right and allowed the
councils to elect their own presidents, the employers frequently

lost their office when they did not all attend to vote. In protest they took to boycotting the whole institution. In Lille in particular the councils ceased to function for several years. The trade unions took to organising the elections to them, demanding a promise from those they supported always to decide in favour of the worker. The employers argued that the councils had ceased to be fair, and were out of date besides, for they no longer dealt with technical matters but with disputes which ordinary judges could well decide, if only their procedure were less cumbersome: three-quarters of the councils' cases in 1892 concerned wages. Many workers, however, considered this institution as potentially very valuable, as a first step to greater equality between master and man. Numerous bills were introduced into parliament to reform and extend it. A few got passed by the deputies but were rejected by the senate.

In 1905 finally a law allowed appeals from them to go to the ordinary law courts (*tribunal civil*): previously appeals were to the *tribunaux de commerce*, composed exclusively of employers. A law of 1907 restored the procedure of the Second Republic, that employers and workers were to take it in turn to be president—so ending the bitterness caused by the system of free election established in 1880. Women workers were given the vote but, in the face of the senate's opposition, were not eligible to serve as councillors, even though a great number of cases concerned women. The law allowed the establishment of councils for other industries—notably mines, transport and commerce—but (again owing to the senate's opposition) not agriculture. The workers had long clamoured for this, and for more councillors, so that each trade could have its representatives on the councils. Councils were henceforth to be established not at the government's pleasure but in every town which wanted one. Foremen were to vote as employers or as workers depending on whether they were principally engaged in surveillance or in the physical execution of the work—a compromise reached after the deputies had classified them as employers and the senate as workers. The reforms were rounded off by the issue of medals to all councillors as insignia of office and the promise of further decorations as rewards for long service. It thus took almost exactly a century of argument to establish equality between master and man in these conciliation tribunals.[1]

Again, workers were treated differently from their employers when they combined. They were liable to much higher penalties than them—a maximum of five years' imprisonment as against only one month's imprisonment or a fine for employers. Once the convicted workers had served their sentence they were in addition liable to a further two to five years of police surveillance. Moreover, employers were guilty of the offence of combination only when they tried to reduce wages 'unjustly and abusively', whereas the workers committed a crime however just their demands. The inequality in penalties was ended in 1849 (law of 15 November–1 December) but in practice the discrimination against the worker continued. The prohibition of all trade associations had been made in 1791 in the name of liberty. Rousseau taught that intermediary bodies between the individual and the state were undesirable, and the theory of *laissez-faire* opposed any combination which might hinder the free working of the economy. Though these theories and this justification might have been new, successive governments after the Revolution were merely continuing the practice of the *ancien régime*, of consistently suppressing workers' unions. By contrast, intermediary associations of employers were tolerated and even recognised. Chambres de Commerce had over the years been established in 70 or 80 towns; elected by merchants, they represented them in dealings with the state, giving their views on legislation and organising works and services of common interest. Industrial towns had similar bodies known as chambres consultatives des arts et métiers. These bodies were represented on the national conseil général du commerce and the conseil général des manufactures—partly elected and partly appointed by the government. The workers, by contrast, were allowed no similar organisations and they frequently complained that they were not consulted by the government.

Unions of employers were not recognised by the state, but they were tolerated and the reigns of Louis-Philippe and

---

[1] Robert Baffos, 'La Prud'homie, son évolution' (Paris thesis, 1908); Émile Mallard, *Des Conseils de Prud'hommes. Étude de la loi du 27 mars 1907* (Poitiers thesis, 1912); E. Cleiftie, *Les conseils de Prud'hommes. Leur organisation et leur fonctionnement au point de vue économique et social* (Paris thesis, 1898).

Napoleon III were remarkable for the rise of numerous private employers' organisations. Already under the Restoration local associations of iron masters and of silk merchants had been formed; in 1832 the sugar manufacturers established a committee to safeguard their beet sugar against colonial imports; in 1835 the Committee of Industrialists of the east of France was formed to maintain the protection of the textile industry; in 1840 three committees appeared, of metallurgical interests, machine constructors and colliery owners. In 1846 these various industries were successfully brought together into one Association pour la Défense du Travail National, to counter the activities of the free traders. Its president was Odier, peer of France, a textile manufacturer of the Vosges; its vice-president and principal organiser was Auguste Mimerel, president of the official conseil général des manufacturers; its secretary was Joseph Lebœuf, porcelain and pottery manufacturer and regent of the Bank of France; its treasurer was Joseph Périer (brother of Casimir) of the Anzin mines. It published a newspaper, *Le Moniteur Industriel*, which flourished thanks to plentiful advertising revenue. It was an acknowledged pressure group throughout the Second Empire and was particularly active in organising opposition to Napoleon III's free trade policy. The best-known organisation, the Comité des Forges, which discreetly traced its history back to only 1864, was in existence for some time before this and was only one of a number of employers' associations.

The smaller employers had their unions too. In 1873 it was estimated that there were a hundred of these unions in Paris and between 140 and 160 in the provinces. There were also federations of small employers' unions. In Paris in 1858 Pascal Bonnin, a lawyer, had founded a Union Nationale des Chambres Syndicales, which by 1874 grouped 70 employers' unions in the capital. It published a profitable newspaper, organised insurance schemes, information services, petitions to the government on taxation and legislation. It won control of the elections to the Tribunal de Commerce and this official court recognised it even if the government did not. The Tribunal de Commerce referred many commercial disputes to it for arbitration and settlement. The employers' unions were, however, divided and a second federation, called the Comité Central, was organised as a rival by F. Lévy; there was apparently a third minor federation too. The employers thus set the pattern for the workers in their organisations and in their divisions. To a certain extent they even stimulated the workers to unite by their example: this is specifically stated by several workers in the International Exhibition Report of 1862.[1]

The prohibition on workers' unions was abolished in several stages, with hesitations, delays and reservations which repeatedly deprived the government of any credit among the working classes for its concessions. In 1848 the Provisional Government published a declaration that workers had not only a right to unite but a duty to do so, 'to enjoy the legitimate benefit of their work'; but no sooner was their appetite whetted than the old restrictions on clubs, societies and meetings were restored and savagely enforced. Matters were back to where they had started, except that all combinations by employers or workers were to be equally penalised, whether they were 'unjust' or not (27 November 1849). Later Napoleon III, disliking the harsh sentences of imprisonment passed on workers, and particularly the compositors, for striking in a perfectly peaceful manner, issued numerous reprieves and then ordered new legislation on strikes. By the law of 25 May 1864 the offence of combination ceased to be known to the law. But though strikes now became legal, trade unions remained illegal, and the right to strike, moreover, was limited in two ways. First the use of violence, threats or fraudulent manœuvres in the organisation of a strike was severely punished, more severely than, e.g., in elections. The intention of the main author of this law, Émile Ollivier, was not to allow strikes of the traditional kind, but somehow to transform strikes into a peaceful parley, in preparation for their gradual disappearance from the ideal harmonious society of which he dreamt. Secondly strikers who impinged on the liberties of blacklegs, who interfered, that is, with the 'right to work', were likewise to be severely punished. This law had a didactic, moralising character which made it both impracticable and unpopular. It displeased both employers and workers; and prosecutions for infringing the liberty to work were henceforth almost as numerous as the old prosecutions for combining. But the law was a great step forward none the less and a remarkable achievement for its author, whose

[1] Roger Priouret, *Origines du patronat français* (1963).

idealistic infatuation alone carried it through, for Napoleon had begun to waver in the face of the mounting opposition to it.[1]

In 1868 the imperial government publicly promised to tolerate workers' unions in the same way as it did those of employers—but the reactionary governments which followed the Commune put an end to this temporary suspension of the law. It was only in 1884, after some eight years of intermittent debate, that trade unions were finally legalised. The men who carried this law wished to free the workers, but they also, like Ollivier, had hopes of changing their habits. This law therefore contained restrictions, complications and omissions. But many of its results were unexpected.[2]

Trade unions could henceforth be formed without any special government authorisation provided a copy of the statutes and a list of its officials were deposited at the town hall. This at once made many workers suspicious of the whole law, declaring it to be a police measure, though in fact it ended the police's right to attend every meeting. A good number of unions refused to register and remained technically illegal: some were in consequence dissolved when they came in contact with the courts. The trade union must consist only of men exercising similar professions or professions working together to produce the same goods: this excluded union leaders as soon as they became full-time paid officials—another pretext the courts could use to dissolve them. Thirdly, the unions must limit their activities to the study and defence of economic, industrial, commercial and agricultural interests. This meant they could not engage in politics. In practice of course the prohibition was seldom enforced, but it was resented as yet another threat suspended over the unions. There were occasional prosecutions, as for example when the president of the union of waiters and restaurateurs of Meurthe-et-Moselle was fined 50 francs for urging his

[1] T. Zeldin, *Émile Ollivier and the Liberal Empire of Napoleon III* (Oxford, 1963), 79–85; F. D. Longe, 'The Law of Trade Combinations in France' in *Fortnightly Review* (1867), 220–5 and 296–309; H. Ferrette, *Manuel de législation industrielle* (1909); Émile Ollivier, *Commentaire de la loi du 25 mai 1864 sur les coalitions* (1864); P. L. Fournier, *Le Second Empire et la législation ouvrière* (Paris thesis, 1911).

[2] Isidore Finance, *Les Syndicats professionnels devant les tribunaux et le parlement depuis 1884* (1911); J. Beslier, *Les Syndicats professionnels, leur capacité d'après la loi du 21 mars 1884* (Caen Thesis, 1911); Aimé Chevron, *Les Syndicats professionnels devant la justice* (Bordeaux thesis, Barbezieux, 1909); Pierre Aubry, *Des Syndicats professionnels. Étude historique, juridique et économique de la loi du 21 mars 1884* (Nancy thesis, 1899).

members to vote in a certain way at a municipal council election. But more frequently this limitation was used against religious propaganda—as when the *curé* of Fermel, finding it impossible to get permission to found a Catholic club, organised an agricultural trade union as a cover instead (1892). In the same year a union was dissolved for allowing religious lectures on its premises. The courts gradually established it as a rule that unions could participate in the election of prud'hommes but not of deputies. Civil servants were forbidden to form unions and the courts even held (1903) that the labourers of the Paris sewage system counted as civil servants. The limitation to 'the study and defence' of economic interests forbade unions to engage directly in commercial or industrial activities. This hit the agricultural unions. It had not at first been intended to allow peasant unions at all, and the word 'agricole' had only been inserted as an amendment at a late stage in the discussion of the bill. Rather surprisingly, agricultural unions were precisely the ones which were most stimulated by the law. The courts decided that these unions could buy fertilisers for resale to their members, and provided they made no profit, this would not be classed as an illegal commercial activity. Encouraged by this, the unions began dealing in seeds, machines and finally in all kinds of goods, openly establishing shops. Rival shopkeepers, disgruntled by the loss of custom, sued them and in 1908 the Cour de Cassation ruled—or rather reaffirmed, for it was well known—that trade for profit by unions was illegal. The very existence of agricultural unions, built up to their enormous size almost entirely by their practical use as co-operatives, was placed in jeopardy.

Unions were given the right to sue and to be sued, but they could not own land or buildings beyond what was strictly necessary for their meetings, libraries and professional courses. Their right to receive gifts was uncertain—though the courts soon allowed this. These restrictions reflected an outdated fear of mortmain. It was argued that their consequences were of great importance, because they prevented the unions becoming rich like the English ones, and so conservative like them. In fact the unions did not become rich because they could not collect subscriptions: they never had any money to save. They had the right to own other forms of property—i.e. money or

shares—in unlimited amounts. More important perhaps was
the provision that though they could offer friendly society
benefits, the funds for these should be kept entirely separate and
not used to subsidise strikes. This was an attempt to safeguard
the savings of the worker for pensions and medical insurance,
but in practice it served to discourage trade unions from offering
these benefits in any substantial way. The suspicion of the
working-class movement could be seen finally in the provision,
passed after much resistance by the senate, allowing federations
of unions, but withholding from them the right to own land or
houses, or the right to sue.

The law was so frequently ignored in France, and so increasingly spurned by the revolutionaries, that, unlike in England, it was not so vital to the unions to seek amendments to it.
The courts moreover interpreted the law in a somewhat in-
consistent manner: few cases were taken to the highest court
and even it sometimes avoided the issue. Unions preferred to
dissolve and reconstitute themselves when faced with penalties,
rather than fight their cases to appeal. From their point of view
the major defect in the law was that employers continued to
victimise members of unions. A bill to stop this, passed by the
Chamber of Deputies in 1889, 1890 and 1895, was consistently
rejected by the senate. A law of 27 December 1890 did indeed
allow workers to demand damages from employers who dismissed them for belonging to a union, but it was seldom easy to
prove that the dismissal was entirely due to this reason. The
right to sue for damages was in fact more effectively used by the
employers. Cases in the courts soon revealed that the right to
strike was seriously limited by the law on breach of contract.
The Cour de Cassation ruled (18 March 1902) that a strike
involved a breach of contract unless due notice was given. In
the test case of Loichot, a locksmith of Montbéliard who went
on strike, his employer was awarded damages because Loichot
had not given notice that he would stop working. Several other
cases showed that the law of 1864 did not give the right to strike
but only removed the criminal (but not civil) penalties to which
strikers had been liable. Secondly, the right to strike was limited
also by the means employed. The use of threats could make
a strike illegal. Despite the abolition of article 416 guaranteeing
the liberty of work, picketing was not fully allowed. 'Fraudulent

manœuvres' by the strikers could give rise to damages being awarded to an employer. Thus Rességuier successfully sued Jaurès for seducing his workers during the Carmaux strike by his injurious and defamatory articles and speeches. A third restriction on the right to strike could arise from the aims of the strike. Thus in 1896 the Cour de Cassation held that a strike was legal if its object was the defence of professional interests but not if by 'pure malevolence' it sought to force the employer to dismiss a worker against whom there was no 'serious complaint', nor if it sought simply to force a worker to join the union, nor if it sought to defend private as opposed to general interests. Damages were awarded against a union, for example, in favour of a worker who could not get a job because the unions had blacklisted him and the employers feared to employ him. Likewise damages were awarded against another union for blacklisting an employer after a strike: vengeance was forbidden. This meant that the courts kept the right to investigate each strike, before they could determine whether it was legal or not. Even when the law of 1884 was completed by that of 1901 on associations, which allowed any group of people to join together whether they were members of the same trade or not, there were still many obstacles to the growth of unionism. But it would be a mistake to argue, as is too frequently done, that the law seriously hindered the rise of powerful trade unions. That these did not develop faster was due to more fundamental reasons, connected with the very nature of French society.[1]

Traditions

The size of the proletariat is something no one was or is quite sure about. The industrial sector, as has been seen, occupied between a quarter and a third of the active population. Excluding employers from these totals, one gets 2,700,000 workers under Napoleon III, 3 million in 1876 and 1886, 3,300,000 in 1891, a peak of 4,800,000 in 1931 but only 3,700,000 in 1936. One should then perhaps add a quarter of a million clerks in industry during the nineteenth century and half a million after the war. Of course, not all workers were male, nor were wage earners exclusively in industry. In 1906,

[1] Henri Pouget, *La Grève au point de vue juridique* (Bordeaux thesis, 1907); V. Diligent, *L'Action syndicale ouvrière* (Caen thesis, Roubaix, 1908).

when the total active population was 20 million, 11,700,000 were classified as wage earners, and of these 4,100,000 were women. But 2,090,000 of this supposed proletariat were in fact artisans working on their own—not strictly wage earners—who could barely be distinguished from 2,080,000 other artisans classified as *petits patrons*, though they employed no one. In 1906, only 742,000 people worked in industrial firms having over 500 employees. The statistics must be taken as approximate: detailed research frequently contradicts them. Thus in the Second Empire, despite all one reads about rapid industrialisation, it is by no means certain that the number of workers did rise: what may have happened was that there was an increase in factory workers at the expense of artisans, but little rise in the total of both together. The survival of the artisans can be illustrated by these figures of 1872:

> Mining: 14,000 employers and 164,000 workers;
> Factories: 183,000 employers and 1,112,000 workers;
> Small industry: 596,000 employers and 1,060,000 workers.

The industrial population was then still divided almost equally between small workshops and factories, and it was only in the 1890s that the predominance of the latter became marked. The transformation proceeded at very different rates: the concentration in textiles and metallurgy was rapid during the Second Empire, but in 1914 the building trade (the third largest in manpower) was still almost entirely artisan. Concentration was restricted to a few regions (see Map 3 opposite). Much of the country felt the consequences indirectly. In the 1920s, a new complication was added by the contrast of the mass-producing factories, which created a large class of semi-skilled workers, noticeably distinct from those in more traditional firms.

It is impossible therefore to talk about the proletariat as a homogeneous class, because it was changing all the time, and because the variations within it were very considerable. In the Second Empire some workers were earning five or seven times as much as others. The porcelain makers of Limoges for example, or the glass blowers of the Loire, earning around 10 francs a day were veritable aristocrats to their junior labourers, and they had still less in common with, say, the weavers of Mulhouse earning a mere 1 fr. 65. The average metal worker earned 3 fr. 50 or 4 francs a day, but some working in teams at Le Creusot made 10 to 11 francs, while inferior workers in the same trade got only 1½ or 2 francs.[1] Many artisans were not only manual

MAP 3. The growth of industry, 1906–31. Based on A. Sauvy: *Histoire économique de la France entre les deux guerres* (1961), I. 274

workers but also merchants who sold their own products and were proprietors of their tools and their shops. It is impossible to classify them as necessarily enemies of the bourgeois order.

[1] G. Duveau, *La Vie ouvrière en France sous le second empire* (1946), 302–13.

The inquiry of 1872[1] into working-class conditions revealed that 80 per cent of employers were former workers and a further 15 per cent were sons of workers. The internal divisions among the workers were even more profound than those of the bourgeoisie. The fragmentation of the ruling classes into numerous parties riddled by individualism was more than matched by the workers. This tradition is one of the fundamental causes of the slow growth of trade unionism before the First World War.

The guilds of the *ancien régime* were not the ancestors of the modern trade unions but they reveal the traditional divisions to which the working class was for centuries subjected. It is often thought that these guilds contained all the merchants and artisans of a given region. This was not so. Some towns, like Lyon, had no guilds; some trades did not form them; some artisans abstained from joining, particularly those who worked on their own; and most rural ones were left out of the system. The guilds were really a privileged aristocracy with many working-class enemies. They were not organised on a uniform pattern and allowed varying degrees of equality to their members. Different trades were normally in a state of dispute with each other, just as guilds in different towns and guilds with overlapping skills engaged in perpetual warfare and vicious litigation. The idea of federating was quite inconceivable.

The union of workers against their masters goes back to the organisation known as the Compagnonnage, which deserves more detailed description because it was still a highly influential force in 1848. Just as the middle classes had found in freemasonry an institution from which they would evolve a united attack against the old order, the monarchists and the Church, so the working class, or rather the artisans, had a similar body in the Compagnonnage, with mystic rites as elaborate and secrecy as well guarded. In the case of the artisans, however, this served not to unite but to divide them and it explains why they remained so long absorbed in their own private world, fighting battles against each other much more than against their masters.

The Compagnonnage was an organisation of apprentices and journeymen. Its formation was stimulated by the frequent degeneration of the medieval guilds into oligarchies dominated by the masters, with high admission fees, so that it became

[1] G. Duveau, op. cit., 415; *Journal Officiel* (19 Nov. 1875), 9466.

increasingly difficult to be recognised and admitted as a master. Guilds sometimes decided to admit no more masters for ten or twenty years, or to confine admission to the sons of masters. The journeymen therefore formed their own societies, which had to be secret, and hence the complicated rites of initiation, the passwords and the mysticism. These societies enrolled their members from young beginners aged eighteen to twenty-five, and they became solidly established because they assisted young artisans in their professional training and in finding employment during their *tour de France*. It had become customary for many artisans to spend a few years of their early manhood travelling round France, improving their skill by observing different methods of work, and widening their horizon beyond what they could learn from their fathers. By joining the Compagnonnage, they would find in each town they visited members of their society ready to offer them lodging *chez la Mère* (the inn which had a standing arrangement to give them credit until they found work) and a local official, *le rôleur* or *rouleur*, who would obtain employment for them. As they prospered, the Compagnonnages were frequently able to hold a monopoly of this vagrant labour; by acting as intermediaries they were able to compel employers to pay minimum wages and to prevent journeymen accepting a lower wage with which, as strangers, they might feel obliged to content themselves. They could boycott recalcitrant employers and even organise strikes. In addition they provided useful assistance in case of illness or imprisonment.

However, the Compagnonnage did not produce a united artisan youth but the very contrary. About thirty trades were members but they were divided into three different factions. The *Enfants de Salomon* claimed their order had been established by King Solomon to recompense the artisans who built his temple. The *Enfants de Maître Jacques* claimed a French stonemason from Saint-Romili, who had distinguished himself in the building of the temple, as their founder. The *Enfants du Père Soubise* went back to a carpenter who was Jacques' colleague but who then quarrelled with him and whose followers eventually assassinated Jacques. According to another version Père Soubise was a thirteenth-century Benedictine carpenter and his order dates from a division among the *Enfants de Maître Jacques* during the building of Orléans cathedral. These different allegiances meant that the notion of class solidarity was some-what obscured. Artisans of different orders refused to work together. In Paris the river was a strict dividing line, and rival orders of carpenters, for example, each held a monopoly of employment on the left and right banks. Membership of an order was shown by a different uniform. Each trade in each order wore a bunch of coloured ribbons, in varied combinations and lengths, in their buttonholes or hats; some wore ear-rings with different symbols on them, denoting their trade; nail makers wore their hair long in plaits; all carried canes, the more warlike trades having them long and strengthened with iron or copper. Each order had its own songs or ballads, many of which extolled one order and insulted the others. A number of trades were famous for their *hurlements*, a sort of chanting, with the words so pronounced that only their own order could understand them. Hence some earned the names of Dogs, Wolves, Werewolves, and they rejoiced in these titles.

The three orders were started by masons and carpenters, who gradually admitted other trades and revealed the rites to them. Much disagreement resulted because there were nearly always some trades which considered other trades to be so inferior as to be unworthy of the privilege of belonging to the Compagn-onnage. The farriers for example refused to acknowledge the harness makers. The blacksmiths admitted the wheelwrights on condition that they wore their ribbons in their lower botton-hole, but the wheelwrights failed to keep their undertaking and took to wearing their ribbons as high as the blacksmiths—hence their implacable enmity. The bakers were unable to obtain admission at all, though the carpenters said they would sponsor them in return for the payment of a tribute and a promise to abstain from carrying a cane for seven years. Weavers and cobblers were likewise pariahs, the latter being held in par-ticular enmity because they had discovered the secrets of the Compagnonnage without sponsorship, through the indiscretion of an initiate. It is possible that the well-known radicalism of cobblers in the nineteenth century was due to this contempt shown to them by other workers; for the Compagnonnage in general certainly appears rather to have stimulated conserva-tism and great pride in sectional traditions.

The result of these antagonisms was a great deal of physical violence. When two Compagnons met on the high road they would carry out the ritual of *topage*. 'Tope!' one would shout. 'Tope!' the other would reply. They would ask each other's trade and order. If they were of the same order they would drink from each other's gourds or retire to the nearest inn to celebrate; but if one considered his trade or order superior to the other's, he would raise his cane menacingly and demand that the other should get out of his way. A fight usually ensued, which in due course required revenge. In the towns pitched battles would be held: the judicial newspapers of the Restoration are full of reports of bloody and sometimes fatal conflicts between large groups of opposing *Devoirs*. To tear off a companion's ribbons was the worst outrage one could perpetrate upon him; to capture his cane was a sign of great prowess. Occasionally disputes would be fought out more peacefully by holding a competition, to see which order could produce the better piece of work: a representative of each would be locked up, sometimes for several months, to produce a 'masterpiece': the losing order would then be chased out of town in shame.

The Compagnonnage was an institution for young men who, when they completed their *tour de France*, normally retired from it 'thanking the society'. In many towns the retired frequently formed friendly societies—to provide for old age or unemployment—from which the later trade unions in part developed. Altogether it was estimated that in the reign of Louis-Philippe every three years 100,000 artisans passed through the Compagnonnage.[1] It was clearly an important influence on the working class; but it was then already in a state of decay. It had reached the zenith of its activity under the Restoration, but at the same time it had developed certain characteristics which stimulated future divisions. The aspirants (or novices) increasingly complained of the excessive brutality of the initiation ceremonies, of the high fees which the *rouleur* extracted from them for finding them employment, and of the privileges which the older members tried to arrogate to themselves. Under the July monarchy, as a counterpart to the revolution of 1830 (though as early as 1823 in Bordeaux according to some), many aspirants rebelled, seceded and formed a new order, the

[1] A. Perdiguier, *Le Livre du Compagnonnage* (1841), 1. 68; cf. his *Mémoires d'un compagnon* (1914, ed. D. Halévy), and J. Briquet, *Agricol Perdiguier* (1955).

Société de l'Union alias the Indépendants or the Révoltés, in which all were equal, and in which the initiation rites and mysteries were either abolished or made much more humane. In practice, however, these new Indépendants only exacerbated the conflicts, for they engaged in battles against their rivals in the traditional manner.

It is against this background that one must view the movement for fraternity which reached its climax in 1848. The reformers who preached the union of the working class were not typical of the majority but on the contrary were reacting against the cliquishness that was almost universal. Agricol Perdiguier, a joiner from Avignon, was almost alone in attempting to transform the whole spirit of the Compagnonnage by rewriting the warlike songs of the Compagnons to express more loving sentiments: he stimulated a lot of new ballads which deserve to be studied as genuine working-class literature. In 1839 he published these songs together with a description of the violent practices of the Compagnons and an exhortation to reform. 'We are accused of being barbarians, brigands, assassins . . .', he wrote in a passage which is very revealing about class relationships under Louis-Philippe and about the limited aspirations and mutual antagonisms of the workers. 'The rich and powerful form a poor opinion of our capacity and, perhaps not without some reason, contest our civil and political rights. Most people reiterate the severe judgement passed upon us. If we wish to reduce the just dissatisfaction of our brothers at work, if we wish to merit the respect and esteem of those who possess the public fortune and power, if we wish to approach them and to be really considered as their equals, let us not reject each other, for if we do this, they will have the right to reject us.' Perdiguier won some support, but was also bitterly attacked by many of his fellow artisans, who thought a book about them should have glorified their skill and extolled the virtues of their own particular societies. He roused great enthusiasm mainly among the romantics, and George Sand wrote a sugary novel in praise of the highly idealised *Compagnon du Tour de France* (1841) of the future. In 1848 for a time it seemed as though these hopes for the reconciliation of the artisans would be fulfilled. Perdiguier was elected to the Constituent Assembly by Paris (with more votes, significantly, than

Lamennais). A committee was established to effect a federation of all the Compagnon orders. On 21 March 1848 between 8,000 and 10,000 Compagnons paraded through the streets of Paris in witness of their reconciliation. Several trades, hitherto spurned, were admitted into the movement. Even the cobblers, who in 1847 had won some recognition in Lyon, were, in November 1850, accepted by nine corporations. But the plan for a general unification of all the orders and rites of the Compagnons was thoroughly defeated. New schisms and disputes quickly broke out.

This failure came when the movement was already in decay and it sealed its fate. The Compagnons' narrow exclusivism, their outmoded dress, their cruel rites and their tyrannic treatment of the apprentices made them increasingly unpopular with the younger generation. The railways made travel less of an adventure and destroyed the practice of the *tour de France*. Increased industrial activity disrupted the old routines. The Compagnonnage decayed rapidly during the Second Empire and by 1870 it had lost its importance.[1]

It did not disappear entirely, for in 1900 there were still some 10,000 Compagnons. About a quarter of these belonged to a new Fédération Compagnonique, founded in 1874 (later renamed l'Union) which sought to modernise the institution and to combine all the orders. This, however, was largely an artificial creation: it started new Compagnonnages in trades which had never known it, like the mechanics, and it even claimed an outpost in Buenos Aires, founded by an emigrant. Its self-important congresses revealed it as a collection of archaic, esoteric clubs. The real Compagnonnage survived mainly among the farriers, wheelwrights, blacksmiths, thatchers, tilers and locksmiths, genuine relics of pre-industrial France—but not necessarily of rural France only, for in 1900 there were still over 800 carpenter Compagnons in Paris.

Trade Unions

The way the ambitions of the proletariat developed can be seen, from one point of view, by the way they formed trade

[1] W. H. Sewell, 'La Clause ouvrière de Marseille sous la seconde république', *Le Mouvement Social* (July–Sept. 1971), 27–63, makes an outstanding contribution to detailed study of the various types of workers in this period.

unions. The printers were among the first to organise themselves
effectively. As early as 1830 the compositors of Paris already
had forty friendly societies; by 1833 they had founded an
Association libre typographique with most of the aims of a trade
union: to obtain a uniform scale of wages from all employers,
to provide unemployment benefit and other forms of assistance,
and to improve the moral, material and intellectual condition
of all workers, with a particular emphasis on the development
of the spirit of association.[1] By 1842 they had won their wages
scale—the first ever negotiated by a union with their employers.
They made no efforts to subvert the social or political order:
they quickly made their peace, though reluctantly, with the
Second Empire and accepted a president nominated by
Napoleon III, in order to survive as a legal friendly society.
This even held its banquet in 1861 to the accompaniment of
the music of the thirty-third regiment of the line, placed at
its disposal, as a mark of official benevolence, by the marshal
commanding the army in Paris. It was thus able to negotiate
a new wage agreement in 1862; and when some employers
resisted it and got the strikers arrested and convicted, Napoleon
III gave the strikers a free pardon. With the consent of the
government, the friendly society turned itself officially into a
trade union in 1867. It did not join the International, even
though one of the founders of this body, Limousin, was a printing worker; but though it thus kept on the conservative side of
the working-class movement of this period, it gave generous
donations to revolutionary workers, including 2,000 francs to
the International and 500 francs to the weavers of Elbeuf when
they went on strike.[1]

The printers in the early years of the Third Republic were
in fact almost equally divided politically into three groups: the
Parisians, led by Alary, were mainly interested in establishing
co-operative printing works, i.e. buying out the employers. The
socialists, led by Allemane, derived their support much more
from the provinces and were keen on the federal and international aspects of the workers' movement.[3] Both these were
in due course defeated by the man who was to become the

---

[1] Paul Chauvet, *Les ouvriers du livre en France* (1956), 213.
[2] Ibid., 310.
[3] *Les Associations professionnelles ouvrières* (1899–1904), 1. 846–7, 860.

leader of the moderate wing of the French trade unionists, Auguste Keufer. This remarkable man became secretary of the book workers' union in 1884 and remained in that post till he retired in 1920. Born in Alsace in 1851, the orphan son of a factory worker, he emigrated to Lons-le-Saulnier after the German annexation, and here he was initiated into the doctrines of positivism which became his lifelong and openly professed creed. He was confirmed in his belief in the religion of humanity by the lectures of Pierre Laffitte which he attended when he moved to Paris.[1] Keufer remained rather unusual, from the point of view of his political inspiration, in the working-class movement. However, his opinions suited his own union perfectly. He was opposed to a class struggle and to violence. He believed that a better society could not be achieved by revolution, but only by a modification of mentality, by the substitution of altruism for egoism. Meanwhile trade unions should work to improve conditions, which was a necessary preliminary: and he favoured negotiating with the employers, through mixed commissions, using strikes as a very last resort.[2]

A critical year in the history of the printers was 1878 when a strike to force up wages not only greatly impoverished the union but also caused a number of important employers and notably Mame (the chief producer of Catholic books) to migrate to the provinces where wages were lower. This stimulated the Parisians to found a National Federation in 1881. It was Keufer who built this up into an exceptionally powerful and wealthy organisation. Unlike other federations, this one kept central control of funds and of strikes, only the details of administration being left decentralised. Its subscription was among the highest in the country: Keufer raised it gradually from 35 centimes to 2 francs a month between 1881 and 1904, and so his union was able to offer and pay substantial benefits. Far from breaking away from bourgeois society, he maintained close relations with both employers and government. In 1895 the master printers and the book workers held their congresses at the same time in the same city (Marseille): they exchanged

---

[1] Jean Montreuil, *Histoire du mouvement ouvrier en France* (1946), 200–1; Société Positiviste Internationale, *Auguste Keufer* (1925).

[2] Auguste Keufer, *L'Éducation syndicale: exposé de la méthode organique* (1910), 14–15, 43–4; id., *Rapport sur l'organisation des relations entre patrons et ouvriers* (1920).

friendly messages and Keufer accepted an invitation to lunch with the master printers. Mixed commissions were instituted on a national scale in 1898. Keufer was frequently to be seen in the ministries: Fontaine, in charge of the *Office du Travail*, and Finance, one of its officials, were both positivists, as was Fagnot, a former typographer who became an official of the ministry of public works. Keufer served for long on the Conseil supérieur du Travail, of which the minister of commerce was president and he vice-president. He was thus able to get employment for his men in the Imprimerie Nationale (the largest printing works in the country), as well as other jobs and decorations in the government's gift. His treasurer Gaule was given the Legion of Honour, though he himself refused it.[1] Keufer's independence was shown in 1906, during the movement for the eight-hour day. He got his union to declare openly that they considered this an impossible ideal to achieve immediately, that they would seek at first only a nine-hour day and that they would not join the national strikes of May 1906 until they had exhausted all possibilities of negotiation. He met the national organisation of employers in Paris, who decided by 232 to 179 against granting the nine-hour day. He tried then to get agreements at a local level with smaller groups of employers and only when these failed did he allow a strike. It was generally successful, for he was able to spend over half a million francs on the campaign. But the struggle was very hard in the Nord, where there was almost no contact between employer and worker.[2] This regional variation is significant. It is impossible to generalise in simple terms from the experience of the book workers and to argue that, had other unions followed the same policy, the embitterment of the working class might have been avoided.

The miners were slow to organise themselves and even when they began to do so they remained somewhat isolated from the rest of the working class. They placed great faith in the state and looked to it to improve their lot. Having won a privileged

[1] Maurice Harmel, 'Keufer', in *Les Hommes du jour* (27 Aug. 1910), no. 136 (this includes a portrait of him).

[2] A. Keufer, 'Les Grèves de mai dans l'industrie du Livre', *La Revue syndicaliste* (July–Sept. 1906), 51–5, 83–9, 109–15.

position through special legislation, they took care to be moderate in order not to lose it. They showed little sense of solidarity, refusing to make common cause with other workers, and even with miners of other provinces. For long their organisation was self-contained—though torn by numerous and varied disagreements. They could have been a major force in the emancipation of the working class and theirs was a trade capable of a really mass movement: but they were paradoxically hostile to the general strike. So the revolutionary agitation remained largely the monopoly of trades quite incapable of implementing their threats.

Already under Louis-Philippe bloody strikes had broken out in the coalfields of both the Nord and the Loire but they were spontaneous outbursts of anger, and not the work of trade unions. In the Loire, the rudiments of a union existed but their programme and organisation were very elementary. In contrast to the politically conscious artisans of this region, the miners were generally peasant immigrants from the backward mountains around (Haute-Loire, Creuse, Puy-de-Dôme).[1] They were stimulated to unite largely by the union of their employers, who merged their companies into one, the Compagnie de la Loire. In 1852 the miners' vigorous and effervescent leader Garon went to Paris and obtained an interview with the Prince-President of the Republic. As a result the miners were given some concessions and the employers were forced to split up into four companies. The miners were clearly backward looking, yearning nostalgically for the days of the small unmechanised mines, run not by distant engineers but by gang leaders chosen by the men themselves.[2] The appeal to the state was revived a dozen years later by the next leader to rise up, Michel Rondet. He, however, unlike Garon, did not expect the state to emerge as the protector of the workers of its own accord. His plan was to force it to act by seeking out issues on which it would be hard for it to abstain. He showed that the employers were acting illegally in their handling of the miners' provident fund. He successfully sued them, using Jules Favre as barrister; and as

[1] Pétrus Faure, *Histoire du mouvement ouvrier dans le département de la Loire* (St. Étienne, 1956), 39.

[2] P. Guillaume, 'Grèves et organisations ouvrières chez les mineurs de la Loire au milieu du 19e siècle', *Le Mouvement social* (Apr.–June 1963), 5–18.

a result the government allowed him to create an independent fund, run by the miners themselves (*La Société Fraternelle*). This turned out in fact to be half-way to a trade union, but it could not control the miners, and their spontaneous and disastrous strike of 1869 destroyed all Rondet's work. Rondet himself was sentenced to seven months' imprisonment and the flirtation with the empire was over. On 5 September 1870, proclaiming the republic at Ricamarie, he shattered the statue of Napoleon III to the applause of the crowd; he took part in the St. Étienne Commune and was sentenced to five years' imprisonment. These clashes with authority did not, however, turn him into a revolutionary, and indeed with time he became increasingly moderate and conciliatory. He concentrated on a practical programme: the eight-hour day, pensions, miners' delegates for accident prevention and a *conseil de prud'hommes*. In 1882 he went to Paris to canvass the deputies, seeing among them Waldeck-Rousseau, who promised his help. Soon the first bills were introduced: Rondet became nationally known, always as an advocate of gradual improvements by legislative means. Even his ultimate ideal was to be achieved peacefully: 'The government', he said, 'should purely and simply withdraw the coal concessions from the companies and the state should *buy* up the equipment of the mines and exploit them itself to the profit of all.'[1] Rondet toured the mining areas of France and engaged in active propaganda to encourage the formation of unions. He organised the first Miners' Federation in 1883, of which he was secretary until 1896. For all his energy, however, he made little headway in his own department. At the end of 1897 there were still only 3,497 miners organised in unions in the Loire, out of 17,663. They were moreover divided into ten different unions, and Rondet's, the largest, had only 1,127 members. He had sought to stimulate interest by founding a library and a friendly society, but the latter was joined by only sixty miners. The small rival unions waged a bitter campaign against Rondet in the Departmental Federation, which he had himself started but of which he lost control—as he soon lost control of the National Federation.[2]

[1] Office du Travail, *Les Associations ouvrières professionnelles* (1904), 1. 344.
[2] C. Bartnel, 'Un Oublié, Michel Rondet', *La Vie ouvrière* (5 Jan. 1913), 15–24; cf. André Philippe, *Michel Rondet* (1948).

The power of the federation for long remained slight and the initiative passed to the miners of the Nord and Pas-de-Calais, who were suddenly becoming by far the most numerous group in the country.[1] Though they had had sporadic strikes in the 1870s all attempts to found a union had failed and it was only through the encouragement of Rondet that one was established at Denain in 1883. The secretary of this, Basly,[2] was to be the leading figure among the miners till 1914. He followed the same policy of moderation as Rondet, with two differences: he entered parliament himself (deputy for Paris 1885, defeated by a Boulangist 1889, deputy for Lens 1891–1928) and so worked for legislation discreetly, and he had none of Rondet's views on solidarity. He did not seek to spread unionism beyond his region and he kept the welfare of his own union uppermost in his mind. Within a year he had enrolled half the 7,000 members, but in 1884 a strike at Anzin, unsuccessful after fifty-six days and followed by a thousand dismissals, shattered the whole movement in the north. No union arose again in Anzin for fourteen years. The Anzin Company, which had been able to resist the strike largely because of the slack demand for coal, developed a very careful policy of recruitment, engaging new workers only from among the sort of men it knew it could rely on. It established a near monopoly of shopping facilities, becoming the principal baker, grocer and clothes merchant of its workers, so that these had no alternative source of supply or credit should they strike. Whenever there was a strike elsewhere, it told them that they would receive the same advantages as might be won by the strikers.[3] The strikes of 1884 had been supported by the small tradesmen who were hostile to the Anzin Company's co-operative and the Company wished to

---

[1] Miners in Pas-de-Calais—1886: 10,000, 1890: 36,000;
     „   „   the Nord—1886: 15,000, 1890: 19,000.

E. Lozé, *La Grève de 1891 dans les bassins houillers du Nord et du Pas-de-Calais* (Arras, 1891), 36. The two departments produced 32 per cent of France's coal in 1869 and 63·3 per cent in 1903. E. Levasseur, *Questions ouvrières et industrielles en France* (1907), 35.

[2] Émile Joseph Basly, 1854–1928. He was also mayor of Lens 1900–28. His heroism during the German occupation, and his organisation of the reconstruction of the town afterwards prolonged his popularity.

[3] C. Lespilette, *La Vérité sur la grève des mineurs du Nord et du Pas-de-Calais en 1893* (Lille, 1894), 83–6.

destroy them too. Paradoxically, small shopkeepers were for long to be the principal financiers of workers' strikes, by giving credit for purchases, whereas the co-operatives were often instruments of capitalism. This is not surprising, however, for the shopkeepers were frequently former miners who had made good. Basly, who had started work in a mine at the age of ten, was dismissed for his union activities: he then earned his livelihood as a café owner.[1]

In 1889 improved economic conditions stimulated a revival of unionism in the north (except at Anzin) and a series of strikes won wage increases of 20 per cent. Membership soared but at the same time the union leaders showed less and less combativeness and vigour. They preached caution and moderation lest the gains of their negotiated agreement (the 'Convention d'Arras') be lost. Their regional victory increased their isolation from the miners in other parts of the country, and from the union movement as a whole. In moments of crisis they invited the socialist deputies, not the leaders of other trade unions, to come down to help them. The government's threat to withdraw its troops had helped to compel the employers to yield in 1891, and the miners were encouraged to look to it even more for aid against the companies. The companies for their part were driven to unite more effectively among themselves.[2] In 1893 they were able to obtain their revenge, when an unofficial strike, which the leaders had tried to avoid, revealed how precarious the miners' organisation was. Basly quickly made peace, to save the union's funds. Rondet on his side refused to bring out the Loire miners in sympathy. The intervention on this occasion of a quite extraordinary number of troops (thirty-five companies of infantry, ten squadrons of cavalry and 220 gendarmes) and the march of some of the strikers to liberate Anzin, the 'Bastille of the Nord', gave the impression of a veritable insurrection. The revolutionary elements were, however, a very small minority (there were only

[1] Basly was somewhat ashamed of this, however: the café was only in his name, he was never there, he said. See his evidence in *Procès-verbaux de la commission chargée de faire une enquête sur la situation des ouvriers de l'industrie et de l'agriculture en France* (1884), 225–6.

[2] Marcel Gillet, 'L'Affrontement des syndicalismes ouvriers et nationales dans le bassin homiller du Nord et du Pas-de-Calais de 1884 à 1891', *Bulletin de la Société d'histoire moderne* (Mar.–Apr. 1957), 7–10.

500 marchers in fact) and, as in most revolutions, there were
paralysing divisions among them.[1]

The revolutionary minority urged a general strike but Basly
repeatedly foiled them. He at length agreed to a referendum
being held to decide the issue when 1,800 Montceau miners
were dismissed in 1901 after an unsuccessful strike. The vote
was in favour of a general strike (though more than half the
miners abstained). Basly ignored the vote and negotiated with
the government. Twice again referenda were held, producing
increasing approval of a general strike—but still Basly refused
to accept it. When a general strike was at last held in 1902, he
effectively sabotaged it by regionalising it. The general strike
was seen to be far less disastrous for the national economy than
the bourgeoisie feared or the miners threatened. The miners
in fact did not hold anything like the important position their
English counterparts did.[2] The miners of Montceau, together
with some other small unions, now withdrew in protest from
the National Federation and formed their own Union Fédérale.
Again, following a strike at Commentry which Basly likewise
refused to assist—accepting government arbitration instead—
a breakaway union was formed against him in the Pas-de-Calais
by the anarchist Broutchoux.[3] These divisions postponed still
further the admission of the miners into the C.G.T. Basly had
no sympathy for its revolutionary aims. It feared to admit a
moderate union of such enormous size which would inevitably
be a drag on its forward policy. Only in 1908, in a moment of
emotion caused by the arrest of leading unionists, did the
miners join—but the divisions were not therefore diminished.[4]
Broutchoux's young union failed to make the majority of the
northern miners revolutionary: Basly's hold there remained. In
June 1913 Basly indeed withdrew his union from the Fédération du Sous-Sol and established a separate miners' federation

[1] C. Lespilette, *La Vérité sur la grève des mineurs du Nord et du Pas-de-Calais en 1893*
(Lille, 1894) is full of interesting detail.

[2] Comité Central des Homillères de France, *Documents relatifs à la grève des
mineurs de 1902* (1903), 23, 94, 231.

[3] J. Julliard, 'Jeunes et vieux syndicats chez les mineurs du Pas-de-Calais (à
travers les papiers de Pierre Monatte)', *Le Mouvement social* (Apr.-June 1964),
7–30.

[4] G. Dumoulin, 'La Fédération des Mineurs et la C.G.T.', *Le Mouvement socialiste* (Nov. 1908), 321–38.

of more moderate character. Violent polemics were exchanged between the opposing groups.[1]

The railway workers also had it in their power to organise a really influential trade union. There were 44,000 of them in 1854, 240,000 by 1883 and 310,000 by 1914. Their employers—half a dozen major companies—were a clear target. They were subjected to fairly uniform conditions of work, so that unity should have been possible. Their conditions stimulated many grievances. The companies consciously worked their men to the limit. A driver threatened with dismissal in the 1860s for failing to stop at three stations, replied that he had been driving for thirty-eight consecutive hours, and had simply fallen asleep. A petition to the National Assembly in 1871 revealed that drivers frequently worked forty hours without rest and often went for twelve hours without food.[2] It was only in 1891, after numerous vain exhortations by the government, that their working day was limited to twelve hours. However, the companies long continued to subject their men to a rigorous discipline: an elaborate system of fines penalised unpunctuality, insubordination, drunkenness and a whole list of carefully foreseen professional mistakes. There were plenty of mistakes made. For example, on the Nord Railway in the years 1900–10, there was on average one accident a day. 43 per cent of a sample of retired railwaymen at the turn of the century had suffered at least one injury during their employment. The companies did indeed pioneer a pension scheme, which was at first a great attraction, but with time the workers complained that this was an instrument of bondage, since they forfeited their contributions if they were dismissed. In the early years railwaymen had to some extent been privileged members of the working class, but after 1900 their wages failed to keep up with the rising cost of living. The drivers themselves, once an élite, now earned very little more than well-paid Paris artisans; the permanent way men were getting considerably less than navvies.[3]

[1] G. Dumoulin, 'La Fédération des mineurs', *Le Mouvement socialiste* (Oct. 1908), 241–57 (an informative history). E. Merzet, 'L'Unité minière', *Le Mouvement socialiste* (Jan. 1907), 75–83; G. Dumoulin, 'Le Dernier Congrès des mineurs', *La Vie ouvrière* (5 June 1911), 671–80; G. Dumoulin, 'Avec le bureau fédéral des mineurs contre Basly', *La Vie ouvrière* (20 Jan. 1913), 65–79.

[2] Cf. C. A. de Janzé, *Les Serfs de la voie ferrée* (1881).

[3] Guy Chaumel, *Histoire des cheminots et de leurs syndicats* (1948), 19–23, 87–99;

However, before 1914 a mere fifth of the railwaymen had joined a trade union. The history of their efforts to combine is particularly revealing. The first union was a *Société Fraternelle des Mécaniciens Français* founded in February 1848, whose main purpose was to press the companies to employ French rather than English drivers: at that time one-third of the drivers on the Nord lines and all those on the Paris–Havre railway were English. Haphazard strikes to compel the expulsion of the English failed completely and the society disappeared by the end of June 1848. The *Association des Travailleurs des Chemins de Fer Français*, likewise founded after the revolution of February, had as its vice-president a representative of the employers, whose donations alone kept it going for a couple of years. It had no revolutionary ambitions, any more than did the *Société de l'Union Fraternelle* (1871). This latter hoped to save its subscriptions to build a small local railway of its own—to safeguard its members against unemployment and to enable them to become independent. In 1880 Gambetta and Carnot helped to found another union, which was likewise devoted to self-help, providing pensions, sickness benefits and mortgages. Some members wished to use it to agitate for legislation to improve railwaymen's conditions, but the engineers and directors of the company infiltrated it as honorary members and kept it virtually a friendly society. Again the *Syndicat Professionnel* (*Association Amicale*) was founded in 1884 by well-intentioned but bourgeois deputies. Under their influence, it sought to solve its members' problems by a long-term plan of buying shares in the railway companies: it proclaimed itself an organisation devoted to conciliation and it opposed the use of strikes. It attracted little more than 3,500 members by 1890 and 12,000 by 1906.

A really large and independent railwaymen's union, the *Syndicat National*, appeared only in 1890. It prospered rapidly, claiming within ten years 45,000 members (much exaggerated, no doubt). It found in Guérard, who at the age of thirty-four became its secretary and remained so for eighteen years (1891–1909), an organiser of unusual talent. He believed that the

F. Caron, 'Essai d'analyse historique d'une psychologie du travail: les mécaniciens et chauffeurs de locomotives du réseau du Nord de 1850 à 1910', *Le Mouvement social* (Jan.–Mar. 1965), 3–40.

great problem was to unite the workers into powerful federations and he devoted himself unremittingly to this task of
building up numbers. He preached the general strike and
organised two, in 1891 and 1898, both woefully unsuccessful,
because only a tiny minority of his members stopped work.
Though Guérard was outstanding in the C.G.T. as one of the
principal advocates of the general strike, he became more
moderate in course of time. In the nineties he had secured
the passage of a bill (loi Berteaux, December 1897) giving
pensions to all railwaymen but the senate postponed passing
it into law till 1909. This failure of parliamentary methods, and
the refusal of the employers to negotiate with him, stimulated
him to organise the general strike of 1898; but its pitiful failure
caused him to modify his revolutionary ideals. He was soon
accused of having excessive relations with bourgeois parlia-
mentarians, of attending a dinner given by Millerand and
indeed of preaching doctrines very much akin to those of the
moderate Keufer. The limitations imposed by the senate on the
Railways Pensions Law of 1909 produced so much dissatisfaction that the upper hand was won by the revolutionaries.
Guérard resigned and a strike was declared in 1910. It failed,
not surprisingly, and the revolutionaries were once more
voted into a minority. This is enough to show how the revolutionary unions were far from being irreconcilably hostile to the
regime. Their alienation was in large measure due to the in-
transigence of the capitalists and the government. But the
politics of the railwaymen should not be seen in terms of seizure
of power by clear-cut rival groups with antagonistic views. There
was much gradual evolution of attitudes in opposing directions. Thus while on the one hand Guérard gave up revolutionary for parliamentary agitation, the once conservative
engine drivers of the North, who had remained in a separate
union so as to avoid joining any revolutionary movement, who
had epitomised responsibility and loyalty to their employers,
and who had largely accepted the benefits of paternalism,
surprisingly came out on strike in 1910, in greater numbers
than any other group—70 per cent of them. Of those of them
who were dismissed as a result 38 per cent were aged over
40 (not far from the retiring age of 50), which shows that
some older men had changed their minds about strikes. The

employers on their side were on the one hand increasingly conciliatory after 1900 and, without avowing it, began negotiating
with the unions (which is why Guérard could change his
tactics); but on the other hand they felt they could not make
more concessions, because receipts were diminishing (and the
law imposed a ceiling for fares), while their expenses were
rising inexorably with costs.[1] However, for all the new currents
at work among the railwaymen, traditional attitudes clearly
continued to prevail. Only about 20 per cent of them were
members of a union as late as 1914. This figure, moreover,
included many moderates, as, for example, the *Est* Railwaymen's Union, which had refused to join in the movement of
1910, the majority in it being hostile to strikes altogether.[2]

In 1900 it was estimated that there were about 100,000
workers in the building industry. Only some 30,000 of these
were members of unions, and they were divided between no
fewer than 357 organisations. The Compagnonnage had been
extremely powerful in this industry, with old-established and
deep-rooted loyalties, and it kept the building workers separated not only by craft but in groups within each craft. The trade
unions rose up as a challenge to it, stimulated by a desire to
end the privileges or monopoly enjoyed by the Compagnons
in obtaining employment. However, the unions were themselves
distracted from the task of unification by their interest in establishing co-operative associations, for which the building trade
was particularly suitable. The exclusiveness of these co-
operatives, and the fact that they frequently paid their members
even less than the exploiting employers, in turn produced a reaction against them. However, repeated attempts to organise
a national federation (1882, 1892, 1902) had only limited and
very temporary success. The craft unions, led by the powerful
masons and carpenters, preferred to build up their own
independent national federations, until the strikes of 1906
revealed their weakness and the dangers of these traditional
divisions. It was only then that the *Fédération Nationale des
Travailleurs de l'industrie du bâtiment* came to be widely accepted.

---

[1] Caron, 34–40.
[2] Anon., 'Le Congrès des cheminots de l'Est', *La Vie ouvrière* (20 Jan. 1911),
120–2.

Its membership rose from 9,000 in 1905 to 30,000 in 1908, but the union frittered away its funds: in 1911 it gave away no less than 60,000 francs to the C.G.T., to help pay for its journal, *La Bataille Syndicaliste*; so when the strike of 1912 broke out, it had no money to support its men. Membership at once fell drastically and even more so when the federation raised its subscriptions in 1912. It was feared as a revolutionary monster, which periodically expanded and deflated, but it was less menacing than it seemed.[1] For example, despite its nominally uncompromising demand for an eight-hour day, on a national scale, it was in practice content to accept considerably longer hours, for in some regions builders worked as much as twelve hours a day, and they realised an immediate adoption of short hours was impracticable. The varied social conditions of France compelled them to be opportunists in practice.

The extremes to which craft particularism could go are illustrated by the trade unions of cooks. Under Louis-Philippe there existed in Paris two groups of cooks: *La Laurentine*, which was a social club, and the *Société des Pieds Humides*, so called because its members used to meet in the mornings at Les Halles in search of employment. In 1840 these two united to form the *Société des Cuisiniers de Paris*, whose sole object at first was to serve as a labour exchange. At the Revolution of 1848 they changed their title to *Société Centrale des Artistes Culinaires*, and in 1853 again to *Société de secours mutuels et de prévoyance des cuisiniers de Paris*, for this was the only kind of organisation the Second Empire would tolerate. It continued to concern itself with employment but at the same time it gradually developed a pensions fund, which by the end of the century was one of the most successful of its kind. The concentration on pensions was not surprising, for the cooks opposed the introduction of notice before dismissal into their craft; they wished to be free, as temperamental artists, to leave an employer without notice at any time. The concentration of this union on pensions, however, started a certain amount of dissatisfaction. A separate *Cercle d'etudes sociales et professionnelles des Cuisiniers de Paris* was founded in April 1899, borrowing its statutes from the *Cercle d'études sociales des proletaires positivistes de Paris*: about fifty Comtist cooks joined this. A demand for more attention to professional education gave birth in 1882 to a *Union universelle pour le progrès de l'art culinaire*, which a year later obtained the prefect's authority to call itself instead the *Académie de Cuisine*. It purposely allowed itself only thirty full members, though an unlimited number of associate members. Candidates for full membership had to present a written thesis, which was read before the Academy. In 1884 the cooks of Paris were divided into seven different organisations. There were three friendly societies (serving also as employment exchanges) and four unions each with a slightly different emphasis: a *Chambre syndicale*, a *Cercle de la Fraternité*, a *Société des Cuisiniers français*, and the *Académie de Cuisine*. When in 1898 the *Fédération ouvrière des cuisiniers* (founded 1887) joined the C.G.T., it brought with it only a minority.[1]

Syndicalism

The impression left by traditional descriptions of the rise of the trade union movement is one of an increasingly revolutionary force, openly threatening to overthrow the whole social order, and refusing all compromise with it. The proceedings of the workers' congresses may perhaps have justified the terror of the bourgeoisie. The first of these congresses, held in 1876, revealed, it is true, no wish for revolution. It resolved that the emancipation of the worker would be achieved by the formation of co-operative associations; it condemned strikes; it said nothing about property, except that the worker should own his tools, and that interest on capital should be abolished. Some thought that it was idle to expect reform from the bourgeoisie, but their remedy was that the workers should elect their own representatives to parliament. Gradually, however, principally under the influence of Guesde, socialist views and the theory of the class struggle were introduced. The third congress of 1879, held

[1] *Les Associations professionnelles ouvrières*, 1 (1889), 515–49. P. Hubert-Valleroux, 'Les Syndicats professionnels en France', in *Revue sociale et politique* (Brussels, 1892), 431.

at Marseille, decided on the formation of the Party of Socialist Workers. Had this survived, the unions might have become the backbone of a French version of the Labour Party; but two factors prevented this. First, the socialist leaders (as will be seen in another chapter) were deeply divided and the party quickly split into several factions. Guesde's triumph was brief, and he had in fact never really captured the workers' movement. The Marseille congress was packed with his supporters and widespread indifference among unions allowed him to pass his resolutions in their absence. When they later began to attend congresses more conscientiously, they had relatively little difficulty in evicting him. For, secondly, there now became manifest among them a desire for direct action, as opposed to agitation through parliament. They wished to avoid entanglement in bourgeois politics, or in politics at all, for that served only to divide them. In 1892 they adopted the general strike as their method of action—against the policy of Guesde. Three years later Guesde had seceded and his Federation of Unions quickly faded out of existence. The workers' movement became completely independent, with anarcho-syndicalism as its creed.

This suggests the adoption of a thoroughly revolutionary attitude. The workers proclaimed themselves enemies not only of the capitalists but also of the state and of democracy. They openly preached violence as the only possible means of winning their objectives: the strike, boycott, expropriation. They had no intention of postponing the day of victory till all the workers were behind them. They believed in the rights of minorities. They joined, that is to say, to the socialist criticism of the capitalist order, and its belief in the class struggle as the method of emancipation for the working class, the anarchist horror of the state as an inevitable source of tyranny, and the desire to abolish it as a centralised organisation. They were less optimistic than the socialists, however, in that they did not believe that capitalism was bound to collapse from its internal contradictions. They insisted that the revolution would be achieved only through the efforts of the workers themselves. This, together with the belief that once the revolution was successful, the new order should be run by the workers themselves, organised in unions, is the real essence of syndicalism. But syndicalism was for many only a new form of the old working-class ideas of independence and dignity on the one hand and production associations as a means of achieving this on the other. In proclaiming themselves syndicalists the workers were often reiterating an old belief more than they were innovating.[1] Pelloutier's description of the new order they would establish is not all that different from Proudhon's.

It is true that syndicalism now no longer meant simply mutual help but was anarchist and revolutionary. The workers claimed to reject the bourgeois order rather than attempt to find a niche for themselves in it. They believed that strikes were their best instrument, instead of rejecting them as they had once done; indeed they even looked upon them as good things in themselves, a method of education in class consciousness. However, more careful examination of their attitudes, and even of their actions, reveals that they were far less uncompromising than all this talk of revolution suggests. Though they dismissed the Millerandists as traitors, though they contemptuously denounced partial reforms conceded by the bourgeois state as worthless, and though they considered the mutual benefits offered by the moderate unionists as diversions from the class struggle, in practice there were very few trade union leaders who did not work for the immediate improvement of the workers' lot by gradual reforms. They called it 'revolutionary reformism'—but whatever may have been their ultimate goal, it was reformism in practice. Their problem was to prevent the government reaping the reward of its social legislation and winning the workers away from the revolutionary struggle. They sought, that is, to satisfy the workers' immediate complaints but to keep them dissatisfied, to distinguish the short term from the long term.

The C.G.T. as a body was revolutionary but the majority of its members and of the unions in it were not revolutionary. This paradox is explained by the voting system. Every union had a vote, irrespective of its size. The small unions, which tended to be revolutionary because their small membership gave them no hope of ever achieving anything by peaceful

[1] For a good analysis of revolutionary syndicalism see Félicien Challaye, *Syndicalisme révolutionnaire et syndicalisme réformiste* (1909). This contains valuable references to articles by workers on this subject, which he unfortunately does not differentiate from the works of intellectuals from outside the movement. See also F. Ridley, *Revolutionary Syndicalism in France* (1970).

means, thus dominated the C.G.T. The six smallest unions, with a total membership of only twenty-seven, had as many votes as the six largest, which had some 90,000 members.[1] A minority of 45,000 unionists had enough votes, because they belonged to so many different small unions, to decide every issue.[2] The executive committee held about one-third of the votes by proxy, from small unions unable to afford sending their own representatives to congress. The C.G.T. was in fact almost run on the basis of rotten boroughs.[3] It justified its unrepresentative character in the name of the rights of minorities, but in its own proceedings it was ruled by majority votes.

The leaders of the C.G.T. were far from being the slaves of anarcho-syndicalism or indeed any theory at all. Griffuelhes, who was its secretary general from 1902 to 1909, not only made a point of emphasising this, but even went so far as to say he had not even read the theorists. 'I read Alexandre Dumas', he used to say contemptuously. The working-class movement, he repeated, was the product not of principles but of day-to-day events. Some of the members argued about the kind of society it would one day establish, but he did not consider that very profitable. 'It is always easy to formulate theories, it is harder to put them into practice.' Griffuelhes (1874–1923) was a cobbler, who specialised in making shoes for the luxury market in Paris, working for a wage under a humble master who was little more than an artisan himself. He had a hard life and joined his union 'to fight against the employers, who were the direct instrument of my enslavement, and against the state, which was the natural defender, because it was the beneficiary, of the employers. It is from the union that I drew all my strength for action, and it is there that my ideas began to grow precise.' He was essentially a trade union man, who worked consistently for the independence of the movement, for its interests, and not for the service of any party or theory. In his youth he was for a few years a follower of Blanqui, but his entry into the trade union movement quickly caused him to abandon political action. He considered it his task as a union

[1] Mermeix, *Le Syndicalisme contre le socialisme, origine et développement de la C.G.T.* (1907), 200.

[2] Guérard in *Humanité* (31 May 1907), quoted by F. Challaye, *Syndicalisme révolutionnaire* (1909), 132 n.

[3] Victor Diligent, *Les Orientations syndicales* (1910), 170.

leader to reflect the ambitions of the members of his union, without worrying about consistency of principle. 'The workers' movement', he wrote, 'has been a series of daily efforts linked to efforts of the previous day, not by any rigorous continuity but uniquely by the attitude and state of mind ruling the working class. The action of the working class has not been, I say it again, ordered by formulae or by any theoretical affirmations; nor has it been a demonstration following a plan foreseen in advance by us.'[1]

Griffuelhes was above all an organiser and an administrator. He had neither a brilliant mind nor any particular oratorical gifts; but he was able, efficient, disinterested and by nature a man who could command obedience. His great achievement was to give coherence to his thoroughly divided movement. Though he worked to maintain the supremacy of the revolutionary wing, he always kept his polemic against the reformists within reasonable bounds and took care not to force them out of the C.G.T. by any inordinate extremism. His essentially practical common sense should have been adequate guarantee that he would never have supported any premature revolution.

Griffuelhes's deputy at the C.G.T., Émile Pouget (1860–1931), was no demagogue either, with even less gift for public speaking. Pouget was a journalist, of *déclassé* bourgeois origin. His father had been a notary but died young, so compelling Pouget to earn his own living. He began as an assistant at a Paris department store (the Bon Marché), read *La Révolution sociale*, was converted to anarchism, spent three years in prison for taking part in one of its demonstrations, and then started a remarkable periodical called the *Le Père Peinard*, reminiscent in style of the *Père Duchesne* of the Revolution. He wrote this entirely himself. It at once attracted attention because it was written for workers in their own slang and with great verve. He claimed their language was entirely different from that of the bourgeoisie whom they could barely understand. When in 1900 the C.G.T. founded its own (weekly) paper, *La Voix du Peuple*, Pouget was made its editor. He always longed to run a daily, but his efforts to found one repeatedly failed. He wrote novels of working-class life (not very genuine ones). He was a friend of many of the impressionist painters—Pissarro and Paul Signac

[1] V. Griffuelhes, *L'Action syndicaliste* (1908), 8.

illustrated some of his writings—and he accumulated a sizeable collection of their paintings, given to him as presents. He ended his days as a salesman of catalogues which he arranged to have printed for art galleries. He was thus, like Pelloutier, something of an outsider in the movement. However, he played a very important part, by his leading position in the C.G.T.'s propaganda, in increasing the numbers of revolutionary syndicalists. He preached the class war as essential to all progress, but he did not reject partial reforms as worthless. If reforms came as gifts from the government, they must be received with caution, because they would inevitably contain a bias towards the employer, but they were acceptable if they were won from the government by force. The workers should organise so as to force reform by direct action, instead of waiting for the government to make presents to them.[1]

Yvetot, the secretary of the Bourses section of the C.G.T., was a vigorous antimilitarist (author of the celebrated *Manuel du soldat*, written in prison and published partly with funds from the government subsidy to the Bourses). His father had been in the *garde impériale* and the *gendarmerie*. He himself was educated by the Frères de la Doctrine Chrétienne, and never became an anticlerical. Merrheim, secretary of the metallurgists and in charge of the C.G.T.'s relations with the provincial federations, was a puritan from Roubaix who was horrified by the demagogy and immorality he found in Paris. Intellectual curiosity and a remarkable seriousness of purpose alone kept him from giving it all up and returning home. He insisted that it was impossible to defeat the capitalists by blind attacks. The workers needed to study their enemy. He undertook careful and thorough surveys of the organisation of the employers; his favourite reading was company reports. Pataud of the electricians on the other hand was the very opposite of Merrheim. He was an exhibitionist who loved nothing better than to be photographed and interviewed by journalists, but who took care to exchange his habitual bowler hat for a more democratic beret before he allowed the cameras to get to work. He plunged Paris into darkness by a strike in 1908, with a marvellous sense of publicity. Only the Bourse du Travail was allowed any

[1] Christian Demay de Goustine, 'Emile Pouget' (unpublished thesis in the Library of the Faculty of Law, Paris, 1961).

electricity and there Pataud received the journalists to show them his power. On another occasion he got the electricians of the Opéra to go on strike in the middle of a gala performance given for a foreign sovereign: they got their wage increase after a few minutes of negotiation in the darkness.[1]

The threat of revolution from the C.G.T. is seen to be even more superficial when one realises that between a third and a half of its members were not revolutionary syndicalists but reformist syndicalists. As such, they hoped, no doubt, for the same ultimate goal as the revolutionaries. They wanted, as one of them said (in language which has an interesting antique flavour) the complete emancipation of labour by the suppression of wage earning and the replacement of bourgeois capitalism by the association of workers. But their programme, as opposed to their ideal, was one of immediate practical reforms.[2] They did not believe in revolution by minorities but, admiring the wealth and numbers of the British and German unions, they wished to draw the majority of the French workers into unions. They believed that only a mass rising could ever be successful, or rather that when all the workers were union members, they could one day simply say to the capitalists: 'We have had enough.' The way to attract the workers into the unions was first to respect their different opinions and beliefs, avoiding politics, whether socialist or anarchist. Their neutrality was expressed as aparliamentarianism, not as antiparliamentarianism. They rejected the idea of forming a Labour Party.

Secondly, as Niel of the book workers' union wrote, 'Syndicalism will be passionately loved by all the proletariat the day it proves that it wants and is capable of bringing the working class immediate alleviation and consolation, which numerous naïve persons still hope from religion, from the employers or from the politicians.' They demanded revolutionary reforms rather than revolution. They continued to call themselves revolutionaries, but explained this as meaning simply that 'every reform which snatches a piece of capital or a piece of authority from the employer, to give it to the worker, is a

[1] M. Leclercq and E. Girod de Fléaux, *Ces Messieurs de la C.G.T.*, *profils révolutionnaires* (1908); J. Julliard, *Clemenceau, briseur de grèves* (1965), 115.

[2] Maurice Claverie (of the Paris gas workers' union), 'Révolutionnaires soit, mais réformistes d'abord', in *Action ouvrière*, 1 Dec. 1909, quoted by Pierre A. Carcanagues, *Sur le mouvement syndicaliste réformiste* (Paris thesis, 1912), 36.

revolutionary reform ... We are revolutionaries because we have proved that historically the Revolution is destined to take place [la Révolution est fatale].'[1] Keufer said the workers were just not ready to take over the means of production, in their existing state of ignorance. The total failure of the general strikes organised in the early years of the twentieth century produced a disillusionment with the idea of the general strike and even with the ordinary strike itself as a method of advancing the cause. Eight reformist trade union leaders, questioned about their attitude to the general strike, dismissed it as an illusion, a bluff or a decoy; three others approved of it only provided the workers were first educated, three were not certain whether it would be the method they would use, one thought it a useful sword of Damocles.[2] 'A new attitude is spreading among the unionists', wrote P. M. André of the railwaymen. 'The workers, led astray by the mirages of the theories of creative violence, have finally come to see that we [the reformists] have been right, that these theories were entirely childish. Unionists are considering themselves less and less as "revolutionary pioneers". They have never gone on strike in order to learn the art of revolution, but always to further their professional interests.'[3] The reformists now said that strikes should be used only as a very last resort; they insisted a referendum should be held among the workers involved before any strike was actually declared.[4] Increasing use of collective bargaining was urged, with the idea that ultimately the unions could tender for work from the employers and so gradually run the economy themselves.[5] *Action* was the revolutionaries' demand: '*useful action* is our motto.'[6]

The principal reformists were Keufer of the book workers,

---

[1] L. Niel, 'Les Réformes révolutionnaires', *Bulletin de la Bourse du Travail de Reims* (15 June 1909), and id., 'Évolution ou révolution', *Travailleur syndiqué de Montpellier* (Dec. 1901), quoted op. cit., 36, 39.

[2] Carcanagues, 21 and appendix.

[3] P. M. André, 'La Débâcle du socialisme anarchisant', *Le Socialisme* (9 Nov. 1909), quoted op. cit., 43.

[4] F. Challaye, *Syndicalisme révolutionnaire et syndicalisme réformiste* (1909), 120 n. 3.

[5] Carcanagues, 68.

[6] Challaye, 127. Cf. A. Keufer, 'Le Syndicalisme réformiste', *Mouvement socialiste* (Jan. 1905), 18. The main reformist organ was *La Revue syndicaliste* (1905–10), later *La Revue socialiste* (1910–14), which contains informative articles on union life as well.

Compat of the mechanics, Renard of the textile workers and
Guérard of the railwaymen.[1] The builders and the metal-
workers were the most prominent revolutionaries. But it is once
again impossible to divide the unions neatly in this way.
Moderate leaders, among the miners for example, had to con-
tend with growing revolutionary minorities within their ranks.
Able leaders with a strong hold over unions gave them a political complexion which was not truly representative of their
followers. The moderate Guérard was in due course evicted
from his leadership of the railwaymen, but in the 1911 strike
the East railwaymen refused to take part, and their secretary,
Le Leuch, was hostile to any strikes at all.[2]

The C.G.T. was particularly weak financially. In 1910 its
income was only about 20,000 francs (£800). To support the
general strike of 1 May 1906 it had appealed for funds—and
received the ludicrous total of 5,000 francs (£250). The national
federations likewise were very poor, but they kept what money
they could collect largely to themselves, so that they retained
a considerable measure of independence as against the C.G.T.
The National Federation of Printers was actually ten times
wealthier than the C.G.T. Its annual income was 220,000
francs (£8,800). The strikes of 1906 for the eight-hour day had
totally absorbed its reserves, for it paid 3 francs 50 a day strike-
pay to its members and 2 francs a day to non-unionists who
made common cause with the strikers. It had been able to
spend 628,000 francs (£25,120) on the strike, helped by gifts of
163,000 francs from foreign unions and the International
Printers' Federation and by an equal sum raised by a 5 per
cent tax on its members not on strike. In June 1906 it had a
deficit of 14,000 francs. Three years later it had already paid
this off and accumulated savings of 212,000 francs. These
figures are those of the richest union in France, outdistancing
all others by far; but though the French printers had the third
largest membership in the International Printers' Federation,
it was only the eighth in wealth. The London and Provincial
Compositors, with an equal membership to it, had an income

[1] J. B. Séverac, *Le Mouvement syndical* (1913), 74 n. and 75 n.
[2] 'Le Congrès des cheminots de l'Est' (anon.), *La Vie ouvrière* (20 Jan. 1911),
120–2); cf. A. Picart, 'Le Troisième Congrès du bâtiment', *La Vie ouvrière* (5 May
1910) 547–58, 552.

five times as large. The next richest trade, but far behind the printers, was the miners'. Their federation, it has been seen, existed mainly on paper, and so though it had 30,000 members, its subscription was only 5 centimes a month per member; its total income was under 10,000 francs (£400) a year. The regional unions were the bodies which kept the real power among the workers, and by far the largest of these was that of Pas-de-Calais; but even they had great difficulty in accumulating any reserves at all. It was only after the bloody strike of 1906 that the need for funds was accepted. The subscription was raised from 50 centimes to 2 francs a month; but of this 2 francs, only 50 centimes went to the union—as before. The rest was placed to the credit of each unionist, remaining his individual property, to be used in case of strike or long unemployment. It was only by this subterfuge, that is by opening a sort of savings bank, that the Pas-de-Calais federation was able to accumulate 779,000 francs by 1909, from its 24,000 members; and no other union at that time could compare with this. But it is interesting that this was achieved at the expense of all the socialist principles. In the event of a strike, each member would draw a different amount of pay, in proportion to the savings he had made. In the textile industry the national federation had an income of only 26,000 francs (£1,040) from 20,000 to 25,000 members. The textile union of Roubaix, with 6,000 members, was five times richer. Frequently, as with the metallurgical or building workers, rival craft federations split up what little income was collected. All in all, it was estimated that in 1910 French trade unionists paid 1,353,000 francs a year, which came to about 2½ francs a head—viz. 2 shillings a year each. Low though subscriptions were, the workers seemed to find them not worth their while; it was seldom that, of the subscriptions promised, more than a small proportion was ever paid. The federations could not offer attractive benefits: only the printers had a fund for funeral and sickness benefits and only they and the mechanics offered unemployment pay. Travelling money was more frequent. Many federations promised strike pay, few of them ever paid it. There were enormous regional differences in the willingness of workers to pay subscriptions. The glove makers of Chaumont paid 5 francs a month, those of Milhaud and Grenoble only 60 centimes. In such circumstances effective federation was impossible. The worker continued to trust only the small local union where he was individually known. The notion of national solidarity, though sometimes strikingly shown by union leaders in generous donations to other unions, was rarer among the mass of their followers, among whom peasant thrift and individualism had not always been extinguished.[1]

The best account of trade unionism before 1914 was written by Griffuelhes himself.[2] His tour of France in 1911 revealed how fragmentary was its organisation, how unequal its provincial foundation, how dependent its strength on personal factors. The majority of strikes were still entered into without any preliminary union organisation.[3] The strikes of the miners themselves in 1902 and 1906 had been the work of minorities opposing the union leaders. There were still numerous regions where unionism had hardly even won a foothold, and these sometimes included highly industrialised parts of France. 'The Vosges are full of weavers whom syndicalist propaganda has been unable to galvanise so as to produce any profound or vigorous movement. Protected by [the obsessive] hate for Germany, there has been established a bourgeoisie whose power is colossal. Against it a weak trade union movement can be seen showing itself by a few revolts, after which a deep calm reappears.' In Franche-Comté likewise there was little unionism despite the very considerable industrialisation. Apart from the watchmakers of Besançon, there had been no conflict in this region since 1899.[4] Rural areas, like the Cher, by contrast had been deeply penetrated by the movement. In Grenoble a period of revolutionary activity had been ended by the secession of the deputies, who had become independent socialists, and so more favourable to the government. Lyon was torn by personal and electoral competition. In Marseille the union movement was superficial; the dispersion and heterogeneity of the city's

[1] Charles Rist, 'La Situation financière des syndicats ouvriers français', *Revue économique internationale* (Brussels, Jan. 1911), off-print in Musée Social.

[2] Victor Griffuelhes, *Voyage révolutionnaire* (1911); cf. also his *L'Action syndicaliste* (1908).

[3] *Statistiques des grèves*.

[4] Cf. Jean Charles, *Les Débuts du mouvement syndical à Besançon: la fédération ouvrière 1891–1914* (1962).

inhabitants appeared as grave obstacles. The dockers, suffering from unemployment in the last decade of the century, were powerless: improved conditions after 1899 made possible a sudden organisation, and a succession of strikes, culminating in success; but after 1904, a lock-out shattered the movement and largely re-established the dominance of the employers.[1]

The situation in the Vosges was exceptionally interesting. Another observer wrote in 1906: 'The sentiments of the workers towards their employers were for long ones of submission and respect, not to say servility and subservience. Their only political opinion was patriotism, acute chauvinism, which made them rally behind Boulanger or against the Jews. This has changed since the formation of the unions. The socialist spirit is penetrating little by little into their heads. But, despite the strikes and the agitation, its progress is still very slow.' There were no unions at all before 1884. A few were then founded but the only really successful one was that of the book workers—which was of course very moderate. Then the cotton crisis of the early years of the century, causing the wages of the textile workers to be reduced, led to an outbreak of strikes. Four textile unions were founded—but, very significantly, not by the textile workers themselves but by Pernot, the leader of the Vosges Book Workers' Union. He also founded a federation of the unions in the department and started a newspaper for it. It was only then that the central trade union leaders, Renard of the textile workers and Keufer of the book workers, came on a tour of the Vosges and stimulated the formation of other unions. It was always to Pernot, however, that workers in distress in the department appealed. It was he, for example, who organised the paper workers at Étival and brought them out on strike. In due course his federation had 18,000 members. His leadership of it was at first very moderate indeed: he belonged to the *Alliance Républicaine* which had employers among its members and he accepted government subsidies for an anti-alcoholic campaign in his paper. Under the influence of the general trend in France, however, he was driven to adopt a more socialist line and the moderate radical editor of his paper was forced to resign. Significantly, it was prin-

[1] M. Lartigue (*née* Vecchie), 'Les Grèves des dockers à Marseille de 1890 à 1903', *Provence historique*, 10 (1960), 146–79.

cipally the refusal of the employers to deal with him that made
Pernot abandon his hopes of agreement with them by conciliation and mixed unions. They preferred to set up their own
'yellow unions'. It was in this way that a potentially moderate
department became revolutionary.[1]

The Bourses du Travail

The growth of national federations was considerably delayed
by the rise of a rival form of federation of unions, the local
Bourse du Travail. It was under this name that the unions in
any one town grouped themselves, sharing the same building
for their offices. The Bourses have some resemblance to the
English local trades councils (e.g. a union could be a member
of both the trades council and a national federation) but they
differed from them in many respects and the name is best left
untranslated. First of all, the Bourses du Travail owed their
origin, unlike the trades councils, to official action. They were
given free buildings by the municipality and substantial subsidies to meet their administrative expenses. The Bourses were
expected to perform a number of public functions—the most
important of which was that of labour exchange. The demand
for labour exchanges was an old one. It was first canvassed by
a Catholic social economist, Molinari, in the 1840s.[2] The provisional government of the republic of 1848 decreed that every
town hall should have one—a dead letter like so many of its
decrees. The idea then spread that some shelter should be
provided where the unemployed could gather; for traditionally
they congregated in certain streets, or wine shops, where employers seeking workers met them. (The Place de Grèves, now
the Place de l'Hôtel de Ville, was one of the principal meeting-
places, and it is from this that the word grève came to be used
to mean strike.) The initiative was finally taken by the city of
Paris in the 1880s under the stimulus of the new attitude towards
the workers symbolised by the law of 1884. The employment
exchange, it was now considered, should be run by the workers

[1] G. Airelle, 'Le Mouvement ouvrier dans les Vosges', in *Le Mouvement socialiste*
(Feb.–Apr. 1906), 218–31, 333–63, 455–75.
[2] See G. de Molinari, *Les Bourses du Travail* (1893), 121–5. His proposal was
first published in the legitimist newspaper *La Gazette de France*.

themselves. and be one of the services which the trade unions—
in which there was then unbounded optimism—would render
to the community. The Bourse indeed became a means of
encouraging the growth of trade unions. In 1887 the city of
Paris opened one in the rue J.-J. Rousseau and in 1892
donated a sizeable new building to it. The Bourse was essential,
said the municipal council, to prevent trade unions leading a
precarious existence, because the subscriptions they levied to
meet their expenses kept away the majority of the workers. The
Bourse would provide a free meeting-place and offices, so that
all could come without fear of incurring financial obligations
beyond their means. 'The free and permanent use of meeting
rooms will allow the workers to discuss with greater maturity
and precision the many questions which interest their industry
and which influence their wages. They will have there to guide
them all the information, news and statistics they need, an
economic, industrial and commercial library, facts about trends
of production in each industry not only in France but throughout the world.' The Bourse was thus intended at once to
encourage the formation of unions, to keep their expenses down,
to diminish their isolation from each other, and to enable them
to work together for their common interests and education.
Though the president of the municipal council inaugurated
the Bourse in the name of 'solidarity and social peace', he also
declared that its purpose was 'to enable the workers to fight
capital with equal and legal arms . . . By permitting the demands of the workers to manifest themselves freely, scientifically
and legally, the Bourse du Travail will give the republican
government the means not to snuff out these demands but to
understand them and to work for a social order more conforming to justice.'[1] Paris was quickly copied by other towns
and by 1908 there were no fewer that 157 Bourses all over
France.

In this way there grew up an original form of workers' association. The Bourses became not so much employment exchanges
as societies of trade unions, grouped on a local basis. Though
subsidised by the authorities, nearly all of them were run by

[1] F. Pelloutier, *Histoire des Bourses du Travail* (1902), 63–4, 74; L. Le Theuff,
Histoire de la Bourse du Travail de Paris (Paris thesis, 1902), 35; E. Briat, 'La Bourse
du Travail de Paris', *Le Mouvement socialiste* (1899), 52–6.

revolutionaries, who frequently used these subsidies to attack the government. They managed to do this partly because many municipalities at this time were captured by socialists and public money could thus be voted to attack the bourgeois state. (Socialist municipalities used to vote money even to support strikes.) But even where the Bourses were subsidised as a form of charity, the financial dependence did not turn them into hirelings of the bourgeoisie. The fortunes of the Paris Bourse illustrate this interestingly. At first the subsidy was used by the workers in part to agitate for socialism, but even more to line the pockets of the organisers. An inquiry in 1891 revealed considerable peculation, large travelling expenses, grants to friends for imaginary duties.[1] This was soon remedied, but the propaganda continued. Governments reacted differently according to their political complexion and optimism.

Dupuy in 1893 closed down the Paris Bourse completely, on the grounds that nearly half the 270 unions which used the Bourse (a small minority of those in Paris, it should be noted) had not registered themselves in accordance with the law of 1884—because they were too revolutionary to accept that law. He used troops to occupy the Bourse: some unions talked of an armed rising to expel them. In 1896 the radical Bourgeois reopened the Bourse but with a new constitution which compelled the workers to share their control with representatives of the government and municipality. This arrangement met with considerable hostility among the workers, whose state of mind can be seen in their refusal of a subsidy to establish a statistical department, because they preferred not to give information to the prefect of police or the government. Millerand and Waldeck-Rousseau in 1900 restored full control to the workers. The municipality, controlled after 1900 by nationalists, opposed this, and replied by ending its subsidy—which it offered instead to individual unions (of appropriate political views). The Bourse was split and two rival ones coexisted. In 1905 official tutelage was reimposed.[2] The dependence on subsidies raised many problems and kept the Bourses absorbed by their relations with the authorities. The vicissitudes

[1] Charles Franck, *Les Bourses du Travail et la C.G.T.* (Paris thesis, 1910), 36–7.
[2] L. Le Theuff, 59–89; A. Boivin, *Les Bourses du Travail en France* (Lille thesis, 1905), gives a useful summary of relations with the government.

of the Paris Bourse were reproduced in different ways elsewhere, though with a time lag. Provincial Bourses generally
started as a result of a petition from a number of unions to the
municipalities, which would benevolently grant a building and
a subsidy. The members quickly revealed that they were divided
in their attitude to the authorities. Some thought they could
accept the republic—and in the 1890s the republic was young
enough for it to be reasonable to expect social legislation from
it—but others wished to turn the Bourses into instruments of
the class struggle. These latter on the whole rapidly prevailed,
for the Bourses were nearly always run by minorities among the
unionists, who were themselves a minority of the workers.[1]

Three factors gave the movement its particular character.
First, it became a haven for anarchists. Secondly, the Paris
Bourse, jealous of the National Federation of Unions which
had been captured by Guesde, set up a rival federation of B.D.T.
in 1892, from the dozen then existing, mainly in southern
France, in a bid to keep its hegemony over the workers movement. Thirdly, in 1895 Fernand Pelloutier became secretary
of this Federation of B.D.T. and by 1901, when he died, he
had made it an extremely vigorous and active body.

Pelloutier inhabits the pantheon of working-class mythology.
He died while still only thirty-three and so, like Gambetta, he
had no time to fall into discredit before a younger generation.
The information about him is all one-sided and must be received
with some caution. Gambetta's career, on investigation, justi-
fies the high opinion spread about him by his many friends.
That of Pelloutier has still to be investigated.[2] The only biography of him is written by his brother. Pelloutier was not a
worker but the son of a civil servant. The family was clerical
and legitimist; his grand-uncle was made a baron by Charles X
and Pelloutier himself was educated in a church school. However, his grandfather, as an exception, had been a republican
journalist and Pelloutier quickly followed in his steps. He was
expelled from his *petit séminaire* for writing an anticlerical novel.
At the Collège de St. Nazaire he started a school newspaper and

---

[1] Maurice Poperen, 'La Création des Bourses du Travail en Anjou 1892–4',
Le Mouvement social, 42 (1962), 39–55.

[2] Jacques Julliard, *Fernand Pelloutier* (1971), an excellent study, appeared after
this book was sent to press.

failed his *baccalauréat* (because of 'an inadequate English essay').
He was an idle, erratic boy, and he had already contracted the
tuberculosis which was to kill him and which soon manifested
itself in a frightful facial lupus; but he had a *personnalité rayon-
nante* which won him friends everywhere, and a feverish energy in
pursuit of what he really cared about—though it took him a
long time to discover what this was. He founded a number of
ephemeral reviews, and contributed to the *Démocrate de l'Ouest*,
Briand's radical journal. In 1899 he was briefly editor of a paper
founded to support Briand's candidature in Saint-Nazaire. But
then he had to take eighteen months' rest on medical grounds,
and he emerged from this transformed, disabused by politics and
believing that salvation lay in economic action. After a brief
period as a deputy secretary of the committee for the establishment of a workers' glass factory (a co-operative) and as a dissident member of Guesde's Parti Ouvrier Français, preaching
the general strike with Briand, he obtained the post of Secretary
of the Federation of B.D.T. in 1895. Here he laboured to exclude
all politics, to ignore such problems as anticlericalism, mili-
tarism, patriotism, parliamentarism, and to concentrate on the
organisation and education of the proletariat.

Pelloutier is an interesting man, because he consciously
devoted himself to separating the working class from the bourgeoisie and to developing institutions to enable them to live as
separate a life as possible. The cleavage of classes in French
society owes something to him. Of course, the idea that the
workers should rely only on themselves had been propagated
long ago by Proudhon and Tolain in the 1860s, but their ambition had been to turn the workers into petty proprietors, and
Tolain had quickly compromised with the bourgeois state. In
a society in which Tolain represented the general pattern
which careers followed, Pelloutier is original in that he voluntarily turned against the bourgeoisie, moved into the working
class and succeeded in becoming one of the very few bourgeois leaders of an exclusively working-class movement (which
the Bourses du Travail, unlike the Socialist Party, were).

Pelloutier was a bourgeois disillusioned by his own class,
a *déclassé*, a sceptic, a pessimist, an invalid who knew he was
dying and who imagined that the society around him, for
which he felt only disgust, was dying too. He claimed to despise

all bourgeois values. He declared himself to be the irreconcilable enemy of all its moral and material despotisms, a rebel against everything, 'without God, without master, without country'. The one gleam of light in his world came from the working class. He was fascinated 'as a student of social pyschology' by its sudden rise in a movement which was threatening to overthrow, as he believed, the whole political and economic order. At once he made common cause with it, and sought to guide it towards the creation of a truly free society. The workers alone could regenerate the world, destroy the hierarchic organisation of the bourgeois state and replace it by a free association of anarchist producers. In the Bourses du Travail he found his ideal instrument, for these would not only prepare the revolution but form the embryo from which the new order would spring. They would be 'within the bourgeois state a veritable socialist (economic and anarchist) state'.

Pelloutier deeply influenced the working-class movement in three ways. First, as an anarchist, he helped to detach it from co-operation with the bourgeois state, to spread scepticism about the parliamentary system, disillusionment with its social legislation and contempt for its ideas of the conciliation of classes. Secondly, as the organiser of the Bourses du Travail, he did a great deal to diminish the rivalries between trades which the unions and federations tended to preserve or strengthen, to introduce solidarity among the workers (which the politicians were trying to establish between classes in the nation as a whole). Thirdly, he popularised the idea of association among the workers by making the Bourses du Travail of immediate and practical use to their members, instead of simply being organisations which fomented strikes or which served as springboards for the ambitions of traitor politicians. He drew up a plan of work which gave the Bourses a uniform goal, with detailed advice on how best to use their meagre financial resources. This was taken up as a model by the numerous Bourses whose creation he stimulated. It gave them four objects to pursue: first to provide mutual benefits, unemployment pay, accident insurance, journey money for those travelling in search of work, and above all an employment exchange. Secondly, they should offer education to the workers since this alone could fit them for their new role: they should open libraries, social museums, information offices, classes of professional and general instruction. They should, thirdly, engage in propaganda among the uninitiated, spreading the word among the peasantry and sailors, and organising unions of them as well as of industrial workers. Fourthly, and it is significant he put this object last, they should have a section dealing with strikes, and with agitation against undesirable legislation.

Pelloutier gave himself up to his task as secretary with the almost superhuman energy of a man who knows he cannot have long. When he could no longer afford to have his journal printed, he set it up in type himself, after having written most of it on his own as well. He called it *L'Ouvrier des Deux Mondes* (was this title only accidentally reminiscent of Le Play?) and set great store by it, for he insisted that 'what the worker lacks above all is knowledge of his misery'. He undertook to inform him particularly in a series of articles which were later printed as a sizeable book entitled *La Vie ouvrière*—a great jumble of sombre facts, made to look more sombre still. His energy was rewarded, for by 1901 there were 74 Bourses in France and they were among the most vigorous elements in working-class life.[1]

However, while Pelloutier lived, no effective union between his federation and the national federations could be achieved. The Federation of B.D.T. had of course originally been formed in 1892 as a rival to the National Federation of Unions which was dominated by the Guesdistes; but even when the Guesdistes were ousted by the partisans of the general strike (of whom Briand, prompted by Pelloutier, was the leader), and the Confédération Générale du Travail was formed, devoted like the Bourses exclusively to economic action, Pelloutier remained jealous of his independence. Though he talked of the need for union, he was not willing to have it at any price. Personalities played some part in bringing this about: Pelloutier despised the secretary of the C.G.T., Lagailse, who was indeed a mediocrity, and apparently a traitor too (he was said to have given the government advance warning of a plan for a general strike). But Pelloutier claimed that the C.G.T.'s constitution in fact stimulated division under the banner of a false union. By accepting any union, whether local, departmental, national, craft or industrial, it did not force unions to organise themselves

[1] Jean Montreuil, *Histoire du mouvement ouvrier en France* (1947), 157.

into large federations. He claimed that politics played too great a role in the C.G.T. and he wanted a confederation on the same lines as that achieved by the Bourses, where adherents of different types of socialism put aside their political differences and concentrated on industrial activities. The C.G.T. moreover expected a revolution to take place very soon indeed and therefore ignored the long-term education of the workers. This was still the romantic age of strikes: any small workshop on strike appeared as the harbinger of the millennium and filled the C.G.T. with a fever of excitement. Pelloutier on the other hand was becoming increasingly practical in his outlook.

He grew disillusioned. In 1900 he sadly admitted that for every disinterested militant in the unions, there were nine egoists. His optimism about the transformation which education would effect was modified. Before his death, he even ceased to believe in the general strike.[1] It has been suggested that had he lived longer he might have evolved on the lines of Briand, his former associate, and become increasingly willing to co-operate with the state. His early ideas had certainly been confused and he had not always succeeded in clarifying them. For example, he had said that universal suffrage could not be used to solve the social question, because the law of supply an demand meant that no one man could become richer without another becoming poorer.[2] Later, writing on the possibilities of partial reform, he admitted that the state need not necessarily be evil in itself if the men who ran it were improved. He willingly accepted subsidies from the government and the municipalities. He agreed that co-operatives need not necessarily be egoistic. He abandoned his antimilitarism to the point of saying he would fight in a defensive war.[3] These modifications in attitude did not necessarily spread to all his movement; but some members certainly did become reformists. The Bourses should not be seen too clearly as one type. Pelloutier himself should not be regarded as their only leader. It just happens that more is known about him but there were many others, some of them of outstanding ability. Pelloutier's importance tends to be exaggerated, owing to the inadequacy of the sources. He did

[1] V. Dave's preface to Pelloutier's *Histoire des Bourses du Travail* (1906), vi.
[2] Maurice Pelloutier, *Fernand Pelloutier, sa vie, son œuvre 1867–1901* (1911), 76.
[3] Montreuil, 168–70.

not create the Bourses, of which there were already fifteen
when he joined them, and their federation was formed before
him, with Cordier as the first secretary. He was not an isolated
leader, but an exceptional example of a rich crop of organisers
who flourished in the last years of the century.[1]

Though the Bourses were full of life in this period, their
achievements should not be exaggerated either. Their employment exchanges, one of their main attractions, were not very
successful and provided jobs for only a small minority of workers,
for employers not surprisingly disliked dealing with them.
Their war against the commercial employment exchanges was
crowned by a victory in the law (9 March 1904) allowing
municipalities to abolish these, but the municipalities which did
so then tended to set up their own free exchanges at the town
hall. The Bourses now had to fight these instead because they
were rivals and because they feared the municipalities would
decide that they made the Bourses superfluous. The Bourses
had the advantage that they had a national organisation, and
so could theoretically give information about jobs all over the
country. Attempts to organise this in practice, however, failed
dismally. The viaticum (journey money for unemployed
workers) was used as an inducement to win recruits. Angers
Bourse, for example, gave 1 fr. 50 to unionists and 1 fr. 25 to
others travelling in search of a job, and in addition offered
coupons for free meals and lodging—but in 1896 only 186
coupons were issued. Some Bourses like Nantes did not send
men to hotels but transformed their offices at night into dormi-
tories with hammocks, where they harangued their guests with
suitable propaganda. But gradually as these benefits, available
to anyone, became known, a new race of idle tramps arose who
travelled round the country parasitically making use of them.
Pelloutier's great efforts to produce a national viaticum scheme
(one was already effectively in operation among the book
workers) failed because of local particularism, and because the
large Bourses claimed the small ones could not offer truly
reciprocal benefits. The question was canvassed and debated
without issue for many years. Pelloutier's statistical office, to

[1] E. Dolléans, 'Pelloutier et le réveil du syndicalisme', *Société d'histoire de la
Troisième République* (May 1937), 36–40, especially the comments of Zévaès and
Halévy.

collect information on unemployment, collapsed in 1906. The government subsidy dried up when his successors refused to give an account of how they spent it (in fact, on propaganda); it ceased to serve an impartial public purpose when it kept labour away from strike areas. Pelloutier's scheme for unemployment and accident funds remained a paper one. His libraries, designed to spread enlightenment and knowledge, were disappointing. That of the Paris Bourse, by far the largest, still had only 2,700 volumes in 1910, many of them novels. Professional classes made rather more headway, but again on a small scale. Pelloutier had interesting ideas about winning the peasants over, saying that they should not be forced into unions of the industrial type, but instead should be offered co-operative ones adapted to their needs and admitting small proprietors with under 25 acres (10 hectares). In 1910, however, there were still only 9,320 agricultural workers in the C.G.T. His seamen's hostels did not prove popular, since the individualist fishermen rebelled against the urban workers' propaganda that was served up there, just as much as they disliked the Catholic bourgeois hostels. Only among the dockers were advances successfully made. In general, therefore, the Bourses remained in a precarious state. Pelloutier, though pleased with the success of his recruitment, feared that many of the Bourses which were formed were very weak and bound to collapse if official aid was withdrawn. He came to feel that no more should be created until the existing ones had become stronger and more independent, and had spread into the surrounding countryside.[1]

The reliance on public subsidies not only put the Bourses in a delicate and dangerous position but fomented quarrels within the movement as to whether the subsidies should be accepted at all, or whether they were a source of corruption. After Pelloutier's death, Yvetot, his successor, changed the character of the Federation of Bourses considerably, using it more and more for revolutionary and antimilitarist propaganda, as opposed to the purely working-class purposes Pelloutier had favoured. Many Bourses either lost or renounced their subsidies. In 1912, however, they still received 369,915 francs from municipalities and 52,900 francs from departments.[2] On

---

[1] Charles Franck, *Les Bourses du Travail et la C.G.T.* (1910), 71–199.

[2] *Annuaire des syndicats professionnels* (1912), xliv–xlix.

the eve of the war, the Bourses had still not solved the question of their financial independence, and one of their leaders rightly described them as being in a state of crisis.[1]

The Yellow Unions

At the right wing of the working-class movement stood the Yellow Unions, who for a time were probably not much fewer in numbers than the revolutionaries, though their existence has now been rather forgotten. The Yellow Unions were so called after the badge they adopted, the yellow flower of the broom. Their origins go back to the independent trade unions founded by Catholics, principally in Paris and the Nord. In 1887 Brother Hieron had founded a union of shopworkers in Paris, membership of which involved religious obligations, though after 1900 this requirement was dropped in an effort to widen its appeal. In 1898 and 1899 similar unions were founded for the book, metal, building, furniture and clothing industries. All of them offered a large number of mutual benefits, insurance and co-operatives. In the Nord the Catholic unions were so successful that they combined in a federation and even published a newspaper. All members of this federation had to undertake never to go on strike until arbitration had failed.

These unions, however, remained relatively restricted because of their over-close links with the Church and the employers: the initiative in their formation always seems to have come from above. Some of their leaders argued that they should openly declare themselves Catholic and openly engage in right-wing politics, and one of them, Delcourt-Hoeillot, started a Catholic miners' federation, the *Union des syndicats Sainte-Barbe*.[2] There were few employers, however, who were sufficiently demagogic or astute to start trade unions, the very idea of which was too awful to contemplate. The yellow movement therefore did not follow on from these Catholic unions, but was started independently by workers or at least by men who were not employers.

[1] Paul Delesalle, 'Les Bourses du Travail et leurs difficultés actuelles', *Le Mouvement socialiste* (1908), 161–70; cf. F. Marie, secrétaire de l'Union des Syndicats de la Seine, 'Les Méfaits de la manne officielle: le subventionnisme et l'organisation ouvrière', *La Vie ouvrière* (Oct. and Nov. 1911), 507–26, 635–54.

[2] Maurice Gros, *Étude du mouvement syndical ouvrier en France: syndicats jaunes ou indépendants* (Dijon thesis, Paris, 1904), 319.

The first proper yellow union was founded at Le Creusot by the blacklegs in the strike of 1899. Its leader, Mangematin, was a young house painter of twenty-eight who had experienced several spells of unemployment and was tired of strikes.[1] His union flourished. A similar one was formed in the mines at Montceau, and others followed rapidly. An employee of the Orléans Railway Company, Lanoir, established an independent Bourse du Travail in Paris, uniting these various unions. Laroche-Joubert, the Bonapartist paper manufacturer of Angoulême, came to his aid. The new nationalist majority of the Paris municipal council voted him a subsidy, which the socialist minister Millerand promptly cancelled. Nevertheless the president of the republic Loubet received Lanoir at the Élysée in 1901 and assured him of his sympathy for his work. Méline's Republican Association declared their support for him, but at the same time some accused him of being the tool of Waldeck-Rousseau. It seems that several political parties hoped to profit from his aid in the elections of 1902. Lanoir claimed he had 200,000 members, in 317 unions affiliated to his Bourse. The true figure was perhaps one-third of that. The movement nevertheless seemed to be an important one. Lanoir, who had a gift for political intrigue and negotiation as well as an insinuating personality, won a reputation as an innovator in influential circles.

However, internal discord knocked down the whole edifice like a house of cards when Lanoir's deputy, Pierre Bietry, rebelled against his authority. Bietry was an incorrigible agitator, a vigorous orator and an able organiser of masses. Born obscurely of humble parents, he had spent an adventurous youth in Algeria in various jobs (selling watches in native clothing according to some). He had learnt to read and write only when he joined up to do his military service. He rose to be a corporal but was demoted for misbehaviour. He then worked for a time as a watch-maker, but quickly got involved in organising strikes and unions, among several professions in the Doubs. On one occasion in 1898 he organised a march of 10,000 strikers towards Paris. He was a delegate to socialist congresses, where he opposed the general strike. An article he published in Lanoir's paper led to his expulsion from

[1] Mangematin later became assistant station master of Lyon. Gros, 139–43.

the Socialist Party. After working for Lanoir, he was expelled
by him in turn, and founded his own Fédération des Jaunes,
which soon eclipsed its rival. (Lanoir retired to Juan-les-Pins,
with a pension—it is not stated from whom.) In January 1903
Bietry transformed his federation into a political party and
called it the National Socialist Party. The French may claim
to have invented even that. The party lasted for only one year
and little is known about it, but the Fédération des Jaunes was
soon revived.

It is uncertain at what stage the movement won the patronage
of Japy, who employed 7,000 watch-makers in the Doubs.
Bietry had once worked for him, attacked him, but they then
appear to have come to an agreement. Lanoir had been skilful
at obtaining subsidies from industrialists and politicians. Bietry
took some time to learn this art, so that for a while poverty
kept his activities to a minimum. His headquarters was a single
room, later only a share of a room (unlike Lanoir's Bourse of
no fewer than twenty-seven offices). Bietry's socialism was also
quickly changing. He had at first been simply a heretic among
the socialists. He now opposed not only strikes, but also the
class struggle and expropriation. He preached the need for
a piece of property for every man. He now found the means
of achieving this in Japy's creed of participation in profits.
Laroche-Joubert, the paper manufacturer, had long practised
this and he too became a patron of the federation. Half a dozen
other industrialists joined in and the federation flourished. In
1906 Bietry was elected to parliament for Brest, as a candidate
of the workers but against the extremism of the revolutionaries;
a supporter of his, Dupourqué, was also elected. They claimed
400,000 members in their federation at this period (obviously
exaggerated).

However, Bietry's position now grew difficult, because of
the danger of weakening his federation by introducing politics
into it, and because of the accusations which were levelled
against him, that his unions existed only to further his political
ambitions. He tried to resolve his dilemma by founding in 1908
a political party which would be separate from the unions: Le
Parti propriétiste anti-étatiste. Its object was the capture of
power by its members—which it thought would take ten years—
so as to facilitate the acquisition of property by the largest

possible number of people and to limit the role of the state. Bietry thus ended up where one would have thought he would have begun, a defender of property, but property for the small man. He remained hostile to 'speculating capitalists' and to the Jews. He proposed, when the Western Railway was nationalised in 1908, that it should be run by a company of its employees. He envisaged compulsory unions and regional parliaments representing industry and agriculture, to which relevant legislation would be referred. On the subject of co-operatives his movement was divided: some favoured them but others objected on the ground that they might ruin small shopkeepers. Bietry differed from the social Catholics in that he objected to charity: he wished the workers to have a share in running industry; and Japy declared himself to be 'unfortunately' a bad Catholic and no clerical. The Yellow Union movement had some resemblance to later fascism, but Bietry, for all his considerable qualities, did not have the makings of a dictator, or even of a party leader. He retired from politics—it is not clear why—in 1910 and went off to Indo-China, where he died in 1918. The phenomenon which he represented was to reappear after the war.[1]

To get a true picture of trade union life, one should not look only at the few large national federations, which contained only a minority of the unionists of the country. The more typical unit was the local provincial trade union, of which there were in 1912 over 5,000. On average, each of these had around a hundred members; some had as few as eight or twelve.[2] They were spread thinly over France and inevitably frequently led an isolated existence. If one looks not at Paris or the Nord, but at, say, a poor department like Ardèche, one can see these small unions in a rather different perspective. They appear more as clubs than as part of an organised movement. In the whole of the department of Ardèche, the only important industrial town which could possibly have unions of any size was Annonay, and this had a population of only 16,000. The old trades of leather dressing and paper making were its prin-

[1] Auguste Pawlowski, *Les Syndicats Jaunes* (1911); Pierre Bietry, *Le Socialisme et les Jaunes* (1906); J. Jolly, *Dictionnaire des parlementaires français*, 2 (1962), 599–600.
[2] *Annuaire des syndicats professionnels* (1912) gives a full list.

cipal occupations and in the 1850s it had only three factories
with more than 100 workers. The early unions were, therefore,
really only fraternities. In 1848 some 40 or 50 men formed
a union of leather dressers, but it was dissolved in 1851. Several
other small groups appeared briefly: *La Belle Étoile*, *Le Soleil*
(the president of this was an innkeeper), *L'Union des Travailleurs*
(the president was a commercial traveller): these names are
enough to show that they were friendly societies of the traditional, mutualist character. A strike in 1855 was thus held
without any union being involved at all. The first union of
leather workers to last was established only in 1880, with 400
members, rising quickly to 1,000. It won many concessions, but
it was mainly prized for its co-operative bakery (founded 1885,
which by 1907 had a turnover of 100,000 francs) and for its
pension scheme. Another union of *Ouvriers Mégissiers Palis-
soneurs* with 500 members in 1900, and 350 in 1912, showed
even more strikingly how much akin to the old restrictive
guilds these provincial unions often were: it concentrated on
protecting its members against rival competition, and on
limiting apprenticeships. In other words, the leather workers
of this town had only a small minority of unionists among them
and even these could not agree to form a single union. The
proliferation of small groups was the rule. There were in addition a large number of tiny unions for various trades round the
department. Not one of these unions belonged to the C.G.T.
The only revolutionary one, which was not just local and
corporatist, was not a working-class one at all, but that of the
Instituteurs. The largest union in the department was in fact
an agricultural one, founded by a priest in 1896. It had 1,223
members, who annually celebrated the feast of St. Vincent by
attending a special mass, drinking military and agricultural
toasts and listening to speeches on social concord from a deputy
who simultaneously defended the liberties of the Church and
the privileges of the alcohol makers.[1]

Proselytism by individuals and the accidents of personality
often explain the unequal spread of unionism in different parts
of the country and their varying political character. Thus
Limoges during the Second Empire was not industrialised but

[1] Élie Reynier, 'L'Organisation syndicale dans l'Ardèche', *La Vie ouvrière*
(July–Aug. 1913), 19–26, 93–6, 147–54.

it was an important centre for porcelain making and so had numerous highly paid artisans. Suddenly in 1870 (before the war) these formed a union. Why did they choose this particular moment? The stimulus came from outside. In fulfilment of the decisions of the International, two porcelain workers from Sèvres were sent by the Paris unions to Limoges and their public lectures started the movement. In the same way the more revolutionary activity of the Limoges porcelain workers was originated by the lecture given in that town in 1883 by Allemane.[1] The spread of the movement to the countryside was in turn due largely to the lithographer Noel who toured from village to village, establishing an agricultural union. It is interesting that Allemane's influence did not, however, survive, at least in its original form. The leader of the trade union movement in Limoges, Treich, a porcelain turner, soon abandoned Allemane's leadership and became a Possibilist, and then a Millerandist. When Millerand visited them in 1899 Treich declared: 'Now that you are minister, we have become free workers.' Treich ended up with a *bureau de tabac* given to him by the minister as a reward for his services. The effect of his long leadership was to make the federation and Bourse du Travail he established distinctly moderate, rejecting the general strike. This moderation reflected the dominance of the porcelain workers in Limoges. Here the union movement originated among the best-paid workers and was gradually spread by their propaganda to the less privileged. It is instructive to see the kind of strikes the movement produced. A large number seemed to have been reactions against competition—from machines, women or apprentices. There was a strike in 1895 by workers who resented the increasingly strict rules of discipline imposed in the factories: they claimed the right to go out when they pleased, and on this occasion struck because they were not allowed to attend *en masse* an exciting trial concerning the exhumation of a corpse. In the same year the first women's union in the region, that of the corset makers, went on strike

---

[1] Allemane was likewise a decisive influence in starting the union movement among the slaters of Trélazé: François Lebrun, 'Ludovic Menard et la naissance du syndicalisme ardoisier', *L'Actualité de l'histoire* (Oct.–Dec. 1959), 6–7. Menard is another example of a single individual creating a whole movement. The slaters later joined the miners' federation, reinforcing the revolutionary element in it. The proselytising work of Allemane deserves study.

to end the compulsory religious practices their employer demanded. The Limoges unions became a radical centre for the spread of socialism, but just as the type of artisan predominating in the city modified the nature of the socialism that was received from Paris, so in turn the peculiar economic characteristics of the surrounding countryside modified the teaching as it was received there. The socialist deputy, appealing to the peasant electorate, came out firmly in favour of private property (except that sharecroppers would become proprietors). Antimilitarism in these unions meant no more than that troops should not be used to suppress strikes.[1]

The case of André Lyonnais—totally unknown on a national level—illustrates the way the movement could spread locally. The son of a journeyman stone cutter, he had worked at Le Creusot for seventeen years, since the age of thirteen, until he was dismissed because the man who guided his youth, a doctor, had asked him to bury him in a civil ceremony, which he did at the time of Broglie's Ordre Moral. He moved to Le Havre as a book-keeper, and there organised no fewer than fifteen unions. 'I am not an enemy of capitalism,' he said, 'because I am a partisan of co-operation and therefore, as such, I wish to become a capitalist. I am not a partisan [either] of the interference of the state in industrial affairs . . . I have studied England for ten years now; I am filled with English ideas, I admit it, but not to the point of wishing to copy our friends across the channel servilely. . . . We want to achieve our deliverance by ourselves, and it is the law on trade unions [of 1884] which will be the instrument of this emancipation . . . In two or three years time the employers will negotiate with us and there will be no more strikes . . . We have no hostility towards [them] . . . we wish to increase the number of employers . . . and to equalise the profits of capital and labour.'[2] The English influence of this man was probably not typical, but due to contacts in Le Havre; the influence of the radical doctor, however, is a fairly frequent phenomenon. Lyonnais was clearly a unionist of the first generation. His evidence raises the question of whether, or

[1] Pierre Cousteix, 'Le Mouvement ouvrier limousin de 1870 à 1939', *L'Actualité de l'histoire* (Dec. 1957).

[2] Evidence of Lyonnais to the *Commission chargée de faire une enquête sur la situation des ouvriers de l'industrie et de l'agriculture en France, Procès-Verbaux* (1884), 103–10.

to what extent, the workers in France were more irreconcilable enemies of the employers and the state than in other countries.

Workers and Employers

In 1901 a well-known journalist, Jules Huret, went round a number of employers, asking them their views on unions, strikes and arbitration. The verbatim reports of his interviews reveal a very striking conservatism. These employers are a minute sample, but they are representative all the same. Rességuier, the head of the glass works of Carmaux, said: 'The workers have no personal ideas, no initiative, they are like sheep . . . [they] need to be led.' The arrival of trade unions meant only that they 'had changed masters' and the trade union leaders now terrorised them. He spoke with angry hatred of these leaders and of the socialists. He was an example of the employer who resisted any change in relationships within the factory and there were clearly a vast number of others, who, like him, could not see that the introduction of democracy in the political field (which many regretted) could not but affect the industrial and commercial world. Teste, vice-president of the federation of employers' unions in Lyon, insisted that compulsory arbitration of disputes would destroy 'order and prosperity, because it would destroy the authority of the employer'. This hierarchical view of society was shown likewise by an employer of Lille who refused to recognise trade unions: 'In my factory, I tell my workers that if they have any complaints, they may send the two oldest employees and I will talk with them, because I am sure they would be reasonable.' This refusal to negotiate with elected representatives left violence as the only resort of the workers. In the documents of strikes in this period one meets again and again instances of employers who haughtily ignore the unions and do not even answer their letters. 'The principal obstacle to harmonious relations between employers and workers', wrote an author who knew the industrial world well, 'is most often to be found in . . . the fact that the employers are sometimes, as happens to injured husbands, the last to know the aspirations, extent and intensity of the real or imaginary grievances of the workers'.[1] Many employers heard their

---

[1] E. Lozé, *Conciliation et arbitrage dans le bassin homiller du Nord et du Pas-de-Calais, 1889-1898* (Paris and Nancy, 1899), 53.

workers' grievances only through the foremen but these were far from being considered the workers' friends. The disputes about which side of the Conseil de Prud'hommes they should serve on show their equivocal position; numerous strikes against their behaviour reveal that it was often more the foremen than the employers who exasperated the workers. Foremen were notorious for their favouritism. They not infrequently had grocery shops or cafés kept by their wives and they preferred workers who were their customers. Their shops represented a patronage system additional to that of the employers.

According to Ribot there had been a transformation among employers in the course of the last thirty years of the century. 'One meets far less often today those absolutist employers who do not even consent to discuss with those who receive wages from them.'[1] An example of the new kind can be seen in Savon, who employed several thousand dockers in Marseille. 'The days of the employer's arbitrary power are past, unfortunately', he said. 'Till these last few years we did what we pleased with the worker, or almost. And things did not go any worse then. But, well, it is finished . . . The worker has opened his eyes or at least men have taken it upon themselves to open them for him. He is conscious now of what he is, of his power, of his omnipotence. We must reckon with him from now on. For long we could hope to subdue these trade unions that rose against our authority. We seduced their presidents, and won them over to our side. That too is finished, over. Then we had the idea that it was the fault of the government. We asked ourselves if a good despot, a king, an emperor, a Boulanger, strong, tough, could not quickly bring these men to reason and bring all the old things back to their old condition. That was not true either. We see around us monarchical governments more frightened than ours before the workers' movement . . . Let us therefore be sensible and philosophic. A wave threatens to submerge us; let us not try to prevent it advancing, that is impossible. Let us analyse it, let us build dams.'[2]

Examples of this kind of philosophic resignation are, however, rare. Briand insisted that the French unions could never resemble the English ones because of a fundamental difference in the mentality of the employers in the two countries. 'Between

[1] Jules Huret, Les Grèves, enquête (1901), 140.   [2] Ibid., 60–4.

English employers and workers, it is simply a question of money. . . . If in the course of a strike the employer sees that his interests are threatened, he does not hesitate to capitulate.' But in France the workers had to obtain a victory not only over material interests but also over 'sentiments of pride, arrogance and the caste spirit of the employing class'—so intimidation and force were inevitable. The French employer was usually guided more by prejudices about his authority than by his industrial interest, which he was willing to sacrifice to maintain appearances, to be able to say: 'I wish to be master in my own house.'[1] The contrast with England is perhaps based on too elementary a view of the English problem, but there was some truth in Briand's idea.

Even Henri Japy, described as one of the most liberal employers in France, and noted for giving participation in profits and pensions schemes to his 7,000 watch-makers, exhibited an attitude which many workers could not but find equally intolerable. The workers, he said, were not sly cheats trying to outdo their masters, but warm-hearted and honest, 'However, they are children, big children who want only protection and who think about revolting only when they feel they have lost this protection or that it tries to turn into domination.' For all his philanthropy, his aim was to preserve his influence over the workers. He gave them a share of profits not because he was a socialist but to give them a share of the pleasures of capital.[2] In the same way the chocolate manufacturer Devinck in 1874 had said that the way to conciliate the classes was to 'moralise the worker', to give him, that is, bourgeois standards and aspirations. 46 per cent of the children born in the tenth *arrondissement* of Paris were illegitimate. 'We must re-establish morality, without which there will never be order.'[3]

The fact that many employers were former workers who had made good did not improve matters. Frédéric Lévy, who for twelve years, during the Second Empire as a mayor in Paris, tried to bring workers and employers together in mixed unions and then admitted his failure, said that 'it is the workers who have become employers who are always the most difficult and

---

[1] Huret, 166-7.
[2] Ibid., 117.
[3] Fernand Desportes, *Enquête sur les associations syndicales* (1874), 85.

the most recalcitrant.'[1] These new men were certainly conscious of the breach between them and their workers, though
they seem unable to explain it. The president of the carpet-
weavers employers union of Paris complained in 1884 that
when he became a master, he took with him some of his old
work-mates—'to me they were not workers but friends'. But
when a strike broke out, they joined it—which gave him great
pain.[2] A lithographic master printer likewise declared that in
his trade nine-tenths of the employers were former workers, but
'from the moment you are at the head of a firm, you are despite
everything and *de parti pris* their enemy'.[3]

The workers resented being looked down on by their employers and being pariahs in the social order. However, they
might perhaps have borne this if they had been more convinced of their masters' superiority, but few employers were
successful enough to command their respect. Mediocrity and
incompetence were so prevalent that the workers had good
reason to despise many employers. It is very interesting to see
workers in the 1880s criticising not so much the capitalist
system as the inability of its leaders to run it successfully. Tolain,
one of the pioneers of the union movement, considered that
the recurrent economic crises were due to the ignorance of the
employers. The employers stupidly thought that wages were the
only flexible item which should respond to competition. They
neglected transport, credit and sales methods. 'The majority of
our industrialists are men with rather limited outlook, who see
work as simply a necessity to which they must subject themselves
for a certain time, so as to be able as soon as possible not to play
a role in the world but to go and live on their savings in some
distant corner and, as is vulgarly said, grow cabbages. The
industrialist who is in this position, who looks upon retirement
as the dawn, lets his equipment rot. He does not keep up with
what goes on in foreign countries. As soon as he has acquired
enough money to be able to take a rest, he sells his firm or if
need be liquidates it and goes off.'[4] The president of the Paris
Chamber of Export Commerce and Jacques Siegfried, the self-
made business magnate, both admitted the truth of this picture:

[1] Ibid., 148.
[2] *Procès-verbaux de la commission . . . sur la situation des ouvriers* (1884), 279.
[3] Ibid., 89.   [4] Ibid., 127–31.

French manufacturers, they agreed, hardly tried to sell their
goods, to adapt their production to the needs of the world
markets.[1] Tolain claimed that the hostility between master and
man was increasing not only because of the growth of factories
but also because of the open profiteering which spread during
the Second Empire, when speculators cynically devoted themselves to making money by any and every means, ignoring all
moral considerations. The worker could not feel bound by duty
in such conditions.[2]

It certainly became clear that the workers were not getting
a fair share of the profits of increased prosperity. Between 1806
and 1891 the value of the shares of the Anzin Mine Company
increased 23 times; those of the Courrières Mines were worth
in 1891 over 150 times their value in 1851; those of Lens were
90 times their value and yielded annually in dividends 3 times
their original cost. During the same period the miners' wages
rose by only a fraction, remaining roughly at subsistence level
and they were even reduced pitilessly whenever there was an
economic setback.[3] The employers on the whole systematically
fought against any change in the redistribution of wealth.
In the majority of cases they systematically fought the growth
of unionism. With time a few began to realise that this attitude
had contributed to making the French union movement more
threatening to their position than it need have been. An
employer told the Congress of the Federation of Industrialists
in 1907: 'Hitherto, the employers have done all in their power
to prevent reasonable workers from forming unions; the result
is that it is the unreasonable ones who are masters of them.'
Japy added: 'If the employers had not ignored the unions, we
should not be in the position in which we are.'[4]

Working-Class Culture

The trade union leaders, interesting though they are, tell one
about only one relatively small section of the proletariat. They

[1] *Procès-verbaux de la commission . . . sur la situation des ouvriers* (1884), 272, 274.
[2] Ibid., 130.
[3] E. Lozé, *La Grève de 1891 dans les bassins homillers du Nord et du Pas-de-Calais*
(Arras, 1891), 22–3, 41.
[4] G. Olphe-Gaillard, ancien inspecteur du travail, *L'Organisation des forces
ouvrières* (1911), 295. Cf. Peter Stearns, 'Employer Policy towards Labour Agitation
in France 1900–1914', *Journal of Modern History* (1968), 474–500.

were an élite, usually with above average qualifications and education. They were, increasingly, the sons of workers, rather than new recruits into industry. Among others in this same situation, they were untypical in that, though well qualified, they were unwilling to try to climb out of the working class; they rejected the ambition of setting themselves up independently in their own business, and they had low expectations of promotion.[1] Conflict soon broke out between these militants and those they sought to represent, and the next stage of trade union history was dominated, to a considerable extent, by this.

In the growing manufacturing industries, a large proportion of the workers were peasants, and very often peasants trying to better themselves. It is obviously difficult to discover or to generalise about the motives that led people to forsake the land for the factories, but one investigation, carried out by a doctor in the Tarn, found that the ambition of these migrants was, in descending order, higher wages, more regular work throughout the year, insurance against illness and accident, and the prospect of a pension.[2] These certainly were advantages which agriculture could not offer in this period. For long, the newly arrived peasants kept many of their traditional ideas. In the mines of Carmaux, for example, they often kept a piece of land on which they grew much of their food; they expected their wages as miners to provide them with cash for the extras they could not produce, and for savings with which to buy or build a house. Far from reducing their hours of work by going into the mines (where hours were limited by law), they now worked much longer, because before or after their shift underground they would carry out in addition about half a peasant's day of labour on their plots. Friction inevitably arose between them and those who had lost contact with the land, because they, growing a lot of food themselves, could afford to work for less. The full proletarianisation of these peasants was a slow process.

In Carmaux at the turn of the century, some 37 per cent of the miners owned their own houses, and 44 per cent owned allotments. They were not primarily seeking better housing

[1] Marc Maurice, 'Déterminants du militantisme et projet syndical des ouvriers et des techniciens', *Sociologie du travail* (July–Sept. 1965), 254–72.

[2] Dr. Valatx, *Monographie sur le mouvement de la population dans le département du Tarn de 1801 à 1911* (Albi, 1917), quoted by Rolande Trempé, *Les Mineurs de Carmaux 1848–1914* (1971), 1. 184–5.

conditions, because they preferred to own inferior shacks rather than live in the new model housing estates the employers put up. In Carmaux, the mining company built 91 bungalows (each with two rooms and an outhouse) for its workers in 1866, but it managed to let only 20, because the workers hated having their rent deducted from their wages, having to pay compensation for the damage they caused, and generally having the company interfere in their private lives. This was a phase some workers moved out of. In Pas-de-Calais, the six largest mining companies succeeded in getting 51 per cent of their employees into company housing, and in the Nord some companies housed as many as 85 per cent. The peasant-workers, however, even refused the loans offered to them by their employers, preferring to borrow privately, at a higher rate of interest. The cash they put down as a deposit for a house was accumulated in the traditional peasant way, with help from their fiancée's dowry, or from their own inheritance. The sums they had at their disposal were tiny, but they won their way into the status of proprietor, even though they had to content themselves with buying only half a house, or one room—but always with a fraction of a garden and of a pigsty too. A sociological study carried out in the 1950s showed that these workers of agricultural origin remained far more optimistic about the possibility of moving up in the world than unskilled workers of urban origin. They had smaller families, they complained less about the disagreeable physical conditions they encountered, because they saw the factory only as a stopping place. Their level of education was generally lower than that of their factory mates, but perhaps because they were more ignorant of the world, they had high hopes of a better job, at least for their children. They generally had no desire to remain factory workers. They talked politics far less than other workers; they did not see society as ruled by class antagonisms. The very fact that they themselves had escaped from the land showed, as they believed, that individual effort could overcome social obstacles.[1] The constant influx of these peasants regularly diluted the militancy of the revolutionaries.

Going into the factories, however, brought the peasants serious new problems. In the first place, regular employment was far from assured: they became victims now of economic

[1] Alain Touraine and O. Ragazzi, *Ouvriers d'origine agricole* (1961).

crises, which they could not predict, instead of the seasons, which they could. One can see this in the mines of Carmaux, on which Rolande Trempé has recently thrown such precise light, by the simultaneous use of workers', employers' and public archives. The company frequently laid off its workers when it could not sell its coal—for as much as fifty-six days in 1886 for example. It stopped recruiting altogether from time to time; the fear of being sacked dominated the town. The workers felt victims of obscure forces. A new tyranny also irked them. When they first came into the mines, if they retained their links with the land, they would seldom work the full six-day week. Absenteeism was practised on such a large scale—sometimes reaching 50 per cent—that workers were given prizes if they achieved a mere twenty-three days' presence a month—a rare feat. Mondays were used to recover from Sundays; fair days and festivals were seized upon as an excuse to lay down tools. One of the major battles the company waged was to instil discipline into these men, whose irregularity cost them a lot of money. By 1914, absenteeism was down to 4 per cent. The company used fines, dismissals, threats, but in the end evolved new methods of payment as the best solution. This was another major source of conflict. The Carmaux company survived because it pursued a rigorous policy of reducing costs and increasing productivity. This was achieved partly by technical improvements but also by making the men work harder. The increased agitation of the unions was a clear reply to this tightening pressure. By 1890, the company had most workers at its mercy, because the majority of them were by then proletariatised, dependent on their wages, and it pushed its advantages to the very limit. No understanding of each other's position was ever reached between employers and workers. The workers had no knowledge of economics, or of the trends in the national market, and so they blamed all reverses on the company, interpreting every effort at economy as a sign of ill will, or as an attempt at revenge to compensate for the workers' success in a strike. Merrheim was one of the first trade unionists to make any real study of company finances, but that was only after 1910.[1] The mine company for its part was guided by the

---

[1] Christian Gras, 'Merrheim et le capitalisme', *Le Mouvement social*, 63 (1968), 143–63.

problem of production costs, ignoring that of the cost of living which was what the trade unions were worried about. Wages rose, but so too did prices and, even more, the expectations and needs of the workers. The retailer, into whose debt the workers were constantly falling, paraded tempting new foods before them which they soon found indispensable. In the 1890s they began complaining not just about the cost of food but also about 'many other needs essential to our existence'. In particular they took a greater interest in their clothes. The company directors could not understand this change, condemned their demands as mere 'pretensions', and continued to consider their frugality as 'natural'. Inevitably, therefore, there was increasing hostility between the workers and the employers and endless bickering about the details of payment. Since there was a vast multiplicity of different tasks, each paid for differently, and each with different rates of unemployment, antagonisms continued between the workers, but by the 1890s a sense of solidarity appeared to have overcome these. For a time the trade unions were able to bring the workers together. The struggle took on a political character, and the whole capitalist system was called into question. But then the splits in the union movement greatly reduced its prestige. Animosities built up against their leaders, who had become a new power, exciting jealousy and mistrust. The vigorous resistance of the employers led many workers to follow the prudent course of abstention. Repeatedly unsuccessful strikes, combined with a reduced demand for labour, made even the unions more circumspect. The union movement thus came to a halt, and its problems with its own followers became almost as difficult as its relations with the employers.[1] It will be seen how co-operation with the state was to be the unions' way out of this impasse. Just as the republicans, in the end, made a deal with the state, so many of the unions ended up being a channel of communication between worker and the state, much more than a representative of the former. The history of the trade union movement after 1914 is largely the history of how this came about.

The more or less uniform programme of the union leaders could not reflect accurately the wide variety of attitudes among the rank and file. Alain Touraine's work has shown how the

[1] R. Trempé, *Les Mineurs de Carmaux* (1971), a first-rate, highly instructive thesis.

Paris workers, who have more relations with other classes, see the world in a unique way: they are far keener to have their children pursue their studies and they are more ambitious for them. Their optimism is partly based on the fact that they are better paid than workers in the rest of the country; but they also have a far wider view of the class to which they think they belong, and form their judgements in political more than professional terms. Their situation contrasts markedly with that of workers in purely industrial towns, and again with that of workers in medium-sized towns, which are dominated by the state bureaucracy, and where workers are three times as keen to have their children become civil servants. These regional variations—which are much emphasised by every local study—are cut across by important professional distinctions. Thus gas workers think they have twice as much chance of promotion as miners do and their attitudes vary accordingly. Building workers have little class consciousness and often aim to set themselves up independently. Metal workers, among the most combative of unionists, have been particularly insecure in their rapidly changing industry, and have been staunchest in their loyalty to the working class, defending it rather than trying to escape from it; but even within their ranks, there are considerable differences according to the kind of factory and speciality. Thus to the question posed by Touraine of whether there were any people whose interests were absolutely opposed to the general interest, 44 to 47 per cent of metal workers in factories employing over 500 answered that the capitalists were the enemies, but in factories of 10 to 50, only 12 to 15 per cent gave this answer. There is a further difference between qualified, partially skilled and unskilled workers. The first category stress professional advancement and economic gain as their main ambition, but the semi-skilled are less optimistic about their chances and they are content that their children should remain workers. However, because they are in the working class to stay, they are often more determined to defend it as a unit. Insecurity in employment also varies enormously; in some sectors and grades it was as high as 60 per cent, in others it fell as low as 6 per cent.[1] Mobility of labour—on which more

[1] A. Touraine, *La Conscience ouvrière* (1966), 55, 60, 106-7, 138, 173, 119-215, 242.

historical evidence is needed—was shown to be high in Chombart de Lauwe's investigation of working-class families in the 1950s, with 24 per cent of his sample having changed their place of work eleven times or more, and 42 per cent having changed their trade four times or more. 73 per cent of unskilled workers, 78 per cent of skilled workers and 59 per cent of highly qualified ones expressed a desire to change their trade. This mobility was the workers' answer to monotony, insecurity and repression, but it was barely compatible with tight union organisation. Again, the distinction between the different grades of workers was very strikingly revealed, as late as 1954, in the statistics of children who died under the age of one year. The rate was 61·7 per thousand for unskilled labourers' families, 51·9 for average workers, 42·5 for qualified workers, 34·5 for shopkeepers, 32·4 for master craftsmen, 30·5 for clerks, 23·9 for industrial employers and 19 for the liberal professions.[1]

The divisions between workers were often accentuated in their recreational pursuits. Thus in St. Étienne, the miners tended to join gymnastic clubs, while the armourers formed rifle clubs; the shopkeepers and artisans were keen on pigeon shooting, while pigeon breeding was a particular speciality of miners. The armourers were, however, of two kinds, depending on whether they worked for the state or in small artisan workshops: the latter were vigorously anticlerical, but also hostile to unionisation.[2] Even drinking, which was the principal recreation of many workers, was carried on in remarkably particularist groups. In the nineteenth century there was a vast increase in the number of cabarets, which the bourgeoisie condemned as dens of debauchery and clandestine agitation, but where the workers found warmth, comfort, sociability and a meeting-place for their clubs. Between 1856 and 1858 the number in Lille rose from 909 to 1303. In St. Étienne (which came second only to Paris) there was, in the early Third Republic, one cabaret for every 62 inhabitants, which meant one for every 15 electors or every 3 houses. These cabarets may have reinforced the network of relationships among neighbours and were an important social factor. The kind of particularism that

[1] P. Chombart de Lauwe, *La Vie quotidienne des familles ouvrières* (1956), 7 n., 25.
[2] Janet Jacobs, 'A Working Class Community: St. Étienne 1870–1914' (thesis in preparation at St. Antony's College, Oxford).

prevailed is illustrated in Lille, where friendly societies under the Second Empire were known to have expelled members who drank more than half a litre of beer in a cabaret other than that where the society met. Lille during the Second Empire had 63 drinking and singing clubs, 37 clubs for card playing, 23 for bowls, 13 for skittles, 10 for archery, 18 for cross-bow archery. They had their presidents, deans, treasurers, and numerous officials; they organised boisterous banquets and festivals, at which they sometimes used up all their savings. So the worker could have a very busy life, quite apart from the unions.[1]

It was not necessarily to the unions that he would look for the solution of his private frustrations. One of the most striking differences between the factory worker and the rest of the population was that he often did not come home to lunch, as they did. The amount of time he spent with his family was far shorter—because of his long working hours—than was normal among the bourgeoisie, whose complaints that he did not practise their own domestic virtues seem strangely hypocritical. His housing conditions were often so appalling that there was no room for him to do much but eat and sleep at home. Overcrowding was notorious in Lille, for example, where in 1864 there was a tenement building inhabited by 271 people, with an average of 1·70 square metres of living space each. In the 1950s, the living space of unskilled Paris workers was 7 square metres per person, and 11 square metres for highly qualified workers. This does not mean there was a gradual improvement. New suburbs were sometimes as bad as the slums they were designed to replace. An inquiry into the leisure activities of workers carried out in 1924 showed that patterns of behaviour were often unaltered by changing conditions. Thus those who worked ten hours a day did little else; but those who had their hours reduced to eight often got part-time jobs, which raised their total to twelve. More leisure stimulated a return to older ideals. In St. Étienne, the eight-hour day increased the demand for gardens tenfold. The life of the miners of the Moselle was barely altered: they got up at 4 a.m. went to work at 6, finished at 2 p.m., got home at 3.30, ate at 4 and went to bed at 6. The greatest change of the twentieth century was the end of irregular work: lazy Mondays and Tuesdays were no longer tolerated by

[1] Pierre Pierrard, *La Vie ouvrière à Lille sous le second empire* (1965), 302.

employers.[1] The self-made Denis Poulot, writing from personal experience, said that in 1870 a good worker who did 300 days a year was very rare; ordinary ones usually worked only 200 to 225, and changed their employment three to five times a year.[2] An English mechanic, Henry Steele, who spent twenty-three years working in France, wrote in 1904 that discipline in French factories was less tough than in England, more freedom was left to the worker, more respect accorded to him by foremen and masters. There are suggestions that, in the twentieth century, particularly in certain new and modernised industries, this laxity was tightened. It took some time for the transition to be accepted. Steele noted that French workers tended to enjoy themselves, as far as possible, without paying, unlike the English workers who spent vast sums on their bank holidays. This probably changed even later, perhaps not till after 1936.[3]

The possibilities open to the workers can be seen from the autobiography of one of them, Georges Navel. His father (whose thirteenth child he was) spent forty years working as a labourer in the Pont-à-Mousson factory. His work, his children and the republic had all proved disappointing to him. He was completely resigned. 'The earthen pot', he used to say of the C.G.T., 'will never break the iron pot.' His only consolation in distress was drink. Georges's eldest brother also spent his whole life in the same factory, but he accepted his lot more readily, because he found satisfaction in hobbies, gardening and a happy family life. Georges himself, however, was a rebel from childhood. He never learnt anything at school because he was usually sent outside the classroom as a punishment for mis- behaviour. He could not bear the factory, and wandered off to every part of the country, in a large variety of jobs. He hated his status as a wage earner, which he considered undignified, a vestige of ancient slavery. He felt he belonged to a class looked on as animals, isolated in ghettos and despised. This was impossible to bear without faith in revolution or social pro- gress: political activity, he said, was the only cure for *la tristesse ouvrière*. This family illustrates three distinct attitudes.

[1] Jean Beaudemoulin, *Enquête sur les loisirs de l'ouvrier français* (Paris thesis, 1924), 212–36.

[2] Denis Poulot, *Le Sublime, ou le travailleur comme il est en 1870 et ce qu'il peut être* (1872).

[3] Henry Steele, *The Working Classes in France: A Social Study* (1904), 17, 121.

All three raise the question of the isolation of the proletariat. Georges Navel said that the only things he knew about bourgeois life were what he saw at the cinema: as a young man they had appeared to him 'a superior race, which spoke and dressed better than us, and knew everything that was taught in the schools'.[1] Even his attitude towards the bourgeoisie was not one of simple hostility: there was also a hint of admiration or envy.

This can be seen more clearly in René Kaës's interviews with workers in the 1960s. Only 21 per cent of his subjects thought the workers ought to have their own culture. 70 per cent were against this, because they defined culture as communication. What they lamented in their condition was their isolation. What they admired the liberal professions for was that their members were able to meet many different types of people, be at ease with all of them, work when they liked. Only the most highly qualified workers dreamt of their children getting to such a status. But admiration for commercial travellers, shop assistants and state employees, common among the least educated workers, was for the same reason, that such people came in contact with the world, heard news, could read and write easily, and had dealings with the public. They welcomed education as an escape from their isolation, to help them achieve dignity. Far from rejecting the bourgeoisie's culture, and even their study of Latin, only 37 per cent were in favour of purely technical education, while 6 per cent were in favour of the traditional classical course and 50 per cent of both together. A carpenter defined 'culture' as the opposite of humiliation, which ignorance stamped on them. The primary-school master was much admired. The educational work of the Third Republic was thus appreciated, and the values it represented were at least partially shared by the workers. They believed that education was something acquired in the schools; only 10·5 per cent were dissatisfied with the schools and most regretted that they had not had more schooling. It was not just knowledge that they wanted, but even more the 'ability to live in society', to know how to conduct themselves in circles different from their own, to talk well and tactfully, to be at ease with people. The great divide came on the question of what chance a worker really had of reaching this ideal. 39 per cent thought he could, 31 per cent

[1] Georges Navel, *Travaux* (1945), 28, 66.

thought it impossible, 17 per cent thought it possible but very difficult.[1] This is what workers thought in a period of prosperity, and in a welfare state. It is impossible to argue back from these figures, even to guess about the division in a different situation. But more research in social mobility might, at any rate, reveal how the realities corresponded to the dream.

After 1914

1914 is a crucial date in the history of the trade union movement. The C.G.T. had repeatedly affirmed that it would reply to a declaration of war by a general strike, which would be tantamount to a revolution. But it did nothing of the sort. Jouhaux (its secretary 1909–47) turned a somersault and supported the war.[2] The propaganda of antimilitarism was suddenly replaced by patriotism. This has long been looked on as something of a mystery. To the bourgeoisie, threatened with civil war, it was a miraculous escape. The myth of the general strike was shattered. It was the end of revolutionary syndicalism as a threat that had to be taken seriously. The union leaders explained their volte-face by saying that if they had not supported the war, their members would have shot them as traitors: they claimed they were pushed from behind, but the evidence for this is rather slight. The episode raised the whole question of the relationship between the leaders and the masses. Jouhaux appears to have acted instinctively, without consulting his colleagues; and it is said that he was principally moved by a desire to prevent a violent repression of the working class which would occur if it did resist. This was not so much a collapse of the old syndicalism, as a revelation of what it was really like. The extremism had often been superficial, and it was not unanimous. Jouhaux may have been expressing what he felt was the profounder desire of the workers, to be integrated into the nation (in the way that Jaurès understood the nation). The C.G.T. had hitherto tried to raise a barrier between the workers and the rest of France, but 1914 suggested it was a barrier of hurt pride rather than of alienation. The attitude of the masses

---

[1] René Kaës, *Images de la culture chez les ouvriers français* (1968). On isolation, see also Maurice Halbwachs, *La Classe ouvrière et les niveaux de vie* (1913), 119–23.

[2] Bernard Georges and D. Tintant, *Léon Jouhaux* (1962), 102–58.

is difficult to discover. A recent study of the metal workers shows that there was never any enthusiasm for the war among them. They looked on the patriotic *union sacrée* as the work of their leaders. Their mood appears to have been one of indifference: neither integration, nor alienation. The force they were most conscious of was the presence of the police, and the threat of being sent to the front if they misbehaved in their factories. They felt their union leaders had made a deal with the state. Their reply was to disown them and find new leaders, nearer to their own preoccupations. Their sense of autonomy was not radically changed. The integration of the working class into the nation, which some have seen as the significance of 1914, is by no means proved.[1]

1914 marked a change in the position of the trade unions, much more than in the workers. They were transformed from opponents of the state into institutions which were increasingly almost part of it. During the war leaders of the C.G.T. served in government commissions, co-operating with members of all classes.[2] In trade disputes, they appealed to the government for support and intervention. After the war, they negotiated and obtained the eight-hour-day law of 1919.[3] This was largely a declaratory law of principle, requiring ministerial decrees to enforce it in individual industries: there was therefore need for further negotiation. (By 1926 probably about 5 million workers were affected by it, though all sorts of exemptions reduced the effect.) The trade unions before the war had sabotaged the 1910 insurance law, but in 1928 they co-operated to secure the passage of a new one. Their attitude was different now: they sought to defeat the employers, who set up paternalistic insurance schemes to woo their workers away from the unions, by enrolling the assistance of the state to do the same or better. The 1928 law, in which workers and employers each contributed 5 per cent of wages, was compulsory for all workers earning

[1] Jacques Julliard, 'La C.G.T. devant la guerre (1900–1914)', *Le Mouvement social*, 49 (Oct.–Dec. 1964), 47–62; A. Kriegel and J. J. Becker, *1914, la guerre et le mouvement ouvrier français* (1964); M. Gallo, 'Quelques aspects de la neutralité et du comportement ouvriers dans les usines de guerre 1914–18', *Le Mouvement social*, 56 July–Sept. 1966), 3–33.

[2] Roger Picard, *Le Syndicalisme durant la guerre* (1927) (Carnegie Endowment for International Peace; Economic and Social History of the World War: French Series); Alfred Rosmer, *Le Mouvement ouvrier pendant la guerre* (1936–59).

[3] Cf. Robert Veyssié, *Le Régime des huit heures en France* (1922).

under 18,000 francs a year, and was designed to give a 40 per cent pension after thirty years. The senate had held this up because it originally involved a state subsidy: as it was now established, it cost the state nothing, but the state emerged as the intermediary between worker and employer. The law required union co-operation in establishing insurance funds, and the unions henceforth gave much of their time to organising these. They met the employers increasingly in government offices. They participated in more and more official bodies, and most notably in the National Economic Council in 1924. They no longer hesitated to accept government subsidies for their unemployment funds, which even the communist C.G.T.U. received. The Bourses du Travail became simply state-financed employment exchanges. The C.G.T. even supported the bill of 1925 which would have required compulsory government intervention in all labour disputes. It used strikes sparingly now, and largely to draw the attention of the state to troubles it wished to cure, rather than to defeat the employers. This was known as the *politique de présence* which meant that the C.G.T., while rejecting actual participation in government, obtained a place for itself in every discussion concerning the working classes. In other words, the unions increasingly saw their role as one of lobbying and bargaining with the state.[1]

This relationship reached its climax in 1936, when the state imposed the Matignon Agreement on the employers. By this agreement the employers were forced to recognise the unions, and to negotiate collective bargains with them, but under state supervision. The unions, though they represented a minority, were, through government support, given the status of representatives of the whole labour force. The ministry of labour further decreed that the C.G.T. should normally be considered the 'most representative union' with which the employers should negotiate their collective agreements. Collective bargaining had been organised by a law of 1919, but by 1933 only 7·5 per cent of wage earners had been affected by it, mainly in mining and shipping: in the metal industry only 1·4 per cent of workers had been affected. The resistance of the employers

[1] Georges Lefranc, *Le Mouvement syndical sous la Troisième République* (1967), 283 ff. gives a useful description of this from the C.G.T. point of view. Lefranc was a leader of the teachers' union.

and their refusal to recognise the unions had kept France way behind her neighbours in this matter. All this changed in 1936, but one of the most significant features of the new order was that in the event of unions and employers failing to agree, and in the event of disputes arising about collective agreements, the deadlock was to be resolved by government arbitration. As it turned out, in the succeeding years, all but 4 per cent of disputes were decided by the government. Labour relations and strikes depended increasingly, therefore, on the state, and on public opinion, rather than on the attitudes of the rival parties. The strategy of social conflict was thus fundamentally altered. The C.G.T. never faced up to this and never really discussed the new problems which were created. Its 'Minimum Programme' of 1918 talked only of the nationalisation of key industries and a greater share for the workers in economic decisions. Its plan of 1934 showed it had no immediate desire to abolish private enterprise beyond that, though it favoured national economic planning with worker representation. In 1944–5, therefore, it was the state, not the unions, which emerged as the principal challenge to the employers, and which took over the battle to reduce the latter's remaining independence.[1]

These developments can be partly explained by the peculiar composition of the trade unions. The unions had extraordinarily little success in winning recruits from private industry, and they became instead representatives of the state workers and the civil servants. For most of the inter-war period there were only about one million unionists. Their number shot up enormously in two periods of agitation and enthusiasm. In 1918–19 they almost doubled; in 1936 they shot up from one to over five million. However, in the textile, metal and building industries, union membership in 1930 was lower than it had been in 1914. The great permanent increase in unionisation was in the public sector, or in related industries which were partly controlled by the state, like mining, transport and the docks. The state

---

[1] There are some good American books on inter-war labour relations, notably Val R. Lorwin, *The French Labor Movement* (Cambridge, Mass., 1954); Henry W. Ehrmann, *French Labor from Popular Front to Liberation* (New York, 1931). See also François Sellier, *Stratégie de la lutte sociale. France 1936–60* (1961); Pierre Laroque, *Les Rapports entre patrons et ouvriers* (1938); Adolf Sturmthal, 'Nationalisation and Workers' Control in Britain and France', *Journal of Political Economy*, 61 (Feb. 1953), 43–79.

encouraged this because it formed mixed commissions with them. In the civil service it was claimed in 1930 that unionisation was as high as 90 per cent, that it was 75 per cent among miners and 60 per cent in semi-public utilities, but (apart from the printers) below 20 per cent elsewhere. These figures are all much too high, but the variations appear to be in the right proportions. A recent author gives 6·3 as the percentage of workers in private industry who belonged to unions.[1] In 1935, at any rate, of the C.G.T.'s 775,000 members, 350,000 were civil servants or public employees and 165,000 were railwaymen (whose conditions were regulated by special statute).[2]

When the masses came into the unions, in periods of crisis, the old leadership could not cope with them. The new members, on the whole, represented a different kind of worker, usually the semi-skilled employees of industries in the process of being rationalised, with more recent peasant origins and no traditions of solidarity. In 1936 there were 1,063,000 industrial workers in firms with over 500 employees and another 1,393,000 in firms with between 100 and 500 employees. Mass production brought them together in larger numbers but these workers were trained in a week, instead of the old slow apprenticeship. This created a new atmosphere in factories. The strikes of these new recruits often almost completely by-passed the regular trade unions. Thus in May 1919 the C.G.T. organised a demonstration to mark its return to agitation after the war and this was followed by a succession of strikes all over the country, which suggested a massive onslaught on the capitalist system. But in fact there was very little connection between the different strikes, which confined themselves to winning concessions on a strictly local basis. In 1920 the railwaymen, who formed at that date the largest union in the country, went on strike and got the C.G.T. to declare a general strike to support them. The result was disastrous. Only about 40 per cent of the railwaymen came out. The vigorous resistance of both the state and the middle classes prevented the economic chaos that could have resulted. The C.G.T.'s timid policy, of launching its

[1] Saposs, 127; Ehrmann, 25. For detailed calculations of trade union numbers, see Annie Kriegel, *La Croissance de la C.G.T. 1918–21* (1966), and Antoine Prost, *La C.G.T. à l'époque du front populaire, 1934–39: essai de description numérique* (1964).
[2] For the civil servants, see Georges Mer, *Le Syndicalisme des fonctionnaires* (1929).

general strikes in successive waves proved totally ineffective. An extremist minority, led by Monmousseau, had captured the railwaymen's union, and forced the C.G.T.'s hand, so internal disagreements paralysed the movement. 12 per cent of the railway strikers were dismissed (about 18,000 men, or 5 per cent of all workers in the railway's employ). The victory of the employers was total, and profound discouragement almost immediately halved union membership. The C.G.T. had proved incapable of leading the working class. Important strikes had broken out without its consent, and within individual federations, local unions had likewise defied their leaders. This was particularly noticeable among the metal workers, who disowned their union's agreements with the employers on the eight-hour law. Then the workers repudiated their local unions.[1]

The union movement was further discredited by its split in 1921, when the anarchists and communists seceded to form a rival to the C.G.T., the Confédération Générale du Travail Unitaire. The Russian Revolution had a profoundly important effect on the working class. Its influence, and the rise of the communist party in France, are subjects which require separate treatment.[2] But from the trade union point of view, the result of this split was not only that the strength of the C.G.T. was gravely reduced (to 250,000, against 500,000 secessionists) but also that the C.G.T.U. created a new type of union. By 1924 the communists had captured the C.G.T.U. and expelled most of the anarcho-syndicalists. This reduced their strength to as little as 230,000 (the membership they claimed in 1935).[3] But they controlled this rump with an all-powerful, permanent body of leaders who took their orders from the communist party. They created a bureaucracy to run the unions, completely against the anarchist traditions of elected and rotating leadership. Their unions thus became a source of protection and security, rather than a meeting-place for free discussion.

[1] A. Kriegel, *Aux origines du communisme français* (1964), 1. 359–547, contains a thorough study of the railway strike, based on a wide range of new sources, including the employers' archives. E. L. Shorter and Charles Tilly, 'Le Déclin de la grève violente en France de 1890 à 1935', *Le Mouvement social* (July–Sept. 1971), 95–118, shows that after the 1914–18 war, violent strikes were six times less frequent than before it. They argue that this shows an increase of integration of the workers.

[2] See Zeldin, *France 1848–1945*, vol. 2, chapter 23; Zeldin, *Anxiety and Hypocrisy*, chapter 9 (forthcoming).

[3] The C.G.T. by then was three times as large, thanks mainly to the adhesion of the civil servants.

The communist view was that unions were simply one way of organising the workers, but what really mattered was membership of the party, for the workers by themselves were incapable of acquiring a revolutionary conscience. Discipline, for which the factories had prepared the workers, must be the keynote of union organisation. In 1936 the C.G.T.U. rejoined the C.G.T. By 1938 the communists had a majority in this reconstituted C.G.T. The position of the worker in his union was now considerably different.[1]

The transformation was completed by the events of 1936, when the workers went through what was in many ways the most moving and important experience of the century for them. The change was remarkable and paradoxical. It has been seen how the Popular Front Government used these events to force the employers to negotiate with the C.G.T. and the unions. But while they had their status thus enhanced, and though their numbers increased in an unprecedented manner, they did not succeed in becoming the true representatives of the will of the workers. The fivefold increase in the number of unionists in the space of a single year totally changed the character of the unions. In the chemical industry, unionisation increased sixty-fold, in the glass industry twenty-three times, in metals eighteen times (whereas by contrast the civil servants and teachers, the backbone of the C.G.T. in the 1920s, rose by less than 50 per cent). There was now at last something approaching mass unionisation, at least by French standards, for the over-all level was just over 50 per cent. But this meant that the unions were swollen with semi-skilled workers with no experience of organisation, and the leadership was unable to deal with them. It is said that the organisers spent all their time just collecting dues. That is how the communists were able to move in and provide a bureaucracy to run and direct these masses into political channels. Belonging to a union, after 1936, was no longer an act of rebellion; it was rather the man who did not join who attracted attention. Membership of the communist party became a far more significant political gesture.

In 1936 the C.G.T., with its reformist traditions, was anxious to maintain order and negotiate peacefully. Three-quarters of

[1] Maurice Labi, *La Grande Division des travailleurs, première scission de la C.G.T. 1914-21* (1964).

its members did not participate in the strikes of that year. These were spontaneous outbursts by unorganised workers, acting independently. The occupations of the factories have become a legend in revolutionary history, and they were revolutionary in that for a time the workers felt themselves to be freed from the disciplinary restrictions of their work. They brought the employers to their knees and the relations between the two looked as though they could never be the same again. But it is important to note that these strikes were united only in their method: the occupation of factories suddenly appeared as a new weapon, and it spread by spontaneous imitation, not under any central or union orders. The workers saw their action as signifying that it was no use relying on unions, or even on governments; they were taking matters into their own hands. They negotiated therefore each with their individual employers, for advantages for their own factories only. The occupations, at their peak in mid June, involved about one million workers but they were settled at a local level in different ways. Almost none seemed to have envisaged any destruction of the capitalist system: there were sit-ins, occupations, but not take-overs. Red flags were flown, but the public services were not affected, and no effort was made to rise against the bourgeoisie as a whole. The trade unions did increase their membership, but in the course of the strikes the workers rejected their direction. When they wanted help from outside, they called in the local deputy or mayor or municipal councillors. A director of Huntley and Palmers' biscuit factory at La Courneuve who was imprisoned by his workers—not as widespread a phenomenon as is believed —said that he could easily have reached agreement with the workers, but for the constant interference of the local communist deputy, who urged them not to give way.[1]

After 1936, the trade unions had more to do with the employers, but from the workers' point of view they were almost superfluous, since it was the government which decided in disputes. There were many who felt that the union leaders had taken over the role of the politicians, and become masters

[1] Salomon Schwarz, 'Les Occupations d'usines en France en mai et juin 1936', *International Review for Social History*, 2 (Amsterdam, 1937), 50–104; Alexander Werth, *The Destiny of France* (1936), 296–310, vivid journalistic reports for the *Manchester Guardian*.

rather than servants of their followers. By 1946 indeed the C.G.T. had between 5,000 and 6,000 permanent officials. Political action was nevertheless seen to be all-important now, and this is what the communists offered, in a new way. But again, it is rash to generalise too much about the significance of the unions before the war of 1939. Unions still meant different things in different regions. The well-organised mass unions of the north and north-east, based in large factories, were distinct from those of the centre and west, based in workshops, with more individualist militants, looser coherence, and loyalty to nineteenth-century revolutionary traditions. In the south political and temperamental considerations were predominant, with the individual rather than the party as the unit. In Paris, Lyon and Marseille, again, the mixture of classes in these towns meant that professional grievances were not in the forefront as much as elsewhere.

It is not possible to conclude simply therefore about class consciousness at the end of this period. At one level, the workers seemed to be segregated into a separate party, hostile to the whole capitalist order, but their successful participation in politics was also a sign that they had a recognised place in it. At the cultural level, their position was ambiguous, but far from irretrievably antagonistic. In the crisis of 1936 they had forced unity upon their leaders, but it was a fragile one. Many workers, moreover, stood completely outside the union movement, and a small section—soon to grow much larger— organised themselves separately in Christian trade unions. The traditions of the proletariat and the pressures upon them were too varied to make their behaviour predictable.[1]

[1] Michel Collinet, *L'Ouvrier français. Esprit de syndicalisme* (1951), and id., *Essai sur la condition ouvrière 1900–1950* (1951), are valuable and stimulating analyses. See also Jean Bruhat and Marc Piolot, *Esquisse d'une histoire de la C.G.T. 1895–1965* (1966). For subsequent developments, Richard F. Hamilton, *Affluence and the French Worker in the Fourth Republic* (Princeton, N.J., 1967).

Part II

11. Marriage and Morals

THE family, as organised in France in these years, had an effect on people's lives as profound as any political regime or any economic force. It was a powerful institution which resisted change with remarkable vitality—the counterpart, in private life, of the administrative centralisation of the *ancien régime* which, for all the attacks on it, survived into the mid twentieth century. It deserves attention as much as the changing governments and the industrial revolutions, but it seldom receives it because there are very great difficulties—many of them insuperable—in discovering the facts about it. Its activities were inevitably hardly ever recorded and research on it is still fragmentary. It has too often been described simply as one of the values to which the bourgeoisie paid greatest homage. Certainly in 1940 the Vichy government included *Famille* in the new motto it devised for France, with *Travail* and *Patrie*. Perhaps only in the Students' Revolution of 1968 was a real threat to its organisation widely noticed and the tensions concealed in it revealed publicly. The ambitions and frustrations the family produced have more than a private interest. But the historian cannot easily assign dates to developments in it. Rather than talk about changes and gradual evolution he is conscious of haphazard personal influences—of people reacting against their upbringing but of others perpetuating traditions, of different classes, professions, regions having their own peculiar customs. The history of domestic relations cannot be written in the same way as the history of international relations and any description of them must be tentative and incomplete.

In a work published in 1883, the marriages of the day were described as being of three kinds: those contracted for convenience, those produced by sympathy or love, and those entered into from duty.[1] Is it possible to discover what the proportions between these varieties were, and how they changed during this century? In public opinion polls held in 1947 men

[1] Alexandre Laya, *Causes célèbres du mariage ou les infortunes conjugales* (1883).

and women agreed, to the extent of 71 per cent and 78 per cent, that love marriages were the best kind. But it does not follow that this represents the triumph of the romantic ideal. Even the most calculating matchmakers of the nineteenth century hoped that if love did not precede a marriage—and it could hardly do so if the couple had barely met—it should result from it and be the basis of its strength: the girl married off for reasons of convenience had a duty to love her husband. Views about how to contract a marriage may have been different in the nineteenth century, but not necessarily the way the marriage functioned. When in this same opinion poll of 1947 people were further asked what they valued most in life, only 1 per cent of men and 5 per cent of women considered love as most important. 47 per cent of men and 38 per cent of women thought money was more important: health, peace, wealth, a nice family and hope were preferred in that order.[1] In an inquiry among 10,000 young people in 1966, both boys and girls placed fidelity as the first attribute they sought in their ideal spouse—before love, beauty or intelligence.[2] When in another inquiry, women who had, to the extent of 83 per cent, mentioned attachment to a man as necessary in order to be happy, were questioned further about what they hoped to get from this, only 22 per cent talked about love; 41 per cent wanted 'a good husband', variously described as faithful, understanding, courageous and kind, who stays with his wife and children; and 20 per cent wanted 'a good home', with mutual understanding, harmony and peace. 54 per cent of the women said they were definitely not romantic, and the figure was only a little lower for those still in their twenties: romanticism survived rather interestingly most strongly in rural areas and small towns, where the figure rose to up to 60 per cent; it was lowest in the cities (47 per cent). Only 44 per cent of women believed in the idea of the *grand amour*. Only 61 per cent of single women under twenty-five believed in it. Only 29 per cent of all women claimed to have experienced a *grand amour*: these came twice as often from professional and white collar families as from farming ones. Peasant girls might claim to be romantic, but few apparently had the opportunity to be

---

[1] Georges Rotvand, *L'Imprévisible Monsieur Durand* (1956), 131.
[2] Roberte Franck, *L'Infidélité conjugale* (1969), 86.

so. It is important to distinguish between what happened in real life and the ideals and fantasies obsessing the novelists. The changes that did occur were more subtle than a radical rejection of the values of the past.[1]

How should a man choose a wife, what should he expect of her and what could he expect their relations to be? The answers throughout the period were varied. So long as obedience was the principal virtue inculcated into children, so long as girls were brought up to be models of innocence, to be ignorant of the world, skilled in domestic arts, and destined for marriage, then the choice was made by the parents, using their own criteria. Parents seem to have been influenced by the position they held within their class. The marriage of their children was a public valuation placed on the parents' position, and it was also a method of improving that position. The great problem was to avoid a *mésalliance*, which was why love was the great enemy, the rebel against parental authority which could bring disaster on all their plans. The aristocracy laid greatest stress on the antiquity and nobility of the families they married, though if they were strong themselves in the matter of antiquity, they were willing to marry for money—provided the sums to be acquired were very large—and many did. In any case, it was generally accepted that property arrangements had to be satisfactory, to maintain both the couple immediately and their children after them. The bourgeoisie accepted these values. Marriage was for them the great means of social ascension. The larger the dowry they could obtain for their son, the better the situation he could buy and the more optimistic his prospects. In the lower commercial bourgeoisie, the combination of two fortunes was often used to start up or expand businesses. The peasantry had the same practice on a more modest scale, with the accumulation of land into larger units as the aim. Only the poorest industrial workers were the pariahs of this society. Quite often in the nineteenth century they did not marry at all, because they could not afford the expense of the ceremony. Rootless in the city, there was not the same family pressure. But when they rose to the artisan class and accumulated some property, they followed the same pattern.

[1] French Institute of Public Opinion, *Patterns of Love and Sex: A Study of the French Woman and her Morals* (1961), 133-49.

This picture of a society basing its domestic arrangements on financial considerations is only part of the truth. It was certainly in this way that a large number of people described marriage throughout these years. As late as 1912 a justice of the peace of the tenth *arrondissement* in Paris issued a judgement which began: 'Whereas in antiquity marriage was based uniquely on the love of two people of different sex; whereas, since the advent of Christianity, the morals of marriage have undergone substantial changes; so that during the past century and more particularly nowadays the social system considers it as a veritable financial contract to hold in check possible trickery between the two parties and to reassure the silent distrust of the future spouses, because the true reason of modern marriage is money; the husband seeks a dowry and the woman buys at once a protector and a manager considered more experienced for the administration of her property . . .'[1] After the war of 1914 emancipated girls were complaining that men never mentioned marriage without talking about the size of the dowry. Men even advertised for dowries in newspapers and a notary would tell a young man that 'at the present time, given the high cost of living, a young man should not marry a girl who has less than 100,000 francs of dowry'.[2] The situation does not appear to have changed drastically since 1806, when Joseph Droz, of the French Academy, wrote his *Essay on the Art of Being Happy*—a book which reached its seventh edition in 1853 and which was placed on the open shelves in the Bibliothèque Nationale, presumably as an accepted guide. He said: 'Marriage is in general a means of increasing one's credit and one's fortune and of ensuring one's success in the world.'[3] France, it was pointed out, was the one country in Europe which did not have the custom of long engagements. Young people were unwilling to wait and to save before getting married. They expected to be able to keep up the style of life they were brought up in, and the dowry was therefore essential.[4] The dramatists of the Second Empire wrote innumerable plays on this subject, to resolve the question of what constituted a good marriage.

[1] Jules Thabaut, *L'Évolution de la législation sur la famille* (1913), 17 n.
[2] H. Bordeaux, *Le Mariage* (1921), 167.
[3] J. Droz, *Essai sur l'art d'être heureux* (1853), 189.
[4] Armand Hayem, *Le Mariage* (1872), 152.

They took it as an axiom that the financial question was of major importance. The safe moral, which men like Émile Augier preached, was that the most successful marriages were likely to be those in which the wealth of the two partners was equally balanced: the ideal marriage was the fair bargain. He showed the scrapes people got into when they broke this rule, which they obviously did. Merit could to a certain degree be translated into monetary terms; but the wife should not be much richer than the husband, or she might treat him the wrong way, nor should she be poorer, or she will be called a schemer. Alexandre Dumas fils, after thirty-five years of writing about marriage, concluded that though the love marriage might be the ideal, it was not a practical reality, and people must not expect too much from marriage: they must be thankful for whatever happiness they might find. The use of marriage for social climbing presented conflicts and difficulties. Marriage was, as Dumas said, 'not only the union of two people but the alliance of two families'. Relations were most likely to be satisfactory if the social climbing was gradual and the two families capable of talking to each other, and using each other for their mutual aggrandisement.[1] Thus marriage, like education, was a way of bettering oneself. It fitted in best with the prevailing mania for social advancement when conceived in this way. In so far as equal opportunity and the rule of merit failed to be fully introduced, this attitude to marriage survived.

However, the marriage dowry was not simply a method by which men acquired wealth. A marriage usually involved a marriage contract—not just among the rich, but even sometimes among servants and labourers with only a few hundred francs each. The way this contract was drawn up was crucial in determining the nature of the household which would result. For though the Napoleonic code made the husband the guardian and administrator of his wife's wealth, numerous obstacles could be placed in his path and the wife could retain powerful rights against him. The practice in the north and south of France was originally very different. In the areas where Roman law had prevailed the *régime dotal* gave the husband use of the

---

[1] C. E. Young, *The Marriage Question in the Modern French Drama (1850–1911)*, Ph.D. Wisconsin, in *Bulletin of the University of Wisconsin*, no. 771, Philology and literature series, vol. 5, no. 4 (Madison, Wis., 1915), 19, 44.

income from the dowry, but the capital was inalienable. It was conceived of as a guarantee against widowhood and could remain in the control of the wife's family. In the north, where customary law was followed, these restrictions did not apply and the husband could even sell the dowry to pay his debts. The position of wives was thus different in the south: but in the years 1835–60 the dotal system was largely abandoned in the south-west. The change can be precisely dated from the reports of the notaries who drew up the contracts. The reason given for this change was that the dotal system suggested both suspicion of the husband and doubts about the wife's capacity to look after herself, independently of her family. The system was best suited to a stable society; merchants and industrialists were the first to abandon it, and it lasted longest, well into the twentieth century, among rentiers, civil servants, the nobility and the very rich who were content to live off their capital. It made an active investment policy difficult; it made frequent recourse to loans necessary; and involved high legal costs. Not least, it deprived the wife of any share in the profits her husband might make by using her money.

The courts, for their part, attempted to maintain the strict inalienability of the dowry, claiming that it was in the public interest to strengthen the family, so that if, for example, the husband went bankrupt, the dowry, under this system, could not be seized and his wife and children were safeguarded. The notaries, at the request of their clients, attempted to foil this inalienability by introducing greater flexibility; but increasingly they encouraged its abandonment. The change in the south-west can be partly attributed to a generation of notaries educated at Bordeaux, who spread the practices of the merchants there to the surrounding countryside. Now instead marriages became joint partnerships, by the widespread adoption of the *régime d'acquêts*. By this both spouses shared equally in the profits of the marriage. It is interesting to find notaries reporting that couples came to them saying they wished to be associates and equals and to have a contract drawn up accordingly. The Civil Code prescribed that if no contract was made, property should be owned in common. Now this, paradoxically, gave a predominant power to the husband. Most of those who abandoned the dotal system therefore preferred the alternative of separation of property, by which what they brought in continued to belong to each separately, and only the common profits of the marriage were shared. With the reintroduction of divorce in 1884, there were even stronger reasons for adopting this latter course. Between 1900 and 1949 therefore the percentage of contracts adopting separation of property rose as follows:

	per cent		per cent
1900–9	9–15	1930–4	47
1910–14	14	1935–9	45·5
1915–19	21	1940–4	56
1920–4	22	1945–9	66·1
1925–9	40·7		

These are figures from one sample taken in Paris and must be interpreted with the appropriate reservations (they include marriage contracts by divorcees and widowers; if these are eliminated the rise is from 7 to 48·5 per cent). The survival of the dowry system has not been studied statistically. Only when the notarial archives for the late nineteenth and early twentieth century are opened will it be possible to appreciate accurately exactly what the role of money in people's marriages was. The complexity of the arrangements, however, reinforces the view of marriage as very much a business affair, whatever may have been the equality with which it was conducted. 'For the great majority of the bourgeoisie', wrote Paul Bureau in 1927, 'marriage is the greatest financial operation of their lives.'[1]

The history of the emotional relations between married couples is even more difficult to trace. The flowering of the romantic ideal did not of course necessarily mean an increase in domestic intimacy. On the contrary, the idealisation of women placed even greater distances between them and men. The cult of their purity made them inaccessible: pleasures in sexual intercourse could not in such circumstances be sought with them, who were dedicated to motherhood. Romanticism probably made the prostitute even more necessary. It has been argued that positivism had a not dissimilar effect. 'Materialism and the hate of all metaphysics destroyed enthusiasm and

[1] Albert Eyquem, *Le Régime dotal. Son histoire, son évolution et ses transformations au 19e siècle sous l'influence de la jurisprudence et du notariat* (1903); Jacques Lelièvre, *La Pratique des contrats de mariage chez les notaires au Châtelet de Paris de 1769 à 1804* (1959), 391; P. Bureau, *L'Indiscipline des mœurs* (1927), 60.

closed up the doors of the infinite. So, in literature, in art and in life, men threw themselves into physical love with a violence exacerbated by their intellectual refinement and their subconscious spiritual needs. From this resulted the brutalities, and the perversions, the sadism and hysteria which infect recent conceptions and paintings of love . . . [This has worsened] the war of the sexes.'[1]

Anticlericalism likewise divided the family. It was very common for husband and wife to be in fundamental disagreement about religion. In the prevailing atmosphere of polemic and strife over the power of the clergy, the wife appeared as the instrument of the domination of the *curés*, benighted by medieval prejudices, so that the inclination to regard women as an inferior species was strengthened rather than reduced in the nineteenth century. A *lycée* schoolmistress pointed out that in the eighteenth century girls were simply taught the catechism, but their minds were at least left empty, so that, thanks to early marriage, they were soon free to read and converse with men. In the revolutionary conflict of the following century, however, greater efforts were made to instil reactionary principles into girls. They entered marriage encumbered with theories which made it impossible for them to be friends with their husbands.[2] Men like Michelet complained that a liberal husband did not feel free in his own house: his wife spied on him on behalf of the priest, to whom she told all his secrets in the confession. The priest was the only man who claimed the right to talk to a wife alone, in private, whenever he pleased.[3] It was with a mistress or at a café therefore that the husband sang and laughed.[4]

The intellectuals, for all their liberalism, were incapable of solving this dilemma. Michelet wrote several books in praise of women's marvellous qualities, of the beauty of love, of the delights of a harmonious, cosy home. He urged that worship of theological abstractions should be replaced by the religion of the home. He demanded that women should become no longer

[1] Édouard Schuré, art critic, quoted by Ph. Pagnat, *Enquête sur l'amour* (1907), 60–2.

[2] Marie Dugard, *De l'éducation moderne des jeunes filles* (1900), 51.

[3] For the relation of the confession to sexual relations see Theodore Zeldin (ed.), *Conflicts in French Society* (1970), 13–50.

[4] Léon Richer, *Lettres d'un libre penseur à un curé de campagne* (1868), chapter 14, 'Ce qui se passe dans la famille'.

the slaves nor the enemies of men, but their associates and companions, and that couples should bring up their families together in touching unity. He found nothing so moving as seeing workers scurrying home in the evening to get back to their wives. Michelet is usually listed among the heroes of female emancipation. A criticism of his books by a woman, Adèle Esquiros, shows, however, how inadequate his proposals were from the point of view of women. Her book on love, much more than his, deserves to be ranked as a classic of women's liberation literature. She is appalled by Michelet's arrogance, which she regards as typical of middle-class men. Michelet says he wants men to stop shutting themselves up in their jobs and claiming superiority from their specialised knowledge; he claims that he wants men to share their lives with women, but in effect he only imposes a new tyranny upon women. His idea is that men should educate their wives, fashion them in their own mould, tell them what to think. He claims to liberate them but he only really wants them to acknowledge their husbands as their God. 'I do not believe', writes Madame Esquiros, 'in the homoeopathy of M. Michelet, who wants to cure the [old male] pride by an increase of pride.' She complains that marriage should be a source of happiness but so many men make it a pain. Women only went to the priest for confession because husbands did not perform the function themselves. Michelet says that wives got bored with their husbands and became frigid. 'I regret, monsieur, that you have neither found nor sought the cause of this frigidity which exists in almost all marriages.' The reason for it, she says, was that men were either 'brutal, gross and savage' or else they thought they were being respectful towards their wives by not being demonstrative. There was a common prejudice, in the middle classes particularly, that familiarity breeds contempt. The only result was that wives became dry and peevish prudes who said that they knew what their duty was, while their husbands were respectfully egoistic, shutting themselves up in the performance of duty with a similar sobriety and strictness. 'Strange respect and strange duty!' The husband ought to get his wife to know him, to become more truly familiar with him, and among people with feeling, familiarity will produce respect. Men should stop being concerned so much with themselves, they should not try to take more than they give, they should try to understand their wives. Women had their own ideas, caprices and sensitivities and men still had everything to learn from them. Dissimulation would then be replaced by confidence and freedom. She had no use for the poet who once told her: 'To love, is to admire one-self in another.' (Half a century later, Valéry could still write 'Love is the way to love oneself absolutely'; Proust discussed love as an illusion created by men in their own image.) Men had monopolised all the jobs, honours and pleasures of the world. They were consumed by pride, tobacco, spirits and evil passions. They had destroyed women by degrading them into nonentities. They would have happy homes only when they appreciated that women had much more to offer than men at present admitted.[1]

There certainly were advocates of intimacy and friendship between the sexes from an early date. In the debates about marriage during the first revolution, Oudot, deputy of the Côte-d'Or, had demanded the abolition of paternal consent after the age of twenty-one so that there should be no obstacles to 'two people uniting themselves, when they were really suited, as came about when there was conformity of character', even if considerations of ambition, avarice and pride opposed themselves.[2] There were the utopians, above all Fourier, who wanted relations between the sexes to be totally free. But it is more interesting to find pillars of respectability beginning to feel that men ought to have more fun in their married lives. Already in 1806 Joseph Droz (1773–1850), member of the French Academy, and descended from a long line of magistrates, in his manual on how to be happy, urged that marriage should cease to be simply a way of improving one's status and should become a means of being happy. Women should be given a chance in it to correct the pedantry, pride and severity of men. He rejected the idea that love would follow from an arranged marriage. 'I am of the opinion that one should not marry a woman except after one has won her love, for it is doubtful whether love will be inspired by a husband.' But he did not go anywhere as far as Mme Esquiros. He still thought

---

[1] Adèle Esquiros, *L'Amour* (1860).
[2] Dr. Louis Fiaux, *La Femme, le mariage et le divorce. Étude de physiologie et de sociologie* (1880), 27–8.

of the husband as being older than the wife, and educating
her. To marry as heroes married in novels was dangerous: 'The
dreams of lovers spoil the reality when they are married.' The
man, he still thought, must exercise the authority in the household: the wife should only have influence over him. Joseph
Droz marks a first stage, which does not go beyond Michelet.
Gustave Droz (no relation) trained at the École des Beaux Arts
(the son of a successful sculptor, grandson of a director of the
mint), a journalist and for long Buloz's assistant in the *Revue
des Deux Mondes*, wrote a best seller in 1866 called *Monsieur,
madame et bébé*. This went through 121 editions between 1866
and 1884. He said he proposed to do what no one else had done:
write about love in marriage. People had made marriage
sound so grim and frightening, overwhelmed by duty, but the
men who propagated this notion were husbands exhausted by
prostitutes and rheumatism, who wanted to make marriage an
asylum of retirement, of which their young wives would be the
angels. He felt he had to convert women from this role. 'It is
nice being an angel, but, believe me, it is either too much or
not enough . . . A husband who is stately and a little bald is all
right, but a young husband who loves you and who drinks out
of your glass without ceremony, is better. Let him, if he ruffles
your dress a little and places a little kiss on your neck as he
passes. Let him, if he undresses you after the ball, laughing like
a fool. You have fine spiritual qualities, it is true, but your
little body is not bad either and when one loves, one loves
completely. Behind these follies lies happiness. Thank heaven if
in marriage which is presented to you as a career you find a side
that yields laughter and joy; if in your husband you find a
loved reader of the nice novel you keep in your pocket; if in
your husband you find a . . . But if I say the word you will cry
Scandal!' A great battle would have to be fought, said Droz,
before women overcame the inhibitions imposed on them by
their education which made them so stuffy. He held up the
ideal of the married couple who were lovers.[1]

The notion that women could obtain pleasure from sexual
intercourse was no invention of the twentieth century and
Marie Stopes has wrongly been credited with inventing the
female right to orgasm. The works of the seventeenth-century

[1] Gustave Droz, *Monsieur, madame et bébé* (published by Hetzel, 1866), 112.

Dr. Nicolas Venette, frequently reprinted in the nineteenth, painted a picture of women as being naturally more lascivious than men, and offered advice on how to meet their sexual demands. A doctor who produced a revised edition of Venette's book on conjugal love in 1907, like Droz, urged married men to treat their wives sexually in the same way as they treated their mistresses.[1] Among the numerous guides to sex and marriage published in the nineteenth century, there were some moralistic ones, but quite a few stressed the importance of satisfying women emotionally. One particularly successful one, by a retired army medical officer, which went through 173 editions between 1848 and 1888, was quite specific about women enjoying intercourse as much as men. It advised men that whereas some women go into a delirium of pleasure at the least contact, others require frequently repeated caresses to reach orgasm. For extreme cases of inhibition he prescribed flagellation, but his main advice was to win women by tenderness and kindness. He said that doctors were agreed that a married man between twenty and thirty should only exercise his conjugal rights two to four times a week, but always with an interval of a day; twice a week till forty, once till fifty, once a fortnight till sixty, but never beyond that age. Over-activity—'five or six times a day as many young men do'—produced regrets later. Women were capable of indulging more often than men, but they should restrict themselves because it could lead to diseases and to cancer. 'The solitary masturbation practised by many women dissatisfied with their husbands' should be avoided for the same reason.[2]

Another doctor, who published *A Little Bible for Young Spouses* (1885), though writing with more discretion, stressed the need for husbands to give their wives sexual pleasure and to aim for simultaneous orgasm.[3] But all this advice had to work against firmly engrained prejudices in both sexes. There is a case recorded of a wife demanding a divorce because of the excessive zeal and 'unnatural caresses' of her husband: he pleaded that he was only trying to please her and increase her affection for him:

---

[1] Dr. Nicolas Venette, *Tableau de l'amour conjugale* (new edition by Dr. Caufeynon (pseudonym for Dr. Jean Fauconney) (1907)).

[2] A. Debay, *Hygiène et physiologie du mariage* (n.d., 54th edition).

[3] Dr. Charles Montalban, *La Petite Bible des jeunes époux* (1885), 36, 56.

the court found in his favour.[1] In 1887 a book advocated a reform of the art of love-making, on the ground that adultery was caused by husbands not satisfying their wives: women had a right to orgasm.[2] In the 1950s in a poll of married women, 68 per cent said sexual relations were an important part of marriage, 22 per cent said they were only for a minority, and 10 per cent would not answer. But only 46 per cent of these women considered that physical love in marriage proved satisfying; as their ages went up, an increasing number spoke of disappointment.[3]

The lady who asked for a divorce because her husband's love-making alarmed her was very likely the victim of the conflict produced by the hostility of many conservatives to the enjoyment or discussion of sex. The doctrine preached by the Catholic clergy was that the purpose of marriage was definitely not pleasure, but the constitution of families and the procreation of children. In 1920, Abbé Grimaud, in a work which was to go through at least 33 editions and which was crowned by the French Academy, summarised their attitude well when he said that 'God foresaw in his wisdom that couples would not accept the heavy obligations of paternity unless they were pushed by the charms of pleasure'. But sexual pleasure should not be an aim in itself. The clergy generally spoke of the husband as having sexual urges and the wife as submitting to them. Taking their own practice as an ideal, they urged the repression of sexual desire as the ultimate aim: Joseph and the Virgin Mary, who loved each other but never copulated, represented ultimate virtue. Few people could be expected to reach these heights, but, after procreation, continence by mutual consent in marriage was recommended as desirable, even though it would mean abstention from all touching, looks or words of affection, which might reinflame desire. The clergy were genuinely concerned with the dignity of women, but sometimes conceived it in a way which restricted women's intellectual aspirations. Thus Abbé Grimaud, in discussing what kind

[1] Georges Anquetil and Jane de Magny, *L'Amant légitime ou la bourgeoisie libertine* (1923), 518.
[2] J. P. Dartigues, *De l'amour expérimentale ou des causes d'adultère chez la femme au 19ᵉ siècle. Étude d'hygiène et d'économie sociale, résultant de l'ignorance du libertinage et des fraudes dans l'accomplissement des devoirs conjugaux* (Versailles, 1887), 124, 188.
[3] French Institute of Public Opinion, op. cit., 173.

of wife a man should choose, vigorously advises men to steer as completely clear of intellectuals and professional women (unless they were willing to give up their jobs) as of prostitutes. A woman must be primarily a mother devoted to bringing up her children as Christians. For all his belief in the equality of souls, he likewise urges men to marry only girls of their own class. If a man feels that he is about to fall in love (he likens it to being attacked by a microbe) his first thought should be to go to his parents and ask them to ascertain whether the girl was suitable. Then, when all the demands of reason were satisfied, he could allow his passion to capture him. Passion would of course pass rapidly and could not be the basis of marriage. That is why it was so deplorable that employers were putting 'young men and girls to work at the same tables. Go into a bank, for example, and in a flash, if you are just a bit of a psychologist, you will appreciate how much a young man, even though he would like to remain honourable, is menaced by the possibility of contracting an unhappy marriage. Next to boys—often very distinguished ones, who have studied, and come from a certain level of society—one sees typists, among whom are some of excellent education, but also many others less *sérieuses*. One can judge what the majority of these girls are like from the clothes they wear. One suspects that in this mixed company it will not be the good quiet girls, modest like nuns and reserved like mothers of families, who will attract the men's glances. They will be called boring and unattractive. The others on the contrary will not fail to please the young men rapidly, because they do not hesitate to surround them with the most provocative attention.'[1]

The Church's view of marriage laid stress on gravity, devotion to duty, the bringing up of children, resignation, acceptance of one's lot, and consolation from prayer and piety. It was vigorously opposed to contraception and, through the confession, some clergy even pressed women to resist their husband's embraces if they practised *coitus interruptus*, which was the commonest contraceptive method employed in this period. It sought to maintain morality by preaching self-control. It offered a great deal of emotional consolation, but it was God and prayer, not the husband, who were the consolers. The only

[1] Abbé Charles Grimaud, *Futurs Époux* (1920), 287–90, 301–15.

true and full love women could have, one author pointed out, was love of God. Bishop Dupanloup in the 1860s stressed that marriage brought dignity to the mother but it also gave authority to the father. In 1920 when General de Castelnau issued his Declaration of the Rights of the Family at the Estates General of the French Family (an anti-contraceptive organisation), he defined the family as being 'founded on marriage, hierarchically constituted under the authority of the father, having as its goal the transmission, support, development and perpetuation of human life'. The stress was on the family unit against the rights individuals claimed against it.[1] Sexual education was seen mainly as an exhortation to piety, chastity and repression. The Church opposed sexual education in schools and insisted that it should be left to the parents.[2] One author held up as a model on how the facts should be told the history of a pious father who, when his son reached the age of eighteen, summoned him to his study and told him: 'My son, I have some great truths to tell you. Let us kneel and say an Ave Maria.' Asking whether his son had understood the prayer he explained the divine mystery of the Incarnation, and from that moved on to show the less sublime origins of miserable humanity; then he pointed out our duties, the dangers that would be encountered and the precautions to be taken. The boy listened, hardly asking any questions, and understood the ideas which would transform him. 'I felt', he said, 'that I became a man.' The conversation ended with a prayer as it had begun.[3] Marriage was thus seen as a duty, second best to the complete dedication of the self made by the nun or the monk.

The moderate liberal tradition took a very similar view of marriage. Jules Simon founded a fortnightly *Revue de Famille*, which lasted for twenty years, aiming at the revival of the country's morals by the family spirit. Bishop Dupanloup had thought that hierarchy could not survive in politics or social life unless it was maintained in marriage. Simon, similarly, thought only family virtues could save France from communism. 'The more one is attached to one's home, the more one is ready to die for

---

[1] H. Bordeaux, 208–10.

[2] *L'Église et l'éducation sexuelle*. Proceedings of the seventh national congress of the Association du Mariage Chrétien (1929).

[3] Grimaud, 37–8.

one's country.' The liberals were as anxious to promote duty rather than pleasure as the Catholics, but they slightly moderated the latter's stringent austerity. They agreed it was legitimate to enjoy sex in marriage in moderation, though they were unwilling to discuss it and discouraged people from thinking too much about it. They saw women as performing clearly separate functions in the family. One doctor who wrote a guide to *The Health of Married People* gave this as his advice: 'Happiness in marriage is not possible unless each keeps perfectly within his role and confines himself to the virtues of his sex, without encroaching on the prerogatives of the opposite sex.' The husband, who provided the element of force and activity, had as his function 'to represent the family or to direct it in its relations with the external world and to ensure its preservation and its development. The wife, so well endowed with grace, intuition and a ready emotional sympathy, has as her mission to preside over the internal life of the house, whose well-being she ensures by her knowledge of domestic details.' The children were the result of this union, and were the reward or punishment of it, depending on how successful it was. He recommended marriage between persons of differing temperaments—the bilious should marry the lymphatic, the sanguine should unite with the nervous—because the children produced would be healthier mixtures in this way.[1] This is not to say that intellectual compatibility was regarded as a disadvantage. Many authors were keen to stimulate it, though they often seemed to think of it as coming after marriage. Paul Janet, a leading university moralist in the second half of the nineteenth century, thought the husband ought to be the head of the family because men had a superior power of reason, more suitable to command, having greater breadth, logic and impartiality. Women had reason too, but of a different kind, and their subordination was necessary only because it was best to have one person in charge. Otherwise there should be 'moral equality' between husband and wife.[2] A contemporary of his, Amédie de Margerie, in a strange work praising the virtues of the family but clearly uneasy that there was something wrong with it, urged men to spend their evenings talking with their

[1] Dr. Louis Seraine, *De la santé des gens mariés* (2nd edition 1865), 112–16.
[2] Paul Janet, *La Famille* (4th edition 1861).

wives and, when their conversations died out, to read together. This man was keen to increase the moral influence of the wife in marriage, because she was more often religious and her mission was to convert her husband. 'The times we live in need strong women.' Wives must save the family from the indifference of men. Indeed, he said, 'though their official position in it was subordinate, their influence in it is preponderant'.[1] The subject of the preponderant wife is one which will be discussed later in relation to its effect on children.

In 1920 there was an interesting debate in the press about what relations between husband and wife should be. It is one of the few occasions when, from the letters ordinary people wrote, one can obtain direct evidence of trends in common behaviour, and when one can see revealed widespread dissatisfaction with the traditional kind of marriage. One should not conclude that this was produced by the war, by the absence of men for several years and the increased responsibility women bore, though that certainly brought some tensions into the open. Adèle Esquiros's book had voiced complaints sixty years earlier. But the war broke routines and enabled people to see what habit had concealed from them. 'This unanimous explosion of independence among women, provoked by the absence of husbands,' wrote one letter writer, 'suffices to show what forces and aspirations were repressed in them even by the most loved of tyrants . . . Conjugal affection, the joys and worries of motherhood make them accept in silence many vexations.' The explosion was by no means unanimous, but quite a number of women now had a different view of marriage. They objected to men's expecting their wives to be domestic servants. They demanded that husbands should treat them as friends and companions. But the war had also increased the opportunities for men to develop new interests in life, which took them increasingly away from the home. A railwayman wrote that far from having a higher regard for women because they had done men's jobs in the war, he now saw women as economic rivals. 'Women no longer want to obey . . . We talk about marriage between men and women as people talk of peace between the Boches and the French.' And on the other side a judge refused a divorce to a disgruntled husband, saying he must use gentleness not firmness to win back his wife.[1] In the 1950s the opinion polls said one-third of wives thought their husbands had changed for the worse since marriage, but almost exactly one-third also thought they themselves had deteriorated. This is the nearest one can get to any statistics about the extent of disillusionment with marriage.

An important factor in determining the nature of marriages was the age of the couple at their wedding. 'In general', wrote a member of the French Academy in 1917, 'a man does not consent to take a legitimate wife until the moment when life, of which he is a bit tired, begins to bore him.' It was natural therefore that he should expect submission and docility from his wife. The wife was usually much younger and could hardly challenge him. Léon Blum wrote a book in his youth suggesting that until there were identical codes of moral behaviour for girls and boys, inequalities of experience were bound to produce friction. He made the bold proposal that both sexes—instead of just men—should marry only after they had sown their wild oats and were willing to accept monogamy voluntarily.[2]

In the working class, inequalities of age and experience tended to be smaller and it was claimed by some that family life was accordingly friendlier, more one of equality and companionship. Possibly here women acquired more influence earlier, since they did not have to fight against the husband's technical prestige. For long the problem with the industrial workers was to get them to marry. Moralists saw marriage at this level as a means of shackling the men, of keeping them off the streets, of reducing crime and of instilling love of property in the poor.[3] It is by no means clear that love played a greater role in their marriages: in the country in particular local customs concerning courtship—which differed considerably—maintained the authority of parents and the haggling over dowries continued to the very humble levels. There were areas where marriages were generally fixed at Christmas time—provided the harvest had been a good one—by the parents. On

[1] H. Bordeaux, op. cit.
[2] Léon Blum, *Le Mariage* (1907).
[3] Institut de France, *Statistique: mariage civil et religieux des pauvres* (1846).

occasion it was the girls who proposed to the boys. Intermediaries were used to a considerable extent—travelling
tailors seem to have been particularly active in this role.[1] In the
towns of course marriage bureaux flourished. They offered their
services, it should be noted, to parents more than to the parties
concerned.[2] (After the Great War, they were supplemented by
divorce agencies, with fees fixed in inverse proportion to the
time they took to obtain the decree: 2,000 francs for one year's
delay, 5,000 francs if it was completed in three months.) It was
claimed by an author comparing France, England and the
U.S.A. that French women had less freedom in choosing their
husbands, but once they were married, they acquired more
influence.[3] In many ways it will be seen that the marriage
system oppressed children more than wives. Wives, after all,
could look forward to increasing power as they became mothers,
grandmothers and matriarchs.

Money played such a large part in marriage, sexual relations
were subject to so many restrictions, wives were so keen to
transform themselves from brides into matriarchs that inevitably adultery and prostitution were essential to the working of
this system. An additional reason, not usually appreciated, is
the slow elimination of women's gynaecological diseases. Too
much attention is perhaps given to the diseases which killed,
like smallpox and tuberculosis, and not enough to those which
simply made life unpleasant. One such was leucorrhea. In 1865
a doctor estimated that, particularly in cities, as many as 80 per
cent of women suffered from it.[4] Another doctor, writing in
1868, described the large number of other diseases, metritis,
ulcerations, inflammations, tumours, haemorrhages, etc., many
of which he attributed to irritations caused by amateur contraceptives.[5] A work commended by the Academy of Moral and
Political Sciences in 1872 pointed out that because of these
diseases it was very often impossible for husbands and wives to
copulate, putting aside all the other illnesses which could

---

[1] Évariste Carrance, *Le Mariage chez nos prèes* (Bordeaux, 1872).

[2] *Journal Matrimonial. Gazette des familles* (1 May 1850).

[3] Auguste Carlier, *Le Mariage aux États-Unis* (1860), an interesting criticism of
Tocqueville.

[4] Dr. Louis Seraine, *De la santé des gens mariés* (1865), 136.

[5] Dr. L. F. E. Bergeret, *Des Fraudes dans l'accomplissement des fonctions génératrices.
Dangers et inconvénients pour les individus, la famille et la société* (1868).

nauseate like eczema, rheumatism, tumours, etc. The proportion of young people who were both healthy and attractive was comparatively small. No figures are available for women, but the facts revealed by conscription about boys are appalling. An analysis published in 1872 said that of the 325,000 young men of twenty called up, 18,106 were under 4 foot 10 inches tall. There were 30,524 of 'feeble constitution', i.e. suffering from rickets or consumption, etc. 15,988 were cripples, mutilated or sufferers from hernia, rheumatism, etc. 9,100 were hunchbacks, club-footed or flat-footed. 6,934 had defects of the ears, eyes or nose. 963 had speech defects and 4,108 were toothless. 'Precocious debauchery' had ruined 5,114. 2,529 were victims of skin diseases, 5,213 of goitre and scrofula, 2,158 were paralytics, convulsives or cretins, and 8,236 had miscellaneous troubles. In all therefore 109,000—that is, one-third—were infirm or deformed, and this was at the age of twenty.[1]

The great bogy the moralists used to keep people chaste was the danger of catching syphilis. It was indeed a major blight on the country. Flaubert, in his *Dictionary of Received Ideas*, defined it as being almost as common as the cold: 'More or less everybody is affected by it.' At the turn of the century insurance company records revealed that between 14 and 15 per cent of all deaths were from syphilis. Another source gave a figure of 17 per cent. Between the wars a third estimate suggested that probably one-tenth of the population suffered from it, i.e. four million people, and that 140,000 lives were lost annually from it. Over 40,000 still births a year were attributable to it. It was one of the principal causes of madness. Half of syphilitics caught the disease between the age of fourteen and twenty-one. In the bourgeoisie a tenth caught it at school. One could draw up a list of many distinguished figures in French history who are said to have had the disease, from Gambetta to Baudelaire.

The main reason why it survived so tenaciously was that every government ignored it in hypocritical silence. The Academy of Medicine appointed a commission to find means of checking it in 1887; a Society for Sanitary and Moral Prophylaxis was founded in 1901, but though parliament at last got round to discussing it in 1907, it did nothing. The war

[1] Armand Hayem, *Le Mariage* (1872), 243.

stimulated some governmental activity, particularly in the army; in 1924 a National League against the Venereal Peril was founded and there were many other societies. But there was nothing like the compulsory treatment established in the U.S.A. In the nineteenth century the treatment available was very inadequate. Few beds were allocated to it in hospitals and some hospital nurses refused to allow syphilitic patients to be admitted. Until 1871 the main hospital in Paris devoted to it, Lancine, had underground cells for the punishment of patients considered morally reprehensible. The fact that going to this hospital involved public admission of one's disease kept many away. A real change came only in 1880 when Alfred Fournier had the first chair of venereal diseases established for him. He opened a clinic at an ordinary hospital, with privacy assured, and in 1882 had 31,000 cases come to him, whereas only 4,800 went annually to Lancine. The whole question was confused by the myth that it was the prostitutes who were responsible and that the only need was to control them. Another great obstacle to a reduction of the disease was the vast number of charlatans offering bogus cures. Their advertisements covered the walls of public lavatories, and one of the main activities of the societies was to fight the charlatans. Syphilis was one of the major causes of misery and suffering in this period.[1]

Extramarital sexual relations were a normal feature of life throughout it. Moralists always look back to a golden age of purity. But already in 1865 a doctor wrote: 'Today people do not think they can get rid of the burden of chastity early enough.'[2] 'It is rare', wrote another, 'to find in the present state of our morals boys who are virgin after seventeen or eighteen.'[3] Flaubert makes one of his heroes say of a brothel: 'That is the only place where I have been happy.' Pierre Louÿs's *Aphrodite* was looked upon as a breviary in praise of prostitution. Published in 1896, it had by 1904 sold 125,000

---

[1] E. Jeanselme, *La Syphilis. Son aspect pathologique et social* (1925); *L'Église et l'éducation sexuelle* (1929), 156; Louis Fiaux, *Le Police des mœurs devant la commission extra-parlementaire du régime des mœurs* (1907–10), 1. cxxxix, cxlvi; A. Fournier, *Les Dangers sociaux de la syphilis* (1905); id., *Syphilis et mariage* (1880); id., *Traité de la syphilis* (1899–1906).

[2] Dr. Louis Seraine, 23.

[3] Dr. Louis Fiaux, *La Femme, le mariage et le divorce* (1880), 43.

copies and inspired three plays and four opera libretti, and since then it has been regularly reprinted.

Visits to prostitutes started at school. On holidays and the Thursday half-day the brothels swarmed with schoolboys.[1] This precocity was encouraged by the massive war that was waged against masturbation. The danger of masturbation was one of the prime obsessions of parents and schools. The efforts used to extirpate it were so enormous they can only be likened to a new version of the medieval witchhunts.[2] Manufacturers produced excruciating corsets for children to make it impossible. Books were filled with advice on diet, exercises and clothing best suited to prevent it. Priests fought against it in the confession, and teachers at school. They preached self-control, which they thought ought to last ideally until the age of twenty-five, for young fathers produced feeble children and young debauchees were ruined for life. Some church schools were said even to periodically bleed pupils who revealed excessive sexuality.[3] Prostitutes played an important role in the life of the adolescent. Even in an inquiry among practising Catholic married males, 60 per cent admitted to having had premarital sexual activity, and 47 per cent of these said they had been initiated by a prostitute. This is a radically different situation to that in Britain or the U.S.A. today.[4] Whether there is more premarital sexual activity today in France than there was a hundred years ago is impossible to say. In the 1950s, 30 per cent of a sample of married Frenchwomen interviewed admitted to intercourse with their husbands before marriage. The figure, however, was only 24 per cent when the husband was a farmer but 43 per cent when he was a worker and 34 per cent when he was an executive or professional man.[5] Male and female attitudes towards this remain contrasted. In the poll of 10,000 young people held in 1966, 60 per cent of the girls were against premarital sex, and 66 per cent of the boys were for it.[6]

[1] Abbé Timon-David, *Traité de la confession des enfants et des jeunes gens* (1865, 14th edition 1924); cf. C. Féré, *La Pathologie des émotions* (1892), 269–71.

[2] J. M. W. van Ussel, *Sociogenese en evolutie van het probleem der seksuele propaedeuse* (Amsterdam thesis, 1967).

[3] Dr. J. Agrippa, *La Première Flétrissure* (3rd edition 1877).

[4] Henriques, 259.

[5] French Institute of Public Opinion, op. cit., 121.

[6] Roberte Franck, 86.

After marriage, adultery was almost inevitable.[1] It has been seen how, in this same poll, all boys and girls placed fidelity first as the quality they sought in their future spouse, above love, beauty or intelligence. But 84 per cent of the boys thought that it was possible to deceive one's wife without ceasing to love her: only 18 per cent of the girls agreed. Only 52 per cent of the boys, as against 74 per cent of the girls, thought that adultery necessarily damaged married life. They were agreed (79 and 76 per cent), however, that divorce was not preferable to adultery. The institution of marriage was not threatened, because it was not interpreted in the way the Church demanded. A recent study of the sexual habits of the French married man reveals that adultery is maintained precisely by the survival of traditional moral doctrines. An industrialist of fifty who was interviewed said: 'I make love with my wife when I want a child. The rest of the time I make love with my mistresses. Wives are to produce heirs. For pleasure men seek other women.' The low divorce rate conceals many marriages in which sexual intercourse is totally absent and in which husbands normally seek their satisfaction elsewhere. This study shows the existence of a separate world, maintained more or less secret, sometimes with elaborate subterfuges, hidden behind the respectable façade of married life.[2]

In the 1850s it was estimated that London had about 24,000 prostitutes but Paris, with almost half the population, was said to have 34,000.[3] Until 1946 the state regulated their activities, on the principle that their existence was inevitable and that they should practise their trade in the least offensive manner possible. Public opinion was less outraged by their trade, than by their trade being carried on publicly and in a manner which constituted a nuisance for those who did not require their services. A *police des mœurs* was established and prostitutes were required to live in brothels (*maisons de tolérance*), subject to medical inspection. The number of these official brothels in Paris was 180 in 1810, 200 in 1840, but they gradually fell to 145 in 1870, 125 in 1881 and 59 in 1892. The reason was the growth in

[1] Pierre Veron, *Paris vicieux: le guide de l'adultère* (1883); T. Revel, *L'Adultère* (1861); E. Cademartori, *L'Adultère à Marseille* (1866).

[2] Jacques Baroche, *Le Comportement sexuel de l'homme marié en France* (1969).

[3] Henriques, 224.

clandestine brothels, which the police estimated contained some 15,000 prostitutes in 1888. In the years 1871–1903, some 155,000 women registered as prostitutes but the police arrested 725,000 others suspected of prostitution. In 1900 the prefect of police, Lépine, carried out a reform designed to take into account the new habits. He authorised *maisons de rendezvous*, that is to say, establishments in which prostitutes did not reside but merely came to work: provided the entrance fee was above 40 francs, the police did not make any demands of registration or inspection. The pleasures of the middle class were thus liberated from state control.[1] Lépine viewed prostitution as a perfectly normal activity, and not in itself offensive. His regulation included this sentence: 'Since brothels are considered as public places, any person committing, in an establishment of this kind, in the presence of other persons, an act of immorality constituting a public outrage to modesty (*pudeur*), will be prosecuted.' His aim was to abolish perversions, and to establish a new kind of clean brothel: 'No more peep-holes, no more turpitudes' was his motto, but in vain. Flexner, the American investigator into European prostitution during the war, was amazed by Paris's specialisation in every kind of perversion, and the way the brothels rivalled each other in inventiveness. In the 1960s the Paris police estimated that the brothels of the city—with about one million adult males in it—had 40,000 clients a day; and this suggests that perhaps a quarter of all Parisians had relations with prostitutes.

In the provinces the situation was slightly different. Each town made its own arrangements and regulations. The Second Empire practised a *laissez-faire* attitude, but in the 1880s the government attempted a revival of control. Of the 557 known regulations about prostitution, only 219 date from before 1880. The majority, which were made after this date, varied enormously from town to town. Compulsory medical visits varied from two a week to two a month. In Vichy every prostitute had to deposit three photographs at the police station. At St. Étienne they were forbidden to walk in the streets in clothes other than those of 'respectable women'. Autun and Melun imposed restrictions on their hairstyles. In southern towns and

[1] On part-time prostitution in all classes see L. Fiaux, *La Police des mœurs* (1907–10), I. 37; Roberte Franck, *L'Infidélité conjugale* (1969), 224.

in the ports—most famous of all, in Marseille—the medieval whores' quarter survived. Regulations had little effect because the public prosecutors in general abstained from bringing scandals into the open. When between the wars a number of cities, notably Strasbourg, Grenoble and Nancy, attempted to close down their brothels, there was little change in men's habits and publications immediately appeared to supply clandestine addresses. Every garrison provided a substantial clientele. Soldiers were officially forbidden to visit brothels but the army created them specially in the colonies. It was claimed that prostitutes had to work far harder in these military brothels than in any private establishment exploited by an unscrupulous ponce. It was this exploitation and the white slave traffic that led to the official ending of *maisons de tolérance* in 1946. The abuses were certainly very real, but there is also evidence that a liberalisation of conditions in brothels occurred in the late nineteenth century, with increasing numbers of them being non-residential.

In the nineteenth century the brothel was a place of relaxation as ordinary and as natural as any other. Maupassant in a story of a provincial town describes one where respectable businessmen and young men met regularly, just as in a café, and where the Madame was treated with respect. The streets of the cities were plagued with importunate prostitutes in the same way as with beggars. Around 1900 there were 115 *brasseries* in Paris, which were ordinary cafés, except that the girls employed there made themselves available and took clients to a hotel. These got their best custom from schoolboys and students. There were many other establishments, like perfume shops, baths and massage institutes which performed the same functions. An annual *Guide rose* provided a full directory to all the opportunities. In addition theatres and luxury stores were recognised as amateur haunts. The rumour that middle-class women sometimes worked part-time as prostitutes, to earn money to keep up with the neighbours, has been confirmed by a recent sociological survey. (One suffragette wrote a book to demand brothels for women.) Some students, before they took to sleeping with each other, lived with *grisettes*—working girls who wanted a lover rather than a client and who had ambitions to rise in the world. When one of these *grisettes*, wrote an observer in 1840, had a child, she would set him up as a printer, or, if a girl, send her into the theatre—anything to avoid their having to do needlework like their mother. The *grisette* 'whom the student loves a little better than his dog and a little less than his pipe, madly throws away the best years of her life to love, pleasure and temporary liaisons'. She wears a mask of jollity but underneath is generally sombre, with a great contempt for life. She is greedy, and will accept a dinner from anybody; she is easily picked up at balls. But she consoled the students in their depressions and nursed them in their illnesses.[1]

Brothels always existed to cater for every class, but with time some became more like department stores, offering mass-produced luxury at a popular price. Between the wars several old firms in Paris were expanded from grubby slums into palatial establishments with armies of girls always available, including Saturday and Sunday, and offering themselves at a low fixed price. These brothels changed hands for large sums. Some owners built up chains of them. More and more girls, however, set themselves up as luxury prostitutes operating more discreetly. It was estimated that whereas in 1789 only 10 or 20 per cent of prostitutes were luxury ones, about a half are today. Their total number, it is claimed, has risen considerably. At the Revolution Poncet de La Grave in his *Considerations on Celibacy* (1801) estimated that there were 100,000 of them in France. In the 1960s, by which time the population of the country had doubled, a figure of 400,000 was suggested. But in the 1960s the young appear to have begun to abandon using them and a new morality now coexists with the old.[2]

The position of different forms of relaxation in French life may be indicated by the comparative incomes of different institutions of culture and licentiousness in Paris in the 1920s. The receipts of the Opéra were 12 million francs, but the Folies Bergères came second with 10 million francs, more than either the Comédie Française or the Opéra Comique. In 1923

[1] Alphonse Esquiros, *Les Vierges folles* (1840, new edition 1873).
[2] Dr. Félix Regnault, *L'Évolution de la prostitution* (1906); Fiaux, op. cit., containing numerous documents. The best history is by two *agrégés*, J.-J. Servais and J. P. Laurend, *Histoire et dossier de la prostitution* (1967). See also Marcel Rogeat, *Mœurs et prostitution. Les Grandes Enquêtes sociales* (1935), and the pioneering work of Dr. Parent-Duchâtelet, *De la prostitution dans la ville de Paris* (1836), enlarged edition 1857).

already the Paris cinemas had receipts of 85 million, against
110 million for all the Paris theatres. From the reports of
the antipornographic societies, it is not clear what could be
classified as culture. They complained of the cinema's 'gross
and brutal art, the scenes of crime and passion' exploited by
profiteers without taste or scruples and the grave dangers of
the medium for children and adolescents. But equally the
theatre tried to titillate the bourgeoisie with plays about
adultery, free love and divorce, on the pretext of portraying the
times; the competition was who could 'push furthest scenes of
the phases preparatory to love-making, beds included'. In 1914
Le Temps asked that copulation should take place on the stage
so that at last the police could intervene. In the music halls and
café concerts, there were certainly 'tableaux and scenes which
went so far as to represent sexual intercourse'. No one has yet
studied these or the vast outpouring of pornography, of books,
magazines and photographs, for which colossal sales were
reported and which constituted a not insignificant part of
the country's entertainment.[1]

The history of modesty—of what was considered permissible
and what was not—and the history of repression in the name of
public morality are both complicated subjects. Littré defined
licentiousness as what offends modesty and obscenity as what
offends modesty openly. The law tolerated the former but not
the latter; and it made the distinction that the licentious could
be defended on the ground that it was 'artistic, excluding all
idea of lucre and addressing itself to an élite', whereas the
obscene had 'low and pecuniary aims'. As one court ruled in
1884, 'obscenity exists where . . . art does not intervene to raise
up the ideal and where the appeal to the instincts and the gross
appetites was not opposed or defeated by any superior sentiment'.[2] In the second half of the century it was gradually
agreed that art could not be obscene, but new forms of it
always took time to be recognised. Flaubert's *Madame Bovary*
was adjudged obscene because, it was claimed, it did not hold
up an ideal against adultery. In the same way, a totally boring

[1] Paul Bureau, *L'Indiscipline des mœurs* (1927); Paul Gremähling, *L'Immoralité péril pour la race* (Bordeaux n.d., about 1925, published by Le Relèvement Social and the Ligue pour le Relèvement de la Moralité Publique).
[2] Tribunal de la Seine (11th Chamber), 11 Feb. 1884.

book about the life of a woman of easy virtue, who moved from one man to another, but with nothing scatological at all in it beyond that, was condemned a few years later, for much the same reason.[1] At about the same time a merchant of chamberpots, on the bottom of which was painted an eye, with the words 'I see you', was also convicted for obscenity. But a man who distributed cards announcing the opening of a brothel was acquitted. In 1902 a court ruled that the simple representation of the human form, however indiscreet, could not be condemned as obscene because that would place too great a burden on art, which, whatever it portrayed, 'aided morals within certain limits and purified thoughts by making them more elevated'.[2] At the same time as newspapers and cheap reprints of the classics began pouring from the presses, so the flow of pornography increased, and the invention of photography added to it. Illustrated pornography made its appearance on the mass market. But the public prosecutors brought almost exactly the same number of cases for obscenity each year. Between 1876 and 1906, when this explosion took place, there were regularly around 55 cases a year, involving about 85 people. Very few cases were brought before juries (only 34 in the twenty years 1881–1902) because so many were acquitted (42 per cent). Parliament passed a law in 1898 increasing penalties and extending the definition of obscenity, and ministers of justice issued circulars urging the stricter enforcement of the law, but with little actual effect. Only Fallières in 1891 succeeded in doubling the number of prosecutions, but the situation quickly returned to normal. The main change was the multiplication of puritan societies: the first Congress against Pornography was held in 1905. The League for Public Morality, the Central Society against Licence in the Streets, the National Association for the Protection of Workers were a new way in which the middle classes defended order.[3]

---

[1] Claude Fougerol, *Scènes de la vie galante. Les Amours d'une ingénue* (1862).

[2] Tribunal de Vervins, 29 Nov. 1902.

[3] Albert Eyquem, *De la répression des outrages à la morale publique et aux bonnes mœurs ou de la pornographie au point de vue historique, juridique législatif et social* (1905); Jules Gay, *Bibliographie des ouvrages relatifs à l'amour, aux femmes, au mariage et des livres facétieux, pantagruéliques, scatologiques, satiriques etc.* (4th edition 1894); F. Drujon, *Catalogue des ouvrages, écrits et dessins de toute nature poursuivis, supprimés ou condamnés 1814–77* (1879).

There was one aspect of sexual behaviour, however, in which repression noticeably subsided. Homosexuality was universally condemned at the beginning of this period. 'With all its disgusting and ignominious horrors, how can it exist in an advanced civilisation like ours?' asked the *Encyclopédie Larousse* in the 1860s, which was otherwise liberal and was not too horrified by the ideas on heterosexuality of men like Fourier. There was a curious class consciousness in its condemnation. 'Unbridled debauchery, blasé sensuality can to a certain extent explain homosexuality but it is difficult in many cases not to admit a veritable mental derangement in the moral faculties. What can one say indeed of one of these men come down from a high position to the lowest degree of depravation, drawing into his home sordid children of the streets before whom he kneels, whose feet he kisses with a passionate submission before begging from them the most infamous pleasures?' This can only be 'the most shameless madness'. In the middle of the nineteenth century male prostitution and blackmail was said to have become 'an industry of almost unbelievable dimensions'. From time to time the police descended upon this world. In 1845 there were 47 accused in the *affaire de la rue du Rempart*; and in successive prosecutions after that numerous homosexuals were brought to trial. The Second Empire, in two swoops, arrested another 97 and 52 people. Several murders, including one of a certain Ward, brought public attention to the matter and one magistrate, Busserolles, showed particular energy in trying to repress homosexuality. Research has not revealed when or why the prosecutions ceased; it would be worth elucidating the context in which men like Montesquiou were able to flaunt their tastes, and in which Proust could write about it and Gide openly confess it. These men drew attention to the torments involved in it, and perhaps modified public opinion. In 1937 it was claimed that homosexuality was coming out into the open in all classes, and that there were at least a quarter of a million homosexuals in Paris, with the police keeping files on some 20,000 of them. The clubs, restaurants and baths they frequented made them into something of a separate world, to which theatrical and literary celebrities gave both notoriety and respectability. They claimed the protection of the Napoleonic Code, one of whose authors, Cambacérès, was said to be a homosexual, but they were still subject to bullying from the police. In the state *lycées*—where it flourished much more than in the church schools—it was of course still vigorously and unsuccessfully repressed.[1] The notion that homosexuality was a symptom of the aberrations in family life was very slow to be accepted.

[1] Ambroise Tardieu, *Étude médico-légale sur les attentats aux mœurs* (7th edition 1878), 195–217; Michel du Coglay, *Chez les mauvais garçons* (1937); *Larousse du XIXe siècle*, 'Pédérastie'; *Le Crapouillot*, issue on 'Les Pédérastes' (1970).

12. Children

THE myths about marriage are paralleled by myths about children. A large proportion of France's children did not have a full family life. Around 1900 for every fifteen families which had both father and mother alive, there were six families incomplete (four of them having a father dead and two a mother dead). Only 54 per cent of marriages lasted longer than 15 years: 15·6 per cent were cut short by death within 4 years, and 29·7 per cent within between 5 and 14 years, and only 31·3 per cent lasted over 25 years. 45 per cent of children were orphans in their teens, and a very significant number were so before then.[1] The First World War perpetuated this situation: in 1931 a further 646,000 families existed who had lost their fathers in the war. There were then also 1,322,000 children with fathers who were mutilated or injured by the war.[2] Of the children born in the year 1875, 93,000 were abandoned by their parents. One out of every fourteen was illegitimate.[3] A considerable number were sent away by their mothers, immediately after birth, to be reared by professional wet-nurses in the country.

It is generally believed that the basic transformation of the family has been the rise of children to the position of central importance in the home, after centuries of neglect, and their being accorded the right to a life of a special kind, different from that of adults and with different expectations placed upon them—this again after centuries in which they were treated simply as adults of miniature size, but to be dressed and to work as adults. Philippe Ariès has argued that the change took place in the eighteenth century. Before that there was no social prestige to be derived from being a good parent, and none to be lost by being a bad one. The family was not primarily a sentimental unit. Conservatives like Villèle sought to maintain primogeniture because they believed that emotions were too fragile a basis

[1] Statistique des familles (1906 and 1936).
[2] André Scherrer, La Condition juridique de l'orphelin de la guerre de 1914–1919 (Nancy, 1933), 11.   [3] Vicomte d'Haussonville, L'Enfance à Paris (1879).

for the family's existence; but the abolition of primogeniture is one sign of the end of the family as a unit which was almost a business firm. The increasing interest people took in their children, says Ariès, did not mean liberation from restraint. On the contrary, neglect was replaced by an obsessive love which greatly increased the demands made on children. Discipline and reason were forced on them with a new severity. Instead of being left to their own devices, they had the notion of guilt instilled into them. They were no longer allowed free sex play, as they were in the sixteenth century. The classics were expurgated for their benefit and it was claimed that their innocence had to be protected.

Ariès's pioneering work has been advanced and modified by that of David Hunt, who has studied the childhood of Louis XIII—on whom there is, by chance, a great deal of intimate information. Hunt has shown that it is difficult to distinguish different forms of child rearing into clear chronological periods. Adults did play publicly with Louis XIII's penis when he was a baby; he was allowed to masturbate, to satisfy his sexual curiosity and to read pornography, and he was subject to very little toilet training. But it is untrue that there was a total lack of repression in this period and that children enjoyed a freedom from the modern kind of problems. There was a conflict in society about sex even then: some believed in freedom and some preached continence. The child was still subject to anxieties; the details of sex were still a mystery to him; and his relations with his mother were not unrestrained. It was six months before Louis XIII's mother embraced him and his relations with her remained cold until his father died. Till then the mother belonged to the father. While their fathers were alive children could not get at their mothers. There is some doubt about whether paternal authority did in fact diminish in the *ancien régime*: there are those who claim that the authoritarian monarchy bolstered it up. In any case, the old order has not completely passed away: neglect of children still exists and children are not always the centre of families today. Hunt shows that generalisations about children are as difficult to make as generalisations about any other group of such enormous size.[1]

[1] P. Ariès, *Centuries of Childhood* (1962); D. Hunt, *The Psychology of Family Life in Early Modern France* (1970).

Disagreement about the rearing of children, and about their place in society was almost as great as disagreement about politics, and in the years covered by this book different attitudes coexisted. It is not enough to read the medical manuals in order to trace changes. There certainly were radical alterations in the advice these manuals gave, with a dramatic break in the eighteenth century. Till then the books advocated that new-born babies should be purged, that wet-nurses were preferable to the mother, that feeding should not be scheduled, that swaddling, cradles and cold baths were a good thing. After that, there was instead increasing stress on keeping babies warm, on the avoidance of sex play and masturbation, on the undesirability of thumbsucking (this last appears only in the mid nineteenth century). There was more mention of the need to show babies affection, but also increasing limitations were placed on ways of doing this, for fear of overstimulating them.[1] There was ambiguity, however, in some crucial aspects of this advice. Above all, the advice rather resembles the moralising of the Church. Breast feeding by mothers was advocated long before Rousseau, apparently in vain since the doctors repeatedly complained of the neglect of their advice. After him, it was still not totally accepted, and wet-nurses flourished till the end of the nineteenth century, to be ended not by the force of ideas, but by the new developments in medicine, which made animal milk safe for babies. Rousseau's views on breast feeding, though so famous, were in fact adopted by him almost as an afterthought, when it was pointed out to him that he had omitted any treatment of infancy in his *Émile*. He said he knew nothing about it; a friend gave him a contemporary work by Desessartz, from which he copied almost word for word.[2] Much more important about Rousseau is his giving a philosophic basis for a new treatment of the child. He publicised the view of the child as pure and innocent, who should be left free to develop his own individuality, who was neither a beast nor an adult, but possessed of peculiar ways of thought, with reason being acquired only at the age of fifteen and love even later.

---

[1] Alice Ryerson, 'Medical Advice on Child Rearing 1550–1900' (Harvard Ph.D. thesis, 1960, unpublished).

[2] Congrès international pour la protection de l'enfance: *L'Évolution de la puériculture* (1933), 114.

This conflicted of course with the Catholic view of the child as sinful, in whom obedience must be instilled, and with the empiricist view that the child was infinitely malleable, all of whose characteristics were the effect of experience. These varied traditions all survived in the nineteenth century and if any generalisation can be made—tentatively owing to the dearth of evidence about the behaviour of families—it is that perhaps Rousseau's notions of innocence did not gain anywhere near universal acceptance. Rousseau's thought was a major turning-point in the history of theory rather than of practice.[1]

Throughout this period, the majority of books published about children reflected not Rousseau's views but conservative and indeed reactionary Catholic opinion. It must be remembered that tradition, handed down from mother to daughter, played a decisive role in influencing conduct, that women were not subject to the same pressures from new educational ideas as men were and that differences in opinions and attitudes between men and women were a fundamental feature of society. One should not argue that these Catholic guides determined conduct, but rather that they reflected *ideals* which were current. It is unlikely that families were brought up in full conformity with any one ideal. Some of these Catholic ideals persisted in the doctrines of liberal and advanced thinkers, and equally some of the latter's views modified the teaching of some Catholics. The over-all picture in child rearing is a wide variety of positions, but also considerable hesitation and confusion, induced by the difficulties which the theories met in practice. This was not a period therefore when Frenchmen were brought up in one particular way, but a period of uncertainty. The conflicts experienced by successive generations were to a significant extent conflicts resulting from the unreconciled coexistence of varying aspirations and traditions in parents.

The conservatives believed that values should be transmitted to children through the exercise of authority and by the instillation of respect. The family was a reflection of the divine order; the father was the delegate of God and exercised power akin to God's. A work addressed to children on the subject of filial love, published in 1862 in Hachette's best-selling Bibliothèque Rose Illustrée, said: 'Your parents, in receiving from

[1] See Roger Mercier, *L'Enfant dans la société du 18ᵉ siècle (avant Émile)* (1961).

God the mission to educate you, receive at the same time what is necessary to fulfil it . . . It is the voice of God that you hear in their voice.'[1] In 1946, Robert Rochefort showed how such a relationship worked out in practice. In his memoirs, he talked of his childhood as having been spent 'in the Kingdom of Father'. 'I lived in his strength; in his will, in his presence, as a believer lives in God. There was no room for choice, for acceptance, refusal or doubt. But we were joined in every part so closely that we could not suspect that another world was possible. The face of Father was usually impenetrable. One hardly dared look him in the face at meals, so thoughtful was his face, so charged with clouds.'[2] Coldness and distance had been characteristic of relations between some fathers and sons in the eighteenth-century aristocracy. Mirabeau said of his father: 'I never had the honour to touch the cheek of that venerable man.' Talleyrand doubted whether he had slept two nights running under the same roof as his parents. Chateaubriand was transformed into a statue by the sight of his father. This coldness was sometimes copied by the bourgeoisie. Quinet so dreaded his father that even at the age of fifty he did not dare help himself to food at his father's table, and when once he did, he was given a sermon by his mother.[3]

One of the causes to which moralists attributed the decline in paternal authority was excessive familiarity. Joseph Droz thought that *tutoiement* was damaging to the relationship of subordination which ought to exist and it introduced a 'ridiculous equality'. A successful manual for *Well Brought Up Children* repeated in 1886 the importance of traditional formalities. It told children to stand up when their parents entered the room. 'When you have the honour to be admitted into the salons of your mothers, you must behave yourself in such a manner that they do not regret having accorded you this favour . . . You will, rightly, not dare present yourself in a salon without your gloves. Provincials are even more rigid observers of this etiquette than we.'[4] A study of *Badly Brought Up Children* (1890) insisted that the way to be successful with children was to be authoritarian.

[1] T. H. Barrau, *Amour filial. Récits à la jeunesse* (1862), 375.
[2] Robert Rochefort, *Dans le royaume du père* (1946), i, 4.
[3] Hippolyte Durand, *Le Règne de l'enfant* (1889), 7.
[4] Comtesse de Ferry, *Les Enfants bien élevés* (Mame, Tours, 1836; reprinted eight times before 1913; 1924 edition), 45, 49.

'By the exercise of authority, one makes one's sons respectful and men of duty.' Children should not be treated as the equals of parents, but rather—the simile is the author's—'like dogs'. 'If a man has a dog, he tries to attach it to himself, to make it know and like his house; he does not let it wander according to its whim. He takes care to make it obey by employing threats sometimes and caresses at other times. Well, he ought to take at least the same amount of trouble with his child . . . At the least calculated resistance, punish with real severity, that is the great secret of authority. Obedience must be demanded without restriction.' Another way to obtain it was to make the child accept that he was not in this world to enjoy himself. From an early age he should be taught that the ideals of sacrifice and resignation should guide him, that life was a trial not a pleasure and that success was rare and ingratitude frequent, that his own egoistic desires were his principal enemy. This book argued that a child had only one basic instinct—a fear of suffering. Beyond that 'the child will appreciate people and events in accordance with the education he receives'. Filial gratitude and obedience were thus not natural and there was widespread agreement that it was far weaker than maternal love. So it devolved on parents to instil these feelings of gratitude, and people wrote books for children to recite, enumerating the benefits they owed to their parents.[1] Nevertheless there were some writers who rejected this view; they claimed filial affection was the natural consequence of shared blood and they attacked the psychologists for denigrating the relationship of mother and child.[2]

One of the features of this system of education was that it looked on life as a succession of dangers and temptations which had to be avoided. A book about what children should do on holidays, published in 1935 by a canon and recommended by a bishop, begins with a chapter on the dangers of holidays. Its opening sentence is: 'The first duty of parents is to understand the risks involved in holidays.' Children were left to themselves

---

[1] Fernand Nicolay, Les Enfants mal élevés. Étude psychologique, anecdotique et pratique (1890).

[2] Louis Doucy, Introduction à une connaissance de la famille (Éditions familiales de France, 1946); Abbé F.-M. L., Devoirs des enfants envers leurs parents (Librairie Catholique, Lyon, 1896); anon., Dieu et famille, l'enfant et la conception laïque de ses droits et des devoirs des parents (n.d., about 1925).

more, unwatched by their teachers, so that they unlearnt all the moral lessons instilled into them at school and picked up bad habits from the wider range of children and amusements they might meet. 'People excuse this lack of surveillance by quoting the example of America, but, apart from a difference in temperament between the French and Americans, one can assert that America is hardly a model of family life: little intimacy, many divorces, few children.' The fear of the child's friends was an obsession: better to invite one's cousins, about whom one could be more sure. Guided visits to isolated mountains and nature study were safe, much safer than holidays by the sea, which were a serious threat. In 1934 the accumulating apprehensions of parents burst into a 'Fight against the Immorality of Beaches'. The semi-nudity was a sign of debauchery and of an atrophy of the moral sense. 'Christians, remain Christians on the beaches' was the cry. Avoid the 'manners, exhibitions, and frolics reminiscent of pagan antiquity, the savage tribes of central Africa and ancient Germany'. Doctors were found to warn that sunbathing should be indulged in only under medical supervision. 'Games are agreeable but they are extremely dangerous.' Henry de Montherlant in his advice to his son, wrote likewise: 'You are in a canoe, which is a new toy for you, on an ocean of dung, which is the world. It will be a miracle if you do not capsize.'[1]

In this school of thought the most serious danger facing children was the awakening of sexual desire. The most serious duty falling on parents was to postpone as long as possible its manifestation and curiosity about reproduction. Repression was advocated unanimously by the conservatives with as much vigour as it was denounced by the Freudians. A work by Jean Viollet, which sold widely in the inter-war period, may be taken as an example of their views. He insisted that 'it is false and dangerous to put the child brutally face to face' with the facts of life. The child must be taught first to have a mystic regard for parents, so that he looks on marriage more as involving a moral responsibility of great dignity than carnal relations. Then he must be habituated not to seek his physical well-being and bodily satisfactions: love of food and comfort should be repressed. His will-power should be developed by

[1] Henri Pradel, *Les Devoirs de vacances des parents* (1935), 5–8, 233–45.

giving him the habit of renouncing things he wants and being used to the sacrifice of personal pleasure. He must be isolated from friends who might lead him astray. That this policy sometimes worked is seen in the cases he quotes of the appalling ignorance of convent-educated girls about sex. One rushed to the confession after a man in a train had put his arm around her: she believed she was pregnant as a result. A curious analysis of letters in Italian popular women's magazines in the 1950s reveals similar instances and confirms that the facts of life and the most elementary notions of anatomy have successfully been kept from many girls well into adolescence.[1] But Viollet laments that this complete innocence was becoming increasingly rare. He was conscious of a rising tide of opposition to his views. 'The purity of the young', he wrote, 'appears to the majority to be an anomaly and a sign of inferiority.'[2]

The stress on authority was not preached blindly, even though in some extreme cases the impression is of a demand for total and constant repression. The works of Bishop Dupanloup, published in the 1860s but continuing to be read and quoted throughout this period, were inspired by a genuine and moving love of children, and written by a priest who began life as a highly successful teacher. Dupanloup was not ashamed to quote Rousseau, though more frequently he quoted Fénelon and at enormous length—showing how influences are perpetuated for centuries. Republican writers in their turn, like Janet, were not averse to quoting from Dupanloup. There was a lot of interpenetration of ideas between the parties. Dupanloup represented a middle view based on a great deal of experience. He warned parents that if they neglected their children, their children would neglect them when they grew up. He stressed, like most conservatives, the need for authority, respect, innocence, purity, obedience. He said the main reason why these virtues were found less and less (always assuming a golden age when they did exist) was that parents had been too lazy to accept their responsibilities, too vain to admit any defects in their children, and too uncertain about their own

---

[1] Gabriella Parca, *Italian Women Confess* (1963). Cf. also F. J. Kieffer, *L'Autorité dans la famille et à l'école* (1916, 14th edition 1924).

[2] Jean Viollet, *Éducation de la pureté et du sentiment* (1925, 32nd thousand, 1944), vi, 1, 33, 50, 69 n., 78–80.

ideas to know what exactly they ought to instil into their children. From Dupanloup's books—and he knew a lot of families intimately—one gets the impression that the control of the young in his period was fitful, sporadic and arbitrary. What he attacked more than anything else was the spoilt child. But it was by no means always in the interests of the children that parents yielded to the whims of their offspring and could find no wrong in them. They resented any criticisms of their children from teachers, they demanded academic success irrespective of the gifts of the child. Dupanloup wrote in praise of authority, but also in defence of the child. He attacked pride, sensuality and cupidity as the worst faults of children: he rigorously forbade boys at his school to adorn themselves with perfume or gold chains, or to give excessive attention to their hair and clothes. He fought against masturbation, homosexuality and all sexual interests in his school. He tried to extirpate indocility, independence (which he classified as a vice) and contradiction from them. But he also defended their rights against their parents, so that his book on *The Child* has been called a charter for children. The child had a right to respect of his individuality, of his intelligence and his vocation. 'I have a religious respect for children,' he wrote; 'I have even learned to fear them.' Each one needed different treatment. The first task of a parent was to study the child's nature to discover what he was capable of. The great enemy of the child was parental egoism, ambition and vanity, which too often sought to push the child into a job unsuited to it. The worst offenders of all were the parents who goaded their children hard to obtain academic success and then forced them into jobs they considered respectable.[1]

Lay psychologists and educationists for long took a view of children which was not all that different from these opinions based on an acceptance of original sin. Bernard Perez, who wrote one of the earliest books specifically devoted to *The Psychology of the Child* (1882), drew his inspiration from science and evolution, but he was far from championing the innocence of the child in the manner of Rousseau. He stressed the importance

[1] Bishop F. A. P. Dupanloup, *Le Mariage chrétien* (1869), *L'Enfant* (1869), and *L'Éducation des filles* (1873-4). Cf. the odd but significantly titled work by Angely Fentré, *Contre le mariage actuel. Tout en faveur des enfants* (1882).

of hereditary factors in determining the child's behaviour and the innate vices which were as powerful (though he did not say it) as original sin. Children were innately victims of fear, anger and jealousy. They lied naturally, for 'cunning was innate in every animal.' Their minds were similar to those of animals but inferior to adults and to experienced animals. Despite these innate qualities, like animals, one could 'with justice and kindness, make almost anything one wanted from a child'.[1] Gabriel Compayré, a leading republican educationist who wrote on the *Intellectual and Moral Evolution of the Child* in 1893, attacked original sin and exonerated the child of many of the evil qualities Dupanloup attributed to him. The child's cruelty, he said, was due to ignorance, his lying to fear or playful imagination, and defective education was to be held responsible for any faults he developed. Even so, Compayré did not go the whole way with Rousseau. The child he said, did have an evil base (*un fond mauvais*) which no indulgence could explain away. He was not only perverted by social factors: he was naturally perverse. He had innate antisocial instincts.[2]

The scientific study of children was slow to develop in France and foreign ideas penetrated with difficulty. In the 1860s Caron tried to give a course of lectures on the art of bringing up infants—to which he gave the name Puericulture—but though he was supported by Victor Duruy, the Empress Eugénie judged it indecent, and he had difficulty in finding an audience. In 1865 when he tried to speak on this subject at the meeting of the Provincial Learned Societies at the Sorbonne, the chairman refused permission on the ground that the subject would 'provoke hilarity'. It was only in 1919 that a School of Puericulture was founded, but at the instigation of the American Red Cross, as a souvenir of its work in the war.[3] Alfred Binet, France's great pioneer in intelligence testing, waged an almost lone campaign to modify the monolithic educational system to suit individual needs. Writing in 1910, he complained that very few people asked whether the child was anything other than a miniature man, and most assumed that there was a

[1] Bernard Perez, *La Psychologie de l'enfant: les trois premières années* (1882, 11th edition 1911), 70–90, 123–6, 329.

[2] G. Compayré, *L'Évolution intellectuelle et morale de l'enfant* (1893), 307, 315.

[3] Paul Tissot, *Notes pour servir à l'histoire de la puériculture* (Chambéry, 1959), 4; Dr. B. Weill-Hallé, *La Puériculture et son évolution* (1929), 9.

standard type of child, whom all resembled more or less. Teachers concentrated on the value of what they taught rather than on the aptitude of the child. But Binet was unable to advance knowledge of the emotional needs of the child. His work was essentially on the measurement of intelligence, memory, vision and hearing. Though he recognised the inadequacies of a relationship with the child based on reason, he could not get beyond the traditional ideals of authority, respect and altruism.[1]

In the inter-war period, the most ostensibly scientific books on children stressed the determining influence of physical factors, to the extent of appearing to regress to Zola's emphasis on heredity. Dr. Victor Pauchet (whose work was given a prize by the French Academy in 1929) attributed the characteristics of children to their physical constitution, to the extent of 90 per cent, and he thought the best way of curing their defects was to subject them to thyroid treatment. However, he too could not refrain from repeating the traditional statements about the need to exercise authority over infants, using the same example of the dog; and his remedy for timidity, which he called moral feebleness, was the old one of self-control, taught by rational argument. He welcomed Freud, and praised efficiency as a virtue, but the lip-service to new doctrines could not obliterate ingrained attitudes.[2] Another child psychologist, G. Collin, writing in 1943, was all in favour of the ideas of Montessori, Dewey, Decroly, etc. penetrating into kindergartens and the first forms of primary schools (but that was as far as he went) and he regretted that psychologists had studied the intelligence of children much more than their emotions. However, in discussing how infants could be cured of fear, he suggested two methods: improve their physical health, so that their strength will immunise them against fear, and 'appeal to their reason'—end their ignorance.[3] The intellectualist approach survived powerfully. And it had its effect on the children. It is precisely in the intellectualism of the French child that Laurence Wylie sees the principal difference between

[1] Alfred Binet, *Les Idées modernes sur les enfants* (1910); Edith J. Varon, *The Development of Alfred Binet's Psychology* (1935).

[2] Dr. Victor Pauchet, *L'Enfant* (1929), xv, 91, 227–8; id., *Le Chemin du bonheur* (1929).

[3] G. Collin, *Précis d'une psychologie de l'enfant* (1943), 49, 64–8.

him and the American child. The French child, as a result, learns to control his impulses, to see education as the memorising of categories established by others, to behave in each segment of life in the way deemed appropriate.[1]

The weakness of French psychology in this period is partly to be explained also by the strength of *characterology*, a peculiarly French science. It was a development of the ancient doctrine of the four humours: sanguine, bilious, phlegmatic and melancholic. When the science of anatomy disproved the physical existence of these humours and showed instead the importance of the nerves, the system was modified and made psychological rather than physical but the classification into a definite number of types was retained. In the nineteenth century further subdivisions were added and the categories reorganised. Dr. Fourcault reduced it to three basic types, dominated by the nervous, sanguine or cellular systems, which could be combined to produce seven other types. In 1858 Dr. Eugène Bourdet, in his work on *Diseases of the Character*, produced 36 different types. Professor Azam in his work on *The Character in Health and in Sickness* (1887) produced 120 subdivisions. It would be tedious to enumerate the large number of variations of increasing complexity—and also of Platonic simplicity—in the many works written about this. This was no aberration limited to the nineteenth century. The popular versions of the same idea were physiognomy and graphology, and it should not · be forgotten that the graphological test was used by employers as readily as Americans used the psychological ones.[2]

The liberals—those who were liberal in other spheres—did not offer a radically different method of upbringing. Jules Michelet—who described himself as a spoilt only child, who flew into a rage at the least contradiction and sought constant pretexts for disobedience, who lived isolated, with only one friend and a couple of favourite books, who was so maltreated

---

[1] Laurence Wylie, 'Youth in France and the U.S.', in E. Erikson, *Youth: Change and Challenge* (N.Y., 1963), 243–60.

[2] E. Bourdet, *Des maladies du caractère* (1858); Azam, *Le Caractère dans la santé et dans la maladie* (1887); B. Perez, *Le Caractère de l'enfant à l'homme* (1891); Ribot, 'Sur les diverses formes du caractères' in *Revue philosophique* (Nov. 1892); F. Paulhan, *Les Caractères* (1894); F. Queyrat, *Les Caractères et l'Éducation Morale: étude de psychologie appliquée* (1896); Abbé J. H. Michon, *Système de graphologie* (1878); J. Crépieux-Jamin, *L'Écriture et le caractère* (4th edition 1896; 7th edition 1921).

at the *lycée* that he felt he hated all men—proclaimed that children were born innocent, illuminating and purifying all by their innocence. He sung the praises of family life. But he was too astute to think that family upbringing was producing satisfactory results. By itself, he said, it was capable of suffocating children and making them wholly unfit for the world. Parents were ceasing to abandon children to the care of vicious domestic servants, but instead they spoilt them by making them participate in their own vices of drinking and obscenity. They allowed the awakening of the children's senses and so destroyed their ability to educate them. Michelet therefore urged not a closer intimacy in the family but on the contrary more formality. 'The child—for his own good—ought to be a little apart, watched and held lovingly, but always at a certain distance, and not mixed indiscriminately in the life of his parents, as is done today. He will be more modest, if he thinks that the family consists of only two people, and that he is an accessory. Its intimacy should be closed to him.' This interesting passage suggests that contrary developments were taking place at the top and the bottom of the social scale. The bourgeoisie were tiring of formality, but at the very same time the upper levels of the working class, rising into the petite bourgeoisie, were attempting to abandon their traditional easy-going approach.[1]

By contrast with Michelet, Paul Janet, writing about the bourgeois family in 1861, praised 'the intimacy, confidence and liberty that reigns today in families'. He insisted that this did not represent the decay of the institution. Parents spoilt their children more now, but they also looked after them better. Formerly they imposed respect on them but neglected them. Neglect had not disappeared: 'There are houses today where children see their mothers only at certain hours of the day.' But Janet applauded that parents were now seeking to win respect not by discipline but by love.[2] The apparently conflicting approaches of Michelet and Janet, however, conceal a basic similarity. In both cases the child remained an instrument for the gratification of parental aspirations—producing either higher social status, or affection. From this point of view the changes in methods of upbringing in this century were often

[1] J. Michelet, *Ma Jeunesse* (1884), *Nos Fils* (1869, reprinted 1903), 94–5.
[2] Paul Janet, *La Famille* (1856, 4th edition 1861), 145.

less important than contemporaries thought, and less a diver-
gence from the traditional avowed subjection of the child to
the interests of the family. That is why the rebellion of the young
was not diminished, as will be seen.

The longing for affection can be seen in that wildly successful
book *Monsieur, madame et bébé*, previously mentioned. After
urging men to be friends with their wives and to have fun with
them, Droz told them to do the same with their children. He
pitied fathers 'who do not know how to be *papas* as often as
possible, who do not know how to roll around on the carpet,
play at being a horse and a great wolf, undress their baby. These
are not simply agreeable forms of child's play that they neglect
but true pleasures, delicious enjoyments . . . How simple it is
to be happy.' But he went on to say that paternal love was
more calculating, less instinctive than a mother's love. The aim
of this frolicking was to win the child's affection. 'To be loved
all one's life by a being one loves, that is the problem to solve.'
Filial love did not grow naturally: it had to be won and
deserved, and so was done best of all by amusing the baby.
'Be his playmate a little, so as to have the right to remain his
friend.' Droz acknowledged it was no simple thing, for he said
that children had great acuteness of judgement and that those
who were subject to clumsy pressure became rebels. The
sentimentalism of this approach concealed a serious purpose.
Droz was important not because he was advocating a new
approach towards children—numerous instances could be
quoted from the seventeenth century onwards to show that this
kind of familiarity was not new—but because he saw the
difficult problem of communication and understanding between
generations. His jolly solution was almost one of bluff.[1]

In almost the same year as Droz published his book Ernest
Legouvé (a member of the French Academy) noted that the
change Droz was advocating had already taken place. 'Children today', he wrote in 1867, 'occupy a far larger place in the
family. Parents live more with them, and live more for them.
Either by an increase of prudence and affection, or from weakness and relaxation of authority, they think more about their
children's well-being, and listen more to their opinion.' But
the result of it was, he said, that 'these poor little creatures of

[1] Gustave Droz, *Monsieur, madame et bébé* (1866), 339–45.

three or four are enervated by this attention and indulgence; at seven they are egoistic, despotic, greedy masters of the house; at twelve they gravely go up the street to school with a cigar in their mouth; at seventeen they argue with their father and yield neither before age nor before superiority; at eighteen they discuss politics and art and are even atheists; at twenty they are idle and demand a share of their father's wealth to satisfy their private tastes.' Legouvé (and others) discussed the need for parents to learn from their children but avowed a kind of helplessness before the problem of how to avoid the tyranny of the child that resulted.[1] At the same time as people were praising the family as a source of bliss and morality, they were also lamenting that it would be this if only it did not go wrong so often. The tyranny of the child was the most frequent complaint. When he was paid attention to, he was seen to be uncontrollable. Gavarni's cartoons, *Les Enfants terribles*, showed the reverse side of the joys of intimate family relations.

Alain, the philosopher of republicanism, provided an acute analysis of the problems which were being created in this way, and showed how matriarchy was a corollary of the child being king. In discussing the married couple, he decided that the *real* couple was in fact the mother and child, not husband and wife. Marriage without children was only 'an idea, not a fact'. The love between mother and child was the only *real* love. The relations between the child and his father were necessarily difficult, particularly in the case of boys. The father was a stranger to his child, because he moved in the world where childhood and the laws of affection which governed it had to be forgotten, whereas the mother remained with the child in the other world ruled by affection where things could be obtained by asking and begging. The child wants to win the affection of his father but the father is too demanding; he expects the child to achieve what he himself has failed to achieve. The child copies the mother in obeying the father, but the father is severe and impatient, so the child cannot really admire the father. The child is often a humiliation to his father because he has not been freely chosen. The father is expected to love him independently of his merits, but this conflicts with the rules of

[1] Ernest Legouvé, *Les Pères et les enfants au 19e siècle (enfance et adolescence)* (1867), 1-3, 347-52.

reason which govern the father's world. The child in turn
cannot consider the esteem of his parents adequate because they
love him irrespective of his personal qualities. Family life thus
involves conflict with society. The family fails to share the
values of the world outside it: it does not judge the value of
individuals and of actions impartially. In the outside world,
things are weighed in the light of the criterion of real services
rendered, but the family bases itself on favour and chance. If
left to itself, the family is 'savage'. 'Because so much is expected
in it, disappointment often takes the shape of hatred. It is thus
that paternal love sometimes turns into unmeasured severity
and, in return, a child can show signs of bitter hatred. And
because each one knows that reconciliation is not far away, and
is even already effected, the trouble is all the worse.' Pride
forbids any total reparation for anger, and these crises in the
home often lead to an injured silence, quite apart from boredom. The different system of rewards in the school and in the
home complicates the child's life. But Alain insists that the
school can remedy the defects of family education. The school
must be the influence which 'civilises' the child, draws him
into the real world, gives him universal ideals by its teaching of
the humanities, and offers him the chance to make friends outside his narrow circle.[1]

Alain's brilliant essay deserves to be read as a supplement to
the better-known but more conservative work of Durkheim on
Moral Education (1938). Durkheim, like Alain, insisted that the
family by itself was incapable of giving the child an adequate
upbringing. He argued, in a rather abstract fashion, that it
caused the birth of the child's first altruistic tendencies, but
that these were of a limited kind, being based on affection
rather than duty. The school was therefore an essential supplement to the family and only it could inculcate into the child
wider perspectives and the spirit of discipline, which Durkheim
prized as much as any Catholic did.[2] Durkheim, concentrating
above all on the interests of society and the preservation of
cohesion in it, had an approach which neglected the psychological reactions of individuals to the marvellous solidarity he

[1] Alain, 'Les Sentiments familiaux' in *Cahiers de la Quinzaine*, 18th series, no. 8
(1927).
[2] E. Durkheim, *L'Éducation morale* (1938), 168.

hoped to impose upon them. Since he thought that society made individuals what they were, he could see no justified conflict arising between them. His conclusion strongly resembles that of the Catholics. Alain is a useful reminder of the divisions that existed among republicans, as among Catholics, and of the survival of an unquenchable individualism.

It will be obvious by now that there was no Dr. Spock in France in this period: no one book dominated child rearing, but if anybody came anywhere near to Spock's position, it was perhaps Dr. Gilbert Robin. He was a doctor with a gift for incisive and down-to-earth prose and he published at least a dozen volumes in the inter-war period about children. His works mark a real advance, in that the subjects he treated showed that at last people were realising that ordinary children, as opposed to chronically sick ones, could have important psychological problems. He wrote a book called *Hate in the Family* which listed the many perfectly natural relationships which could produce tensions and animosities. He wrote about *Difficult Children, The Dramas and Anxieties of Youth* and *Nervous and Psychic Troubles of Children*. He had no radically new remedies to offer and most of what he said had been said before. He represented a moderate eclecticism, and quoted both Freud and Father de Buck (author of *Difficult Cases*). He was typical enough of his times to believe that comfort was mortally dangerous, because it weakened will-power, and he advised parents against using central heating, comfortable armchairs or 'pick-up' gramophones which saved the child the trouble of changing the record. But he was important for combating the myth that all would be well if children stayed meekly at home and obeyed their parents. He is interesting also for revealing how the individualism of Alain, and the whole tradition Alain represents, could be reconciled with conformity. The child, says Robin, is not more difficult to satisfy than the adult. He demands before all else to be free and like the adult, it is not liberty to do what pleases him that he is keenest about, but liberty of thought. 'In return for this liberty, you will obtain from the child, without effort, submission to habits and to rules of hygiene, punctuality, cleanliness, politeness. The hours devoted to study cease to be burdens. They are on the contrary the instruments indispensable to the installation of the child's kingdom. They serve as marks of respect to others and to win respect from them, to live in good accord with everybody, to give every man his due, so as to be repaid likewise. Thus, these habits are useful to ensure his liberty. The child has paid for his seat: he believes in the dream-show he gives himself.'[1] This fits in very well with what Laurence Wylie observed in his comparison of French and American children. Wylie stressed that the reason why the French child appeared to accept the formal requirements of his elders, was that he was skilled at withdrawing into his own private world where he was free.

Suspicions that maternal love could, in certain circumstances, have disastrous results took an increasingly positive form. Dupanloup had inveighed against the doting mother, very perceptively but perhaps in old-fashioned language. Marie Dugard, an interesting writer, pointed out in 1900 how spoiling and domination by mothers was a result of the transitional stage through which girls' education was passing. The conflict between what was taught to girls at school and what was taught at home produced internal tensions which manifested themselves when girls became mothers. On the one hand marriage was still regarded as being the aim of a girl's life, brains were considered an obstacle to marriage and the best marriage was one of convenience, to someone she barely knew. On the other hand germs of ambition were inculcated into girls. 'Incapable therefore of either the submissions of the past or the duties of the present', inadequately prepared to assume responsibility, taught in their convents 'to regard anyone who thought as suspect, and anyone who was independent as a rebel, guided by the instinct which pushes us to model our children on ourselves and by the passionate love Frenchwomen reserve for their children, they surround their sons and daughters with anxious surveillance, keep them jealously at home, and so as to be able to possess them longer, repress energy and all initiative in them.'[2] However, the sacrosanct image of the

[1] Dr. Gilbert Robin, *La Guérison des défauts et des vices chez l'enfant. Guide pratique d'éducation* (1948), 59. Cf. also his *Les Haines familiales* (1926); *L'Enfant sans défauts* (1930); *Les Drames et les angoisses de la jeunesse* (1934); *Les Troubles nerveux et psychiques de l'enfant* (1935); *Comment dépister les perturbations intellectuelles et psychiques des tout petits* (1936); *L'Éducation des enfants difficiles* (1942); *Enfances perverses* (1946), etc.

[2] Marie Dugard, *De l'éducation moderne des jeunes filles* (1900), 52–3.

mother, even if she did react against enforced femininity and against her indifference towards her husband, by overpossessive love of her children, was perhaps less an object of attack than the image of the authoritarian father, which invited denigration more readily.[1] The deposition of the father had wider implications. The great challenge to him came when the sons of the illiterate learnt to read and for the first time could judge their parents. This side of the campaign against illiteracy was still to be investigated. The one thing that Julien Sorel's illiterate father could not forgive him was his passion for books. Upward social mobility, to which families were so devoted, eroded the bases at the same time as it outwardly strengthened the structure of the institution. Freudian ideas entered France only very slowly but, by the end of this period, there were those who saw hate of the father as the initial conflict of perhaps the majority of men. Jean Lacroix, writing on the strengths and weaknesses of the family in 1948, pointed to the family as the crucial factor in most human resentments, and 'the principal obstacle to men's most profound desires and most essential demands. One could explain a large part of the present-day democratic movement by the desire for parricide . . . The death of the father was necessary to man's liberation.' Atheism was only another form of this same parricide.[2]

The idea of youth as the happiest time of one's life began to be challenged. As from around 1890 books about adolescence began to appear in increasing numbers: by 1930 at least 100 novels had been published on this theme. The peculiar problems of this period of life were recognised as unique, forming a separate category between infancy and adulthood. Psychologists and educationists wrote special studies of adolescence.[3] In the two years preceding the First World War, there were no fewer than five 'inquiries' by journals on the problems of youth, of which Agathon's was only the most famous.[4] In 1929 a whole

---

[1] On overprotective mothers see André Rouède, *Le Lycée impossible* (1967).

[2] Jean Lacroix, *Force et faiblesse de la famille* (1948), chapter 1. Cf. G. Mendel, *La Révolte contre le père* (1968).

[3] P. Mendousse, *L'Âme de l'adolescent* (1909); G. Compayré, *L'Adolescence* (1910); Auguste Lemaître, *La Vie mentale de l'adolescent et ses anomalies* (1910); Paul Gaultier, *L'Adolescent* (1914).

[4] Henri Mazel, 'Nos Enfants, à quoi rêvent-ils?', *La Revue des Français* (Jan.–Apr. 1912); F. Laudent, 'Enquête sur la jeunesse', *Revue hebdomadaire* (Mar.–June 1912); Agathon in *L'Opinion*, reprinted as *Les Jeunes Gens d'aujourd'hui* (1913);

issue of the review *L'Éducation* was devoted to 'the crisis of adolescence'.[1] A study of crime in 1905 revealed that the number of minors accused of homicide, arson, assault, vagabondage and theft was almost double that of adults accused of the same crimes.[2] Henry Bérenger declared adolescence, far from being a period of delightful innocence, was one of 'anxiety of the mind, of the emotions and of action'. Jules Laforgue entitled one of his poems *The Complaint of Difficult Puberties*. Romain Rolland, in *Jean Christophe*, depicted the adolescent in all his aspects. Formerly, education had been devoted to curing people of adolescence, to urging them to grow up. Between the wars a cult of adolescence developed in protest against adult values. In 1923 the first novel by an adolescent was published, written by Raymond Radiguet, aged seventeen. Five years later another one, by Jean Desbordes, made an even more powerful impression, because it substituted a technique of shock and impudence for Radiguet's sobriety. It was greeted as a manifesto by the young, as Barrès's work had been thirty-five years before, but it had a different significance. This represented more than a revolt against the opinions of the previous generation. There is a new social malaise, wrote Henry de Montherlant in 1926, *adolescentisme*, a new competitor against feminism. The cult of sports which became fashionable at the turn of the century was giving new prestige to youth.[3] After the war Abel Bonnard said that respect for the old was yielding to a cult of youth.[4] Edgar Quinet had been told on his seventh birthday that he had reached the age of reason, but now people were willing to take longer to grow up. André Gide wrote for adolescents and prided himself on keeping contact with them. Moreover, he told them to cultivate those very qualities which were not considered adult: he praised restlessness, anxiety and desire and hated everything the family stood for. 'Families, I hate you', he said; the phrase was to become a motto. His homosexuality was the

Émile Henriot, in *Le Temps*, reprinted as *A quoi rêvent les jeunes gens* (1913); Gaston Riou, *Aux écoutes de la France qui vient* (1913).

[1] *L'Éducation* (Oct. 1929).

[2] G. L. Duprat, *La Criminalité dans l'adolescence* (1905).

[3] Pierre de Courbertin, 'Le Sport et la société moderne', *Revue Hebdomadaire*, 6 (1914), 376–86.

[4] Abel Bonnard, 'Le Préjugé de la jeunesse', *La Revue de Paris* (1 Dec. 1922), 655–63.

decisive discovery of his life—he was interested in young men, not in relationships with women, which were the standard mark of adulthood—and he discussed his sexual problems openly, against the rules of adult society. Adults moreover read him too. The attentive interest in young people, and the serious curiosity about their emotions and thoughts, was a new phenomenon. It certainly increased the self-confidence and self-consciousness of the young. And the young emerged from this scrutiny, as an isolated group, shut off from adults, as Mauriac said, 'by a wall of timidity, shame, incomprehension and hurt feelings'.[1] Gide asserted that it was impossible for any member of his family to be a friend of his.[2] However, this was more than a confrontation of generations in the traditional sense. The extent of the conflict was not as great as some of the participants thought. Of the hundred novels on adolescence in the period 1890 to 1930, only fourteen deal with revolt against authority, and only five of these give this a large part. Far more frequent was the subject of sexual awakening and its problems.[3] The young were still only trying to understand themselves.

It is useful to examine the impression made by the novels protesting against the myth that parents always knew best. Jules Vallès's autobiographical novel of his childhood was one of the most powerful and moving.[4] It described a boy whose mother acted in accordance with the moral precepts enshrined by tradition. He was taught to read in a book which said he must obey his father and mother, but he felt no affection for either. He was ashamed of his father who was a poor, timid, ill-dressed teacher, the son of a peasant who had cringed his way up the ladder of social promotion. The mother was anxious that her son should continue this climbing. She forbade him to play with the cobbler's boy, because that was degrading; she wanted to make him *comme il faut*; she wanted to save him from the fate of being a peasant, as she had once been. She beat him every day because she thought he ought not to be spoilt. She refused him food he liked and gave him what he disliked, so as to develop his self-control. She promised him

---

[1] F. Mauriac, *Le Jeune Homme* (1926), 79.
[2] A. Gide, *Le Retour de l'enfant prodigue* (1922).
[3] Justin O'Brien, *The Novel of Adolescence in France* (New York, 1937), 187.
[4] Jules Vallès, *L'Enfant* (1879).

pennies if he was good, but then put them into a savings box which he could not touch. She was so keen for him to have some capital when he grew up that she never gave him any pocket money. 'To be clean and hold oneself straight, that summed up everything.' He was never conscious of any love in the house. He felt thoroughly guilty. The more his mother beat him, the more he was sure she was a good mother and he an evil boy for being so ungrateful to her. To the outside world he was just an ordinary boy, and this was an ordinary respectable family. Neither the world nor the family knew how he felt. The *coup d'état* of December 1851 gave Vallès a chance to escape. He participated in the republican opposition. His father replied (this happened in real life) by having him sent to a lunatic asylum. Vallès protested: '[My father] has the right to have me arrested, to treat me as though I were a thief; he is master of me as of a dog.' He went into socialist politics, and when the Commune was proclaimed he greeted it with deeply felt personal emotion. 'Here it is at last, the moment hoped for and waited for since the first cruelty of my father, since the first slap from the usher, since the first day spent without bread, since the first night passed without lodging. Here is the revenge against school, against poverty and against December.' In exile afterwards, Vallès attempted to found a league for the protection of the rights of children and he dedicated his novel 'To all those who died of boredom at school or who were made to cry at home, who during their childhood were tyrannised by their masters or thrashed by their parents'. His book was a protest also against another deeply ingrained prejudice of his time, that a child should follow in his father's profession, and should keep on climbing the social ladder. He did not want his father's job of a 'learned dog'. He longed to be an ordinary peasant, on whom there was—in his idealised view—no pressure. Though he escaped into revolutionary activity, he concluded 'it seems that there will always remain from my childhood gaps of melancholy and painful wounds in my heart.'

The reaction this book received from the critics (in 1879–86) was one of anger. Brunetière began his review: 'It is of an evil man that I am going to speak' and castigated Vallès as an example of exaggerated conceit. Brunetière characterised this as the illness of the century, so he was conscious of dealing with an important phenomenon, whose right to existence he preferred to deny. 'This father and mother', he wrote, 'at bottom committed no other wrong except to have brought up their child perhaps severely, but we in our turn have the right to say that they brought him up too gently, since he was to become the man we have known.' He protests that Vallès is immoral, because he questions the very existence of society. Another reviewer remarked that what was unpardonable was that Vallès should have written the book as a novel with the son accusing the mother: the public should legitimately protest against that.

Fifteen years later a curiously different reception greeted Jules Renard's *Ginger*.[1] This again was an autobiographical novel, protesting against the myth of family harmony. It portrays a boy made vicious and miserable by lack of love, ignored by his father, cruelly teased by his elder brother, always criticised by his mother—again with the aim of instilling moral principles into him and producing more conformist behaviour from him. In this equally respectable family, the boy feels himself an orphan. At school he sees a young master kiss a boy. He reports him, and when the master is sacked, Poil de Carotte shouts after him: Why did you not kiss me? Renard offers a different explanation of his parents' behaviour. He sees his taciturn father (an engineer, later mayor of his village) being driven into silence, withdrawing from family life, seeking consolation in unfaithfulness, by the fact that he had nothing in common with his wife, whose domination exasperated and frightened him. Renard attributed her alienation to her being a pious Catholic, which the husband was not; but he makes the father say that it is his own neglect of his wife which had driven her to get her revenge by taking it out on her son. The boy complains to his father: 'My mother does not love me and I do not love her.' The father replies, 'And I, do you think I love her?' But this did not bring the two together: the boy was never admitted into the confidence of the father: harmony was totally absent. Later, when Renard got married, his mother tried to dominate his wife and it was this that spurred him on to write his novel. The reception of the book was, however, strangely favourable. What critics objected to most was the realistic

[1] Jules Renard, *Poil de carotte* (1894); dramatic version 1904.

portrayal of the child as an animal, so far removed from the idealised angel in favour. But the attack on the mother was now accepted as true, even as showing something typical, the neurotic mother. The play of the book was put into the repertoire of the Comédie Française and three films have been made of it. However, it should not be thought that the right to criticise the family was thereby won. In 1923 Victor Margueritte had his Legion of Honour withdrawn by President Millerand on the ground that his book *La Garçonne* had calumniated the French woman. It all depended on the way the criticism was made.[1]

In the 1950s, a sample of French people were asked which commandment they considered most important. The fifth, 'Honour your parents', won easily. Only 12 per cent thought the new generation represented progress over the old, and only 27 per cent thought it was more or less equal. 70 per cent considered that discipline was extremely important in bringing up children, and a majority wanted greater severity towards children. 52 per cent of parents were against sexual education for children at school.[2] It is clear that traditional values had survived in the majority, at least as ideals. What parents believed and what they did were not the same thing. An interesting study by a schoolmaster of the psychology of his pupils, published in 1913 on the basis of many years' observation and note taking in a varied selection of schools, stressed that the great majority of parents neglected their children. 'One cannot imagine', he wrote, 'the indifference of the great majority of parents for all that concerns the intellectual and moral advancement of their sons.' In one class, at the beginning of the year, only four fathers came to school to discuss their sons with the teacher—which was a respected custom—out of thirty-three. The peasant was particularly careless: 'Uniquely preoccupied with his land, he abandons his sons to their instincts.' The teacher thought the children he knew got little affection or even intimacy from their parents. 'They are not happy.'[3] The teacher's observations do not of course contradict the findings of the polls. The conflict between principles and

---

[1] I am indebted to Dr. Nicholas Hewitt for permission to use a paper on this subject which he wrote for my graduate seminar at Harvard in 1969.

[2] Georges Rotvand, *L'Imprévisible Monsieur Durand* (1956), 124, 131–4.

[3] J. Fontanel, *Psychologie de L'adolescence. Nos lycéens. Études documentaires* (1913), 56, 82, 262.

practice was another of the sources of tension, and this particular conflict was only one of several. It was not only in the family that children were subjected to opposing pressures.

One important instance of this emerged in children's peer groups. The inevitable reaction of children to the isolation imposed on them by their parents and the authoritarianism of their teachers was that they formed groups at school. It has been claimed that these had a vital and lasting influence upon all their subsequent behaviour. Jesse Pitts has described them as delinquent groups, meaning that what held them together was their hostility to the teacher. These groups provide an outlet for rebelliousness, while preserving loyalty to the family. Since the teachers are a challenge to the authority of the family, the parents do not disapprove of the petty warfare these groups engage in. The co-operation between families and peer groups is, however, tacit and unspoken. Families are not mentioned in the groups: the two are separate worlds, and members are not normally invited to each other's homes. The groups are societies for mutual defence. They are purely negative. Whereas the American peer group is recognised by both school and parents, gives prestige, prepares for distinction in sports and provides opportunities of importance to the whole of the child's social life, the French one has no adult values, it protects the children against the teacher, it involves co-operation only in forbidden pleasures, but perhaps its main function is to guarantee each member the enjoyment of his private interests. It seeks to destroy authority, to discredit the teacher, for example, by making him declare his political views. The teacher replies by trying to subvert the cohesion of the group. This is its test, for the group's solidarity covers a very limited range of behaviour. Distrust of one's fellows remains within it, and the child remains isolated. His isolation is concealed by such things as interest in politics, which appears to place the group on a more universal level. But in reality it only raises the delinquency into a more general rejection of the established political order. This is seen as a root of the ideological opposition of each generation; and also of the shallowness of the opposition. The group involves only an abstract and purely verbal rejection of the adult world. The member can then fall back safely into the comforts of dependence on his family. Jesse Pitts sees the survival of these peer groups—described in Jules Romains's *The Pals* (*Les Copains*), a perennial best seller with adolescents—in the cliques, salons and old-boy networks of adult life. These behave in the same delinquent way, stressing untramelled liberty of speech, violent hatreds against other cliques, with slander and denigration serving to produce blood bondage. When a member of one of these cliques comes into contact with a state official and wants a favour, the interview begins by trying to establish their group memberships, to see whether they can combine in a delinquent community against the state —in which case the favour is granted. In this way there is intense social and political activity, but the *status quo* is saved. The really powerful force, thinks Pitts, that survives beneath the agitation is the family, because only it is really relied upon. Respect for the public interest is thus undermined at the very earliest stage of life. Friendship itself, though paraded, is unreliable.[1] In the light of this theory, one can argue that not only is the emotional development of children stunted by the rigours of the family, but their social capacities are restricted by the nature of their peer groups. They are prepared more for a negative obstructionist and verbal role rather than for co-operation and action.

Indeed, school, family and peer groups each pulled in a different direction. The school nominally sought to develop sociability in the way Durkheim preached, but in fact it did its best to destroy the groups children formed of their own accord. Roger Cousinet, whose pioneering work on child sociology Pitts developed, showed how, for all its lip-service to solidarity, the school continued to be individualist in its influence. It gave very few opportunities for games, it sought to supervise the children as much as possible, it allowed them to play only in breaks, and stopped them when they were noisy. Above all it was one of the principal destroyers of young children's groups by its stress on intellectual achievement. It was the marking system which, thought Cousinet, did as much as anything to split the groups as the children grew up and marks became more important. The family, on its side, feared these school friendships and tried to limit their scope; but on the

[1] Jesse R. Pitts, 'The Bourgeois Family' (Harvard, unpublished Ph.D. thesis, 1957).

other hand it did not accord its co-operation to the school. It paid great attention to social inequalities, which became the other major obstacle to the continuation of young children's friendships.[1]

But while school, family and peer groups exerted contradictory pressures on children, they also maintained a conflict between the world of the child and the adult world. A French psycho-analyst, comparing the French and American child in 1953, pointed out how the French child thought of himself as being different from the adult, of whom he had a deep distrust. His life involved a coerced learning of adult behaviour but without the compensating reward of adult privileges. Whereas adults could be guided by pleasure, children were expected to be *sage*. Life therefore began only with the end of childhood. This is not to suggest that the more spontaneous American child, whose parents took so much pains to leave him free lest he be traumatised, in fact enjoyed greater real autonomy in childhood. He owed his independence to the privileged position accorded by Americans to their children, and he was much more influenced by social and psychological pressures. French parents did not worry about whether they traumatised their children. They made constant use of bogy men to frighten their children into conformity. Though corporal punishment was abolished in schools, the *martinet* whip continued to be widely used; and obliging policemen were employed by parents to threaten children who remained recalcitrant even then. It was an accepted procedure to frighten the child to make him obey—with force, the police, illness or God. The American child learnt about restraint in a noticeably different way from the French child. This analyst claimed that there was far more certainty among French parents about how to bring up their children, but this certainty derived essentially from their own family experience and the belief inculcated into them that the individual was first of all a member of a family. Those who consulted her always gave as their justification what 'in my family' was considered the right thing to do.[2]

[1] Roger Cousinet, *La Vie sociale des enfants. Essai de sociologie enfantine* (1950).

[2] Françoise Dolto, 'French and American Children as seen by a French Child Analyst' in Margaret Mead and Martha Wolfenstein, *Childhood in Contemporary Cultures* (1955), chapter 23.

The consequences of these differences were interestingly noted by Martha Wolfenstein in a comparison of how French and American children played in parks. Each French family kept its toys strictly separate; friendliness between children of different families was not encouraged; parents intervened frequently in games to scold those who broke the rules; the children were not expected to fight their own battles; physical aggression was kept in check and so instead verbal disputes were substituted. French children were content to spend long periods alone with their own families; they were much readier to play with children of all ages, unlike the Americans who divided into age groups cutting across families. The French would only watch children from other families, not join in with them. Though French parents intervened as umpires, on the whole they busied themselves with other tasks and left the children alone, again unlike the Americans who liked to be good sports. The adult world was a separate one, and the children's activities were subordinated to it. Liberation came only after childhood, and that is why Americans think the French had a greater capacity for enjoying adult life, instead of looking back on childhood, as Americans do, as the happiest time of their life, when everything was allowed.[1]

[1] M. Wolfenstein, 'French Parents take their Children to the Park', ibid. chapter 7.

13. Women

THE simultaneous idealisation and repression of women and children was one of the ways by which French society developed its peculiar characteristics. Repression was compensated for and mitigated by giving women considerable power in certain strictly limited fields. There was nevertheless resistance to that repression, which took two forms: psychological and political. The former was by far the most efficacious and widespread: withdrawal, peer groups, alliance with the Church and a variety of personal reactions served as stratagems to limit the rigour of male and adult rule. Children had no other recourse. Some women, however, organised themselves and agitated to protest in public. Their history is interesting, above all because their failure throws valuable light on the ambivalent and subtle nature of their position.

The legal situation of women was very definitely inferior to that of men. The French Revolution had done little for women beyond abolishing male primogeniture. The law still required the wife to obey the husband, in return for which the husband owed her 'protection'. She had to reside wherever he chose and he was entitled to use force to compel her to do so. If she committed adultery, she was liable to imprisonment for a period of between three and twenty-four months, but he could engage in it with impunity. He committed a crime only if he actually maintained a concubine in the conjugal home, and then he was punished only by a fine of 100 to 2,000 francs. If he chanced to discover her committing adultery and killed her, he would not be guilty of murder—but she was not allowed to attack him in similar circumstances. She could not go to law without his permission, even if she had her own business and she could not sell or buy without his approval. Indeed the law treated women as minors. Normally marriage involved community of property, but not community in the management of it. The husband had the sole right to administer the joint estate: he could alienate her personal property, though he could only enjoy the usufruct of her real estate. Even in marriages with separation of property

the wife could not alienate her own real estate without her
husband's consent. Even if the wife obtained a separation from
her husband, she still needed her husband's signature for all her
business affairs; all she gained was the right to live where she
pleased, with whom she pleased, but she could not sell her
property. He had full powers over his children, but when he
died, she must act with the consent of his two nearest relatives.
As a widow she had custody of her children, but if she remarried, the family council met to decide whether she could
keep the children.[1]

Women at the beginning of this period were paid half the
wages of men. Most professional careers were closed to them.
They were offered far fewer educational opportunities. Guizot's
law on primary education omitted to deal with girls. Only in
1850 were communes with a population of 800 required to have
girls' schools, and only in 1867 those with 500—and even then
the lack of properly trained teachers limited the value of the
education. Girls' teacher-training colleges were established in
every department only in 1879. Secondary education for girls
took even longer to get started. Victor Duruy got some fifty
lycées going by a law of 1867, but many of them did not survive
long. Only in 1880 was a regular system of secondary education
for girls established, thanks to the law of Camille Sée (a deputy
aged thirty-three), but the girls were given only certificates
issued by their own school at the end of their course, not the
state *baccalauréat*. Their courses were different and more superficial than the boys'. The Sorbonne excluded women from
attendance at lectures till 1880; the Paris faculty of medicine
till 1868. The first woman to get the *baccalauréat* was a Paris
primary-school teacher, aged thirty-seven, who, after being
refused admission to the examination in Paris, was accepted by
the dean of the faculty of Lyon on his own responsibility. The
Paris faculty of law's first woman student, in 1884, was a woman
'of a certain age' who came accompanied by her husband and
by the secretary of the faculty, frightened that there might be a
scandal. In 1913 there were still only 4,254 women at universities, compared to 37,783 men. Until 1876 five women or

[1] Léon Richer, *Le Code des femmes* (1883); Charles Lefebvre, *La Famille en France
dans le droit et dans les mœurs* (1920); Frances I. Clark, *The Position of Women in
Contemporary France* (1937).

fewer obtained the *licence* each year; in 1913 the number was still only sixty-nine.[1]

The inferiority of opportunities for women was backed by a long tradition of writing on the subject. Rousseau thought that women should be given only a domestic education. Joseph de Maistre said: 'Knowledge is what is most dangerous to women.' Proudhon could see only two possible roles for them, housekeepers or prostitutes, and rated their intellectual and moral value as one-third of that of men.[2] Michelet, as has been seen, wrote in praise of them, but only to extol them in their traditional domestic role. Comte firmly believed that they must stay at home, and that 'man must provide their food for them'. It is true that Montesquieu, Helvétius and Condorcet demanded an equal education for them, but in the nineteenth century feminism was principally supported by the socialists. Fourier invented the word, and argued that the extension of their rights would be the measure of general progress; he envisaged full educational equality for them; his advocacy of a radical marriage reform was far in advance of his time. The Saint-Simonians not only preached equality but practised it in their organisation—again causing general horror. In 1848 Victor Considérant demanded that women should be given the vote, and in 1851 Pierre Leroux introduced the first bill to this effect, though he limited it to municipal elections. It was these *men* who started the feminist movement and ultimately it was they who brought it success.

Unfortunately for the women, their cause was taken up by a minority party, acting on theoretical and disinterested grounds. The majority of the republicans, by contrast, believed that since women went to church much more than men, giving them the vote would mean the triumph of a clerical reaction. The radical party took this danger very seriously and, for all its support of educational reforms for women, it remained a principal obstacle to the granting of the vote. The conservatives, who stood to gain, were too attached to the traditional family system to imperil male supremacy in the home. The trouble was that the feminist cause could not be tacked on to any other. In

[1] Edmée Charrier, *L'Évolution intellectuelle féminine* (1931), a mine of statistics about female academic achievements.

[2] P. J. Proudhon, *La Pornocratie de la femme dans les temps modernes* (1875).

the U.S.A. it was linked to the emancipation of the slaves: if illiterate negro slaves could vote, so could women. But in France, though the socialists always coupled the liberation of the proletariat and of women, these two were in fact economic rivals. The proletariat having got the vote were by no means keen to share it with women. Women's lower wages perhaps needed to be raised to prevent undercutting, but their competition at work threatened unemployment. Thus, though the C.G.T. declared in favour of equal wages in 1898, it unanimously added that it accepted only work by spinsters and widows: in general 'man must feed woman'. Proudhon had clearly expressed a generally accepted view. Only in 1935 did the C.G.T. accept full equality.

Unlike England, where vigorous agitation by women won them the vote in 1918, in France there was comparatively little open pressure on the men, and what pressure there was, was for civil rather than political emancipation. There was no mass feminist movement. Mrs. Pankhurst's explanation of this was that France was run by the backstairs influence of women: Frenchwomen knew they had power and they did not think the vote would increase it.[1] 'Though legally women occupy a much inferior status to men,' wrote Violet Stuart Wortley in 1908, 'in practice they constitute the superior sex. They are the "power behind the throne" and both in the family and in business relations undoubtedly enjoy greater consideration than English women.'[2] Already at the end of the *ancien régime* Necker had said: 'Do you wish to get an opinion to prevail? Address yourself to the women. They will accept it because they are ignorant, they will spread it because they are talkative, they will support it because they are obstinate.'[3] Foreign observers seem unanimous in stressing the exceptional influence of Frenchwomen. 'In most French households, women reign with unchallenged sway.'[4]

The early women feminists were isolated individuals and their activity was at first purely literary or journalistic. Olympe de Gouges is usually credited with being the first woman

[1] L. Sauna, *Figures féminines 1909–1939* (1949), 42.
[2] Violet Stuart Wortley, 'Feminism in England and France', in *The National Review*, 51 (Mar.–Aug. 1908), 793–4.
[3] Amélie Gayrand, *Les Jeunes Filles d'aujourd'hui* (1914), 61.
[4] Miss Betham-Edwards, *Home Life in France* (1905), 89.

feminist, in honour of her Declaration of the Rights of Women
of 1791 (which she had to dictate, for she was barely literate).
The Saint-Simonians produced the first feminist review edited
by women only, *La Femme Libre*—a title which they had to
change, because of the unfortunate meaning placed upon it,
to *La Femme de l'Avenir* and then *La Femme Nouvelle* (1832–4).
Even though this did not demand the vote but only the right
to education and to work, a *Journal des Femmes* (1832–7) was
started to reply to its exaggerations, as an organ of Christian
feminism. In 1836 Madame Herbinot de Mauchamps founded
La Gazette des Femmes, run exclusively by women, to demand
the vote, and the right to enter the professions and the civil
service; but her interest was confined to the bourgeoisie. The
revolution of 1848 produced a number of ephemeral feminist
clubs and newspapers; Jeanne Deroin, on 23 March 1848,
went to the Hôtel de Ville to ask for the vote; in 1849 she stood
for parliament and obtained fifteen votes; she founded a paper,
La Politique des Femmes, to attack Proudhon. Juliette Lamber in
Les Idées antiproudhoniennes (1858) declared that family life was
not enough to absorb women's energy. 'The role of the brooding
hen is doubtless very respectable, but it does not suit all women
and it is not as absorbing as is claimed.'

However, feminism as a continuous movement was really
launched by a man, Léon Richer (1824–1911). He had been
educated for the profession of notary but family reverses kept
him employed for fifteen years as a notary's clerk at Choisy-le-
Roi, at a wage of 1,200 francs. In his spare time he took to
speaking at public meetings, and particularly at the Grand
Orient, on women's rights; he wrote for Guéroult's *Opinion
National*; some of his articles were reprinted as a successful book
entitled *Lettres d'un libre penseur à un curé de village*. The alliance
of freemasonry, anticlericalism and feminism had begun. In
1869 he founded his own paper, *Le Droit des Femmes*, and in 1871
the Association (later the League) for the Rights of Women.
He organised an international congress on women's rights, held
in Paris at the same time as the international exhibition of 1878,
which created some stir and was the first important act of
French feminism. He got Victor Hugo to become president of
his society and so launched feminism as a significant movement.
His aims were limited to legal equality: he did not ask for the

vote, saying, 'The female mind is still too dominated by the yoke of the Church.' He was a journalist well connected in the political world, and able to obtain Victor Schoelcher and then René Viviani to succeed Hugo.[1] The first important woman ally he attracted was Maria Deraismes (1828–94), a lecturer like him at the Grand Orient, and a journalist, founder-editor of *Le Républicain de Seine-et-Oise* (1881–6), an active anticlerical, the first woman to be admitted as a freemason (1882), and later founder of a mixed lodge (1893). Like Richer she favoured gradual and limited reforms—no doubt because of her connections with opportunist republican politicians.[2]

The moderation of Richer and Deraismes soon led to a split in their society and the foundation of a rival one by Hubertine Auclert (1848–1914), France's first suffragette. She was not a *grande dame* like Deraismes, nor highly cultured like her, but an orphan with only a modest private income. She joined the cause soon after leaving her convent school but broke away in 1876 when Richer decided the demand for the vote was impossible. She put all her impetuous and uninhibited energies into agitating in the manner the English were to adopt. Her constant feuds with the authorities, her refusals to pay taxes, her insistence that she would yield only to force, compelled the press to take notice of her. She did indeed succeed in converting a few deputies and she helped win a vote for the political equality of the sexes from the *conseil général* of the Seine (1907). However, her extremism found few imitators and her career marks the failure and abandonment of activist methods at the very start of the feminist campaign.[3]

After her, the feminists behaved like all the innumerable moderate societies in favour of mild social causes. The main reason for this was that they were a definitely bourgeois and upper-class movement, led by the wives of the republican politicians, and they had no desire to threaten a regime to which they were basically attached. Thus the National Council of French Women, founded in 1901, was presided over by Sarah Monod, of a well-known family of academics and divines. In

---

[1] René Viviani *et al.*, *Cinquante Ans de féminisme 1870–1920* (1921).

[2] See her very conservative moral opinions in Maria Deraismes, *Nos Principes et nos mœurs* (1868).

[3] File of her press cuttings and letters in the Bibliotheque Marguerite Durand, the main feminist library, located in the *mairie* of the fifth *arrondissement* of Paris.

1912 she was succeeded by Mme Jules Siegfried (1848–1922), another Protestant, daughter of a pastor, wife of a moderate millionaire politician, organiser of many good works for widows, women workers and unmarried girls. She in turn was succeeded by Avril de Sainte-Croix, who had specialised in the defence of prostitutes and who remained at the head of the council till she was nearly eighty.[1] After her came Marguerite Pichon-Landry, sister of a radical minister, aunt of another, wife of an industrialist member of the Comité des Forges; she continued the tradition of respectability and moderation, content to run her organisation 'as a sort of conservatory of feminist principles discreetly pursuing its little tasks in the shelter of the lugubrious walls of the Musée Social'.[2] The National Council was a federation of some 150 different bodies (300 in 1938), but it completely failed to unify the activities of its members. Numerous, often rival, organisations dispersed the efforts of well-meaning matriarchs. There was a National Union for the Women's Vote and a National Union for Woman's Suffrage. The former was presided over by Cécile Brunschwicg,[3] wife of a professor at the Sorbonne; she did a lot to improve the social conditions of the poor, and to help alcoholics and tuberculars, but the radicals were all personal friends of hers and she agreed with them that female suffrage was too dangerous so long as the republic was in difficulties, which it always was. The second Union was presided over by the duchesse de La Rochefoucauld,[4] a minor poetess and allied to the Catholic and moderate right-wing parties, so it too was unlikely to cause much trouble. Yvonne Netter, a successful barrister and a warm speaker at public meetings, presided over the League for the Emancipation and Well-being of Women: she demanded the vote but she became increasingly absorbed by her professional work and unwilling to fall foul of the law. After the war, two different associations of war widows were founded—one of remarried ones (anxious to keep their pensions after remarriage), and one of widows who had not remarried: they were rivals almost to the point of physical violence—but of violence against each

[1] Secretary general 1901–22, president 1922–32.
[2] Louise Weiss, Ce que femme veut (1946), 41.
[3] Succeeding Mme de Witt-Schlumberger, granddaughter of Guizot, in 1924.
[4] Succeeding its founder Mme Le Vert-Chotard, president 1920–31.

other, not the state. There was a communist league of women for peace and liberty (later 'against war and fascism'). The more numerous the associations, the smaller their individual membership. No reliable figures are available, though it is said that the largest female demonstration before the war, on 5 July 1914, was 6,000 strong.[1] The Conseil National des Femmes Françaises in 1929 claimed 150,000 members; the Union Française pour le Suffrage des Femmes, which had 300 members in 1909, and 9,000 in 1914 (in 45 departments), claimed 100,000 (in 200 groups) in 1929.[2]

The most successful woman's organisation was the Patriotic League of Frenchwomen, which claimed 250,000 members in 1906 and half a million in 1914 but it had nothing to do with the suffrage and scarcely anything with politics.[3] It, like nearly all the others, was run by ladies of leisure for middle-class women. There was no participation by the peasantry and virtually no attempt to interest it. After 1934 Louise Weiss, an energetic journalist, tried to bring new vigour into feminism by introducing the methods of modern propaganda, and standing at elections, drawing the uninitiated into public meetings (which hitherto had often been merely social gatherings of old friends). She was treated coldly by the established organisations and found insurmountable resistance among women outside their ranks. 'The peasants stood open-mouthed when I spoke to them about the vote, the workers laughed, the shopkeepers shrugged their shoulders and the *bourgeoises* repulsed me in horror.' No change in the law would be possible, she concluded, until women changed their opinion of themselves and of their interests.[4]

The war of 1914 did not produce any radical change in feminine attitudes, largely because it did not make all that much difference to the women. The legal difficulties created by the

[1] Li Dzeh-Djen, *La Presse féministe en France de 1809 à 1914* (1934), 208: well-informed and far broader in scope than the title suggests; cf. Evelyne Sullerot, *Histoire de la presse féminine en France des origines à 1848* (1966).

[2] André Leclerc, *Le Vote des femmes en France. Les causes de l'attitude particulière de notre pays* (1929).

[3] Yvonne Delatour, 'Les effets de la guerre sur la situation de la française d'après la presse féminine 1914-1918' (D.E.S. May 1965, unpublished, copy in M. Durand library), 23.

[4] L. Weiss, 24. These memoirs are most amusing and very informative on the bitchiness in the feminist movements.

absence of husbands were dealt with not by reform of the law,
but by temporary legal fictions—particularly the 'tacit consent' of those absent at the front.[1] The peculiar characteristic of
France was that already before the war it had a far higher
percentage of its women at work than most European countries.
In 1906 68·2 per cent of the male population of all ages worked,
and 38·9 per cent of the female population. These figures
remained almost constant for the next thirty years, rising by
3 per cent in 1921 for both men and women, but returning to
68 per cent and 37 per cent in 1931 and in the economic depression of 1936 still remaining at 65·39 and 34·2 per cent. France
first of all had an exceptionally large agricultural population,
which kept women at work. But 20·2 per cent of married
women had jobs outside agriculture in 1906 and the figures did
not increase after the war: 1921 (19·1 per cent), 1926 (16·4 per
cent), 1931 (19·4 per cent), 1936 (18·7 per cent). The only
significant change was the move out of the factories. In 1911
56·6 per cent of women working in non-agricultural jobs were
in industry, 18·6 per cent in commerce, 7·5 per cent in the
liberal professions and 17·3 per cent in domestic work. In 1921
the figures were 52·9, 21·7, 10·6 and 14·8. In 1936 they had
switched to 44, 27·1, 13·8 and 15·1. The change thus came well
after the war and not as an immediate result of the war.
Whereas before the war there were two men to every woman in
a factory, in 1939 there were three men to every woman. The
number of commercial employees rose threefold. Domestic
servants fell in number, but also the *petites patronnes*, the independent artisans, who were now replaced by the shop assistants
and the clerks. The basic fact, however, is that France had
twice as many married women at work as England.[2] The real
importance of the war, in this context, was its effect on the
bourgeoisie, more of whose daughters had to go to work to compensate for their vanishing private incomes. That is partly why
feminism was largely a middle-class affair, for the bourgeoisie
only now became properly aware of the problems of the working woman, to which the poorer classes had long ago adjusted.

[1] André Isoré, *La Guerre et la condition privée de la femme* (Paris thesis, 1919),
481–97.
[2] Jean Daric, *L'Activité professionnelle des femmes en France* (1947), an excellent
monograph, as are also Madeleine Guilbert, *Les Fonctions des femmes dans l'industrie*
(1966), and id., *Les Femmes et l'organisation syndicate avant 1914* (1966).

The *jeune fille moderne* appeared quite early. Already in 1864 the Goncourt brothers had written the first novel about her, *Renée Mauperin*, in which they had attempted a realistic portrait of 'the modern young girl, such as the artistic and boyish education of the last thirty years has made her'.[1] However, an important reason why feminism failed in France was that it came very early to that country, burnt itself out and produced a conservative reaction among women already by 1914. In the middle of the nineteenth century George Sand (1804–76) had not only raised the standard of revolt but had lived the life of an emancipated woman. She told her husband, 'I shall go where I please, without having to render account to anybody.' She left him for most of the year and lived a Bohemian life in Paris. She kept herself by writing novels, which, like her own life, were a protest against the repression of women, against the duty imposed upon them by society to love their husbands, irrespective of their merits.[2] She herself had ceased to respect her own husband, to whom she had been married before she knew her own mind, and she had had the courage to leave him. But George Sand was not a full feminist: her romantic temperament forbade her to be one. She believed in equal education for the sexes, in civil liberty and in 'sentimental equality'. She thought that the servitude in which man kept woman destroyed for her the prospect of happiness, which was impossible without freedom. 'Women', she said, 'are maltreated; they are reproached for the idiocy into which they are plunged; their ignorance is despised; their learning is mocked. In love they are treated as courtesans; in conjugal relations as servants. They are not loved but made use of, they are exploited and all this is designed to subject them to the law of fidelity.' The real crime, she argued, was not for a woman to leave a man for another whom she loved, but to give herself to a man whom she did not love, even if he was her husband. One explanation of George Sand's tormented promiscuity was that she never could obtain sexual satisfaction, and she sought out new lovers in the hope of finding it. She did not seek much more than the right to divorce. She did not want the vote, saying that woman's function was different from man's—'What she must save, in the midst of

---

[1] E. and J. de Goncourt, *Renée Mauperin*, preface to the edition of 1875.
[2] See G. Sand, *Indiana* (1831), Preface.

gross passions, is the spirit of charity.' She did not take up writing to make herself independent, but simply because she needed money. In her years of more serene maturity, she wrote with increasing respect of marriage, and in the end said, 'If I had to live my life again, I should be chaste.'[1]

The tradition of George Sand continued for many years and female rebels against convention are portrayed in numerous novels.[2] However, the rebels were confined to a small class, those who were left wing, or highly educated, or both. By 1914 they appeared out of date to most girls. The Catholic and conservative reaction of the 1900s may have been partly responsible for this. Certainly the Church maintained a traditional view of woman's role.[3] Bishops even fulminated against the 'scandal' of new styles in female clothing, and against 'indecent and provoking fashions'; the Archbishop of Paris joined in a protest to the *couturiers* of his city.[4] An inquiry among girls in 1914 revealed a situation very similar to that prevailing among young men, as shown in Agathon's *Les Jeunes Gens d'aujourd'hui* (1913). The girls were no longer moved by the poetesses in revolt against custom and restraints, who made an 'unbridled appeal to sensual pleasures'. They wanted discipline, order, reason. Alain said that the favourite philosopher of his female pupils was Comte, the advocate of the most rigorous discipline in family and society. 'The first feminists', they said, 'had sought to be friends with their husbands': for the new generation this was not enough: 'We do not wish to lose anything of our feminine prestige.' Coquetry, femininity quickly came back into fashion. The strong man became the ideal, instead of the 'pretty boy' who was admired by the previous generation. They rejected the violent methods of the English suffragettes. They were patriotic. They saw

[1] A. Maurois, *Lélia ou la vie de George Sand* (1952), 125, 147–9, 151, 165, 367–9, 423, 493.

[2] V. Margueritte, *La Garçonne* (1922); Colette Yver, *Les Cervelines* (1903) and *Princesses de sciences* (1907); Gabrielle Reval, *Les Sévriennes* (1900) and *Ruban de Vénus* (1906); Marcel Prévost, *Les Vierges fortes* (1900). Camille Marbo, *Hélène Barraux, celle qui défiait l'amour* (1926); Renée-Tony d'Ulmès, *Histoire de Sibylle* (1904–9); Marcelle Tinayre, *La Rebelle* (1905); cf. Jules Bertaut, *La Littérature féminine d'aujourd'hui* (1907).

[3] Semaines Sociales de France, Nancy, 19th session, 1927: *La Femme dans la société* (Lyon, 1928): 'La femme forte, c'est la mère de famille', 31–66.

[4] Delatour, 84.

motherhood as woman's supreme role. They wanted education
as a means of safeguarding themselves against the compulsory
marriage of the past; with a job, they could choose freely
between a marriage that suited them and independence, but
most were opposed to married women working or even voting.
Only the woman who led a man's life had the right to his
privileges.[1] One of the most popular women novelists of this
period, Colette Yver, protrayed the lives of bluestockings as
lonely and frustrated: 'Woman is made for love, before being
made for knowledge.'[2] The correspondence columns of *Eve*,
a best selling woman's magazine, read by all classes, show an
overwhelming preoccupation with love and literature—and
very little indeed with feminism: novels dealing with personal
relations appealed to the imagination of girls far more than
political programmes for their emancipation.[3] When a more
modern American-style woman's paper, *Marie-Claire*, was
started in 1937, and sold 800,000 copies, it in no way diminished
the circulation of the traditional magazines.[4] Even Simone de
Beauvoir, whose brilliant self-analysis in her autobiography
and whose books on *The Second Sex* provide the best-known
description of the attitudes of the emancipated woman of the
inter-war period, was uninterested by the feminist movement.
Her approach to life was existentialist; she was interested in
herself as a person, rather than as a woman; and her message
was: 'One is not born a woman, one becomes one.' Her books,
however, are full of reservations about the possibility of a woman
achieving an independence equal to man's. Though she lived
with J.-P. Sartre unmarried, in a much discussed liaison, she
also forcibly stressed the difficulties she had in liberating
herself from tradition. The fact that she did not have children
prevented her experiment from being a model for her contemporaries. She wrote of women in the context of a world
dominated by men, but at a time when conditions were begin-

[1] Amélie Gayrand, *Les Jeunes Filles d'aujourd'hui* (1914).

[2] C. Yver, *Dans le jardin du féminisme* (1920), 111.

[3] Fernand Goland, *Les Féministes françaises* (1925), contains numerous extracts
from the female press. Cf. Marcel Prévost, 'Les femmes lisent-elles?', in *La
Revue de France* (15 Oct. 1922), 673–94 and id., 'Comment lisent les femmes', ibid.
(15 Nov. 1922), 225–44.

[4] Geneviève Gennari, *Le Dossier de la femme* (1965), 266; Evelyne Sullerot, *La
Presse féminine* (1963).

ning to change rapidly. She was widely read by the post-1945 generation, but she was also a reminder to the middle-aged of their struggles and failures.[1]

Female emancipation was faced with traditions which could not be easily overthrown. Taine had remarked on the strength of these: 'To postpone the awakening of ideas and of feelings, to keep the soul in primitive candour and ignorance, to teach obedience and silence, that is what education was reduced to, total repression.'[2] Edmond About explained this by saying: 'We want above all to keep women faithful to their husbands. So we hope that the girl will bring to the world an angelic provision of ignorance which will be immune to all temptations.' Thus a father might praise the academic successes of his son, but recommend his daughter for her innocence and for the purity with which she had left her convent school.[3] Scribe was accused of having only insignificant, stupid, timid girls in his plays, puppets who could say only 'papa' and 'maman', but Jules Lemaître defended him saying these were realistic portraits, to be explained by the fact that men had developed a taste for such girls. 'The impossibility of penetrating the secrets of the feminine soul at eighteen, the sentiment of a sort of inviolable mystery are part of the idea we have of the young woman.' The theatre of the Second Empire was full of girls who happily married the man selected by their fathers: Émile Augier and Dumas portrayed them because they existed but partly also to encourage them to behave like this. Madame E. Garnier, in her memoirs of *A Parisian University Family in the Nineteenth Century*, recalled: 'We had confidence in the wisdom of our parents, we did not think we demeaned ourselves by sharing their opinions.' Timidity was long considered a virtue. Guizot told his daughter: 'You have too much pride, that is to say, too much self-confidence. Think always about this defect.' The woman journalist Séverine recalled her youth as one of constant repression. 'Nature had to be conquered. According to my parents it was desirable that children should have no will of their own, that a strong discipline should from the beginning break their

[1] Simone de Beauvoir, *Mémoires d'une jeune fille rangée* (1958), *La Force de l'âge* (1960), *Le Deuxième Sexe* (1949).

[2] H. Taine, *Vie et opinions de Thomas Graindorge* (1867).

[3] E. About, *Le Progrès* (1864).

inclinations, their tastes, the awakening of the personality. Not only ought the child not to say I wish, but preferably it ought even to be ignorant of the possibility of desire.' Madeleine Danielou's successful *Livre de sagesse pour les filles de France* (1950) shows how the ideal of submission and purity survived, particularly in Catholic families.[1] Against those who believed in the spread of girls' education, there were others who insisted that this should be different from that which was given to boys. Xavier de Maistre wrote to his daughter: 'The great defect in a woman is to want to be a man and it is to want to be a man to want to be learned.' Barbey d'Aurevilly's attack on *Les Bas bleus* (1878) represented a view that continued to be strongly held. As parents, women appear to have largely supported this traditional method of bringing up girls and, in so doing, defected from the cause of their own liberation.

It is not surprising therefore that little real progress was made in improving women's legal position, and that when legislation was introduced, law and practice remained at variance in many sections of the community. Two laws of 1881 and 1895 allowed women to open post-office savings accounts in their own names and draw money out of them without their husbands' consent. A law of 1907 allowed a married working woman to keep full ownership and use of her wages. However, these measures were not easily enforceable, particularly since the husband still remained legally responsible for his wife's debts. In practice, most stockbrokers and bankers ignored the law and refused to buy stocks or open bank accounts for married women without the consent of the husband. A story is told of a schoolteacher of Marseille who received two different bills for her taxes, one in her maiden name and one in her married name. She protested in person; the tax-collector apologised for the mistake and asked her to send in a written objection. She did so at once, but he returned it to her saying though the tax was for money she herself had earned, only her husband could sign the letter of protest. 'You exist from the fiscal point of view, but you have no legal existence.'[2] The law only slowly got round to remedying this. One of 1893 gave separated women legal capacity; another

---

[1] M. A. Martin, *La Jeune Fille française dans la littérature et la société 1850–1914* (Rennes, n.d., c. 1930).
[2] L. Weiss, 115.

of 1917 allowed women to be guardians of children. In 1920 married women were allowed to join trade unions without their husbands' consent; after 1927 they could have a different nationality from their husbands. Finally the law of 1938 gave married women legal capacity. This was hailed as a great revolution and as a new 'Family Code'. A commission had been set up in 1904 to revise the Civil Code on the occasion of its centenary. When it had got to article 212 saying, 'The couple owe each other fidelity, help and assistance', Paul Hervieu had suggested that the word 'love' should be added, and this had been adopted. But the commission's proposals had never been turned into law. Now, after taking six years to get through the senate, the law of 1938 repealed article 213, which stated that the wife owed obedience to her husband. The husband's marital power was abolished, at least in name, in the sense that it ceased to be stated as such in the code. Secondly, the wife was granted full legal capacity. The wife could now appeal to the courts against her husband's choice of residence, and against opposition by him to her taking a job. The onus, however, rested on her. In reality, the apparent concessions on examination turned out to be largely illusory. The husband was no longer entitled to obedience, but he was called the 'chef de la famille', which seemed to be taking back with one hand what was being given with the other. The full civil capacity given to married women immediately raised many difficult problems and conflicts with other laws, so that it was virtually unworkable.[1] The law courts generally refused applications to override the husband's objection to the wife's working, since they laid it down that the husband had merely to say that this would be against the family's interest: they did not inquire whether his claim was justified.

Only in the matter of divorce was real change achieved—but then, of course, easy divorce was not a feminist demand. The law passed through several stages. In 1792 divorce was allowed on the grounds of incompatibility or by mutual consent. Napoleon made it more difficult, with adultery, cruelty or

[1] Jane Cérez, *La Condition sociale de la femme de 1804 à l'heure présente, étude de sociologie juridique* (1940), disappointing but not useless; Charles Vacheng, *L'Application pratique de la loi du 18 février 1938 sur la capacité de la femme mariée* (Aix thesis, 1941), solid; Thomas Kallai, *La Notion de chef de famille* (1950).

grave injury as the main grounds. Only about fifty divorces were granted a year in Paris as a result; very few indeed in the provinces. In 1816, however, divorce was abolished altogether and it remained so until 1884. An attempt by Crémieux in 1848 to re-establish it failed. Alfred Naquet (also a Jew) was the man whose tireless advocacy of the cause of divorce carried it through. He was a professor of chemistry, an ardent republican and free thinker, convicted for organising a secret society in 1867 and for publishing an attack on *Religion, Property and Family* in 1869. He at first proposed a return to the situation of 1792, then to that of 1815; he was successful only when he agreed to make divorce a punishment for a matrimonial offence and to exclude divorce by consent. His victory was, however, incomplete. Only in 1904 was the guilty partner allowed to marry the respondent with whom he or she had committed adultery. Adultery, though a ground for divorce, remained a crime and punishable. In practice, prosecutions became very rare, though occasionally token fines were imposed. The law of 1884 was harder than Napoleon's in that all possibility of divorce by consent was eliminated, but the courts made increasingly liberal use of the grounds of cruelty and injury. The mere refusal to return home allowed the deserted spouse to obtain a divorce. One wife obtained a divorce because her husband did nothing when she was insulted by their servant; another because her husband had sold her jewels without her permission; a third because she was allowed no initiative in the internal conduct of the household.[1] On the other hand, one husband sued for divorce because his wife attended lectures at the Collège de France without his permission, showing 'a dangerous spirit of insubordination and adventure'.[2] There were 7,363 divorces in 1900, 15,450 in 1913, 29,156 in 1920, 32,557 in 1921, but the figure was stable at around 20,000 between 1923 and 1939. 5·4 per cent of marriages thus broke down, though the figure in Paris was 11 per cent. By 1930, 450,000 families had been split up by divorce.[3]

In marriage women continued to have an important

[1] André Mollier, *La Question du divorce* (Dijon law thesis) (Besançon, 1930).
[2] Célia Bertin, *Le Temps des femmes* (1958), 39.
[3] Mollier, 90, 95. G. Le Bras and M. Ancel, *Divorce et séparation de corps dans le monde contemporain* (1952), vol. 1, is a useful summary, with a bibliography.

grievance. By the law of 31 July 1920, propaganda in favour of abortion and contraception was forbidden: not just the act or even the intention to abort was punished but its mere advocacy. This was designed to increase the birth rate about which politicians were becoming worried. But juries in fact refused to convict or even the law officers to prosecute. Between 1920 and 1939 only about 350 cases were judged every year, and even the Vichy government did not prosecute more than 2,000. The real effect of the law was to limit the use of contraceptives and to maintain the practice of abortion. Though accurate statistics are of course impossible, it was reasonably estimated that between the wars 400,000 to 1,200,000 abortions took place every year: they were, that is to say, as normal and almost as frequent as childbirth. A study carried out in 1947 showed 73 per cent of those obtaining abortions were married women acting with the consent of their husbands. In 1945, Paris had fourteen 'secret' maternity homes specialising in abortions, and each department at least one.[1]

Equal pay for women came officially in 1946. In 1848 women's wages in industry were around half of men's. In the 1914–18 war they rose greatly in the metallurgical industries: in 1913 they were 45 per cent lower, in 1917 only 18 per cent, but in 1921 they were 31 per cent lower. The collective bargaining agreement in 1936 fixed female wages at 13 to 15 per cent below male wages. In the teaching profession equal pay was accepted in 1927, and equal maxima in 1932. But the civil service as a whole continued to discriminate against women by fixing a limit on women entrants, so as to prevent male unemployment; the Vichy regime in 1940 severely limited the right of married women to work. Careers in the various liberal professions were opened up early enough, but in 1882, there were only 7 women doctors practising, in 1903 95, in 1921 300, in 1929 519. In 1914 there were only 12 women barristers, in 1928 96. In 1930 the universities had 6 women professors. Women certainly won individual distinctions very early on: in 1905 a woman came second in the male *agrégation de philosophie*; in 1913 Lili Boulanger won the grand prix de Rome for music and Odette Pauvert for painting in 1925. In 1936 Léon Blum appointed

[1] Andrée Michel and Geneviève Texier, *La Condition de la française d'aujourd'hui* (1964), 1. 122–4.

three women under-secretaries of state in his government. But as a whole women were still far from sharing equally with men in professional life. In 1960 still only 14 per cent of the jobs in the liberal professions and only 3 per cent of administrative jobs were held by women.[1]

Women received the vote in 1944. The long delay was due to the obstinate opposition of the senate, representing radical, provincial prejudice. The arguments used by the senate reveal how little effect the passage of centuries, and the supposed spread of enlightenment, had had in some quarters. One senator made a very long speech consisting of quotations from ancient authors, whose authority he considered a sufficient refutation of women's claims. 'The woman of the Latin race does not think, does not feel, does not develop like the woman of Anglo-Saxon or Germanic race. Her position in the home is not the same.' The decisive argument to some was that if women were given the vote, then prostitutes would have it too. It would be indecent, said others, for men and women to mix freely in the polling booths. But the real objection was the fear that women, being more frequent church-goers than men, would vote for the clerical parties and so threaten the existence of the lay republic. Viviani had introduced a bill for the female vote in 1901; in 1910 163 deputies favoured female suffrage in local elections; an 1919 the chamber voted for full female suffrage by 344 to 97. The senate rejected it by 156 to 134 and renewed its opposition for the next twenty years on successive occasions. It was only the eclipse of the radical party during the war and the suspension of parliament that enabled General de Gaulle to introduce the female vote by decree in 1944—under the influence of the communists on the one hand, who had many women among their supporters, and of the M.R.P. who hoped to gain from the vote of the Catholic women. Subsequent research revealed that 85 per cent of women voted in the same way as their husbands, and it was largely aged widows and unmarried girls who voted differently from their male counterparts. It is not clear therefore that the vote by itself was all that important in changing the position of women in French society.[2]

[1] E. Charrier, *passim*, and Michel and Texier, 1. 143.
[2] Mattei Dogan and Jacques Narbonne, *Les Françaises face à la politique* (1955), 187–92; Joseph Barthélemy, *Le Vote des femmes* (1920).

Male supremacy was challenged in another way, by the
limitation of paternal authority in the interests of children.
By the Napoleonic code, article 375, a father had the right to
apply to the courts to obtain the arrest and imprisonment of
his child up to the age of 16, in the event of his seriously mis-
behaving; for children over 16, the courts had discretion as to
whether they would agree or not. (A widowed mother needed
the consent of the two nearest relatives of the father to apply
for an arrest.) By article 148, parental consent was essential
for men wanting to marry up to 25 and girls up to 21; but
even up to the ages of 30 and 25 respectively, consent had to
be asked, though it could be ignored after three refusals. Well
after the mid nineteenth century, there were many men and
women, aged 30, 40 or even 50, married and with children, who
were as submissive to their parents as in their childhood. But
a law of 1889 allowed the courts to declare the forfeiture of
parental authority in the event of drunken or scandalous conduct or of ill treatment endangering the health, security or
morality of their children. A law of 1898 allowed the courts to
deprive criminals of the custody of their children. In the early
nineteenth century, the paternal power had been upheld by
the courts against grandparents: decisions of 1825 and 1853
confirmed a father's right to refuse to allow his children to
visit their grandparents. But in 1857 the Cour de Cassation
began the destruction of the father's absolute rule: it laid it
down that others had rights apart from him.[1] The factory and
education laws limited his rights further still. At the same time
the mother's role may have changed when children were kept
at home longer, and as the practice of sending babies out to
wet-nurse in the country, first regulated by the law of 1874,
gradually died out.[2] The roles of both women and children in

[1] Louis Delzons, *La Famille française et son évolution* (1913); Jules Thabaut, *L'Évolution de la législation sur la famille depuis 1804* (Toulouse thesis, 1913).

[2] See Zola's *Fécondité* for a description of the appalling conditions in which the
nourrissons were brought up. E. Sorre, *Des modifications à apporter à la loi de protection
des enfants en bas âge* (Loi Roussel) (Paris medicine thesis, 1903), I, 49, confirms the
accuracy of this description. Bertrand Dreyer-Dufer, *De la protection des enfants du
premier âge* (Paris law thesis, 1900), is a good history of the question. In 1840–60
the death-rate of infants under one rose from 16 to 18 per cent, owing to the spread
of the *nourrisson* system. The publication of detailed statistics by country doctors
showing a death-rate of up to 70 per cent among these infants led to an official

these changing conditions were redefining themselves, but the situation in 1945 was still one of uncertainty and confusion.

The legislative changes effected in these years showed, on the one hand, that there was dissatisfaction with the system of family relations as it existed, but on the other hand that this system, though subject to tensions, was still immensely powerful. The division of the country into self-conscious family units complicated all other relationships. It gave people loyalties, ambitions and a sense of direction which were seldom talked about openly, but which were one of the 'deepest sources of motivation in this period. If all the private conversations which took place in it had been recorded, it might, in theory, have been possible to rewrite the political and economic history of the country in terms of clans and families. But this huge part of daily life is something of which historians have been left almost no records, and their account of the past must, for that reason, always be inaccurate.[1]

inquiry and the passing of the law of 1874. This reduced the death-rate drastically, but some departments ignored the law for many years, until the turn of the century.

[1] Elizabeth Glass of St. Antony's College is writing a thesis on women in 19th-century France, using notarial archives.

GUIDE TO FURTHER READING

THIS note is addressed to those who would like to read more, but who may feel overwhelmed by the choice available. Here are some suggestions to help them to get going, with an emphasis on books that are amusing as well as instructive, and on very recent works not mentioned in the footnotes.

To savour the atmosphere of the period, there is nothing to beat an autobiography, and these are some very moving ones: E. Guillaumin, *La Vie d'un Simple* (1904, English trans. 1921); Ephraim Grenadou and Alain Prévost, *Grenadou, paysan français* (1966); Georges Navel, *Travaux* (1945); Martin Nadaud, *Mémoires de Léonard, ancien garçon maçon* (1895, new edition by M. Agulhon, 1976); Adelaide Blasquez, *Gaston Lucas, serrurier* (1976); J. Ozouf, *Nous les maîtres d'école, autobiographies d'instituteurs de la belle époque* (1967). The six volumes of F. le Play, *Les Ouvriers Européens* (2nd edition, 1877-9), and the periodical *La Science Sociale* run by his disciples, contain vivid monographs on humble people.

For more middle class reminiscences, see Simone de Beauvoir, *Mémoires d'une femme fille rangée* (1958) and *La Force de l'âge* (1960); J. P. Sartre, *Les Mots* (1964, English trans. *Words*, 1967); J. Crouzet-Benaben, *Souvenirs d'une jeune fille bête* (1971); G. Gendarme de Bevotte, *Souvenirs d'un universitaire* (1938); L. Weiss, *Mémoires d'une Européene* (1968); Jules Simon, *Le soir de ma journée* (1901); E. Herriot, *Jadis* (1948-52, 2 vols.); and of course all the other political autobiographies listed in my *Politics and Anger* (1979). There are interesting interviews in André Harris and Alain de Sédouy, *Les Patrons* (1977). For children, see G. Vincent, *Les Lycéens* (1971); J. Vallès, *L'Enfant* (1879); J. Renard, *Poil de Carotte* (1894); and Lloyd de Mause, *History of Childhood* (1974).

One can penetrate into the apparent silences of the countryside by reading some village histories, e.g. R. Thabaut, *Mon Village* (1948); L. Wylie, *Chanzeaux* (1966), and *Village in the Vaucluse* (1961); P. Higonnet, *Pont de Montvert* (1971); E. Morin,

Plodemer (1967); and not least P. J. Hélias *Le Cheval d'Orgeuil* (1975, American trans. 1978), which is good on folklore. These may be put in a wider context through G. Wright, *Rural Revolution in France* (1964), and E. Weber, *Peasants into Frenchmen* (1976).

The atmosphere, of course, changes as you move around the country. There are illuminating books on different regions: M. Agulhon, *La République au village* (1970) on Provence; A. Corbin, *Archaisme et modernité en Limousin, 1845–80* (1975, 2 vols.); G. Désert, *Les Paysans du Calvados* (Lille, 1975); R. Laurent, *Les Vignerons de la Côte d'Or au 19ᵉ siècle* (1958), A. Siegfried, *Tableau politique de la France de l'Ouest* (1913), P. Bois, *Paysans de l'Ouest* (1960), J. Sion, *Les Paysans de la normandie orientale* (1968), G. Thuillier, *Aspects de l'économie nivernaise au 19ᵉ siècle* (1966); R. Beteille, *Les Aveyronnais* (1974); Marcel Laurent, *Paysans de Bâsse Auvergne au début du 20ᵉ siècle* (1976); P. Vigier, *La Seconde République dans la région alpine* (1963); Leo Loubere, *Radicalism in Mediterranean France* (1974); and *The Red and the White* (on the history of wine, 1978); F. Beth, *et al.*, *La Qualité de la vie dans la région Nord—Pas de Calais au 20ᵉ siecle* (1975).

The variety of the urban and industrial scene may be sampled from L. Chevalier, *Classes Laborieuses et classes dangereuses à Paris pendant la première moitié du 19ᵉ siecle* (1958, English trans., 1973); Jeanne Gaillard, *Paris, la ville, 1852-70* (1976); G. Duveau, *La Vie ouvrière en France sous le second empire* (1947); E. Levasseur, *Histoire des classes ouvrières et de l'industrie en France de 1789 à 1870* (2nd edition, 1903–4, 2 vols.), and *Questions ouvrières et industrielles sous la troisième république* (1907), full of curious information, despite or because of their date); M. Perrot, *Les Ouvriers en grève, 1871–90* (1974, 2 vols.); J. W. Scott, *The Glassworkers of Carmaux* (1974); R. Trempé, *Les Mineurs de Carmaux* (1971, 2 vols.); C. Tilly, *Strikes in France, 1830–1968* (1974); R. Pierre, *Les Origines du syndicalisme et du socialisme dans la Drôme, 1850–1920* (1973), and *La Drôme et l'Ardèche entre deux guerres: le mouvement ouvrier, le front populaire* (Valence 1977); M. Gillet, *Les Charbonnages du nord de la France au 19ᵉ siècle* (1973); *Mélanges offerts à J. Maitron* (1976); P. Pierrard, *La vie ouvrière à Lille sous le second empire* (1965); Serge Bonnet, *Mineurs de fer et ouvriers sidérurgistes, 1889–1930* (1976); L. Murard and P. Zylberman, *Le Petit Travailleur infatigable, ou le prolétaire régénéré*

(1976) and *L'Haleine des Faubourgs* (1977); F. P. Codaccioni, *De l'inégalité sociale dans une grande ville industrielle: Lille, 1850–1914* (1976).

How people earned, spent and saved their money has been investigated by Adeline Daumard, *La Bourgeoisie parisienne, 1815–48* (1963), and *Les Fortunes* (1973). See also the articles by J. Estebe and F. Caron in the *Revue d'histoire économique et sociale* (1976), vol. 54, respectively on the wealth of politicians and the 'strategy of investment'. The very rich have been studied by P. Barral, *Les Perier dans l'Isère* (1964), and J. Bouvier, *Les Rothschild* (1960). Successful businessmen are brought to life in P. Fridensen, *Histoire de usines Renault* (1972); E. C. Carter, *Enterprise and Entrepreneurs in 19th and 20th century France* (1976); and J. N. Jeanneney, *François de Wendel* (1976). A. J. Tudesq, *Les Grands Notables en France* (1964, 2 vols.), and L. Girard, *Les Counseillers généraux en 1870* (1967) analyse the leisured classes. See also Laurent Fabius, *La France inégale* (1975); Marc Maurice and D. Delomeme, *Mode de vie et espaces sociaux: processes d'urbanisation et differenciation sociale dans deux zones urbaines de Marseilles* (1976); M. Agulhon, *Le Cercle dans la France bourgeoise, 1830–48* (1977). For the shady side of business, see the biographies of Stavisky, e.g. by J. M. Charlot and M. Montarron (1974) or by P. Lorenz (1974), and the film about him, starring J. P. Belmondo.

The petite bourgeoisie is being studied by a team led by P. Vigier; meanwhile there are ideas to be obtained from D. Borne, *Petits bourgeois en revolte? le Mouvement Poujade* (1977). For artisans, see J. P. Bayard, *Le Compagnonage en France* (1977), L. Sittler, *l'Artisanat en Alsace, jadis et aujourdhui* (1973), and Benard L. Moss, *The Origins of the French Labor Movement* (1976). For bureaucrats, see the recent memoirs of F. Bloch-Lainé, *Profession funcionnaire* (1976), and a review of recent research by G. Thuillier and J. Tulard, 'L'histoire de l'administration du 19ᵉ siècle depuis dix ans', *Revue Historique* (Oct.–Dec. 1977), 441–56; also F. de Baecque *et al.*, *Les Directeurs de ministère en France (19–20ᵉ siècles)* (Geneva, 1976); M. Rousselet, *La Magistrative sous la monarchie de juillet* (1937); and G. Thuillier, *La Vie des ministères au 19ᵉ siècle* (1977).

On the relations of the sexes, there is the new thorough work of A. Corbin, *Les Filles de noce, misère sexuelle et prostitution au*

19ᵉ et 20ᵉ siècles (1978); *Mythes et representation de la femme au 19ᵉ siècle* (1976); J. L. Flandrin, *Les amours paysannes* (16–19ᵉ siècles)* (1975), and *Familles* (1976); M. Guilbert, *Les Femmes et l'organisation syndicale avant 1914* (1966); Y. Knibiehler, *Familles et Pouvoirs* (forthcoming); J. J. Serais and J. P. Laurend, *Histoire et dossier de la prostitution* (1967); E. Shorter, *The Family* (1976); C. Sowerwine, *Les Femmes et le Socialisme: un siècle d'histoire* (1978); Edith Thomas, *Louise Michel* (1971); Paul Hoffmann, *La Femme dans la pensée des lumières* (1977); and Francoise Mayeur, *L'Enseignement secondaire des jeunes filles sous la troisième république* (1977).

INDEX